Assessment Cultures

STUDIA EDUCATIONIS HISTORICA
Studies in the History of Education

Edited by
Marcelo Caruso / Eckhardt Fuchs / Gert Geißler / Sabine Reh /
Eugenia Roldán Vera / Noah W. Sobe

VOL. 3

PETER LANG

Cristina Alarcón / Martin Lawn (eds.)

Assessment Cultures

Historical Perspectives

PETER LANG

Bibliographic Information published by the Deutsche Nationalbibliothek
The Deutsche Nationalbibliothek lists this publication in the Deutsche Nationalbibliografie; detailed bibliographic data is available in the internet at http://dnb.d-nb.de.

Cover Illustration: Hugo Poll, "Die Prüfung," *Über Land und Meer: Allgemeine Illustrierte Zeitung* 2 (1906): 722 (Quelle: Pictura Paedagogica Online, Bibliothek für Bildungsgeschichtliche Forschung, Berlin).

Printed by CPI books GmbH, Leck

ISSN 2195-5158
ISBN 978-3-631-67516-8 (Print)
E-ISBN 978-3-653-06867-2 (E-PDF)
E-ISBN 978-3-631-70023-5 (EPUB)
E-ISBN 978-3-631-70024-2 (MOBI)
DOI 10.3726/ 978-3-653-06867-2

Table of Contents

Assessment and the Construction of 'Deviance'

National Perspectives

Assessment and Psychologisation

Actors of Assessment

Acknowledgements

The editors warmly thank all authors for their willingness und patience to embark on this common project. We are specially indebted to Laura Wiesiolek for her painstaking copyediting of the manuscripts. Finally, we warmly thank Marcelo Caruso, Professor of Humboldt-Universität zu Berlin and co-editor of the *Studia Educationis Historica Series (SEH)* of Peter Lang Publishing. Without his moral and financial support this publication would not have been possible.

Cristina Alarcón & Martin Lawn

Introduction: Assessment Cultures. Historical Perspectives

"We are entering the age of infinite examination and of compulsory objectifica-tion": this forecast, formulated 40 years ago by Michel Foucault, gives a striking description of the current circumstances.[1] There is a boom in national and inter-national assessment tests, and assessment data is used worldwide as a governing instrument of national education systems. Along with this development, scholarly research shows an expanding preoccupation with the topic of assessment. Apart from the more normative research conducted by international organisations, a number of studies deal with the mechanisms, effects, and political gains of Inter-national Large-Scale Assessment (ILSA) programs, such as the Programme for International Student Assessment (PISA)[2] and high-stakes testing accountability[3] in general, or the benefits of assessment data as a governing instrument.[4] More-over, there has been a decades-long dominance of psychological and educational research studies about types, theories, techniques, effects and effectiveness (in-cluding quality criteria) of assessment. In addition, there is philosophical and sociological work on assessment that conceptualises it as an instrument of cultural reproduction (Bourdieu), social control (Basil Bernstein) and a combination of hierarchical supervision and the normalising of sanctions (Foucault).[5] But the balance of this research landscape shows that the conditions of emergence, devel-opment processes and potential path dependencies of assessment have, in general,

---

1   Michel Foucault, *Discipline and Punish: The Birth of the Prison* (New York, NY: Pan-theon Books, 1977), 189. Martin Lawn, ed., *The Rise of Data in Education Systems: Collection, Visualisation and Use,* Comparative histories of education (Didcot, UK: Symposium Books, 2013).

2   See e.g. Heinz-Dieter Meyer, Aaron Benavot and David Phillips, eds., *PISA, Power, and Policy: The Emergence of Global Educational Governance* (Didcot, UK: Symposium Books, 2013).

3   See Larry Cuban, "Hugging the Middle. Teaching in an Era of Testing and Account-ability, 1980–2005," *Education Policy Analysis Archives* 15 (2007).

4   Lawn, *The Rise of Data in Education Systems.*

5   As well as Patricia Broadfoot, ed., *Selection, Certification, and Control: Social issues in educational assessment* (London, UK: Falmer Press, 1984).

remained rather unnoticed.⁶ In other words, the fact that assessment practice is
as old as school itself has been mostly overlooked. Another deficit refers to the
spatial orientation of the studies. Contexts outside of Western Europe (except the
USA) are mostly left aside and the cultural conditioning of assessment has not
received sufficient appreciation.

---

6   With the exception of these valuable contributions: Johann Georg von Hohenzollern,
    ed., *Schülerbeurteilungen und Schulzeugnisse: Historische und systematische Aspekte*
    (Bad Heilbrunn: Klinkhardt, 1991); Karlheinz Ingenkamp, *Pädagogische Diagnostik in
    Deutschland, 1885–1932. Geschichte der pädagogischen Diagnostik, Volume 1* (Wein-
    heim: Dt. Studienverl, 1990); Adrian Wooldridge, *Measuring the Mind: Education and
    Psychology in England, c. 1860 – c. 1990* (Cambridge, UK: Cambridge Univ. Press,
    1994); Nicholas Lemann, *The Big Test: The Secret History of the American Meritocracy*
    (New York, NY: Farrar Straus and Giroux, 1999); Christian Lundahl, *Viljan att veta vad
    andra vet: Kunskapsbedömning i tidigmodern, modern och senmodern skola* (Stockholm:
    Arbetslivsinstitutet, Uppsala Universitet, 2006); John Carson, *The measure of merit:
    Talents, intelligence, and inequality in the French and American republics, 1750–1940*
    (Princeton, NJ: Princeton University Press, 2007); Sheldon Rothblatt, *Education's Abid-
    ing Moral Dilemma: Merit and Worth in the Cross-Atlantic Democracies, 1800–2006*
    (Didcot, UK: Symposium, 2007); Martin Lawn, ed. *An Atlantic Crossing? The Work
    of International Examination Inquiry, its Researchers, Methods and Influence* (Didcot,
    UK: Symposium Books, 2008); Christian Lundahl and Florian Waldow, "Standardi-
    sation and 'Quick Languages': The Shape-shifting of Standardized Measurement of
    Pupil Achievement in Sweden and Germany," *Comparative Education* 45, no. 3 (2009):
    365–85, 10.1080/03050060903184940; Peter Herdegen, *Schulische Prüfungen: Entste-
    hung – Entwicklung – Funktion; Prüfungen am bayerischen Gymnasium vom 18. bis
    zum 20. Jahrhundert* (Bad Heilbrunn: Klinkhardt, 2009); Marie-Odile Mergnac and
    Cécile Renaudin, *Histoire du baccalauréat*(Paris: Archives & Culture, 2009); Rainer
    Bölling, *Kleine Geschichte des Abiturs* (Paderborn: Schöningh, 2010); William J. Reese,
    Testing Wars in the Public Schools: A forgotten History (Cambridge, MA: Harvard Univ.
    Press, 2013); Martin Lawn, "Voyages of Measurement in Education in the Twentieth
    Century: Experts, Tools and Centres," *European Educational Research Journal* 12, no. 1
    (2013): 108–19, doi:10.2304/eerj.2013.12.1.108; Christian Ydesen, Kari Ludvigsen, and
    Christian Lundahl, "Creating an Educational Testing Profession in Norway, Sweden
    and Denmark, 1910–1960," *European Educational Research Journal* 12, no. 1 (2013):
    120–138. doi: 10.2304/eerj.2013.12.1.120; Sherman Dorn and Christian Ydesen, "To-
    wards a Comparative and International History of School Testing and Accountability,"
    Education Policy Analysis Archives 22, no. 115 (2014), doi:10.14507/epaa.v22.1913,
    Sabine Reh and Norbert Ricken, "Prüfungen – Systematische Perspektiven der Ge-
    schichte einer pädagogischen Praxis. Einführung in den Thementeil," *Zeitschrift für
    Pädagogik* 63, 3 (2017): 247–259.

This volume intends to contribute to filling this research gap by investigating both the historicity and culturality of assessment *and* by focusing primarily on pupil assessment. The term *culturality* will be tentatively understood as the dynamic of processing and orientation of meaning, developed by certain actors in a specific setting of time and space, sometimes including, but sometimes going beyond the national frame.[7] The culturality refers both to their emergence and acceptance, as well as to its changing shape while being transferred.

The term *assessment cultures* serves as a key term for this volume. It is not a new term by any means. On the contrary, it has been used for at least three decades and in a variety of contexts. For that reason, it has no clear definition either. As early as 1984, the British sociologist Patricia Broadfoot discussed the gradual "replacement of the psychometric assessment culture" with a "psycho-pedagogic assessment culture" in her book "Education, Assessment and Society."[8] The term 'assessment cultures' was in this instance derived from the underlying sub-disciplines of the assessment practices. Other authors from the field of educational research, especially from educational psychology and didactics, have also used 'assessment culture' as a proper concept.[9] These authors contrast 'assessment culture,' positioned within the paradigm of a qualitative-contextualising constructivism, with the term 'testing culture,' which they consider to be a reference to behaviourism and the psychometric-quantitative paradigm.[10]

---

7   Marcelo Caruso, "Substanzlose Kulturalität. Ein Theorieentwurf für die Erforschung von Bildungs- und Schulkulturen im Medium funktionaler Differenzierung," in *Kulturvergleich in der qualitativen Forschung: Erziehungswissenschaftliche Perspektiven und Analysen*, ed. Merle Hummrich (Wiesbaden: Springer VS, 2013).

8   Broadfoot, *Selection, Certification, and Control.*

9   Menucha Birenbaum, "New Insights Into Learning and Teaching and Their Implications for Assessment," in *Optimising New Modes of Assessment: In Search of Qualities and Standards*, ed. Mien Segers, Filip Dochy and Eduardo Cascallar (Dordrecht: Springer Netherlands, 2003); Dennie Wolf et al., "To Use Their Minds Well: Investigating New Forms of Student Assessment," *Review of Research in Education* 17 (1991): 31–74. doi:10.2307/1167329; Menucha Birenbaum, ed., *Alternatives An assessment of Achievements, Learning Processes and prior Knowledge* (Boston, MA: Kluwer, 1996); Filip Dochy, "A new Assessment Era:: Different needs, new Challenges," *Learning and instruction* 10, no. 1 (2001); Menucha Birenbaum, "Assessment Culture Versus Testing Culture: The Impact on Assessment for Learning," in *Assessment for Learning: Meeting the Challenge of Implementation*, ed. Dany Laveault and Linda Allal (Cham: Springer, 2016), 287.

10 Menucha Birenbaum, "Assessment 2000: Towards a Pluralistic Approach to Assessment," in *Alternatives in Assessment of Achievements, Learning Processes and prior Knowledge*, ed. Menucha Birenbaum (Boston, MA: Kluwer Acad. 1996), Birenbaum,

From another point of view, authors have used the term 'assessment cultures' for spatial delineations. Hence, they examined national 'assessment cultures,' such as the "American testing culture,"[11] "Swedish assessment cultures"[12] or, like recent studies, the diffusion of a "global testing culture."[13] In addition to that, cross-cultural psychology research studies have used the term "assessment cultures" in relation to specific cultural, philosophical, and religious traditions, such as the Confucian heritage culture.[14]

Inspired by these works, we understand 'assessment cultures' in this volume as the totality of interpretation patterns, symbols, discourses, structures, techniques, systems, and/or practices of assessment that have been developed by actors in the context of a specific space and time. The culturality refers both to their emergence and acceptance, as well as to its changing shape while being transferred. While this volume may not systematically analyse the term, it offers a first overview of its different dimensions, both spatially as well as historically. It examines developments in Western Europe (France, Germany, Sweden, Denmark, Norway), Eurasia (Russia), East Asia (Japan), Latin America (Chile, Argentina, Colombia), North America (United States), and in 'international' and/or 'transnational

---

"New Insights into Learning and Teaching and Their Implications for Assessment", 22–23; Wolf et al., "To Use Their Minds Well", 43.

11 Peter Sacks, *Standardized minds: The high Price of America's Testing Culture and What We Can Do to change it*, (Cambridge, MA: Perseus Books, 1999); Audrey M. Kleinsasser and Elizabeth A. Horsch, *Teaching, Assessment, and Learning: Invitation to a Discussion* (Cheyenne, WY: Wyoming University, 1992).

12 Eva Forsberg and Henrik Román, "In Search of Swedish Assessment Culture/s" (23. Policy Studies and Politics of Education, ECER 2008, From Teaching to Learning? Gothenburg, Sweden, September 10, 2008); Christian Lundahl, "The Formation of an Assessment Culture," *Studies in Educational Policy and Educational Philosophy* 2003, 3 (2003): 26810, doi: 10.1080/16522729.2003.11803873; as well as "International Pupil Assessments, National Assessment Culture and Reform History". A 2007–2009 Research Project Funded by the Swedish Research Council (Eva Forsberg, Christian Lundahl, Henrik Román & Florian Waldow, Uppsala University, Sweden).

13 William C. Smith, *The Global Testing Culture: Shaping Education Policy, Perceptions, and Practice* (Didcot, UK: Symposium Books, 2016).

14 John B. Biggs, "Western Misperceptions of the Confucian-heritage Learning Culture," in *The Chinese learner: Cultural, Psychological, and Contextual Influences*, ed. David Watkins and John B. Biggs (Hong Kong, Camberwell, Melbourne, Vic.: CERC; ACER, 1996); Kennedy, Kerry J., "Exploring the Influence of Culture of Assessment: The Case of Teachers Conceptions of Assessment in Confucian Heritage Cultures," in *Handbook of human and social conditions in assessment*, ed. Gavin T. L. Brown and Lois R. Harris (London, UK: Routledge, 2016).

spaces.' Moreover, it covers a broad scope, both in terms of timeframe from the early modern period to today, as well as in terms of different political contexts, such as the welfare state, republicanism, (post-) socialism, post-colonialism, decolonisation, and neoliberalism. To the same end, this volume discusses a highly diverse set of actors as target subjects, producers, experts, mediators, translators, and/or distributors of assessment knowledge. These labels apply to pupils, teachers, psychologists, exam boards, international organisations, and school inspection organisations. Finally, the present volume examines a wide range of assessment types (e.g. formative and summative) and assessment instruments that go beyond standardized tests (in all their formats). Thus, several contributions explore and discuss so-called 'subjective' assessment instruments that are personally produced by a teacher: written and oral examinations, marks, teacher reports, pupil files, cumulative guidance records, report cards, merit boards, rehearsals, quizzes, and memory exercises.

Despite these diverging contexts, eras, and actors, the different contributions reinforce the idea that assessment is a crucial control feature in modern schooling. At the same time, it constitutes a contentious issue at the intersection of society, politics, economics, and science. Therefore, it constitutes a legal-political field of action and power, e.g. a point of dispute between various politico-ideological factions; a professional field of action, e.g. a motive for conflicts between psychologists and pedagogues, as well as a scientific field of action, e.g. the application of scientific research in the service of certain educational policy and reforms. This volume also confirms the central *social* function ascribed to assessment, namely the diagnosis, selection, classification, categorisation, distribution, and/or allocation of pupils. It also refers to the intended and unintended effects of assessment, such as gender, class, ethnicity, sexuality, and ability related normalisation, discrimination and exclusion processes of pupils. The differences between the cases in this volume thus pertain more to the interpretive patterns and techniques that are used to legitimise this control function in discourse, negotiate its political terms, and execute it, as well as to the definition of the 'ideal pupil' an assessment instrument is based on. Despite these divergences, several contributions also refer to the transnational emergence and development of a powerful semantic of scientificity, validity, objectivity, and mechanisation related to the technology of standardized testing.

In the first part of this volume, "Early modern cases of assessment," both authors draw upon a period of time that has so far received little attention with regards to the history of assessment: the early modern period. Both contributions evaluate assessment practices under the teachers' control using the examples of Sweden (Latin schools) and Germany (a Model school).

Christian Lundhal reconstructs a specific assessment culture from an epistemic perspective on the basis of an analysis of Swedish school ordinances (from
1561 to 1724), exhibiting elements of an early practice of knowledge assessments.
These assessment practices mainly served to (re)produce knowledge, which was
supposed to be conducive to the organisation of schooling in two regards: to
the pupils' organisation as well as the organisation of learning processes. The
aforementioned assessment practices contained both summative and formative
elements and, in the context of Lutheran Protestantism, focused on the development of language (speech and writing), memory and judgement skills, and the
promotion of specific spiritual values.

Kathrin Berdelmann looks at practices of pupil observation and assessment
developed at a model school, the *Dessauer Philantropin*, at the end of the 18th century. *Berdelmann* shows how this observation practice developed into an explicit
pedagogic category, as well to an institutionalised precondition for other forms of
assessment, which followed the principles of individualisation and standardisation. Using the example of this model school, *Berdelmann* reveals first signs of a
'modern' assessment culture based on meritocracy as its guiding principle.

The contributions of the second part, "Transnational perspectives," investigate
a specific problem: how do national actors in their national contexts filter, adapt,
or even reject certain international discourses, practices, instruments, and principles of pupil assessment?

The contribution by *Nelli Piattoeva & Galina Gurova* analyses the reception
of ILSA and their underlying "testing culture" in the Russian context during the
last decades. Based on the conceptual framework of discursive institutionalism,
and references to historic developments in the Soviet era, the authors show how
national assessment experts re-contextualise or make relatable the so-called testing culture, especially international assessment data to the local context, and use
it strategically for the conception of specific policy proposals.

Following the perspective of history of concepts, the contribution by *Ángela
Adriana Rengifo Correa* reconstructs the transformation of assessment practices
and their underlying concepts such as "experimental examination" and "educational evaluation" in Colombia over the course of the 20th century. *Rengifo Correa*
shows how the reception of the New School's international discourse, experimental psychology, and the economic discourse of developmentalism led to a
transition from an assessment culture of oral examinations to a testing assessment
culture.

Sverre Tveit analyses specific trends (the meritocracy trend, the accountability trend, the assessment for learning trend) with regards to the research and

education politics of assessment during the 20th century, from a transnational-comparative perspective. He also identifies two different paradigmatic assessment cultures: the "testing culture" and the "examination culture". Lastly, he analyses Sweden and Norway as examples of adoption and resistance dynamics of transnational assessment practices and discourse.

The part entitled "Assessment and the construction of 'deviance'" investigates the central selection and allocation role that is assigned to assessments in the context of modern schooling. Both contributions focus on the normalisation practices that are linked to this selection role in order to discuss the construction of the "deviant pupil."

On the one hand, the contribution by *Christian Ydesen & Mette Burchardt* discusses the connection between the construction of "cultural deviance", and the development of certain assessment practices and cultures in the context of the Danish welfare state during the 1960s and 70s. They reconstruct two cases of state-led interventions on populations in the "inner periphery": school children in Greenland (a former Danish colony) and the children of labour migrants living in metropolitan Denmark. The authors show how educational testing was used in both cases as a "cultural marker" for the purpose of categorisation, selection, and distribution of these children and legitimised using the argument of "cultural neutrality" (objectivity).

On the other hand, the contribution by *Michaela Vogt* focuses on the construction of "ability deviance" from a comparative perspective, with regards to the special education selection process in primary schools in the Federal Republic of Germany and the German Democratic Republic from 1950 to 1970. She analyses professional evaluations (*Profesionelle Gutachten*) as source material in order to define whether the schooling decisions about the ability to attend primary school or the need for special education were made consistently, or whether they instead reveal the existence of a diachronic shift for both German states, in that the special education selection process tended to assess a pupil's social context rather than their performance and learning behaviour.

The fourth part of this volume, "National perspectives," investigates national paths or developments of assessment practices, instruments, and discourse, and takes a look at longer historic periods of time.

María Teresa Flórez Petour analyses the Chilean high-stakes assessment systems from the end of the 19th century to the beginning of the 21st century, uncovering their political and ideological dimension. *Flórez Petour's* central argument is that these systems functioned as a historically constructed "power device" that has hindered change towards more holistic, child-centred, emancipatory ideas in education. She also shows that the underlying assessment culture of these systems adopts a functional view of society, and has therefore always preferred certification and the social purposes of assessment to pedagogical aims.

Jack Schneider & *Ethan Hutt* address the reconstruction of a specific national assessment culture of the United States from the end of the 18th century to the 21st century, its deep historic roots and the ideologies and beliefs linked to them as well as their dominant practices: A to F grading and standardized testing. The authors' central argument is that this assessment culture is characterised by highly contentious and partly opposing principles: consumerism and entrepreneurialism, merit and social mobility, open-access egalitarianism and local control.

Cristina Alarcón investigates the central function that primary school reports (*Grundschulgutachten*) have been assigned in the context of the selection procedure between primary and secondary schools for more than 90 years in Germany: the assessment of a child's personality. Based on the analysis of regulations, teachers' guides, and examples of reports, *Alarcón* tries to retrace the roots of the report, explain its historic persistence and ultimately analyse it as part of a specific German assessment culture.

The fifth part of the book, "Assessment and psychologisation," contains two contributions discussing a concrete assessment instrument: "report cards" serving guidance purposes. Both contributions refer in a broader sense to the process of colonisation of assessment practices by psychological categories, methods and instruments, as well as to the growing involvement of psychological experts in school assessments.

Philippe Bongrand's contribution focuses on the rise and fall of the *fiche scolaire* assessment instrument in France: a pupil report card created by psychologists that teachers were asked to fill in starting in the early 1920s as a form of career guidance. The *fiche scolaire* was conceived as an alternative to marks and examinations, and aimed to assess pupils mostly based on psychological criteria. *Bongrand* discusses the contrast between the assessment culture the *fiche scolaire* was based on, and the assessment culture that has been dominant until today. While the former had the aim of assessing a pupil's personality, interests, and preferences, the latter stands for a summative, quantified, subject matter-based assessment.

Koji Tanaka focuses on the development of the "cumulative guidance record" in relation to educational psychology research in the context of Post-war Japan. Tanaka analyses discussions surrounding assessment theory, which have existed as a dialogue with the theories and discourse of the United States, and in particular with the emergence of different perspectives on pupil assessment, such as "relative assessment" connected to "intra-individual assessment" during the 1960s and "objective-referenced assessment" during the 1970s.

The sixth part represents a summary of contributions that focus on the "actors of assessment," such as teachers, pupils, exam boards, International Organisations, and school inspection organisations. The first two contributions also take up the controversial link between assessment and meritocracy.

Florian Waldow discusses the connection between the "fair" organisation of assessment systems and the realisation of a meritocratic guiding principle. To that end, he conducts a comparative analysis of the assessment systems of Germany, Sweden and England, focusing on the conceptions of fairness that are embedded in the rules and regulations of these assessment systems and in particular on the constellations of actors (teachers and exam boards) stipulated by those rules. *Waldow* shows that the legitimacy of assessment systems as well as the underlying conception of fairness is characterised both in a cultural-contextual and an actor-specific way. *Waldow* also identifies two opposing poles that can be used to define the specific and strongly path-dependent assessment cultures of these three countries.

Alicia Méndez investigates the selective admission regimes of a paradigmatic Argentinian secondary school in connection with the construction of a "meritocratic" elite: the *Colegio Nacional de Buenos Aires*. Based on field observations, interviews, autobiographies, a prosopographic study, and socio-demographic data, Méndez shows how the socio-cultural characteristics of the pupil body would vary on the basis of changing admission regimes. Covering a span of 150 years, *Méndez's* analysis also reveals that this admission regime underlies a traditional national assessment culture in which the assessment of written examinations has a prominent role.

Camilla Addey's contribution focuses on the actor of "international organisations," such as the Organisation for Economic Co-operation and Development (OECD) and the United Nations Educational, Scientific, and Cultural Organisation (UNESCO), as well as non-profit international scientific societies like the International Association for the Evaluation of Educational Achievement (IEA) over a period from the 1950s to 2016. Her contribution aims to analyse the change in their assessment cultures. To that end, *Addey* focuses on the underlying procedures, principles, and goals of administrating international pupil assessment tests and data. She illustrates how organisations like IEA and OECD went from acknowledging difference through in-depth studies of individual countries, to large-scale worldwide comparisons of countries along standardized metrics. The

1990s stand out as a decisive assessment culture shift that had far-reaching consequences for educational policy, practice, and research.

Ultimately, *Martin Lawn's* analysis refers to the current English context, specifically to the problem of how produced assessment data (performance data for every pupil) has become a major way of governing education systems. In England, during the late 20th century, this moved from being personal information about pupils to a major public and commercial arena in which significant performance data is used to order and control the education system. Assessment data now means a complex and changing set of work relations between the centre, the region (or city), and the schools. This new governing landscape is described and its consequences are explored during the 2000s when a new industry of assessment was created.

Literature

Biggs, John B. "Western Misperceptions of the Confucian-heritage Learning Culture." In *The Chinese learner: Cultural, psychological, and contextual influences.* Edited by David Watkins and John B. Biggs, 44–67. Hong Kong: CERC; ACER, 1996.

Birenbaum, Menucha, ed. *Alternatives in Assessment of Achievements, Learning Processes and Prior Knowledge.* Boston, MA: Kluwer Acad. Publ., 1996.

–. "Assessment 2000: Towards a Pluralistic Approach to Assessment." In *Alternatives in Assessment of Achievements, Learning Processes and Prior Knowledge.* Edited by Menucha Birenbaum, 4–29. Evaluation in Education and Human Services. Boston, MA: Kluwer Acad. Publ., 1996.

–. "New Insights into Learning and Teaching and Their Implications for Assessment." In *Optimising New Modes of Assessment: In Search of Qualities and Standards.* Edited by Mien Segers, Filip Dochy and Eduardo Cascallar, 13–36. Dordrecht: Springer Netherlands, 2003.

–. "Assessment Culture Versus Testing Culture: The Impact on Assessment for Learning." In *Assessment for Learning: Meeting the Challenge of Implementation.* Edited by Dany Laveault and Linda Allal, 275–92. Cham.: Springer International Publishing, 2016.

Bölling, Rainer. *Kleine Geschichte des Abiturs.* Paderborn: Schöningh, 2010.

Broadfoot, Patricia, ed. *Selection, Certification, and Control: Social Issues in Educational Assessment.* London, UK: Falmer Press, 1984.

Carson, John. *The Measure of Merit: Talents, Intelligence, and Inequality in the French and American Republics, 1750–1940.* Princeton, NJ: Princeton University Press, 2007.

Caruso, Marcelo. "Substanzlose Kulturalität. Ein Theorieentwurf für die Erforschung von Bildungs- und Schulkulturen im Medium funktionaler Differenzierung." In *Kulturvergleich in der qualitativen Forschung: Erziehungswissenschaftliche Perspektiven und Analysen*. Edited by Merle Hummrich. 43–64. Wiesbaden: Springer VS, 2013.

Cuban, Larry. "Hugging the Middle. Teaching in an Era of Testing and Accountability, 1980–2005." *Education Policy Analysis Archives* 15 (2007): 1–27.

Dochy, Filip. "A new Assessment Era: Different Needs, new Challenges." *Learning and instruction* 10, no. 1 (2001): 11–20.

Dorn, Sherman, and Christian Ydesen. "Towards a Comparative and International History of School Testing and Accountability." *Education Policy Analysis Archives* 22, no. 115 (2014). doi:10.14507/epaa.v22.1913.

Forsberg, Eva, and Henrik Román. "In Search of Swedish Assessment Culture/s." 23. Policy Studies and Politics of Education, ECER 2008, From Teaching to Learning? Gothenburg, Sweden, September 10, 2008.

Foucault, Michel. *Discipline and Punish: The birth of the prison*. New York, NY: Pantheon Books, 1977.

Herdegen, Peter. *Schulische Prüfungen: Entstehung – Entwicklung – Funktion; Prüfungen am bayerischen Gymnasium vom 18. bis zum 20. Jahrhundert*. Bad Heilbrunn: Klinkhardt, 2009.

Hohenzollern, Johann Georg von, ed. *Schülerbeurteilungen und Schulzeugnisse: Historische und systematische Aspekte*. Bad Heilbrunn: Klinkhardt, 1991.

Ingenkamp, Karlheinz. *Pädagogische Diagnostik in Deutschland; 1885–1932. Geschichte der pädagogischen Diagnostik, Vol. I*. Weinheim: Dt. Studienverl, 1990.

Kennedy, Kerry J. "Exploring the Influence of Culture of Assessment: The Case of Teachers Conceptions of Assessment in Confucian Heritage Cultures." In *Handbook of human and social conditions in assessment*. Edited by Gavin T. L. Brown and Lois R. Harris, 404–19. London, UK: Routledge, 2016.

Kleinsasser, Audrey M., and Elizabeth A. Horsch. *Teaching, Assessment, and Learning: Invitation to a Discussion*. Cheyenne, WY: Wyoming Univ., 1992.

Lawn, Martin, ed. *An Atlantic Crossing? The Work of International Examination Inquiry, its Researchers, Methods and Influence*. Didcot, UK: Symposium Books, 2008.

–, ed. *The Rise of Data in Education Systems: Collection, Visualisation and Use*. Didcot, UK: Symposium Books, 2013.

–. "Voyages of Measurement in Education in the Twentieth Century: Experts, Tools and Centres." *European Educational Research Journal* 12, no. 1 (2013): 108–19. doi:10.2304/eerj.2013.12.1.108.

Lemann, Nicholas. *The Big Test: The Secret History of the American Meritocracy.* New York, NY: Farrar Straus and Giroux, 1999.

Lundahl, Christian. "The Formation of an Assessment Culture." *Studies in Educational Policy and Educational Philosophy* 2003, 3 (2003): 26810. doi: 10.1080/16522729.2003.11803873;

–. *Viljan att veta vad andra vet: Kunskapsbedömning i tidigmodern, modern och senmodern skola.* Stockholm: Arbetslivsinstitutet, Uppsala Universitet, 2006.

Lundahl, Christian, and Florian Waldow. "Standardisation and 'Quick Languages': The Shape-shifting of Standardized Measurement of Pupil Achievement in Sweden and Germany." *Comparative Education* 45, no. 3 (2009): 365–85. doi: 10.1080/03050060903184940.

Mergnac, Marie-Odile, and Cécile Renaudin. *Histoire du baccalauréat.* Paris: Archives & Culture, 2009.

Meyer, Heinz-Dieter, Aaron Benavot, and David Phillips, eds. *PISA, Power, and Policy: The Emergence of Global Educational Governance.* Didcot, UK: Symposium Books, 2013.

Reese, William J. *Testing Wars in the Public Schools: A forgotten History.* Cambridge, MA: Harvard Univ. Press, 2013.

Reh, Sabine, and Norbert Ricken. "Prüfungen – Systematische Perspektiven der Geschichte einer pädagogischen Praxis. Einführung in den Thementeil." *Zeitschrift für Pädagogik* 63, 3 (2017): 247–59.

Rothblatt, Sheldon. *Education's Abiding Moral Dilemma: Merit and Worth in the Cross-Atlantic Democracies, 1800–2006.* Didcot, UK: Symposium, 2007.

Sacks, Peter. *Standardized Minds: The High Price of America's Testing Culture and What We Can Do To Change It.* Cambridge, MA: Perseus Books, 1999.

Smith, William C. *The Global Testing Culture: Shaping Education Policy, Perceptions, and Practice.* Didcot, UK: Symposium Books, 2016.

Wolf, Dennie, Janet Bixby, John Glenn, and Howard Gardner. "To Use Their Minds Well: Investigating New Forms of Student Assessment." *Review of Research in Education* 17 (1991): 31–74. doi:10.2307/1167329.

Wooldridge, Adrian. *Measuring the Mind: Education and Psychology in England, c. 1860– c. 1990.* Cambridge, UK: Cambridge Univ. Press, 1994.

Ydesen, Christian, Kari Ludvigsen, and Christian Lundahl. "Creating an Educational Testing Profession in Norway, Sweden and Denmark, 1910–1960." *European Educational Research Journal* 12, no. 1 (2013): 120–38. doi: 10.2304/eerj.2013.12.1.120

Early Modern Cases of Assessment

Christian Lundahl

The Organising Principles of Disciple Assessment in the Swedish School Ordinances, 1561-1724

The history of assessment has often focused on the emergence of scientific psychology and psychometrics. Science has produced instruments for measuring students' knowledge, external in relation to school, which the school has then internalised. In Swedish educational history, for example, the origin of assessment is often described as the ancient temperament theory and the renaissance thinkers who during the 1400–1600s prescribed talent selection for higher education on its foundation.[1] Peter Burke writes in *A Social History of Knowledge* that:

> "Intellectuals are masters of some kinds of knowledge, but other fields of expertise or "know-how" are cultivated by such groups as bureaucrats, artisans, peasants, midwives and popular healers."[2]

The history of knowledge cannot only be understood as the history of erudition. There are other practices that produce and systematise knowledge. In this chapter, a clearly practical pedagogical perspective is adopted, and knowledge assessments are studied as a practice that is shaped within the school. The purpose of the chapter is to, in an early modern context, study some of the relationships that in assessment research have been portrayed as potentially problematic. In the five school curricula printed in Sweden between 1561 and 1724 I examine the historical reproduction of an *internal* assessment tradition with a special focus on the relationship between what is today typically referred to as formative and summative assessments,[3] as well as between knowledge assessments and epistemological approach. When the history of assessment has been written, the connection between knowledge assessments and epistemological approach has rarely been

---

1   Christian Lundahl, "Viljan att veta vad andra vet. Kunskapsbedömning i tidigmodern, modern och senmodern skola" (PhD diss., Uppsala University, 2006).

2   Peter Burke, *A Social History of Knowledge. From Gutenberg to Diderot* (Cambridge, UK: Polity Press, 2000), 14.

3   To simplify, formative assessments are basically ongoing evaluations with an emphasis on processes and how something can be learned, while summative assessments are more final evaluations.

considered, but, as I will show, the epistemological approach of early curricula contributed to the development of certain specific assessment practices. Through observing some of the school's more traditional forms of assessment, such as homework quizzes and examinations, in the light of a time specific epistemological approach, it is also possible to problematize the dichotomy of formative and summative assessment. Many techniques that would today be labelled summative were in fact developed for more formative purposes.

The main theoretical argument is that assessments should be seen as part of the curriculum. From a curriculum theory perspective, assessment then becomes a practice that (re)produces a certain kind of knowledge out of which schools and individuals, as well as teaching and learning within schools, can be organised.[4] The concept of knowledge (re)production signals that assessment in education stands in a dialectical relation to culture and society. When reproducing knowledge, assessments recreate typologies available in culture, when producing knowledge, assessments provide this culture with objects, facts, information etc. At the same time, the assessment system reproduces itself, as the technology that can provide education with the requested objects and information.

A central starting point is that knowledge assessments are *statements* or *comments* regarding an individual's intellectual potential and/or his or her learning. The statements produced within the school institution about children's learning can be used to organise people in the school or to organise the actual learning. An administrative, or summative, assessment practice can then be said to produce a human-organising knowledge, in the sense that it examines who knows what for the purpose of placing or arranging people (e.g. in different classes). A pedagogical practice can be described in terms of how it produces knowledge/information in order to structure, correct or otherwise shape the actual learning (formative

---

4   As a starting-point, this chapter departs from the Swedish tradition of curriculum theory developed in for example Ulf P. Lundgren, *Frame Factors and the Teaching Process. A Contribution to Curriculum Theory and Theory on Teaching* (Stockholm: Almqvist & Wiksell, 1972); Ulf P. Lundgren, *Between Hope and Happening: Text and Context in Curriculum* (Vikoria: Deakin University Press, 1983); Thomas Englund, "Curriculum as a Political Problem. Changing Educational Conceptions, with Special Reference to Citizenship Education" (PhD diss., Uppsala University, 1986), and elaborated in Lundahl, "Viljan att veta." This tradition of curriculum theory has a special interest in diachronic and synchronic production and reproduction of educational ideals, ideas and practices. Also see Ulf P. Lundgren, "When curriculum theory came to Sweden," *NordSTEP* 1 (2015), accessed April 3, 2016, doi: http://dx.doi.org/10.3402/nstep.v1.27000.

assessment). These two practices, the administrative and the educational, can be expected to vary in their harmony with one another from time to time. Here they are studied individually and in relation to each other as the expression of an early modern assessment culture.[5]

The Swedish School Ordinance, 1561–1724

The school ordinances (*Sveriges Allmänna Läroverksstadgar*) from the 1500s onwards are a relatively untapped source material of knowledge assessments' Swedish history. When the first elementary school regulations came in the mid-1800s, and there was a shift in the meaning of the word school in the sense that mass education — a school for the entire people — began to take shape, seven school ordinances had already been published and expended: "The school ordinance of the year 1571 (1561); The school ordinance of the year 1611; The school ordinance of the year 1649;[6] Ordinance concerning Upper Secondary School and Scholar in the Kingdom 1693; his Royal Majesty's renewed School Ordinance 1724; his Royal Majesty's renewed Gracious School Ordinance 1807;"[7] and finally the his "Royal Majesty's renewed Gracious School Ordinance 1820."[8]

These were until 1724 written by men of the church, under the approval and supervision of the king,[9] except the 1611 school ordinance which, according to K.G. Leinberg was never sanctioned by the king.[10] In 1724, the first of the school ordinances approved by the Estates of the Realm was published and thus the clergy's influence over the school ordinances had started to decline, though not

---

5   The analysis is based on Lundahl, "Viljan att veta," part 2.

6   The school ordinances of 1561, 1611 and 1649 as imprints and the two latter in a translation from Latin to Swedish by Rudolf B. Hall et al., *Sveriges Allmänna Läroverksstadgar, 1561–1905. Årsböcker för svensk undervisningshistoria, 1921 vol. IV* (Stockholm: Föreningen för svensk undervisningshistoria, 1921).

7   The school ordinances of 1693, 1724 and 1807 as imprints in Rudolf B. Hall et al., *Sveriges Allmänna Läroverksstadgar, 1561–1905. Årsböcker i svensk undervisningshistoria, 1922 vol. VII.* (Stockholm: Föreningen för svensk undervisningshistoria, 1922).

8   The school ordinances of 1820 as imprints in Rudolf B. Hall et al. (1923): Sveriges Allmänna Läroverksstadgar, 1561–1905. *Årsböcker i svensk undervisningshistoria, 1923 vol. IX.* Föreningen för svensk undervisningshistoria (Stockholm: Föreningen för svensk undervisningshistoria,1923).

9   The school ordinance of 1649 carried Queen Christina's seal.

10 Karl G. Leinberg, *Om snillevalet (selectus ingeniorum) i vår äldre skollagstiftning* (Helsinki: Finska Litteratur-sällskapets tryckeri, 1884), 16.

ended.[11] This school ordinance would remain in place for more than 80 years. The secondary schools in Sweden during this period were basically Latin schools for boys ageing 6–7 up to their twenties depending on if they attended trivium schools or secondary education. Several of them were sons to clergymen, merchandisers and peasants, some orphans. The nobility mainly used private tutoring. In the 1750s approximately 5000 students attended Swedish state schools.[12]

The school ordinances follow a number of common paragraphs. First, a preamble which, simply put, justifies the statute in "God, the kingdom and love of the truth." Then is stated, usually initially, the appointment of the schoolmaster/principal and teachers, as well as the admission of disciples. This is followed by the actual curriculum, what should be learned/read in each class and what should be practised and on which days this should happen. After the reading ordinance, 'some statutes' are, as a rule, specified, in which, inter alia, comments are made about how teachers should relate to some of the books (homework/authors) used for teaching, how the teachers should relate to the disciples, reward and punishment, examinations and grading, teacher salaries and parish walks. Here the variation is great but the teachers' and disciples' relationship to each other (usually under headings such as punishment and reward) and the process of examinations are stated in all school ordinances. Queen Christina's school ordinance of 1649 constitutes the clearest practical pedagogical instructions with the 20 "methodology chapters," including one about the exercise of memory [Swe: minne] and the correction of writing tasks.[13]

The school ordinances were intended to regulate secondary schools. In the church ordinance of 1561 the designation for secondary school is scholar, and the disciples are divided into three circles with different reading ordinances. The classes were not linked to the boys' ages but to a certain curriculum of skills that should be learned. The school ordinance of 1611 announced for example that teachers should probably expect that every disciple would spend two years in each class before the curriculum had been completely attained.[14]

---

11 *School Ordinance 1724*, 20; See Leinberg *Om snillevalet*, 16.
12 Wilhelm Sjöstrand, *Pedagogikens historia, vol.III.* (Lund: CWG Gleerups förlag, 1961), 143.
13 Queen Christina's school ordinance is far more extensive than the others, more than 110 pages compared to about 20 pages for 1561, 1611, 1693, and 46 pages in 1724. In her school ordinance there are also references to pedagogical science for the first time.
14 From the class lists from 1632 it is possible to deduce that the lowest class could accommodate everything from 5-year-olds to 17-year-olds. Rudolf B. Hall, *Valda aktstycken*

It is clear, seen from the way the school ordinances are disposed, that they have been written for at least two organisational purposes, arranging people, i.e. principals, teachers and disciples in classes, and organising skills for learning. The following analysis is mainly about how knowledge assessments are used in both those forms of organisation, starting in administrative, human-organising, practice.

The Administrative organisation of individuals

In contemporary research on assessment in schools, the purpose of assessments is often described as being primarily administrative.[15] Even though the word administration is not used in school ordinances, it is possible to infer the directive of such a practice in the early school ordinances primarily through the concepts of examinations, admissions and transferrals, and in the subsequent ordinances, from 1649 onwards, even more bureaucratic in the sense that these movements would clearly also be recorded, written into the *acts* or *matricula*.

Admission and Selection (delectus ingenium)[16]

If knowledge assessments of pedagogical practice help to organise the actual knowledge, the administrative practice's first function may be to organise access to the house of knowledge. In the translation of the school ordinance of 1611 it is stated that: "No one shall be admitted to school who, firstly, has not been provided with a leaving certificate [Lat. *Testimonium*][17] by the principal at the school that he last belonged to, and, secondly, does not intend to remain a whole year. In the grading it should be specified how far he has come on the study track and which class he has departed."[18] In the school ordinance of 1649, the admittance process

---

till svenska undervisningsväsendets historia (Stockholm: P. A. Norstedt och söners förlag, 1912), 118–19.

15 Patricia Broadfoot, *Education, Assessment and Society. A Sociological Analysis* (Philadelphia, PA: Open University Press, 1996).

16 Selection is a relatively modern word, and in relation to school ordinances the term is actually selective, *delectus*, by inclination and aptitude, *ingeniorum*, more accurately. 'Selection' is however used in the text for smoother reading.

17 The term grades are used in Swedish for the first time in the school ordinance of 1807, interspersed with the words certificate, testimony and evidence. It is not until 1820 that "grades" is used more consistently and this is also where the grades, or "marks", as they are sometimes called in this school ordinance, are given standard designations regarding knowledge degrees for the first time (see School Ordinance of 1820, Appendix Litt. B).

18 *School Ordinance 1611*, 50.

is specified somewhat, partly to take into account those who have not yet attended school and therefore have not yet received a grade, partly to emphasise that it is the student's intellectual and moral qualifications and not circumstances of birth that should be considered most. It says that:

"Disciples who seek entry to a public trivium school are examined by the principal, or on his behalf, by the assistant principal, in order to ascertain 1. whether they possess sufficient aptitude for study, and, in case this matter is approved, 2. to what class they should be referred. / [...] / No one should be admitted into the school without having earnestly promised godliness, diligence and obedience."[19]

Through the school ordinances it also seems possible to conceive a kind of incipient standardisation of admissions requirements in the form of a dual examination. In the 1693 school ordinance it is stated that if the disciple does not correspond with the testimonies at the admissions exam, from the final examination, it may lead to this delivering principal's "tenure's loss."[20] 1724 it is required that the delivering principal should first read aloud the *testimonium in Consistorio*[21] before "it is given to the upper secondary school pupil in hands."[22]

The admissions policies of 1724 were otherwise somewhat 'more softly' formulated compared to the previous school ordinances. While the 1693 school ordinance states that *no one shall be admitted* who is not found to have a particular aptitude for studies,[23] it says in the 1724 ordinance, that *no one should be denied* a place if he is given a good testimony by the parish priest or other credible man, and in "body is brave and healthy."[24] The principal was not allowed however to admit anyone, as in previous school ordinances, without having first examined him.

This relative 'admission generosity' has some similarities with the wording in 1561, where no direct selection thinking yet emerges. The reasons for this can probably be said to be of both a religious and material nature. The church ordinance of 1561 has been partially considered an import from Philipp Melanchthon's Saxon education act of 1528.[25] For his constitution, Melanchthon borrowed,

19 *School Ordinance 1649*, 56.
20 *School Ordinance 1693*, 6.
21 Consistory, with the approximate meaning authority for the church and academy.
22 *School Ordinance 1724*, 27.
23 *School Ordinance 1693*, 3–4.
24 *School Ordinance 1724*, 25.
25 In addition to similar wordings of the two texts, Rudolf B. Hall, *Om Sveriges första läroverksstadga. Studier rörande reformationstidens skola och skolfrågor. Årsböcker i svensk undervisningshistoria*, Vol. 1. (Stockholm: Föreningen för svensk undervisningshistoria,

in his turn, from the Catholic schools,[26] and it should therefore not have been too difficult to reform the Swedish school system from the catholic monastic operation into a school in the service of Protestantism. In the school ordinance of 1571 there are also numerous references to Swedish practice; "General school custom", "such as custom has been" etc.[27] The school ordinance could therefore, in many respects, be understood as a Protestant codification of a Catholic school practice.

For Luther, the purpose of the school was not only to provide God with new tools, which was probably often the case with the monastic schools, but also to spread the word of God — to as many people as possible. This is also what Laurentius Petri initiated the church ordinance with. Preachers were supposed to encourage people to put their children in school, despite the risk "that a big pack of those who came to school would be rogues and villains."[28] The selection process itself was, so to speak, in God's hands — "when and whom God wants to bestow joy and grace, we should do according to God's command and thence place those things in his hands."[29] Even if, as it is furthermore expressed, it is not reasonable to expect that more than a quarter of the crops will bear fruit, one should not stop sowing:

> "scant quarter of what is sown will bear proper fruit, but (as our Lord Christ says) some things will be trampled down and eaten by birds, some things wither, and some things are choked by thistles and all kinds of weeds."[30]

Trying to determine in advance who was skilled enough to undertake studies does not appear to have been the big problem; the big problem was that many were not given the chance to come to school and burst into full bloom. This relates to the Lutheran Protestant stance to not recognise the concept of predestination, but one should only seek out God when faith alone is justification. God will then, along the way, show 'signs' of what one is created for, but this has hence not been settled beforehand. This may be understood in relation to Calvinist Protestantism which

---

1921), 6, invokes that Laurentius Petri had studied with Melanchthon in Saxony. Hall, *Om Sveriges första läroverksstadga*, 6–8.

26   Tore Frängsmyr, *Svensk idéhistoria. Del 1 1000–1809* (Stockholm: Natur och kultur, 2000).

27   See also Hall, *Om Sveriges första läroverksstadag*, 7f.

28   *School Ordinance 1561*, 10.

29   Ibid.

30   Ibid.

assumes that man is predestined and therefore can view individual success as an expression of God's will.[31]

In the difference between the school ordinances and between establishing rules for admission and not establishing rules for admission, respectively, one could say, somewhat simplified, that four often concurrent principles behind the formulations on admission and selection appear. The first could be said to have something to do with the number of individuals in the education system. Historically, this is primarily about the education system's own reproduction, which for many years coincides with the clergy's reproduction. If there was a shortage of disciples, the priests had to actively urge the people to send their children to school.

Later the state's requirement for learned people followed and the church's and state's *different* needs can be said to illustrate the second principle, which has to do with different ways of looking at the usability of education. The strict regulations of suitability for studies of 1693 can be seen in the light that this school ordinance would mainly cater to the needs of the clerical class, while the more liberal admissions system during the age of liberty's school ordinance in 1724 can be understood on the basis that the other classes saw the benefits of educated people.[32] A third principle could be said to deal with different philosophies regarding admission and selection; should it be done at the admittance stage (sort and approve) or should the selection be conducted along the way (sort and refuse).

A fourth principle could be linked to love of the truth. The meaning of love of the truth will become clearer further on in the text, but the fear of false knowledge permeates the school ordinance's knowledge assessment practices in several different ways, including, as mentioned, in relation with the 1693 school ordinance and the dual examination concept. He who could be admitted to school would have to be considered to be or be able to become a bearer of the truth. Whether this was the case had to be thoroughly investigated, i.e. examined.

Examination, transfer and dismissal

Examination should according to the school ordinances take place at the time of admission of disciples, but could also be used for pedagogical purposes. Examinations were also used to support the transfer of disciples between school classes. This adjustment was both spatial and semantic, both physically organised and symbolically controlling.

---

31 Max Weber, *Den protestantiska etiken och kapitalismens anda* (Lund: Argos, 1934 [1978]).

32 See Leinberg, *Om snillevalet*, 17.

The first time the word examination is used in a school ordinance is in the church ordinance of 1561 which formulated that the schoolmaster should examine the children in "evening bible verse" on the one hand,[33] and in the Sunday "paruo Cathechismo" on the other.[34] The examination is also used sparsely in the 1611 school ordinance, only once,[35] and in association with regulations on the school's summer break. The examination was not presented as a purpose for transfer at this point either, even if that was likely the case, but as a verification by the teachers:

> "Every year all lessons are completed on June 1, and for a few consecutive days public exams are carried out: at the cathedral schools in the presence of the bishop and members of the cathedral chapter, at the provincial schools in the presence of a cathedral chapter member as a representative of the bishop and the cathedral chapter, as well as by the clergy in the location. If any of the lecturers is found to have maintained his position in a negligent manner, he shall, after having received a warning time and time again by the bishop and the chapter's ruling, be dismissed from office."[36]

Through the examination of the disciples, the Lord's men were also provided with a picture of how lecturers had done their work. What happened to those disciples who did not pass the examination is not explained. It rather seems as though the primary responsibility for the disciples' knowledge lay with the lecturer — to such an extent that it could cost him his office — and hence not with the individual disciple.

In the 1649 school ordinance it is also made clear, however, that the administrative purpose of the examination is to *transfer* the disciples.

> "After the completion of the examination, the examiners, principals and classroom teachers meet and deliver their reviews about each disciple's diligence and knowledge. Those deemed worthy to attend school are transferred upwards to a higher class or are sent to upper secondary school."[37]

Transferral after the annual examination was, according to this school ordinance, not the only way to advance within the school system. If any disciple as a result of either a "very fortunate talent or through individual teaching" finds himself

---

33 *School Ordinance 1561*, 17.
34 Ibid., 18.
35 This applies both to the Latin original footprint and the Swedish translation.
36 *School Ordinance 1611*, 35.
37 *School Ordinance 1649*, 88.

ahead of the appointed time for his department's course, he should be offered the opportunity to immediately transfer to a higher class.[38]

In the 1693 school ordinance an attribution is added saying that the upper secondary school principal during the month of examinations shall "record" how far each class has come in its prescribed lessons, and that these records shall be submitted to the bishop prior to the annual examination, *Examen Anniversarium*.[39] Here is consolidated, for the first time in school ordinances, a production of written data of an administrative nature. In the school ordinance that follows, the 'need' for such written information is highlighted more clearly. In one particular chapter, "About Ephori Office,"[40] it says that the "overseers," i.e. the bishops and the superintendent of secondary schools, in the name of God and the realm, should seriously ensure that schools work well and make certain that:

> "[…] carefully examine the school boys, record in the Protocol the names of those who give good hope for themselves, with more of importance that has been found; Send the same to the Consistorium, to there be added to the records for keeping until next year, so that when the examination Solenne occurs again, it will be possible to compare the boys' advancement from one year to the next."[41]

The organisation was until 1693 described primarily as a spatial organisation, a transferral from one classroom to another, or within the classroom. For example, the statutes in the 1649 school ordinance declare that "Diligent and conscientious disciples ought to, by the teachers, be given prominence and provided with a place in the class before the negligent and ignorant" and that the "lazy should be put on the donkey stool (*scamno asinorum*) or carry the donkey effigy (*asini picturam*), be placed after the others, be excluded from positions and honorary posts in school, etc."[42] As a result of the 1693, and especially the 1724 ordinances, it is dictated that this order between disciples should also be put into writing. This can be said to constitute a shift from the spatial present to the extensions in time. *Differences*

---

38 Ibid., 57.
39 *School Ordinance 1693*, 11.
40 *Ephorus*, from the Greek. "*Efor*", "*eforerna*" – overseer. Designation *Ephorus* office ['Ephori ämbete'] accounted for episcopal supervision of secondary schools. This function was retained until 1904, when parliament decided to place the entire responsibility for supervision on the secondary school board. The Eforus institution remained, however, saddled with some unimportant administrative tasks until 1958 according to Bengt Thelin, *Exit Eforus. Läroverkens sekularisering och striden om kristendomsundervisningen* (Stockholm: Liber Utbildningsförlaget, 1981), 244.
41 *School Ordinance 1724*, 56.
42 *School Ordinance 1649*, 89, 90.

become historical, they are put down on paper. The disciples can through these records be compared with themselves and with each other from one year to the next. Hence their accomplishments become temporal. Knowledge becomes visible and can be reproduced in order to compare performances over time.[43]

This is likely not a practice that occurs in 1724, or even 1693, but it is at that point in time that it appears important to *formulate* its statute in the school ordinances. For example, the educational historian Rudolf B. Hall has presented a number of summaries of grading lists (*betygslistor*) from catalogues of pupils from Västerås in 1632, which clearly state, among other things, how many pupils who possess which grades, what ages they are and what their fathers' professions are.[44] Peter Burke argues that the church has, since the 1400–1500s, had a penchant for documenting "the spiritual and economic status;" a practice that the state "took over/after."[45] This practice can gradually be said to write a story, based on which strategic decisions can be made and forecasts prepared. The past comes closer and the ability to mirror oneself in one's own short history leads to an extension of the story into the public sphere; into public statistics and into politics.[46]

This tendency to stipulate that assessments be put into writing reappear in the last of the administrative assessment practices that could be identified in the school ordinances, dismissal. Dismissal should be understood in the dual meaning, taking leave (leave school after completing the course of study) and being fired. In many of the school ordinances, leaving the clergy was not the intention. The first school ordinances dwell on getting capable individuals to attend school, both teachers and disciples. Incompetents should be sifted out at the admission stage. For the remaining pupils there were high hopes that they would be able to stay within the church/school. Only in 1649 the possibility to dissuade disciples

---

43 Recorded performances make it, as Hoskin has expressed it, possible: "to generate a 'history' of each student and also to classify students in masse into categories and eventually into 'populations with norms'." Keith Hoskin. "The Examination, Disciplinary Power and Rational Schooling," *History of Education* 8, no. 2 (1979): 137, doi:10.1080/0046760790080205.

44 Hall, *Valda aktstycken*, 106–119.

45 Burke, *A Social History*, 121.

46 See Karin Johannisson's *Det mätbara samhället: statistic och samhällsdröm I 1700-talets Europa* (Stockholm: Norsted, 1988) for a more general description of how this type of order, the "political arithmetic", emerged in Sweden right around the beginning of the 1700s. Sweden, for example, was a front runner in Europe with its national population register and the development of an institution for this bookkeeping: Tabellverken, later SCB (Statistiska centralbyrån, Swedish Statistical Agency) (see also Burke, *A Social History*, 135).

from further education was decreed. At that time the right to a *testimonium* for disciples who had completed the education was also stipulated for the first time. "To those who have left school, he [the principal] should give, if they so request, reliable and conscientious credentials of behaviour and knowledge."[47] Most likely, this was the custom already in 1611, because the schools did not admit anyone who could *not* demonstrate *testimonium*.

The school ordinance of 1693 did not decree the *right* to a leaving certificate in particular, even if such may have been regarded as self-evident, based on the sharp formulations that no one may go further in the system without an excellent *testimonium*.[48] The school ordinance of 1724 has, by contrast, clear formulations of the relationship between the final examination and the *testimonium*. Here, the 'bookkeeping' is described in the same way as for the examination in the same school ordinance. The principal's duties include:

> "13 Convey the *testimonium* to those who would like to travel to the Academy or take leave from upper secondary school and go on to another life mission. /[...]/
>
> 16 Enter into the *matricula* all their names, as under their directorate, that they have either been transferred to upper secondary school or, with *testimonium* from there, dismissed, with more than has hitherto usually been recorded."[49]

Until 1724 three organising principles behind the wording regarding dismissal have been clarified successively. The first one is about a development towards ongoing screening. The admission process becomes a smaller absolute determinant for the resignation. Secondly, the resignation becomes more absolute in the sense that it is marked with a mandatory *testimonium*. Thirdly, the resignation becomes historic in the same sense as the transferral above. If the disciples previously disappeared from the school premises, their disappearance is now visible in the *matricula*.[50] The first two of these organising principles behind the formulations can also be linked to the principles of admission above, in such a way that a gradual screening follows more generous admission policies and that the *testimonium* might become more and more important as several representatives

---

47 *School Ordinance 1649*, 55.

48 *School Ordinance 1693*, 6.

49 *School Ordinance 1724*, 59.

50 The "education historian" Hugo Hernlund has, in an early work from 1880, showed that at least most upper secondary schools, in any case around the years 1730–1740, could present records of how many disciples had been rejected by the school. Hugo Hernlund, *Bidrag till den svenska skollagstiftningens historia under partitidehvarfvet* (Akademiska avh. Appendices. Sthlm 1882–92, 1880).

for those 'skilled in books' are added. Even though the school ordinances of the 1800s are not considered here, it can nevertheless be noted that this 'formalisation' of the administrative, human-organising practice, is described in an increasingly clear manner. In 1807, admission, promotion and transition to the academy are governed in a specific chapter consisting of six pages[51] with, inter alia, complete instructions about the *testimonium*; in 1820, corresponding instructions are written in five chapters at a total of 17 pages.[52] The human ordinance was recorded to an increasing extent in both individual documents and master documents. This is how a text-based foundation for knowledge of the difference between schools and disciples differences is built.

The knowledge-organising practice

It is not possible to do the assessments in the school ordinances justice from a knowledge-organising perspective without first trying to understand what kind of knowledge would be evaluated, or which epistemological approach would be maintained. The love of God, truth and language constituted, one could say, the school ordinances' epistemological basis — even if it was slowly subsiding.

God, truth and language

The first secondary schools in Sweden are often called Latin schools. It is difficult to understand these schools' knowledge assessment practices if one does not understand the meaning of a Latin school. The designation leads one to believe that they are so called because the pupils basically just learned Latin and that teaching exclusively took place in Latin. In fact, one probably ought to understand the 'Latin culture' in these schools as an expression of an epistemological approach that made language a central feature. Language organised knowledge.[53] Michel Foucault writes in *The Order of Things* that knowledge during the 1500s and 1600s was to represent the thing with words, the words represented the thing exactly and

---

51 *School Ordinance 1807*, 76–81. Overall, this school ordinance consists of 52 pages.

52 *School Ordinance 1820*, 14–30. Overall, this school ordinance consists of 90 pages excluding appendices.

53 This is also visible in the administrative organisation of school classes in such a way that school classes were organised based on language. The first grade in provincial schools was called, for example in the 1611 school ordinance, the *Alphabetica*, the second *Etymologica*, the third *Syntactica*; the fourth differed from the previous three, however, and was called Classis *Rectoris*. The cathedral school's fourth grade was called *Graeca*, the fifth *Rhetorica* et *Logica* and the sixth, which also is an exception, was called *Theologica*.

being able to organise the words by using grammar rules in fact also meant being able to organise the world.[54] There was, somewhat simplified, no other world than the one that could be expressed in language, and the purpose of studying language was to express the truth. Words give names to things, represent them, grammar provides the representations with an order, forms verbal signs for discourses — sentences (in both the spiritual and linguistic significance). A developed language brought people closer to true knowledge.[55]

During the 1500s and 1600s one had begun to rediscover the classical texts; Plato, Aristotle, Quintilian etc. Antiquity had a renaissance. According to Aristotle, man would be an animal if God had not elevated him and given him the gifts of thought and speech. According to Hall, references to this particular point can be found in several of the Reformation men's texts, with the addition that it was man's task to cultivate these gifts to an extraordinary degree. These were cultivated through language, and when God had handed down a criminal conviction on the national languages of Babel, it could only mean Latin, which had been spared because it was the language in which the Romans had carved the name of Jesus on the cross, and Hebrew, in which the Bible is written. The ancient texts were often written in Greek, and so Greek was also a suitable language for learning.[56] In this way, God and knowledge/science were unified, particularly through Latin/ grammar. To speak not only real Latin, but also, as it is commonly called in the school ordinances, a "beautiful Latin,"[57] was to speak the truth, a truth that God had given us the opportunity to reach by giving us language. Thereby we became humans in the highest meaning; with a trained sense, expressed through language, we were able to set us apart from the animals.

God, truth and language speak consistently in harmony through all school ordinances, but with hints of a more real epistemological approach in 1649 and 1724. A virtuous disposition, language skills and objectivity are a more or less clearly stated goal in the school ordinances. Latin studies appear to constitute the conditions for the other two. The ability of language to express the truth, through, among other things, the verb "to be" fixates truth to language.[58] With language we can talk about what the world is like, the better we speak, the closer we can

---

54 Michel Foucault, *The Order of Things* (London and New York: Routledge classics 1966 [2002]).

55 Ibid., especially chapter 4.

56 Hall, *Om Sveriges första*, 63–66.

57 See *School Ordinance 1649*, 54.

58 Foucault writes about this under the heading *The Theory of the Verb* where one in the English translation has used the verb "to be". Foucault, *The Order of Things*, 101–06.

get to the truth. The truth makes us virtuous. The consequences this has in the school ordinances is that language and exercises in the language take precedence over interpretations and analyses, at least in the lower school years (it is not until the upper secondary school's final grades one can see, in the school ordinances of 1649 and 1693, a shift toward interpretation and analysis, often with a link to grammatical rules, however). Hall calls this *parallelism*; the ancient texts are used mainly for language exercise purposes where the linguistic emulation of the text was more important than the content that the texts conveyed.[59] Hence, the ancient text rarely posed a threat to the truth that the Bible represented. For example, in the 1649 school ordinance it says below the headline "About the interpretation of the authors whose works are read in school" (*The Auctorum Enarratione*):

> "And all the time when the works of most Latin authors in the school are read for the sake of the language and are highly suitable for this purpose (and they are also of great benefit in other respects), it is announced here a representation of the method for the Latin authors' treatment in and for the acquisition of knowledge of this language.
> This method comprises, in general speech: 1. The authors' reading and interpretation; 2. Selection and notes of places in their scripts, and 3. the authors' emulation ["1. *Lectione et Explicatione*. 2. *Selectione*. 3. *Imitatione*"]."[60]

This fairly literal way to stick to the Latin word was also expressed in the school ordinances as a kind of overzealous audit of the pure, real and true. In addition to working very hard toward hiring teachers with real knowledge, as mentioned above, one should ensure that the books the boys used were faultless, the paper should be neat and the style clear and beautiful. Printers who violated these standards would be punished by confiscation of the edition.[61] Furthermore, the boys should also have special notebooks (*liber memoralis*) for each author "so that excerpts from several authors were not mixed together."[62] Another example can be taken from the instructions for language education in the same school ordinance: "It is enough that they [the disciples] during their writings could achieve the neatness and cleanliness of the Latin language; invention and disposition will have to be according to everyone's natural talent."[63]

Knowledge assessments played an important role with this epistemological approach. They were used as a tool to produce and organise this type of 'closed' knowledge. The concept of knowledge assessments is slightly misleading in this

---

59 Hall, *Om Sveriges första*, 60–72.
60 *School Ordinance 1649*, 65.
61 Ibid., 62.
62 Ibid., 69.
63 Ibid., 61.

context, as this practice in the school ordinances was more intended as a kind of didactic instructions. These instructions aim to transfer the content of the curriculum to the disciples through various forms of feedback, which in turn is also partly reflected by the manner in which the relationship between teachers and disciples is decreed.

Feedback through evaluation practices is expressed in different ways in the formulation about homework, about reading by heart, rehearsals, tests and examinations, as well as the corrections of writing exercises. The school ordinances can also be said to be structured in accordance with two principles that follow from the practice of speech and writing, respectively, and their respective conditions – the sound and the character.

Speech — homework and reading by heart

On the 20 pages that the church ordinance of 1561 is comprised of, the word "*lexor*" is used more than 30 times. *Lexor*, from the Latin *lectio*, means reading and is used in the church ordinance in particular with the meaning "piece of reading"/"sermons text": "The pieces of reading/sermon texts should be read from the Swedish bible in the new or old testament."[64] Reading often refers to reading aloud, the texts were supposed to resound before the entire class. "*Lexor*" is used through all the school ordinances studied here with the meaning of the different classes' reading stipulation. At the same time, over-reading of homework was encouraged outside the education framework, and the term *lexor* in these contexts is given the same meaning as "homework" in modern Swedish (*läxor*). In the church ordinance of 1561 it is stated, for example, that the disciples "From when the clock turns two until she turns three, they must sit by themselves and read the homework and verse."[65] *Homework* is decreed for the first time in 1611: "when school is dissolved, so-called holiday homework is given, which the disciples should read from memory upon their return from the parish walk."[66]

This pattern is repeated in the subsequent school ordinances as well. There was a stipulation of homework to read, and some of these had to be known by heart. This is most clearly stated in the 1649 school ordinance where the reading ordinance for each class is present in a headline: "By heart should in this class be read [...]", or in Latin, "*Memoriae* [...]" or "*Ediscenda hic ad Verbum*", which also

---

64　*School Ordinance 1561*, 6.
65　Ibid.
66　*School Ordinance 1611*, 36.

can be translated as […] carefully […] or […] literally.[67] The higher the class, the higher the demands on what the disciples should know by heart.

The 'by-heart knowledge' can be linked to speech, even though knowledge such as the rules of grammar, syntax and rhetoric are also, of course, of use in the script. It was during the dissertations that the disciples should be practising their *Lexor memoriter*, by quickly being able to provide examples of sentences and words of wisdom that strengthened their theses. The disciples should also be encouraged to talk to each other in Latin when they were playing.[68] The lessons should be read aloud[69] before specific 'hearers,' who in the early school ordinances have been described as disciples from the higher classes. Learning the lessons by heart required rehearsals and tests, and here learning (memorising) and knowledge assessment in the feedback sense, were united.

Rehearsals and quizzes, memory exercise

Rehearsals and quizzes appear to be, from a review of the school ordinances, the most dominant didactic instruction. Memory and rehearsals were presented in fairly general terms in the statutes of 1561 and 1611, but become entire sections in the 1649 school ordinance. Chapter 14 of this school ordinance is called "About the exercise of memory" (*De memoriae excercitatione*).[70] There it is stated that:

> "The boys should not believe that they know more than they fully retain in memory. The memory can through practice be maintained and strengthened. Therefore, the boys must frequently and diligently practice their memories by learning quite a great deal by heart, including everything from the first school years, when they are still at an age that hardly notices the effort, because it does not weigh it. This age is hence the most appropriate

---

67 *School Ordinance 1649.*

68 This also appears to be the basis for the so-called donkey punishment. Any disciple who was caught talking in his native language and not in Latin had to wear a specially manufactured donkey head on his shoulders. By exposing someone else who was speaking in his mother tongue, he was allowed to place the donkey head on him. This later became a punishment for the lazy (see School Ordinance 1649, 82, 90; see Hall, *Om Sveriges första*, 114, see for a picture illustration: Herman Siegvald, *Om kroppsaga (en historisk psykologisk studie* (Lund: PH. Lindstedts universitets bokhandel, 1932), 9.

69 Silent reading (in school) is described in a journal for teachers as an innovation, toward which one was very sceptical, as late as at the end of the 1800s (*Swedish Teachers' Journal* 1882).

70 The school ordinance's introductory paragraphs about the classes' respective reading ordinances often refer to this particular chapter.

for the learning of the first foundations of knowledge, which a more advanced age finds boring."[71]

The teachers are further encouraged to rehearse and renew the homework aloud so that imprinting occurs via both the eye and ear. Therefore, the pupil should also read aloud to himself and copy down in writing "the paradigm he shall toil to achieve."[72] Order of importance must be observed and it is advisable to rehearse the contents on an empty stomach in the morning and before going to sleep. If the teacher furthermore underlines the usefulness and pleasure of what is to be learned, it becomes easier to learn by heart — "through this the disciples' eagerness is stimulated and reinforced."[73] However, it is important not to let the boys learn too much by heart as "their memories will be overloaded and confused."[74] In grammar and at the authorities, "a great deal [...] needs only in its content be remembered, so that it can be reproduced with similar words."[75]

"Regarding rehearsals and exams" it is stipulated in a specific chapter that these "for several reasons are useful, indeed necessary, so that the school could take as a motto the old word: Homework that is not rehearsed is as though never given" (*Lectio Lecta et non est repetite quais nulla*).[76]

In the 1693 and 1724 school ordinances the amount of text on rehearsals and tests is reduced and so is even the decreed frequency of rehearsals and tests. In the 1693 school ordinance it is proposed that exams are held on Wednesdays, Saturdays and at the end of terms.[77] In 1724, the Wednesday and Saturday examinations are replaced by an examination every two weeks. Proper examinations are presented as more effective for imprint in memory than frequent rehearsals. Furthermore, the term examinations were discontinued, and for the examination *Solenne* (annual examination) the examination of dissertation was introduced.[78]

---

71 *School Ordinance 1649*, 84.

72 Ibid.

73 Ibid., 85.

74 Ibid.

75 Ibid. This type of "psychological consciousness" of the memory's capacity is expressed in all school ordinances. In the 1561 school ordinance is says, for example: "... neither is it useful to inconvenience the children with a great deal of homework", *School Ordinance 1561*, 12; or in the *School Ordinance 1693*: "The [the masters] should take heed, that they do not overwhelm *the disciples* with a great deal of reading by heart, or mix many and several things as well, as both the desire and the memory can be stifled," 7.

76 *School Ordinance 1649*, 86.

77 *School Ordinance 1693*, 11.

78 *School Ordinance 1724*, 54–55.

Compared to what Francis Schrag has written, that the dissertation was the model for the oral examination,[79] it seems that in Sweden the dissertations came to be a part of an already established examination practice. As it is stated in the school ordinances it does not aim, above all, to develop the art of dialogue, but to organise the memory and by-heart knowledge. The main purpose of knowledge assessments, as they appear in the school ordinances, were, with some simplification, memory training and a verification that the memory had been imprinted. The memory was the foundation, the dialogue a possible superstructure.

How this 'memory cult,' which is expressed in the school ordinances, should be interpreted is a more open question. The Swedish educational historian Per-Johan Ödman writes about the first school ordinance of 1561/1571 that: "The recommended pedagogics is based on reproduction and recitation" and that "the educational outcome that one was striving for was not that pupils *understood* what they were doing, but that they *did* the right thing."[80] Ödman's interpretation is likely correct, but it can be developed to a certain extent in relation to the 16th century schools' administrative and epistemological conditions. Firstly, the administrative control requirements certainly played a major role in the maintenance of the recitation and test regime. The schoolmaster appointed, as mentioned above, hearers from the higher classes to help him with the teaching of the younger disciples. These 'helpers' as they are sometimes referred to as, heard (rehearsed) homework, whereupon the school master tested his disciples, not least to make sure that the hearers stuck to the correct texts. This control could also be described as an epistemological and moral amalgamation of actors involved in examinations. Christopher Stray has, for example, shown that the public oral exam in Latin at Oxford University during the 1700s also expressed and shaped participation in the academic community.[81]

---

79 Francis Schrag, "Conceptions of Knowledge," in *Handbook of Research on Curriculum: A Project of the American Educational Research Association*, ed. Philip W. Jackson (New York, NY: Macmillan Pub. Co., 1992).

80 Per-Johan Ödman, *Kontrasternas spel. En svensk mentalitets- och pedagogikhistoria* (Stockholm: Prisma, 1998), 105.

81 Christopher Stray, "The shift from oral to written examination: Cambridge and Oxford, 1700–1900," *Assessment in Education: Principles, Policy & Practice* 8.1 (2001), doi: 10.1080/09695940120033243. Barbara Kehm argues that this has also been an important argument for the oral exam at German universities. At German universities the examiners are also schooled in the art of the oral exam by first serving as assistant examiners to a more experienced colleague. The oral examination can with that arrangement not only be said to be a knowledge control function but also an occasion where it reproduces itself as professional knowledge. In the same way, the

It should also be taken into account that these secondary schools were vocational training for priests for a long time. Things like for example the ecumenical symbols one should simply know. That was an important part of the actual professional skills. Another professional skill was to be able to engage in dissertation, i.e. to determine verbal disputes with references from one's memory to true texts. A more substantive interpretation of this memory cult would indicate that there was a lack of books and that one therefore needed to keep more in one's mind. Knowledge was reproduced orally. This appears to be a slightly less sustainable interpretation, since there are, as mentioned above, statutes about both books and notebooks. From a more pedagogical perspective, one can imagine that teaching, especially in grammar and Latin, was so abstract that it could not be understood, just memorised. That the disciple would not think with the apparatus he had imprinted one knew very well, Hall argues, but the disciple was supposed to memorise it for the future — memory could compensate for any lack of understanding.[82]

One way to try to understand how it was possible to maintain a house of knowledge that had the character of an institution for "knowledge cloning" (one-to-one reproduction), may be to try to understand what function *memory* could have had in contemporary understanding of knowledge.

The obsession with memory of the statutes was probably inherited from antiquity,[83] where memory was used to denote the experience. Galen (about 100 AD) also wrote, in addition to medical writings, some epistemological texts, which have been compiled in *Three Treatises on the Nature of Science*.[84] In Galen's epistemology, memory had a crucial function. Memory was for him the single most important tool; not for the reproduction of knowledge, but for the production of knowledge. Galen presented memory, with the meaning past experiences, as a crucial property in all doctors. But everything cannot be remembered exactly, and all the new observations are unlike all previous experiences, which is why logic becomes a necessary support function. Experience gives us facts, logic offers explanations. The doctor's mission, argues Galen, was to observe a state of

---

abundantly examined disciple may have been trained in the ability to examine, for the benefit the moment he himself would become a teacher. Barbara M. Kehm, "Oral Examinations at German Universities," *Assessment in Education* 8, no. 1 (2001): 30, doi: 10.1080/09695940120033234.

82 Hall, *Om Sveriges första*, 31.

83 Compare Paul Ricoeur, *Memory, History, Forgetting* (Chicago, IL: University of Chicago Press, 2004), chap. 1.

84 Galen, *Three Treatises on the Nature of Sciences*m, trans. Richard Walzer and Michael Frede (Indianapolis/Cambridge: Hackett Publishing Company, 1985).

disease and come to the realisation whether it resembled anything he had seen before, and on the basis of this "transition to the similar"[85] make a diagnosis or prognosis, or provide a treatment.[86]

In Foucault's history of knowledge analyses, the 1500s and 1600s preoccupation with memory is described in a similar manner. Memory was a way to talk about how past experiences could be made present in the moment — "making a past impression present"[87] — to reflect new findings, and from the difference or similarity gain new skills.[88] With such an epistemology, new knowledge becomes completely dependent on what the previous experiences are and how new observations are prepared. Here every kind of experience was not sufficient. A, certainly unique, example of this can be found in the 1561 church ordinance. Under the headline church singing, which includes not only the singing in school but in the church at large, it says that the schoolmaster or the person in charge of singing should ensure that ungodly songs or texts were not read in church. They shall:

> "endeavour to abolish the ungodly memory, that farmers have been in the habit of using a great deal during their feasts and come to use in the same way, some of these Swedish hymns or transform the same memory so that they are consistent with the scripts."[89]

The quotation expresses an aspiration to replace a certain memory, certain experiences, a certain history and, one assumes, a certain pagan behaviour. The school was supposed to provide a new experience foundation based on which new findings could be interpreted. Through rehearsals, tests and examinations the school ordinances appear to want to train the memory and at the same time imprint it with specific skills. Hence, one could say that the school ordinances express an attempt to ensure that the new findings will be interpreted in a manner that is known. Knowledge assessments, insofar that they operate in the Latin and church memory services, were, with this approach, not only about verifying and ensuring the reproduction of the known, but also about organising the production of the unknown. The prevailing world view can be said to be self-validating, new skills will confirm the old. But only up to a certain point. During knowledge transfer, an experience of the actual transfer is also transferred. That too much by-heart

---

85 Ibid., 26.
86 Ibid., 31.
87 Foucault, *The Order of Things*, 76.
88 According to Foucault, it was primarily the similarity one searched for during this period, to be able to say that the new was the same as the already known.
89 *School Ordinance 1561*, 8.

knowledge can inhibit the desire, as it was stated in the 1693 school ordinance is an example of this.

By-heart knowledge and the oral tradition was not the only way in which knowledge was considered able to travel. Writing should also be practised and writing was not in the service of memory but of judgement [Swe: *omdöme*], even if it is only in the 1649 school ordinance where one starts to mention this as two different kinds of characteristics.[90]

The Scripture — the Writing Exercises and the Emulation

Memory was the key characteristic that was supposed to be developed for oral knowledge to be passed down. The methods of this was rehearsals which were assessed via tests. Written knowledge was connected with the ability to have good *judgement*, and this was considered to be best developed with other strategies. In the church ordinance of 1561 it is briefly stated that the disciples should learn to write, and it is not until 1611 that specific writing exercises and writing curriculum are decreed. Writing is organised. In the first grade one should, according to the statues, practice penmanship, the second grade would translate, 'as a style exercise' Cicero's letters and Aesop's fables, as well as practice emulation. In the third grade, verse writing in Latin was added to translation and emulation. This pattern recurs in the fourth grade; Cicero's letters should be replicated, but in this class one could also use Virgil's poetry as a model.[91] The pattern penmanship, translating and emulation reappear in the later school ordinances in 1649, 1693 and 1724.

On the surface, the writing exercises seemingly follow the same pattern as the memory exercises, where a gradually more liberal approach to "the authorities" are permitted the higher up the disciples find themselves in the education system, as well over time between the school ordinances. The regulations for writing exercises highlight, however, more clearly than is the case around rehearsals, hearings and memory, that writing is *not* aimed at what has here been termed 'knowledge cloning.' Instead, there are thoughts about the permitted variations relative to the models. The 1649 school ordinance distinguishes between three *degrees* of emulation.[92] With reference to Quintilianus, Lipsius, Janius and Vives, three different

---

90 Text has actually even been considered dangerous for the memory. This is certainly not how it is presented in the school ordinances, but Plato supported and defended memory to such an extent that he feared written language, texts and books. Platon, *Faidros. I Skrifter. Bok 2*, trans. Jan Stolpe, (Stockholm: Atlantis, 2003).

91 *School Ordinance 1611*, 28–30.

92 *School Ordinance 1649*, 72.

types of emulations are initially defined: the childish emulation (*puerilis*), the incipient development's (*crescens*) and the fully mature man's (*adulta*). In the (*trivium*) school, teachers cannot expect to get much further than the first level, while upper secondary school can approach the second level. The first level is more about "plagiarism" than true emulation, while the so-called learned emulation uses the "stylistic beauty" of the original in a more free manner.[93] The regulation of emulation is the clearest example in the school ordinances of thoughts of qualitative differences in a particular skill:

> "As a result of differences in the degree of knowledge gradations were discernible even in the emulation that we have called the child's. The first and lowest is the one that exclusively takes into account an accurate rendition of the basic grammatical rules and Latin's most general laws / [...] / The second level is reached when the disciples not only try to achieve grammatical correctness and general linguistic correctness but also, as thoroughly, give particular attention to special study of language peculiarities / [...] / The third entails that, except what is now mentioned, the disciples attempt to emulate the very style of Cicero, its periods, leads, rhythm and all its continuous construction [etc. ...]."[94]

On other occasions when differences are indicated in the school ordinances, it is only about degrees of *ingenio*, talent, in the disciple or about differences regarding the amount of homework/curriculum. It is not unreasonable to think that the written text opens, in a different way than speech, for a systematic comparison, a sifting out of distinct qualities in the knowledge that can be linked to perceptions of different levels of comprehension.[95] Thus perhaps the learning process is also reflected in a different way in the writing, which one should then take into account in the assessment/feedback of the text. This also appears to have been the case, at least based on the instructions for the correction of scriptures.

The Correction of Scripture

Just as in the case of tests above, in 1561 it is stipulated that the principal should, in the morning, correct the disciples' writing exercises based on the grounds that he in this way could keep the hearers'/helpers' effort from the previous day under

---

93 Ibid., 78–79.
94 Ibid., 72–73.
95 Walter J. Ong writes in the book *Orality and literacy* that the fact that writing separates the skilled person from what he knows, allows for an increased degree of articulate introspection, which opens the mind in a completely different way than orality, not only in relation to the outer objective world that is separate from the psyche, but also in relation to the inner me, against which the objective world is placed. Walter J. Ong, *Orality and Literacy: The Technologizing of the Word* (London, UK: Methuen, 1982).

observation.[96] From a knowledge-organising perspective the correction does, however, differ from the hearing. Correction, *errata emendera*, of translations, or of writing themes, is not linked, in any of the school ordinances, to the word examination. The writing was not examined; it is corrected over time.

This is most clearly expressed in the 1649 school ordinance. In a particular section, "About the correction of scripture" (*De Emendatione Scriptorum*), the difference emerges clearly to the examination's more absolutely imprinted purpose. *Emendatione* can be translated as "liberate from error." The purpose of the correction process does hence not appear to be to indicate where the disciple had done wrong, but to try to liberate the disciple's penmanship from errors, to gradually improve the writing.

An initial difference from the examinations is that both the teachers and the disciples themselves were deemed to be able to correct the texts:

> "Correction is twofold, the disciples' own and the teachers." The disciples should read their scripts themselves as well as correct and improve them. These corrections should, however, be kept within reasonable limits, so that the disciples do not lose themselves in excessive self-criticism and end up making their essays worse."[97]

When the teacher's correction is decreed, four guidelines are indicated. The teacher should first, with an easily readable style, change and add to the disciples' essay books, and:

> "[the incorrect he shall not completely obliterate, but only underline. This attentiveness on what is written brings, among other things, the advantage that the disciples during the following months, at any time, can return to what they have written in the preceding, and through comparisons satisfy themselves about their progress, avoid the once corrected errors and continue on the road that they find be the right one."[98]

With modern assessment terminology one could call this a sort of portfolio thinking, where the disciple and the teacher can always go back and follow the development process.[99] This is not possible, or at least not as easy, if knowledge, so to speak, does not exist on paper. The teacher was also thought to have other

---

96 *School Ordinance 1561*, 14.
97 *School Ordinance 1649*, 80. Contemporary classroom assessment literature describes the "novel idea" of self-assessment in almost exactly these words. E.g. Dylan Wiliam and Siobhan Leahy, *Embedding Formative Assessment: Practical Techniques for F–12 Classrooms* (West Palm Beach, FL: Learning Sciences International, 2015).
98 *School Ordinance 1649*, 80.
99 For an overview of portfolio or portfolio methods, see e.g. Richard J. Stiggins, *Student-centred Classroom Assessment* (New York, NY: Merrill, 1994).

opportunities to develop the disciples through the correction process. Secondly, it was considered:

> "prudent to not undergo the corrections silently or murmuring, but with a loud voice, so that that all gets a part of everyone's faults as well as virtues, whereby they learn to, during noble competition [*honesta aemulatione*][100] for the future avoid the former and emulate the latter."[101]

This type of "listeners' gain", one could of course also conceive, would occur at oral examinations; likely, it was partly because of this that they considered them to be memory training. The comparison between the individual mistakes and virtues might, however, be easier to make when one has the texts in front of oneself, page beside page. The distance between the species is shrinking – the differences become clearer.[102] Thirdly, it is decreed that the teacher should not only prove that the disciple has made a mistake but that the teacher should also demonstrate the language rule against which the error has been committed. Fourthly, the teacher should differentiate between major and minor errors and "take account of the disciples' levels of development."[103] Minor errors he should merely note in passing, but penalise such faults that breach the "regularity, purity and clarity of the language."[104] If someone committed a major error, the teacher should, according to the instructions, not communicate this to the entire class, but "in a low voice inform him of this in private" and hence avoid making the disciple appear ridiculous before the entire class.[105] The teacher was finally encouraged to go through the text as he himself would have written it, and thereby set an example.

It may seem a bit contradictory that the same school ordinance that stipulates the donkey punishment for those who happen to speak in their native language and not in Latin, want to tread so cautiously in the indication of errors and shortfalls. Perhaps it has to do with the fact that this entire correction process was thought to practice a different kind of characteristic, judgement, or, as it is stated in the 1649 school ordinance; "this will enable the disciple to be incited and supervised to practise more the power of judgement [*judicij*] than of memory".[106]

---

100   "*Aemulatione*" can also be translated as "striving to emulate", which does not connote becoming better than others, or even to win, in the same way as the word competition does.
101   *School Ordinance 1649*, 80.
102   Foucault, *The Order of Things*.
103   *School Ordinance 1649*, 81.
104   Ibid.
105   Ibid.
106   Ibid., 82.

The question is whether what one sees here is two different traditions that mainly have to do with how knowledge is transmitted from speech and writing, respectively, or have to do with how one viewed memory and judgement. It seems reasonable to think that judgement is more readily nurtured by the simultaneous visualisation of the true and the false, i.e. that judgement places itself on the border between two possibilities. Memory, as described in the school ordinances, only dwells on what is real, the true experience. Writing could then be said to more lightly (but not necessarily better) visualise differences based on which judgement can be trained. The process-oriented assessments decreed for the correction of writing in 1649 have consistently almost completely the visualisation of differences as an ordering principle; between right and wrong, between before and now, between the disciples themselves and between the disciples and the teacher. The thin school ordinance of 1693 gives no further guidance on this, but the school ordinance of 1724 clearly distinguishes between the 'sciences' that entirely depend on memory and the disciplines that require a more mature *judicium*. Memory is still basic, but judgement seems to be on its way to becoming a higher goal.[107]

Summary and interpretation: (re)production of the school's and the disciples' respective memory and judgement

This chapter has aimed to describe and analyse differences and similarities in how knowledge assessments were presented in the first Swedish school ordinances from 1561 to 1724, with particular focus on summative and formative assessments and the relationship between assessment and epistemological approach. The main argument is that early modern education (re)produced a particular assessment culture in its way of organising schooling. The starting point was the definition of knowledge assessments as two different kinds of knowledge-producing practices, one of them aimed at organising people and the other aimed at organising knowledge and learning.

Around the administrative practice it was discussed how the examinations in the sense of the production of knowledge about what someone knows, was used to admit disciples, employ teachers, move disciples between classes, monitor

---

107   See *School Ordinance* 1724: §7, 29. If we step outside the scope of this study to the 1807 school ordinance, the tendency toward memory's loss of its special position becomes even clearer: "ought the methods for each discipline be followed, which not only push into the memory what should be taught, but also practise and cultivate the mind and gift of understanding, and awaken and sharpen judgement and the power of thought", *School Ordinance* 1807, 83.

the hearers and finally dismiss teachers and disciples. The former for inadequate knowledge, the latter with either inadequate or full knowledge. From the similarities and the variation that exist between school ordinances it is possible, with some help from older Swedish education historical research, to derive a number of principles behind these statutes. The administrative functions can, for example, be said to be related to the education system's reproduction of itself, with its need to control the reproduction of true knowledge and with education's prospective buyers. Increased mobility within the education system and for those educated outside the education system, in relation to guarantees of the reproduction of truth, leads to a certain formalisation of the examination. This is evident in the calls for 'ephori book-keeping' of the disciples, and the disciples' right to a *testimonium* that serves as a leaving certificate.

This organisation of people was combined with the organisation of knowledge through the examination. One the one hand, the examination was a rehearsal of what was most important and thus ensured that this was imprinted in the disciples' heads. On the other hand, it detected what was imprinted in the heads and transferred this to the school master's head or, alternatively, his notebook. This divides, one could say, the experience. The disciples acquire, from a knowledge-organising perspective, the Christian experience, the Christian memory, at the same time as the actual acquisition of the experience educates a new more administrative experience. The examination as a formative assessment practice produces the conditions for an administrative assessment practice. The transfer of a particular experience was presented as though it could be estimated in absolute terms. Imprinted with a loud voice the text could be written over to memory. Read aloud by heart, memory could be compared with the text. Memory served the spoken text, the one that would be passed unchanged from generation to generation. Things were different with the written text. Cicero should not only be plagiarised, the ideal was emulation. It should also be possible to find his manner of writing in the texts about other things. Here judgement should be trained; which manner of writing is appropriate for what? Judgement was not only trained via rehearsals and it should not be examined, but only gently corrected. In modern assessment terminology we would here speak of reaching an alignment between the goals of education and the methods for assessing them.

In relation to the epistemological approach that characterised the early school ordinances, an epistemological approach that as far as possible tried to reconcile God, truth and language, speech and writing were the skills that should be developed and memory and judgement the spiritual qualities that should be trained. These skills and characteristics were practised with two types of exercises and assessment procedures, out of which only one would be linked to a more administrative examination. Here, however, certain shifts between the early school ordinances and the later ones occur, a change that can be linked to other historical observations around this time period.

The formulations of the school ordinances on memory can be understood as the idealisation by a, in terms of knowledge, close to absolute reproduction of the Christian experience expressed in Latin. David Hamilton writes in *Curriculum History* that this form of 'absolutism' locked knowledge to the language, and it was only by separating the language from the truth that it was possible to organise curricula for other purposes. The key lay in the criticism — language's turn against itself.[108] One could perhaps say, based on the Swedish school ordinances, that the onset of this turn-around in a more general sense can be understood in two tendencies. Firstly, the transfer of memory from speech to text. Memory gets a clear history, forms the basis for comparisons over time. The second tendency is that memory, perhaps by the fact that it can be written down, is downgraded. Judgement — the ability to live in the present with help from the past, rather than trying to live in the past with the help from the present — gets a prominent position. This is also in line with Reinhart Koselleck's thesis that the idea of the past as a collection of examples for the correct life is around the mid-1700s replaced by the concept of history as a process.[109] The passed down experience gets a lower value as an organising principle of society. Instead economy, ideology, management, etc. emerge; institutions with a view to the future, which form their own memory. Memory gets, one might say, its value in the new era, not as a reproduced experience, but as a produced experience. We get a disconnection between the school's learning mission and its administration.

In the school ordinances that I have studied, this gets its most obvious consequence in the administrative recordings of the disciples' progress at the examination. The examination continues to be oral and here a translation, or codification, takes place, of the disciples' memory into written administrative text. It is not until 1859 that it is decreed that essays authored by the disciples throughout the

---

108   David Hamilton, *Curriculum History* (Geelong, Vic: Deakin University, 1990), 30–38; Also see Foucault, *The Order of Things*, 257–70.

109   Reinhart Koselleck, *Futures Past. On the Semantics of Historical Time* (Massachusetts and London: The MIT Press, 1985); Reinhart Koselleck, *The Practice of Conceptual History. Timing History, Spacing Concepts* (Stanford, CA.: Stanford University Press, 2002).

year will be considered at the examination.[110] The disciples' written creations were assessed according to the school ordinances until then to practise judgement, not to administer individuals. At the examination one could hence say that it was the examiner's judgement that should be recorded in writing. At the correction of the writings it was the disciple's judgement that should be trained. In the transition to more modern school systems, it is mainly the administrative practice knowledge assessments that are presented. It is these that are formalised while what we today call the formative assessment procedures disappear from school ordinances and return less clearly justified in later Swedish curricula. The assessment's focus is, in other words, directed more at control than at learning.

The conclusion of this analysis is that in the early Swedish school ordinances it can be inferred how the administrative motives of knowledge assessments were associated with teaching. The association was present in how to present the examination, which, on the one hand organised the person in school or into church, and on the other hand organised memory into, simply put, a Christian experience pronounced in Latin. Based on the epistemological approach expressed in the school ordinances, it was hence possible to combine what we today call summative and formative assessments. Admittedly, this was a rather circular epistemological approach and the union of these two types of assessments applied only as long as it concerned the idea that it was speech and memory that should be trained. As the value of an absolute reproduction of knowledge and the value of a good memory fade as key educational goals in the school ordinances, these characteristics are more strongly tied to an increasingly written and formalised administrative practice. In the transition to modern times, the pedagogical motives for knowledge assessments almost completely disappear from the school ordinances, while the administrative motives are accentuated. By-heart knowledge, as an understated educational goal, is reproduced in school ordinances for mainly administrative, human-organising, reasons. An administrative practice that also educates the school's own memory has become institutionalised. Summative knowledge assessments can hence be said to be reproduced on each occasion that information is produced, in order to be used in comparisons with the past.

The most significant character of the assessments of early modern Swedish education was its capacity to strengthen a curriculum culture aiming for discipline in Latin and Christianity based on memory and judgement. It also strengthens

---

110   The school ordinances of 1856 and 1859 as imprints in Rudolf B. Hall et al. *Sveriges Allmänna Läroverksstadgar 1561–1905. Årsböcker för svensk undervisningshistoria, 1924 vol XI* (Stockholm: Föreningen för svensk undervisningshistoria, 1924), 78.

social order and discipline based on classroom achievement and performances. The close link between assessments and the organising principle of the curriculum contributed to a self-validated curriculum leaving little room for change. Today there is a wider gap between to logic of assessment and those of discipline and learning contributing to, for example, a polarisation between formative and summative assessment. It is difficult to see that one and the same assessment practice today could serve as many purposes as it could in early modern times.

Literature

Broadfoot, Patricia. *Education, Assessment and Society. A Sociological Analysis.* Philadelphia, PA: Open University Press, 1996.

Burke, Peter. *A Social History of Knowledge. From Gutenberg to Diderot.* Cambridge, UK: Polity Press, 2000.

Englund, Thomas. "Curriculum as a Political Problem. Changing Educational Conceptions, with Special Reference to Citizenship Education." PhD diss., Uppsala University, 1986.

Foucault, Michel. *The Order of Things.* London and New York: Routledge, 1966 [2002].

Frängsmyr, Tore. *Svensk idéhistoria. Del 1 1000–1809.* Stockholm: Natur och kultur, 2000.

Galen, *Three Treatises on the Nature of Sciences*, translated by Richard Walzer and Michael Frede. Indianapolis/Cambridge: Hackett Publishing Company, 1985.

Hall, Rudolf B. *Valda aktstycken till svenska undervisningsväsendets historia.* Stockholm: P. A. Norstedt och söners förlag, 1912.

–. *Om Sveriges första läroverksstadga. Studier rörande reformationstidens skola och skolfrågor. Årsböcker i svensk undervisningshistoria. Vol. I.* Stockholm: Föreningen för svensk undervisningshistoria, 1921.

Hamilton, David. *Curriculum History.* Geelong, Vic: Deakin University, 1990.

Hernlund, Hugo. "Bidrag till den svenska skollagstiftningens historia under partitidehvarfvet". Akademiska avhandling. Appendices. Stockholm 1882–92, 1880.

Hoskin, Keith. "The Examination, Disciplinary Power and Rational Schooling." *History of Education* 8, no. 2 (1979): 135–146. doi:10.1080/0046760790080205.

Johannisson, Karin. *Det mätbara samhället: statistic och samhällsdröm i 1700-talets Europa.* Stockholm: Norsted, 1988.

Kehm, Barbara M. "Oral Examinations at German Universities." *Assessment in Education* 8, no. 1 (2001): 25–31. doi: 10.1080/09695940120033234.

Koselleck, Reinhart. *Futures Past. On the Semantics of Historical Time.* Massachusetts and London: The MIT Press, 1985.

–. *The Practice of Conceptual History. Timing History, Spacing Concepts.* Stanford, CA.: Stanford University Press, 2002.

Leinberg, Karl G. *Om snillevalet (selectus ingeniorum) i vår äldre skollagstiftning.* Separattryck ur Tidskrift, utgifven af Pedagogiska Föreningen i Finland 1884. Helsinki: Finska Litteratur-sällskapets tryckeri, 1884.

Lundahl, Christian. "Viljan att veta vad andra vet. Kunskapsbedömning i tidigmodern, modern och senmodern skola." PhD diss., Uppsala University, 2006.

Lundgren, Ulf P. *Frame Factors and the Teaching Process. A Contribution to Curriculum Theory and Theory on Teaching.* Stockholm: Almqvist & Wiksell, 1972.

–. *Between Hope and Happening: Text and Context in Curriculum.* Vikoria: Deakin University Press, 1983.

–. "When Curriculum Theory came to Sweden," *NordSTEP* 2015, 1: 27000. doi: http://dx.doi.org/10.3402/nstep.v1.27000.

Ong, Walter J. *Orality and Literacy: The Technologizing of the Word.* London, UK: Methuen, 1982.

Platon. *Faidros. I Skrifter. Bok 2.* Translated by Jan Stolpe, 307–377. Stockholm: Atlantis, 1997.

Ricoeur, Paul. *Memory, History, Forgetting.* Chicago, IL: University of Chicago Press, 2004.

Schrag, Francis. "Conceptions of Knowledge," In *Handbook of Research on Curriculum: A Project of the American Educational Research Association,* edited by Philip W. Jackson, 268–301. New York, NY: Macmillan Pub. Co., 1992.

Siegvald, Herman. *Om kroppsaga (en historisk psykologisk studie). Pedaggiska skrifter.* Lund: PH. Lindstedts universitets bokhandel, 1932.

Stiggins, Richard J. *Student-centred Classroom Assessment.* New York, NY: Merrill, 1994.

Stray, Christopher. "The Shift from Oral to Written Examination: Cambridge and Oxford, 1700–1900." *Assessment in Education: Principles, Policy & Practice* 8.1 (2001): 33–50. doi: 10.1080/09695940120033243.

Sjöstrand, Wilhelm. *Pedagogikens historia, Vol. III.* Lund: CWG Gleerups förlag, 1961.

Thelin, Bengt. *Exit Eforus. Läroverkens sekularisering och striden om kristendomsundervisningen.* Stockholm: Liber Utbildningsförlaget, 1981.

The school ordinances of 1561, 1611 and 1649 as imprints and the two latter in a translation by Rudolf B. Hall: *Sveriges Allmänna Läroverksstadgar, 1561–1905.*

Årsböcker för svensk undervisningshistoria, Vol IV. Föreningen för svensk undervisningshistoria, 1921.

The school ordinances of 1693, 1724 and 1807 as imprints in Rudolf B. Hall, *Sveriges Allmänna Läroverksstadgar, 1561–1905. Årsböcker i svensk undervisningshistoria, Vol. VII*. Stockholm, Föreningen för svensk undervisningshistoria, 1922.

The school ordinance of 1820 imprints in Rudolf B. Hall, *Sveriges Allmänna Läroverksstadgar, 1561–1905. Årsböcker i svensk undervisningshistoria, Vol IX*. Stockholm: Föreningen för svensk undervisningshistoria, 1923.

The school ordinances of 1856 and 1859 as imprints in Rudolf B. Hall et al., *Sveriges Allmänna Läroverksstadgar 1561–1905. Årsböcker i svensk undervisningshistoria, 1924, Vol. XI*. Stockholm, Föreningen för svensk undervisningshistoria, 1924.

Ödmann, Per-Johan. *Kontrasternas spel. En svensk mentalitets — och pedagogikhistoria*. Stockholm: Prisma, 1998.

Weber, Max. *Den protestantiska etiken och kapitalismens anda*. Lund: Argos, 1934/1978.

Wiliam, Dylan, and Siobhan Leahy. *Embedding Formative Assessment: Practical Techniques for F-12 Classrooms*. West Palm Beach, FL: Learning Sciences International, 2015.

Kathrin Berdelmann

Individuality in Numbers: The Emergence of Pedagogical Observation in the Context of Student Assessment in the 18th Century[1]

"He brought the six black billets upon himself right at the beginning, as he imprudently shouted something (?) against a teacher. His mistakes have dissipated for the good part, and he is praised at times that he became more diligent, organised, valorous and good-natured."[2]

Every assessment of a student's learning, competence or knowledge is the result of previous observation of his or her actions or performance, the form of observation depends on the specific form of assessment in which it is engaged. Thus, observation is a premise of every procedure of assessment, these observations construct a specific image of the student that enables the teacher's assessment of him or her. Irrespective of the actual form of assessment, we can state that student observation serves as a knowledge-producing technique that furthermore, needs to be carried out by every teacher in every kind of pedagogical activity. Observation in both in school and out-of-school educational settings is associated with a cognitive interest: it serves to gain an idea of the state of development; of learning progress and learning requirements; of the child's interests and characteristic traits, from which developmental and learning challenges can be derived. Knowledge about the individual student that is gained on the basis of observation and assessment serves then as guidance for educational interventions. Observation is currently

---

1   This paper refers to my habilitation project "Pedagogical Observation – On the Historical Establishment of a Reflective Category in Pedagogical Practice" which takes an historical-praxeological perspective on student observation in schools. I analysed handwritten sources from everyday school life like notes on students, *censur*-tables, conference records and schools' tables from visitations but also articles form early pedagogical journals and official school regulations. The handwritten sources are form late 17th until end of 18th Century from schools in Halle, Dessau and Gotha. I would like to thank Heinrich Josef Metz (1922–2016), my grandfather, who helped deciphering the handwritten sources that are partly introduced in this paper.

2   Entry on 23 December 1781 on student *Benedikt Andreas von Helmersen* in merit book 2 (*Meritenbuch*), 43, in Anhaltinische Landesbücherei Dessau. All quotes from sources and literature originally in German were translated into English for this paper by K. B.

considered a core element of education, one that constitutes professionalism in teaching.[3]

Apart from the fact that at all times, every person engaged in pedagogical activity had to observe the learner to a certain degree, a question remains: How and when did observation become an explicit *pedagogical* category with such a strong link to professionalism? When taking an historiographical perspective onto the emergence of *pedagogical* observation, its interdependence with different cultures of student assessment automatically comes into view. Observation emerged and was systematised and institutionalised as a precedent to adequate, just, and action-oriented evaluation of a student within the context of a changing assessment culture in 18th century in Germany.[4] It is not surprising that this happens in connection with different reforms within German schools that were jolted by the pedagogy of the Enlightenment.[5] By the end of the 18th century, many schools (above the lower, elementary level) in Prussia put new ideas and methods of teaching into practice that were developed within the so called "new pedagogy".[6] They were elements of the slowly evolving modern school in the Age of Enlightenment. There was an already long-existing tradition of student assessment, e.g. the multi-levelled Jesuit practices of examination;[7] however, in

---

3   See among others: Heike de Boer and Sabine Reh, *Beobachtung in der Schule – Beobachten lernen* (Wiesbaden: VS Verlag, 2012); Kathrin Berdelmann and Kerstin Rabenstein, "Pädagogische Beobachtungen: zur Konstruktion des Adressaten pädagogischen Handelns," *Journal für LehrerInnenbildung* 14, no. 1 (2014): 7–14.

4   Kathrin Berdelmann, "'Sein Inneres kennen wir nicht, denn es ist uns verschlossen' – Schulische Beobachtung und Beurteilung von Kindern im 18. Jahrhundert," *Zeitschrift für Grundschulforschung* 9, no. 2 (2016): 9–23.

5   About the reforms in pedagogy during the 18th century, see Hanno Schmitt, "Die Philanthropine. Musterschulen der pädagogischen Aufklärung," in *Handbuch der deutschen Bildungsgeschichte, Band II: 18. Jahrhundert. Vom späten 17. Jahrhundert bis zur Neuordnung Deutschlands um 1800*, ed. Notker Hammerstein and Ulrich Hermann (München: Beck, 2005); for the duchy of Brunswick, see Hanno Schmitt, *Schulreform im aufgeklärten Absolutismus* (Weinheim & Basel: Beltz Verlag, 1979).

6   Prussia serves as an example for the Germans-speaking countries, Prussian school reforms were registered far beyond its borders and Prussia gained role model function. E.g. Russian and Danish schools were reformed by philanthropists. Wolfgang Dreßen, *Die pädagogische Maschine. Zur Geschichte des industrialisierten Bewusstseins* (Franfurt am Main: Ullstein 1982), 155.

7   See Kathrin Berdelmann, Sabine Reh and Joachim Scholz, "Wettbewerb und Ehrtrieb. Die Entstehung des Leistungsdispositivs um 1800, in Leistung als Paradigma. Zur Geschichte und Theorie pädagogischer Praktiken," ed. Sabine Reh and Norbert Ricken (Wiesbaden: VS in print); Georg, K. Mertz, *Die Pädagogik der Jesuiten nach den Quellen*

the last third of the 18th century the assessing perspective on students shifted and diversified. Not only were religious norms for educational reference relativised, but moreover the student was meant to be recognised in a more holistic manner — and most of all as a unique individual.[8] At the same time, student assessment was strongly expected to be just. My thesis is that in order to handle these challenges in assessment practice, student observation in schools came into the foreground. Within the professional discourse, observation was raised as an explicit category and was systematised and institutionalised as a precondition to these new forms of assessment. Observation thereby gained a specific pedagogical form.

In the following, I will show that in the light of the changing assessment culture, the disciplinary formation of pedagogical observation in was permeated by elements of both individualisation and standardisation — both of which are typical for modern society.[9] This is to say that observation, a new tool for producing knowledge about and insights into the students, was expected to capture their singularity, their individual traits and potentials and to enable an almost psychological view into their inner core, while at the same time accomplishing equity and comparability. This is also associated with the slowly emerging meritocratic system.[10] A consequence was that observation developed with a particular methodology; the student was perceived according to different criteria, and the observations were documented in multi-levelled processes.

In this larger context, this paper focuses on the system of merits (*Meritenwesen*) that was implemented in philanthropic model schools as a student assessment practice, and which was embedded in a framework of merits and desire for honours.[11] The systematic observation and assessment of students against the background of a sophisticated system of merits (*Meriten*), which students

---

von der ältesten bis in die neuste Zeit (Heidelberg: C. Winter's Universitätsbuchhandlung, 1898).

8   Berdelmann, "'Sein Inneres kennen wir nicht, denn es ist uns verschlossen'"

9   See for example Rudolf Stichweh, "Lebenslauf und Individualität," in: *Lebensläufe um 1800*, ed. Jörg Forhmann (Tübingen: Niemeyer, 1998); or Louis Dumont, *Individualismus. Zur Ideologie der Moderne* (Frankfurt am Main: Campus Verlag, 1991).

10   The emergence of meritocratic school systems and entitlement structures that started at the end of the 18th century became prevalent in the 19th century. See Sabine Reh, Kathrin Berdelmann and Joachim Scholz, "Der Ehrtrieb und unterrichtliche Honorierungspraktiken im Schulwesen um 1800 – Die Entstehung des Leistungs-Dispositivs," in: *Leistung,* ed. Alfred Schäfer and Christiane Thompson (Paderborn: Schöningh, 2015).

11   This practice in the developing 'modern' school had an active role in the genesis of an achievement theme, the development of certain practices of representation, acquisition,

could gain by demonstrating certain behaviours, was a vital demand on teachers. This demand explicitly shaped the daily routines of teachers and their exchanges with their colleagues at the *Dessauer Philantropin*. In the following, after outlining some basic characteristics about the philanthropic education, I will introduce the merit board (*Meritentafel*), and the merit books (*Meritenbücher*), which were among the most important documentations of student behaviour at this school (2). While also considering each student individually, these artefacts show evidence of the standardisation of student observation within a practice of student assessment (3). The particular form in which the student came into view, and was constructed by observation, is even more conspicuous when compared to the quarterly censur (*Vierteljahrescensur*). The quarterly censur was a system of student observation and assessment that was implemented only a few years later at another prominent Prussian school (4).[12] There observation was constructed in distinction from Dessau's merit regime. In this sense, the *Paedagogium Regium* of Halle serves as contrasting example. Although both schools implemented new assessment techniques in the last third of the 18th century, the comparison will show that not only did the focus of observation forms of documentation in student assessment differ; so, too, did the information to be gained about the students and the pedagogical consequences thereof. The differing forms of observation produce a particular image of the child: a child as a highly individual being who has to be conceived of in his difference and individuality, or a child who had to be recognised individually but simultaneously must be measured according to certain standardized criteria and only takes on form in relation to other students and their behaviour.

---

and evaluation of achievement in the context of certain institutions and thereby also a readiness to invest effort as an individual trait, see ibid.

12 Both schools were higher schools and in the centre of public attention. Their teachers and principals largely contributed to professional discussion about school and instruction at that time, their schools stood for innovative methods. The *Philanthropinum* was thought to serve as a pioneer and model school for others. Joachim Heinrich Campe, "Von der eigentlichen Absicht eines Philanthropins," *Pädagogische Unterhandlungen* 1, no. 1 (1777a): 14–59. The *Pädagogium Regium* of the Francke Foundations in Halle had a long tradition in pietism, but opened up to 'new pedagogy' and underwent reforms under the principal August Hermann Niemeyer in 1780s.

Billets and Points: The Meritocratic Practices at the *Philanthropin* in Dessau

The philanthropes, initially committed to Enlightenment, were leaders in reforming education and teaching.[13] Educational goals of the philanthropes were to enable students to manage life practically and to lead an individually satisfying and fulfilling life through human kindness — that is, though philanthropy.[14] The group introduced new and innovative ideas about schooling and put them into practice in their own schools, which served as models.[15] The improvement of instruction was one of these practitioners' main concerns. Besides producing, collecting and systematizing knowledge about education, they built a large, communicative network of professionals by publishing journals,[16] papers and books for teachers.

---

13 Its founder, Basedow was strongly influenced by John Locke and Jean-Jacques Rousseau. See Johann Bernhard Basedow, *Das Methodenbuch für Väter und Mütter der Familien und Völker* (Altona: Cramer, 1770).

14 Hanno Schmitt, "Pädagogen im Zeitalter der Aufklärung – die Philanthropen: Johann Bernhard Basedow, Friedrich Eberhard von Rochow, Joachim Heinrich Campe, Christian Gotthilf Salzmann," in: *Klassiker der Pädagogik. Von Erasmus bis Helene Lange. Vol. 1*, ed. Heinz-Elmar Tenorth (München: C.H. Beck Verlag, 2010).

15 See Christa Kersting, *Die Genese der Pädagogik im 18. Jahrhundert. Campes 'Allgemeine Revision' im Kontext der neuzeitlichen Wissenschaft* (Weinheim: Deutscher Studienverlag, 1992); Hanno Schmitt, *Visionäre Lebensklugheit: Joachim Heinrich Campe in seiner Zeit, 1746–1818* (Wiesbaden: Harrassowitz, 1996), 151–157; Jürgen Overhoff, "Johann Bernhard Basedows Frühschriften und die Anfänge der philanthropischen Pädagogik in Sorö, 1753–1758," in *Die Stammutter aller guten Schulen: das Dessauer Philanthropinum und der deutsche Philanthropismus, 1774–1793*, ed. Jörn Garber (Tübingen: Niemeyer, 2008); Ulrich Hermann, "Pädagogisches Denken," in *Handbuch der deutschen Bildungsgeschichte Band II: 18. Jahrhundert. Vom späten 17. Jahrhundert bis zur Neuordnung Deutschlands um 1800*, ed. Notker Hammerstein and Ulrich Hermann (München: Beck, 2008); Ulrich Herrmann, "Campes Pädagogik – oder: die Erziehung und Bildung des Menschen zum Bürger," in *Visionäre Lebensklugheit: Joachim Heinrich Campe in seiner Zeit (1746–1818)*, ed. Hanno Schmitt (Wiesbaden: Harrassowitz, 1996); Austermann, Simone, *Die 'Allgemeine Revision': pädagogische Theorieentwicklung im 18. Jahrhundert* (Bad Heibrunn: Klinkhardt, 2010).

16 See the *Pädagogische Unterhandlungen* an important philanthropic journal that contributed to the constitution of a public pedagogical discourse and was published by Campe and Basedow from 1777 on. See Gerhardt Petrat, *Schulunterricht. Seine Sozialgeschichte in Deutschland, 1750–1850* (München: Ehrenwirth 1979), or Kersting, *Die Genese der Pädagogik im 18. Jahrhundert.*

They aimed to establish a professional discussion and thus forced the development of pedagogy as an own discipline.[17]

The pedagogical view on children and their observations at school were discussed extensively by philanthropes like Joachim Heinrich Campe (1746–1818),[18] Christian Heinrich Wolke (1741–1825)[19] and Johann Karl Wezel (1747–1819).[20] In particular, they emphasised the necessity of undertaking one's own observations in classroom in order to get to know the students individually and "the child" in general and consequently to be a better teacher.[21] Gaining knowledge through the observation of children served an anthropological as well as a practical interest.[22] A new aspect of observation was that observation itself was used as pedagogical measure, and not only in terms of monitoring. The students' awareness of their observation and its connection with merit and honour was thought to have a positive effect on students' aspirations.

The *Philanthropinum* in Dessau was built in 1774. It was the philanthropes' most important reformist, progressive school. The school admitted students regardless of religion or class. However, though it aimed for education for all,

---

17 see Christa Kersting, "J.H. Campes 'Allgemeine Revision' – das Standardwerk der Pädagogik der Aufklärung," in *Visionäre Lebensklugheit: Joachim Heinrich Campe in seiner Zeit, 1746–1818*, ed. Hanno Schmitt (Wiesbaden: Harrassowitz, 1996), 37–8.; Simone Austermann, *Die 'Allgemeine Revision'*

18 Joachim Heinrich Campe, "Anecdote von einem Kinde," *Pädagogische Unterhandlungen* 1, no. 1 (1777): 70–71, and Campe, "Von der eigentlichen Absicht eines Philanthropins"

19 Christian Heinrich Wolke, "Sollte nicht bey allem Reichthum an Erziehungsschriften in unseren Zeiten gleichwohl in der Pädagogik noch eine sehr merkliche Lücke seyn," *Pädagogische Unterhandlungen*, 1 (1778): 1038–1047.

20 Wezel, Karl Johann, "Über die Erziehungsgeschichten," in *Pädagogische Unterhandlungen* 2, no. 1 (1778): 21–43. Published in *Pädagogische Schriften*, ed. Philip S. McNight (Frankfurt am Main: Peter Lang, 1996), 69–107.

21 Campe, "Anecdote von einem Kinde," 70–71. In the already mentioned Journal *Pädagogische Unterhandlungen* both in 1777 and 1778 this is a dominant topic. Campe calls on every parent and teacher to observe their children in order to better understand them and educate more adequately (ibid. 71). Wezel asked the teachers to: "Observe, and the – write!" Wezel, "Über die Erziehungsgeschichten," 100ff, and develops a step-by-step technique for student observation that results in an elaborate *Erziehungsgeschichte* (written story about the observed child).

22 Heidrun Diele and Pia Schmid, "Anfänge empirischer Kinderforschung. Die Schwierigkeiten einer Anthropologie vom Kinde aus," in *Physis und Norm. Neue Perspektiven der Anthropologie im 18. Jahrhundert*, ed. Manfred Beetz et.al. (Göttingen: Wallstein Verlag 2007).

a good portion of students were from aristocratic or wealthy families, as they could afford the fees. The school was famous for its system of merit; invented by Johann Bernhard Basedow (1724–1790), it was set into practice in 1777 by Joachim Heinrich Campe. Basedow was of the opinion that a priority in education was the awakening of *Ehrliebe* — a 'love for merit' — in the children. In this sense, Basedow wrote:

> "If they are blameworthy, one cannot take from them the hope that they will soon again attain virtue. [...] take care to sometimes connect the advantages of honour with other advantages. As the children get older, make a [...] book in which the good, the advantageous, and the poor actions are written. Occasionally read to them excerpts of these books. And at certain times, a family celebration of those good actions to be commended and those poor actions to be condemned, as contained in the book [...] identified and counted against each other, in order to be recognised according to the measure of the difference."[23]

Within this framework of the incitement of ambition, students' behaviour was observed and assessed systematically from its beginning until the school was closed in 1793.

The merit board

On 4 March 1777, merit boards were hung in the entryway to the school. There was a board of virtue and a board of hard work.

---

23 Johann Bernhard Basedow, *Das Methodenbuch*, 95–96.

Image 1: table of hard work, Museum für Stadtgeschichte Dessau

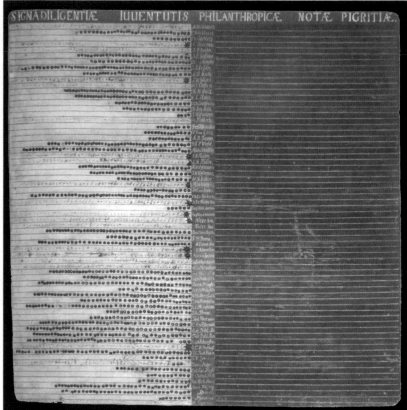

Associated with them was a system of rewards, public within the school, which documented the names of students associated with industrious and virtuous behaviour by a gold star (see image 1 the board of hard work: left side are points and golden stars for hard work (black here); right side are black, iron points for bad behaviour; in the middle column are the students names.) which corresponded to 50 collected billets.[24] For disobedient behaviour, billets were subtracted, and there was a black mark on the right side of the respective board of virtue or

---

24 Campe, "Von der eigentlichen Absicht eines Philanthropins," 14–59; Lorenz, Hermann, "Die Meritenbücher und Meritentafeln des Philanthropinums zu Dessau," in: *Mitteilungen der Gesellschaft für Deutsche Erziehungs- und Schulgeschichte* 12, no. 2 (1902): 93–121.

hard work.[25] During the week, the collected billets and some remarks for each student were put down in books that were kept individually by each teacher. By the end of the week, they were transformed into points and transcribed into the books of merit, where each student was registered with his own page. With respect to the billets that could be earned, virtues and hard work were distinguished. For billets for hard work, the observation of the students took place during instruction. After each lesson, the teacher "distributes billets to those students with whom he was satisfied concerning their attention, hard work and decent behaviour."[26] Billets of virtue could be won when virtuous behaviours were observed by a personal custodian of the student or by co-students, or when the custodian could note that certain misbehaviours had been abandoned after appropriate feedback. For the assignment of credits, a catalogue was provided, written in the book of merit 2 on page 1. The most meritorious behaviours in hard work were, amongst others: 1. "excellent attention," 2. "good behaviour," 3. "order," 4. "own preparations are effects of particularly hard work." Negative or black points were assigned for: 1. "Twelve black billets," 2. "an error with obvious ill intentions could result in several black billets or a whole black point," 3. "persistent disobedience would result in 2–3 black billets and notification of the parents."[27]

---

25 Basedow created this point-system of reward and punishment by referring to the Chinese: "The merits [stars and point on the board, K.B.] will be estimated, like the Chinese do, according to the amount of points [billets, K.B.], to which are sometimes added or diminished." Johann Bernhard Basedow, *Das in Dessau errichtete Philanthropinum* (Leipzig: Crusius, 1774), 14. Also in questions of file keeping about students and in having a moral teacher per class, Basedow was inspired by the Chinese system. See Børge Bakken, *The Exemplary Society: Human Improvement, Social Control, and the Dangers of Modernity in China* (Oxford, UK: Oxford University Press, 2000), 311. There was a long tradition of examination and personnel file keeping in China, in which merits and accomplishments were documented (ibid 288). The European China-reception already started in 17th century through Jesuit missioners, who wrote letters and books and reported about Chinese practices. In the 18th century, a lot of books about China, but also German novels with a plot in China were published in Europe. Especially the aristocrats and educated people were interested in Chinese culture (Adrian Hsia, *Deutsche Denker über China* (Frankfurt am Main: Insel Verlag, 1985), 370. Christian Wolff (1679–1754), for example, discusses the education of moral and virtue in old China's schools. Christian Wolff, "Rede von der Sittenlehre der Chineser," in *Deutsche Denker über China*, ed. Adrian Hsia (Frankfurt am Main: Insel Verlag, [1740] 1985), 58–9. The original Chinese source for Basedow is not reconstructable but I assume it to be within this context.
26 Campe, "Von der eigentlichen Absicht eines Philanthropins", 42.
27 ibid. 39–40.

The assignment of virtue points required careful consideration. The following system was developed: All students were assigned to small groups, each of which had a teacher as a supervisor. Outside of instruction, the teacher or custodian had a slate in his hand and carefully observed the group of students assigned to him and "notes every good and bad action he observes student undertaking."[28] The teacher attempted to:

> "Investigate the main mistakes of each student entrusted to his supervision. When he has discovered them, he makes fatherly suggestions to the students and warns him about them. If the student turns away [from his errors] and the teacher is, after a while, able to testify to the fact that these mistakes have been completely eradicated, the student is rewarded with a golden point. In contrast, he receives a black point on the black side of this board as long as he is prone to the same mistakes he has been warned of."[29]

A catalogue on the criteria for the assignment of points was also compiled. The most noble and meritorious achievements that could earn points on the virtue table were:

1. "Whoever endures injustice without rage or the desire for retribution and freely forgives the insulter with no punishment."
2. "Whoever of their own accord and without later glorification does a favour or service associated with his own effort and self-sacrifice."
3. "Whoever stops his fellow students from acting wickedly or contributes to the betterment of a not-yet virtuous fellow student."
4. "Whoever reports good deeds of his fellow students."
5. "Whoever always shows order and cleanliness whenever the inspector or curator inspects his belongings, clothing, books, and writing materials, etc."
6. "Whoever, after a certain period of time and having been testified to by all teachers, shows that he is always obedient and blameless – will soon by his nature receive a golden point, and billets fitting such a point on the table of virtue."[30]

These catalogues offered not only criteria to evaluate behaviour and measure it by transformation into positive and negative point-capital, but also criteria for observation — the lenses through which the student came into the observer's view. The table of virtue, however, was dismissed, as it made too many problems

---

28 ibid 42.
29 ibid.
30 ibid.

to measure justly and anyway, as Campe stated: "There is no art of measuring virtue at all."[31]

The Book of Merit

Basedow suggested a book for keeping record of good and bad behaviour of each student. Complementary to the merit board, there were two books of merit into which the billets earned were entered alongside a short description of the observed behaviour. The virtue book was no longer maintained after the virtue table was done away with. From then on, any possible observations about virtuous behaviour were recorded with all other observations about students' behaviour in one book. The books of merit had a distinct structure (book of merit 2: see image 2[32]): There were 1–3 pages per student; in the first column was the date, in the second, the points received. Each entry corresponded to a teachers' meeting on Sundays — the Senate — where the teachers jointly discussed their observations about the students and agreed upon a point tally. Any horizontal tally mark represented a "50," or a gold point on the table. The number beneath it is a count of any billets beyond fifty. The praise billets were distributed generously, but could also be revoked. In the next column is a note about the student's current behaviour, and in the final column, negative billets were recorded. 12 negative billets resulted in an "iron point" on the black side of the merit table. Every now and then, the students had the choice between demerits or the reduction of a corresponding number of merit billets, whereby a demerit billet was equal to approximately 20–25 praise billets.[33] Only a few typical examples shall be referred to:[34]

The student *Wilhelm Ernst Wichelshausen Senior* was a good student, who presumably attended the *Philanthropin* school starting in 1781. The entries about him in the merit book start on 7 July 1781. These entries are exemplary of the way many read. They are mostly short, like on 8 September: "orderly, hard-working, obedient." Or "is a joy to teach," "punctual." A dashed line at some dates means that conditions are the same as previously noted. On 11 May, the entry notes "no longer," which in this case means that he no longer is "contrarily conspicuous and attention-seeking,"[35] as had been noted on 16 March and thereafter confirmed by further strikes. The references to prior occurrences are even more pronounced in

---

31 ibid. 51.
32 Meritenbuch 2, Anhaltinische Landesbücherei Dessau.
33 Lorenz, *Die Meritenbücher und Meritentafeln des Philanthropinums zu Dessau*, 110.
34 Meritenbuch 2, Anhaltinische Landesbücherei Dessau.
35 ibid. 132–134.

some of the notes about other students, like for example those about *Ferdinand von Schladen* which on 8 September 1787 noted that "the above is still valid" or "has still not yet improved noticeably."[36] The student *Wichelshausen* furthermore received a large quantity of billets in March 1783. This was documented thusly: "W. received from Assi Sp. an extraordinary (50 billets' worth) of — repeats."[37] Why he received them is not mentioned.

One example that gives evidence of the logic of quantification in the merit system can be found in the entries for *Carl Gustav von Sievers* (image 2). He entered the *Philanthropin* on 13 November 1780. He was a student the teachers were not very pleased with. In his first year, he had only reached 50 points at the end of October, which was commentated with the annotation "during an entire year." His points column shows numerous deductions of points and billets, noted in crossed-out numbers in the same column. For example, on 6 April, he was "conspicuous, neglecting what he was supposed to do." The teachers made note of the value of the many deductions in April to September 1782, like on 18 August of "10, because bad" and, right beneath that "another 10 – still owes 2." and then "another 8 deducted." As the student seems to have been out of billets, he amassed debt. The reasons were documented in somewhat greater detail: "Did not show any great commitment although he announced intention to do so, but seems to think this is all a game."[38]

---

36 ibid. 165.
37 "Assi SP An" is probably an assistant to the teacher.
38 ibid. 123.

Image 2: *Sievers, Meritenbuch 2, Anhaltinische Landesbücherei Dessau*

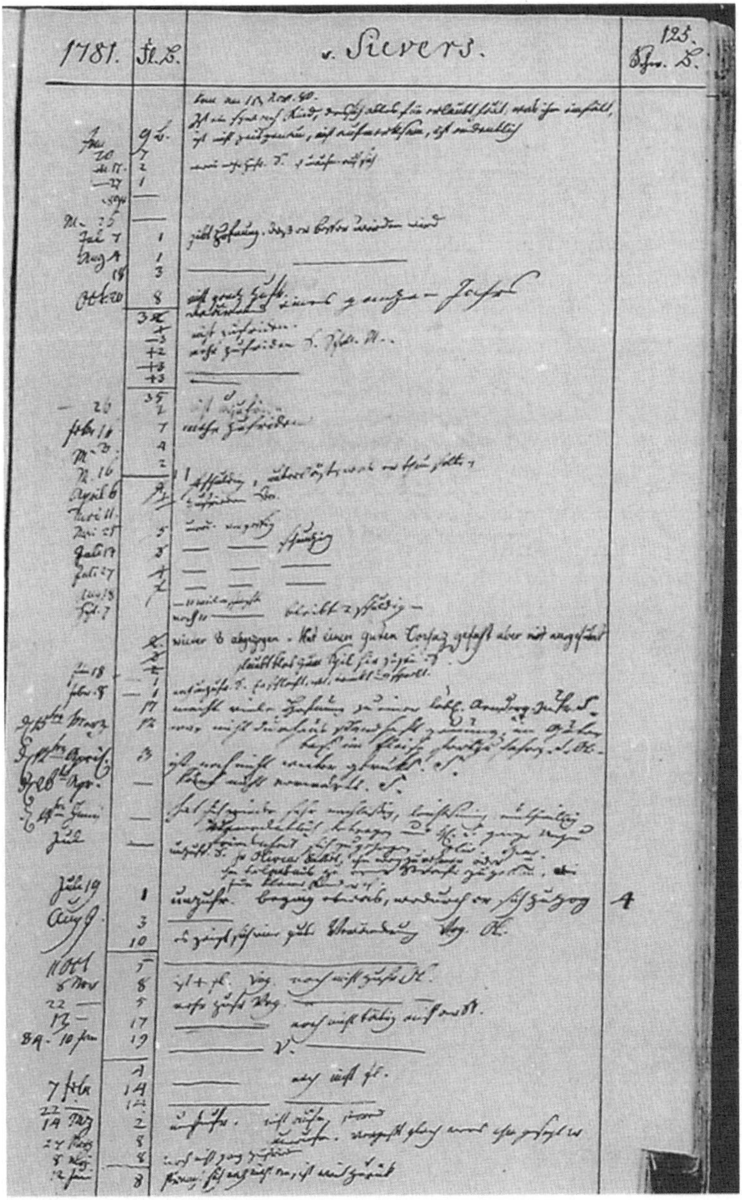

The student *Moozelewski*[39] lost 30 billets because of an offence that was not identified in detail. In certain cases, students could receive billets by different means,
like a particularly good deed that would result in 50 at once, as is shown by the
above example. Furthermore, a particularly bad deed could earn a black billet even
without 12 negative points. A student by the name of *Friedrich von Sandreczky*
learned this on 28 March 1788: "The first gross offence was 8 days ago when he
allowed himself to come into debt by letting himself be gulled into breaking some
window panes. For this spiteful misdeed, he receives 3 black billets."[40] This example demonstrates a somewhat economic accounting logic. Students' behaviour
was observed with respect to a catalogue of criteria and evaluated according to
a point system that made hard work and virtue (at least at the beginning) visible
and measurable. The students could use their behaviour to earn "point capital,"
which both brought them personal honour and allowed them to calculate against
potential dishonour and negative billets. The merit points were traded like currency, with two manifestations — negative and positive.[41]

The notes on the individual students are often brief and refer to one action or
deed. Precisely how points were distributed remained unclear; the system was
accused of arbitrariness. However, a collective exchange between teachers was
institutionalised: on every Saturday, the Senate met, which comprised the curator,
all professors and teachers and some pensioners that were by this rewarded for
excellent hard work and impeccable behaviour. Then all students, one student at a
time, were taken up; and "the teacher indicate 1) how many billets every student in
his class earned over the week; 2) what he observed and documented in good and
bad behaviour. Thereupon the billets are written into the main ledger (*Hauptbuch*,
that is the merit book) accordingly, and secondly, the teachers deliberate how
many billets in addition a student shall receive or lose for this good or that bad
deed. The given number is then entered into the main ledger, too."[42] The observations of the teachers are collected and discussed and practical consequences are

---

39 First name unknown, Meritenbuch des Philanthropins Dessau, 87, Anhaltinische
    Landesbücherei Dessau.
40 Meritenbuch 2, 169, Anhaltinische Landesbücherei Dessau.
41 One teacher's observation that casts a critical light on the merit practices is contained in
    the record on the student *Wilhelm von Lübeck* who on 29 November 1789 received an
    entry that "mainly in this respect, through billets he obtained little by little, he received
    at three today." Teachers at the Philanthropin hotly disputed whether it was appropriate
    to aspire to honour only for the sake of billets. Meritenbuch des Philanthropins Dessau,
    180.
42 Campe, Joachim Heinrich, "Von der eigentlichen Absicht eines Philanthropins," 39–40.

determined. Together, the Senate attempted to measure behaviour in the sum of its goodness or badness through the conversion into points and the short, keyword descriptions in the main ledger.

This system reflects numerous elements of 'professional observation.' A systematisation is recognizable through a determined temporal development as well as through defined forms of documentation and the inclusion and exchange of various observer groups. Campe continually emphasises this reflexive dimension of the observer and exchange with other teachers: teachers should work on their own improvement and further education through "experiments, through observations, and through reflection on and discussions about that which he has observed."[43] This extraction of observational activities from the daily — rather theoretical — routines, as well as the reflection on observation in relation to the teacher's own actions is a fundamental step in the development of observation as professional activity.

Standardisation and individualisation in student observation and documentation

A closer look at the merit book's pages for each student reveals how complex observation and assessment and point tallying were. Every student was assessed individually; it was considered essentially important to know the child. Each student had his own pages within the merit book with his own table that recorded not only the current points and behaviour, but also the history of earned and lost points. Thus, his individual progress and regression came into view, the frame of reference was individual, and the student was comparable with his own previous scores. The entries in the merit books, as short as they sometimes are, show the attempt to take each student into individual account. In an article about the *Philanthropin's* intent and school-practice, Campe writes about the teacher's concern for "circumspection in experiments, differentiation of the individual, bodily, and mental condition of the children, observations about human life in general, and attention to the destiny of any given child in particular."[44] This shift of focus to the individual child is unsurprising. A special and widespread interest for the human being as an individual was typical for the age of Enlightenment.[45] But what

---

43   ibid. 21–22.
44   ibid. 33.
45   Karl Philip Moritz (1756–1793), author of late Enlightenment explained the person as a "maximally complex object" and called for anthropological attention "to the smallest unnoticed splinter." Stefan Martus, *Aufklärung. Das deutsche 18. Jahrhundert – Ein*

becomes apparent here is that pedagogical observational practices systematised around an image of the child that is driven by the concept of an 'inside' or an 'internal' of the child. This interiority becomes describable in many facets as the individuality of this child and thus becomes visible in the first place. The attention to the 'individual' and the 'mental constitution' of the child as well as the child's conduct and the motivating moral traits (including hard work and virtue) — called for by Campe and put into use in merit practices — are evidence of this. This tendency toward individualisation will become more explicit in the example of the *Pädagogium Regium* discussed in chapter 4.

As much as the individual students was taken account of, the system needed to be just, and billet-awarding had be reasonable, too. Observation and assessment of behaviour had to be consistent and enable comparisons. This is why this practice was organised by two measures of standardisation: a) the development of a system of symbols for the documentation of observed behaviour that also provided clear categories for the student perception, and b), the tabular form of documentation.

a) On the second page of the merit book, a list can be found that names all teachers and gives them a single initial to link them to their entries. Below is written: *"Zeichen, daß einer gewesen ist"* ("symbol indicating that someone [a student] was" followed by that stands for a behaviour). Below this is another listing of student behaviours that assigns a symbol to each. Initially, the teachers at the Philanthropin intended to record their observations only by means of these symbols (see image 3). They stood for various categories of student behaviour, like _I_ for "sincere, open, honest"; and I- for "insincere, reserved, dishonest."[46] There were also symbols for resilient, humble, proud and naughty, obedient, diligent and attentive within lecture, diligent at home, lazy, disturbing, sloppy in appearance, inattentive, orderly, disorderly, tidy, untidy, peaceful, quarrelsome, and symbols for general agreeableness or disagreeableness. The idea was that whenever an entry about a student was written into the book, the teacher should only use the symbols to indicate the category of observed behaviour.

Epochenbild. (Reinbek: Rowohlt, 2015), 821. In his magazine for experiential spiritual science, Moritz divided essays according into rubrics of spiritual natural science, spiritual health science, spiritual arts, and spiritual dietics. Karl Philip Moritz, *Gnothi Sauton oder Magazin für Erfahrungsselenkunde als ein Lesebuch für Gelehrte und Ungelehrte,* Volume 1, 1. Stück (Freiburg im Breisgau, Faksimile-Verlag, 1978), 3.

46 Meritenbuch 2, Anhaltinische Landesbürcherei Dessau.

Image 3: symbols for documentation, Meritenbuch 2, Anhaltinische Landesbücherei Dessau

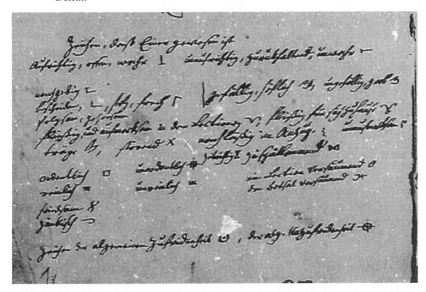

This may seem quite peculiar, but has to be seen within the greater context of the scientification of observation in all disciplines and even spheres of life. Scientific observation was practiced with great enthusiasm through the 18th century, but the volume of observations that were carried out produced new challenges for the integration of the results. Moreover, questions about the coordination of observers, standardisation of instruments and correlation of outcomes arose.[47] Questionnaires and schemes were developed and distributed by authorities aiming to compile observations in universal grids; by the end of the 17th century, even a trend for tables arose (ibid. 90f.); Daston presents "a typical observation notebook from the

---

47 See Lorraine Daston, "The Empire of Observation, 1600–1800," in *Histories of Scientific Observation,* ed. Lorraine Daston and Elisabeth Lunbeck (Chicago, IL: University of Chicago Press 2011), 88–89. Lorraine Daston locates the 18th century in the "Empire of Observation." After observation had long counted as a method for gaining knowledge in astronomy and medicine, it was expanded across all disciplines in the 18th century. Daston writes that around 1750, "observation had also become an epistemic category, that is, an object of reflection that had found its way into philosophical lexica and methodological treatises. Observation had arrived, both as a key learned practice and as a fundamental form of knowledge." ibid. 81.

latter half of the eighteenth Century: pocket format, dated entries further broken down into subentries by a sequence of letters or numbers (...),"[48] in table format. Obviously, the philanthropist's system of symbols did not take hold. Only certain symbols were used, and in the rarest of cases. Nonetheless, they show which criteria mattered in the observation and evaluation of students. More precisely, they were not only categories for assessment and its documentation: they were patterns of perception through which the student is constructed in the teacher's eye. The development and function of this symbolic system was a preliminary standardizing measure. One might even consider it to be a first standardized questionnaire for student observation and assessment.

b) Within the merit books, the tabular observational documentations are worth particular attention because they render visible practices of observation.[49] The table was not unknown to teachers, as they had already been used in schools for keeping track of students' absences, backgrounds, piety, and levels of knowledge (when entering the school) since the 17th century.[50] In the 18th century, teachers were required to keep tables on individual students; these were meant to give them a sense of orientation when reporting to parents and higher authorities.[51] The tables in the merit books and the merit boards differed from these in many respects. While they both served a documentary and informative purpose, the tables in the merit books and on the board also had a pedagogical intent. Namely, the tables did not only document hard work and virtue, but they also were meant to help the students improve. The function of the tables in the merit book and the merit board is disciplinary: The students were aware of the observation and documentation and they knew about the assignment of points and the resulting ranking of students on the public merit board. Tables are systems

---

48 ibid. 99.

49 See about the *tableau*: Michel Foucault, *Die Ordnung der Dinge. Eine Archäologie der Humanwissenschaften* (Frankfurt am Main: Suhrkamp, 1994), 150ff; William Clark, "On the Table of Manners in Academic Examination," in *Wissenschaft als kulturelle Praxis, 1750–1900,* ed. Hans. E. Bödecker et.al. (Göttingen: Vanderhoeck & Ruprecht 1999), 45–6.

50 See Töpfer, Thomas, *Die "Freyheit" der Kinder. Territoriale Politik, Schule und Bildungsvermittlung in der vormodernen Stadtgesellschaft. Das Kurfürstentum und Königreich Sachsen, 1600–1815* (Stuttgart: Franz Steiner Verlag, 2012); Wilfried Hartleb, "Das Beurteilungssystem in der Reichsgrafschaft Ortenburg," in *Schülerbeurteilungen und Schulzeugnisse: historische und systematische Aspekte,* ed. Georg Prinz von Hohenzollern and Max Liedtke (Bad Heilbrunn (Obb.): Julius Klinkhardt, 1991), 111–31.

51 Clark, "On the Table of Manners in Academic Examination," 51–2.

of relation building:[52] for the student, the board enabled comparison relative to others and to oneself. "The resulting relationships are of a dual nature [...] Both the row categories and the column categories construct a factual connection that links this date with other dates in the same row or column and assigns them coherence and comparability."[53] For the merit board, this means, for example, that the student can see and count the awarded — or not awarded — golden and iron stars (or points), and how these compare to others' over a given period of time up to the current day. This in turn leads to information on whether this student is a good or poor student, as others might have earned more or fewer stars over the same period. The broad comparison of all data on the same level leads to multiple relationships between time and date. "This quality [...] potentially leads to every date entered into the table becoming a kind of commentary on each of the others."[54] Like the symbols for student behaviour, the tabular form has an effect on the teacher's perception of the students as Brendecke argues, tables, as a special figure, can have "a vivid function for orientation in the awareness of user (...)."[55]

The entries in the merit book often referred to the above written commentary, and the student in question took on form in comparison to the aforementioned billet counts. Indeed, some individual entries remained legible on their own terms — as solitary records — but only when consciously bracketing out the prior and following comparative values, though, which, in their sum and in relation made a claim about these selected entries.[56] So teachers could classify and evaluate students, and students could locate themselves within a relational field of students and try to alter their position through own effort and responsibility.

The Individual Student: Observation and Assessment at the *Pädagogium Regium* within the 'Quarterly *Censur*'

Another specific form of student evaluation was implemented in different schools in the last third of the 18th century: the 'Quarterly *Censur*.' Besides the above-depicted measures of standardisation with coexisting individual perspective on

---

52 Arndt Brendecke, "Information in tabellarischer Disposition," in *Wissensspeicher der frühen Neuzeit. Formen und Funktionen*, ed. Frank Grunert und Anette Syndikus (Berlin & Boston: Walter de Gryter, 2015), 53.
53 ibid.
54 ibid.
55 ibid. 45.
56 ibid. 53.

students, the *censur*[57] evidences a shift to individualisation in observation and assessment. One pioneer school of the *censur* was the *Pädagogium Regium* in Halles Francke Foundations[58], whose director August Hermann Niemeyer (1754–1828) introduced a system named "The Quarterly *Censur*"[59] in 1786. In contrast to the observation and assessment of students in *Dessaus Philanthropin*, where the emerging image of the child was one mostly based on numbers and tally marks, observation at the *Pädagogium Regium* was close-grained and allowed teachers to capture the holistic progress of the student — a rather psychological knowledge about his nature and his individual potential and dispositions. The sources from the *Paedagogium Regium* show a similarly complex system of student observation and evaluation, which was based on permanent observation and continuous thorough and multifarious description of the students. These observations, evaluations and documentations were also meant to foster improvement by virtue of the students' awareness of their observation. The procedure was as follows:[60] observations were recorded each quarter in a one - to three-page text about each student. Prior to this, three different teachers assessed the student on weekly basis, and this happened over the period of three months. Two of the three *Zeugniszettel* (report cards) referred to the student's progress in lessons and one was for his behaviour in recreational time. Every weekend, students got to read their three cards for feedback, giving them a chance to improve in the following week. By the end of the quarter, the school staff met in a conference and collected, discussed and adjusted their observations on the basis of the report-cards. Together they agreed on the *Gesamtcensur* — the descriptive text on every student, in which his social and moral behaviour as well as his activity and progress in different classes was assessed in great detail. On a Sunday, this text was read to the students in an official event. This is a form of long-term student assessment — an assessment period over three months — and it subdivides into smaller assessment and feedback units. The aspiration in this assessment practice was to get a very detailed, equitable and holistic image; this is why observation had to be complex

---

57 That was implemented i.a. at the *Pedagogium* in Halle, in Friedrich Werdersches Gymnasium in Berlin or at the Klosterschule Amelungsborn in the Duchy of Brunswick.

58 The *Pädagogium* was mostly a school for aristocratic children whose parents paid high fees but also admitted some (talented) students from poor families and such from the orphanage of the Francke Foundations.

59 August Hermann Niemeyer, "Vollständige Nachricht von der gegenwärtigen Einrichtung des Königlichen Pädagogiums zu Halle, 1796," Accessed July 19, 2017. http://digitale.bibliothek.uni-halle.de/vd18/content/titleinfo/4551683. 128–30.

60 ibid.

and multileveled. The following example of the student *Carl von Reck* illustrates the aim of understanding and capturing the child as such (abridged):

> "It is a sad omen when a youngling, who has all the prerequisites for rapid progress in the formation of his intelligence, who has always been requested from all quarters to develop those strengths of his mind for his and others' well-being, who in the love of his parents together with his own ambition and in the expectations, which the country holds of him, should always find the most wondrous motives toward virtue, when this one does not make use of all this, but gradually unfolds all aspects of his nature in a way that the observer must suspect even the absence of an appreciation of the like. This is, as reluctantly as we say it, fully the case with Reckl. Since he is around, we have done everything for him that is required by duty and love. [...] He was encouraged to watch over purity of his soul and to express nothing in his conversations which could give rise to the sad suspicion of the contrary. But he made no use of our hints. His conversations persist as they were, harmful for the unbiased, and witnesses of own foulness. [...] His ambition became evident in small-minded pride about things which had no real value. Tough with others and lenient toward himself, he became consistently unkind in his judgments [...]."[61]

I want to emphasise two aspects of this description: this student's behaviour over the past three months was observed and is assessed in different aspects, and not only his social behaviour causes worry, but also his reactions to any teacherly advice; and secondly, this is even more severe because *Reck* is thought to have the predisposition to be better. The teachers did not only assess the shown behaviour, but also tried to look deeper into the student — into his inside — and estimate his potential: "It is a sad omen when a youngling, who has all the prerequisites for rapid progress in the formation of his intelligence." The frame of reference here is Recks own potential against which he is measured and he has not reached his possible best. But, in this lies an implicit comparison to other students, too, because when looking at this student individually and evaluating his inner potential references values are required to recognise this potential. This is to say that every assessing perspective on a student as an individual implies a positioning within a greater framework (of students).[62]

---

61 This *censur* was written in the early 1790s. AFSt/S A I 199, Blatt 71 in Schularchiv der Franckeschen Stiftungen Halle.

62 An indivualizing perspective on students has to assess and classify him within a spectrum, where all students have their position, too. The examples of the *Philanthropin* and the *Pedagogium* show this, especially, since both had an institutionalised exchange for teachers to talk about their observations and evaluate the students together (the conferences at the *Pädagogium* and the senate at the *Philantropin*) and all students where discussed one after the other.

The rector, Niemeyer himself, argued for a less simple, and instead more complex, view of the students as highly individual in their abilities and disposition. In his opinion, nothing is more worthwhile for a teacher than incessantly observing how his student improved or got worse, which character traits he revealed, in which lessons he deserved praise or admonition.[63] The attempt to understand the 'inside' of a student is even more evident in another example of the student *Julius Goldhagen*, where teachers wonder if a certain behaviour is intentional or just his habit and where they try to understand why he is so withdrawn and does not respond to trustfulness and openness.[64]

Precisely because students are so differently disposed, the teacher needed to recognise what each was capable of achieving and help him attain that.[65] The frame of reference is individually located for each child and according to his potential for improvement. This shows a modern understanding of individualisation and in fact, observation is done for the purpose of individualisation.

Conclusion

In this paper I argued that towards the end of the 18th century, student observation surfaced as an explicit topic in early pedagogical professional discussion because within the context of changing assessment practices, observation became an indispensable necessity. New forms of assessment that were focused on the individual student required observation to capture the child holistically and make the inside visible, to catch sight of his character and moral nature as well as his progress in lectures. Within this pedagogical context, observation was forced to systematize and thus become an important activity and a reflective category for professionals. Furthermore, within this process, observation — as pedagogical activity — developed simultaneously in standardized and individualised forms. Observation integrated elements of both standardisation and individualisation by developing elaborated concepts that were meant to enable equity, comparability and transparency within a close-grained view of the child's individuality. Thus,

---

63 August Hermann Niemeyer, *Grundsätze der Erziehung und des Unterrichts für Eltern, Hauslehrer und Erzieher* (Paderborh: Schöningh, [1796] 1970), 129.

64 "He cites our greatest and most emphatic advice to educate oneself for the world — [but] is silent and lives on as before. Will this obstinacy also lead him through the world? We have often posed this question to him. He leaves it unanswered and remains as he was. […] Whether this is intentional or merely habit, we do not know." (AFSt/S A I 199, Bl. 93, Schularchiv der Franckeschen Stiftungen, Halle).

65 Niemeyer, *Grundsätze der Erziehung*, 309.

individualisation is not considered to be the counterpart of standardisation but always linked to each other in student's observation and assessment.

In *Dessau's Philanthropin*, the behaviour of students was observed and documented in a meritocratically organised system of categories. Hard work and virtue were made visible and assessable. While in Halle's *Pädagogium Regium*, the student was to be evaluated as precisely and particularly as possible, in the *Philanthropin*, students and their behaviour were evaluated under general categories of hard work and virtue. Nevertheless, each child was observed and assessed individually, and the merit books show that there was also an individual frame of reference. The form of the documentation of observation is not insignificant in the evaluation of the students. The tabular entries in the merit book evoke a different observational result — a different image of the student — than the detailed description of the individual student.

There, the documentation in a tabular format was not just a resource for the teacher, as was mostly the case with the "school-tables,"[66] but served an educational purpose, which was to stimulate the desire for honours of the student. The students were held to general expectations of achievement defined by categories of behaviour and, in a sense, put in competition with each other. They then appear as a group with equal chances, who by adoption of responsibility, control, and by orientation of their own behaviour toward certain standards could prove themselves as good and honourable students. This is also not insignificant for the development of what came to be recognised as achievement: Classification and measurability of hard work and virtue based on demonstrated behaviour. Stars, points, and billets were added over a certain period of time and calculated against each other such that students always had to make efforts to attain honour and recognition anew.

Both schools, the *Philanthropin* and the *Pädagogium Regium*, worked on the problem of assessing and observing students and thus made essential contributions to the development of student observation as a pedagogical category. Critical debates about the system of merits and the idea of a 'quarterly *censur*' in the 1780s and 90s in different pedagogical journals and publications[67] give evidence of the

---

66 Clark, "On the Table of Manners in Academic Examination," 50–1.

67 See about reward and punishment discusses advantages and disadvantages of both: the merit system and a quaterly censur: Joachim Heinrich Campe, "Über das Zweckmäßige und Unzweckmäßige in den Belohnungen und Strafen," *Allgemeine Revision des gesammten Schul und Erziehungswesens* 10 (1788): 445–568. This text is commented by many well-known representatives of the pedagogical discourse like Ernst Christian Trapp, Friedrich Gedicke (1754–1803), Peter Villaume (1746–1806) or Johann Stuve (1752–1793); furthermore, August Hermann Nimeyer in a publication about school

importance of these issues and the attention both systems attracted as practice models.

Unprinted sources

Museum für Stadtgeschichte Dessau
Anhaltinische Landesbücherei Dessau
Schularchiv der Franckeschen Stiftungen Dessau

Bibliography

Austermann, Simone. Die 'Allgemeine Revision': pädagogische Theorieentwicklung im 18. Jahrhundert. Bad Heibrunn: Klinkhardt, 2010.

Bakken, Børge. The Exemplary Society: Human Improvement, Social Control, and the Danger of Modernity in China. Oxford, UK: Oxford University Press, 2000.

Basedow, Johann Bernhard. Das Methodenbuch für Väter und Mütter der Familien und Völker. Altona: Cramer, 1770.

Basedow, Johann Bernhard. Das in Dessau errichtete Philanthropinum. Leipzig: Crusius, 1774.

Berdelmann, Kathrin. "'Sein Inneres kennen wir nicht, denn es ist uns verschlossen' — Schulische Beobachtung und Beurteilung von Kindern im 18. Jahrhundert." Zeitschrift für Grundschulforschung 9, no. 2 (2016): 9–23.

Berdelmann, Kathrin and Kerstin Rabenstein. "Pädagogische Beobachtungen: zur Konstruktion des Adressaten pädagogischen Handelns." Journal für LehrerInnenbildung 14, no. 1 (2014): 7–14.

Berdelmann, Kathrin, Sabine Reh and Joachim Scholz. "Wettbewerb und Ehrtrieb. Die Entstehung des Leistungsdispositivs um 1800." In Leistung als Paradigma. Zur Geschichte und Theorie pädagogischer Praktiken, edited by Sabine Reh and Norbert Ricken. Wiesbaden: VS in print.

Brendecke, Arndt. "Information in tabellarischer Disposition." In Wissensspeicher der frühen Neuzeit. Formen und Funktionen, edited by Frank Grunert und Anette Syndikus, 43–60. Berlin & Boston: Walter de Gryter, 2015.

Campe, Joachim Heinrich. "Von der eigentlichen Absicht eines Philanthropins." Pädagogische Unterhandlungen 1,1, 1777a, 14–59.

Campe, Joachim Heinrich. "Anecdote von einem Kinde." Pädagogische Unterhandlungen 1, no. 1 (1777): 70–71.

---

practice at the *Pädagogium Regium* critically discusses the merit system in Dessau while arguing in favour for his quarterly censur. In: Niemeyer, "Vollständige Nachricht."

Campe, Joachim Heinrich. "Über das Zweckmäßige und Unzweckmäßige in den Belohnungen und Strafen." *Allgemeine Revision des gesammten Schul- und Erziehungswesens* 10 (1788): 445–568. Wien & Braunschweig.

Clark, William. "On the Table of Manners in Academic Examination." In *Wissenschaft als kulturelle Praxis, 1750–1900,* edited by Hans. E. Bödecker, Peter Hanns Reill and Jürgen Schlumbohm, 33–67. Göttingen: Vanderhoeck & Ruprecht, 1999.

Daston, Lorraine. "The Empire of Observation, 1600–1800." In *Histories of Scientific Observation,* edited by Lorraine Daston and Elisabeth Lunbeck, 81–113. Chicago, IL: University of Chicago Press, 2011.

de Boer, Heike and *Sabine Reh.* *Beobachtung in der Schule – Beobachten lernen.* Wiesbaden: VS Verlag, 2012.

Diele, Heidrun and *Pia Schmid.* "Anfänge empirischer Kinderforschung. Die Schwierigkeiten einer Anthropologie vom Kinde aus." In *Physis und Norm. Neue Perspektiven der Anthropologie im 18. Jahrhundert,* edited by Manfred Beetz, Jörn Garber and Heinz Thoma, 253–277. Göttingen: Wallstein Verlag, 2007.

Dreßen, Wolfgang. *Die pädagogische Maschine. Zur Geschichte des industrialisierten Bewusstseins.* Franfurt am Main: Ullstein, 1982.

Dumont, Louis. *Individualismus. Zur Ideologie der Moderne.* Frankfurt am Main: Campus Verlag, 1991.

Foucault, Michel. *Die Ordnung der Dinge. Eine Archäologie der Humanwissenschaften.* Frankfurt am Main: Suhrkamp, 1994.

Hartleb, Wilfried. "Das Beurteilungssystem in der Reichsgrafschaft Ortenburg." In *Schülerbeurteilungen und Schulzeugnisse: historische und systematische Aspekte,* edited by Georg Prinz von Hohenzollern and Max Liedtke, 111–31. Bad Heilbrunn (Obb.): Julius Klinkhardt, 1991.

Herrmann, Ulrich. "Campes Pädagogik – oder: die Erziehung und Bildung des Menschen zum Bürger." In *Visionäre Lebensklugheit: Joachim Heinrich Campe in seiner Zeit, 1746–1818,* edited by Hanno Schmitt, 151–57. Wiesbaden: Harrassowitz, 1996.

_. "Pädagogisches Denken." In *Handbuch der deutschen Bildungsgeschichte Band II 18. Jahrhundert. Vom späten 17. Jahrhundert bis zur Neuordnung Deutschlands um 1800,* edited by Notker Hammerstein and Ulrich Hermann, 97–132. München: Beck, 2008.

Hsia, Adrian. *Deutsche Denker über China,* Frankfurt am Main: Insel Verlag, 1985.

Kersting, Christa. "J.H. Campes 'Allgemeine Revision' – das Standardwerk der Pädagogik der Aufklärung." In *Visionäre Lebensklugheit: Joachim Heinrich*

Campe in seiner Zeit, 1746–1818, edited by Hanno Schmitt, 170–93. Wiesbaden: Harrassowitz, 1996.

_. *Die Genese der Pädagogik im 18. Jahrhundert. Campes 'Allgemeine Revision' im Kontext der neuzeitlichen Wissenschaft.* München: Deutscher Studienverlag, 1992.

Lorenz, Hermann, "Die Meritenbücher und Meritentafeln des Philanthropinums zu Dessau." In *Mitteilungen der Gesellschaft für Deutsche Erziehungs- und Schulgeschichte* 12, no. 2, 1902: 93–121.

Martus, Stefan. *Aufklärung. Das deutsche 18. Jahrhundert – Ein Epochenbild.* Reinbek: Rowohlt, 2015.

Mertz, Georg, K., *Die Pädagogik der Jesuiten nach den Quellen von der ältesten bis in die neuste Zeit.* Heidelberg: C. Winter's Universitätsbuchhandlung, 1898.

Moritz, Karl Philip. *Gnothi Sauton oder Magazin für Erfahrungsselenkunde als ein Lesebuch für Gelehrte und Ungelehrte*, Bd. 1, 1. Stück. Lindau im Breisgau, Faksimile-Verlag, 1978.

Overhoff, Jürgen. "Johann Bernhard Basedows Frühschriften und die Anfänge der philanthropischen Pädagogik in Sorö, 1753–1758." In *Die Stammutter aller guten Schulen: das Dessauer Philanthropinum und der deutsche Philanthropismus 1774–1793*, edited by Jörn Garber, 83–98. Tübingen: Niemeyer, 2008.

Petrat, Gerhardt. *Schulunterricht. Seine Sozialgeschichte in Deutschland 1750–1850.* München: Ehrenwirth, 1979.

Niemeyer, August Hermann. *Grundsätze der Erziehung und des Unterrichts für Eltern, Hauslehrer und Erzieher.* Paderborn: Schöningh, [1796] 1970.

_. *Vollständige Nachricht von der gegenwärtigen Einrichtung des Königlichen Pädagogiums zu Halle, 1796.* Accessed July 19, 2017. http://digitale.bibliothek.uni-halle.de/vd18/content/titleinfo/4551683.

Sabine Reh. *Can we discover something new by looking at practices? Practice theory and the history of education,* in: *Encounters in Theory and History of Education* 15 (2014): 183–207. Accessed July 19, 2017. https://ojs.library.queensu.ca/index.php/encounters/issue/view/526.

Reh, Sabine, Kathrin Berdelmann and Joachim Scholz. "Der Ehrtrieb und unterrichtliche Honorierungspraktiken im Schulwesen um 1800 – Die Entstehung des Leistungs-Dispositivs". In *Leistung*, edited by Alfred Schäfer and Christiane Thompson, 37–60. Paderborn: Schöningh, 2015.

Schmitt, Hanno. "Die Philanthropine. Musterschulen der pädagogischen Aufklärung." In *Handbuch der deutschen Bildungsgeschichte Band II: 18. Jahrhundert. Vom späten 17. Jahrhundert bis zur Neuordnung Deutschlands um 1800*, edited by Notker Hammerstein and Ulrich Hermann, 265–76. München. Beck, 2005.

_. "Pädagogen im Zeitalter der Aufklärung — die Philanthropen: Johann Bernhard Basedow, Friedrich Eberhard von Rochow, Joachim Heinrich Campe, Christian Gotthilf Salzmann." In: *Klassiker der Pädagogik Erster Band: Von Erasmus bis Helene Lange*, edited by Heinz-Elmar Tenorth, 119–143. München: C.H. Beck Verlag, 2010.

_. "Versuchsschule vor zweihundert Jahren. Ein Besuch am Dessauer Philanthropin." In *Die Stammutter aller guten Schulen: das Dessauer Philanthropinum und der deutsche Philanthropismus 1774–1793*, edited by Jörn Garber, 169–178. Tübingen: Niemeyer, 2008.

_. *Visionäre Lebensklugheit: Joachim Heinrich Campe in seiner Zeit, 1746–1818.* Wiesbaden: Harrassowitz, 1996.

_. *Schulreform im aufgeklärten Absolutismus.* Weinheim & Basel: Beltz Verlag, 1979.

Stichweh, Rudolf. "Lebenslauf und Individualität." In: *Lebensläufe um 1800*, edited by Jörg Forhmann, Tübingen: Niemeyer 1998, 223–34.

Töpfer, Thomas, Die *"Freyheit" der Kinder. Territoriale Politik, Schule und Bildungsvermittlung in der vormodernen Stadtgesellschaft. Das Kurfürstentum und Königreich Sachsen 1600–1815*, Stuttgart: Franz Steiner Verlag: 2012.

Wezel, Karl Johann. *Über die Erziehungsgeschichten*, in *Pädagogische Unterhandlungen 2*, no. 1 (1778): 21–43. Published in *Pädagogische Schriften*, edited by Philip S. McNight, 69–107. Frankfurt am Main: Peter Lang, 1996.

Wolff, Christian. *Rede von der Sittenlehre der Chineser*, in *Deutsche Denker über China*, edited by Adrian Hsia, 42–72. Frankfurt am Main: Insel Verlag [1740], 1985.

Wolke, Christian Heinrich. "Sollte nicht bey allem Reichthum an Erziehungsschriften in unseren Zeiten gleichwohl in der Pädagogik noch eine sehr merkliche Lücke seyn." *Pädagogische Unterhandlungen*, 1 (1778): 1038–47.

Transnational Perspectives

Nelli Piattoeva and Galina Gurova

Domesticating International Assessments in Russia: Historical Grievances, National Values, Scientific Rationality and Education Modernisation[1]

Recent Russian education policy documents indicate the increasing reliance of policy-making on specialist knowledge based on various kinds of education assessments. In addition to the rise to prominence of "quality education" and "education quality evaluation" in Russian education policy since the early 2000s,[2] the numerical data produced as a result of these procedures has been emphasised in the policy documents in the form of indicators of performance and progress.[3] The latest Government Program on Education contains a long list of performance indicators, some based on the number of international assessments in which Russia participates and the ranks achieved in these.[4] Moreover, in a central policy background paper — the *Strategy 2020*[5] the developments in and priorities for the education sector are presented in detail in light of international assessments and international statistical data. When such comparative numerical data is brought

1   We would like to express deep gratitude to Tuomas Takala, Pertti Alasuutari, Marjaana Rautalin and Tatiana Tiaynen-Qadir for their feedback and support during our work on the chapter.
2   Viktor Bolotov, "O sozdanii obscherossiiskoi sistemy otsenki kachestva obrazovaniia v Rossiiskoj Federacii", *Vestnik Obrazovaniia* 11 (2005): 10–8; Government of Russia, "State Programme of the Russian Federation 'Development of Education' for 2013–2020," accessed May 22, 2015, www.минобрнауки.рф/документы/3409.
3   See e.g. Nelli Piattoeva, "Elastic Numbers: National Examinations Data as a Technology of Government," *Journal of Education Policy* 30 (2015a), doi:10.1080/02680939.2014.937830.
4   Government of Russia, "State Programme."
5   Vladimir Mau and Yaroslav Kuzminov, eds., *Strategiya-2020: Novaya model' rosta — novaya sotsial'naya politika. Itogovyy doklad o rezul'tatakh ekspertnoy raboty po aktual'nym problemam sotsial'no-ekonomicheskoy strategii Rossii na period do 2020 goda* (Moscow: Delo, RANEPA University Press, 2013).

into the political sphere to govern through numbers and comparison,[6] individuals and professional groups possessing such specialist knowledge gain prominence in policy-making.

The authority of experts is based on their ability to develop common categories and a common language, propose evaluation tools and produce evidence to support decision-making in the contested and sensitive arena of education policy.[7] This is particularly important for policies seeking to transcend national borders.[8] Expertise helps to present decision-making as neutral and universal, and gives an impression that policy-makers manage public action through rigid method and rationality. The utilisation of measurement tools in particular is deemed as proof of political neutrality and capitalises on the common currency of scientific objectivity.[9] When utilizing assessment data produced by experts, the government can be seen to construct its political direction on the basis of impartial external sources, while simultaneously appearing efficient and professional. At the same time experts, such as researchers, professionals, leaders, consultants and planners, play a central role as editors and cultural translators of ideas and models that circulate globally.[10] Moreover, global practices and models get adopted not because they work, but because they are made to work through active adaptation, thus necessitating a closer examination of the means and rationales of this process.[11]

Through the conceptual framework of discursive institutionalism in general and domestication in particular, this chapter develops an argument in support of a closer examination of the worldviews and practices of national education experts in explaining the rapid proliferation of large-scale international assessments of student achievement (ILSA). Our general research interest lies with the question as to why international assessments would be welcomed on the national level while they could equally be treated as attempts at international influence on and

6   E.g. Antonio Nóvoa and Tali Yariv-Mashal, "Comparative Research in Education: A Mode of Governance or a Historical Journey?" *Comparative Education* 39 (2003), doi: 10.1080/0305006032000162002.

7   Peter Miller and Nikolas Rose, *Governing the Present: Administering Economic, Social and Personal Life* (Cambridge, UK: Polity Press, 2008).

8   Martin Lawn and Sotiria Grek, *Europeanizing Education: Governing a New Policy Space* (Oxford, UK: Symposium Books, 2012).

9   Ibid.

10 David Suárez and Patricia Bromley, "Institutional Theories and Levels of Analysis: History, Diffusion, and Translation," in *World Culture Re-contextualised*, ed. Jürgen Schriewer, (London, UK: Taylor and Francis, 2016).

11 See Ibid., 146.

exercise of power over the national education system. To this end we examine the ways in which Russian academics talk about and utilize international assessment tools and data in their professional work, bearing in mind the overall context of Russia's regular participation in ILSA since the 1990s and the prominent place of their data in recent national policy documents. As Morgan and Shahjahan[12] argue, while much research focuses on the impact of these assessments at the national level once the results have been made public, much less research is available on the channels of influence during the early stages of test development through exchange of knowledge and practices among experts. Moreover, the authors call for research exploring global governance of education through the production of international assessments from the perspective of local knowledge in a highly connected world and also addressing the role and reach of international assessment tools within local contexts.[13] The chapter at hand seeks to contribute to this line of inquiry by answering the following questions: (1) What ideas motivate Russian experts to support international assessments? (2) How do they make use of international assessments in their own professional practices?

Our chapter also sheds light on the emerging assessment culture among the Russian evaluation experts and researchers at the interface between national context and global education governance through international learning assessments. The analysis is concerned with assessments of school education, purposefully excluding numerous international studies on adult literacy and higher education, in which Russia is likewise a regular participant. We argue that national experts play an important role in translating the methods and results of international assessments to the Russian public and policy-makers. Through their active engagement with the secondary analyses of test results, experts make sense of the studies, offer more detailed interpretations of their findings and prove their value to the national public, and also develop applied policy proposals that go beyond those advocated in the global reports. National evaluation experts perceive international assessments as repositories of scientific expertise in the field, and utilize this image and international knowledge in the form of evaluation techniques and test materials for developing national tools and strengthening the identity and influence of their (re)-emerging professional community.

The study relied upon two main sources of data: interviews with currently active national evaluation experts and academic publications by Russian authors

---

12   Clara Morgan and Riyad A. Shahjahan, "The Legitimation of OECD's Global Educational Governance: Examining PISA and AHELO Test Production," *Comparative Education* 50 (2014), doi: 10.1080/03050068.2013.834559.

13   Ibid., 12.

on the topic of international assessments. The data was originally collected for a larger research project entitled "Transnational Dynamics of Quality Assurance and Evaluation Politics of Basic Education in Brazil, China and Russia", 2014–17 and encompasses interviews with education experts and policy-makers at the national and local levels, ethnographic observations in schools, as well as a sizable collection of academic articles on the topic of assessment published in 1990–2015.[14] For the purposes of this chapter we analysed ten interviews with evaluation experts and a purposeful sample of academic publications specifically focusing on the topic of international assessments and written by evaluation experts and academics working in education research more generally. The interviews were conducted in 2015 in several institutions most actively involved in the development of education evaluation policy and its tools, and/or in the administration of international assessments and the analyses of national and international assessments data for both research and policy-making purposes. Academic publications discussing international assessments were identified from the three leading Russian academic journals in education sciences that regularly publish on the topics of evaluation and assessment: *Voprosy obrazovaniia* (Educational Studies in its English version), *Narodnoe obrazovanie* (Popular Education) and *Pedagogika* (Pedagogy). The search resulted in 42 items published between 2004 and 2015 that referred to one or several international assessments.

The chapter proceeds in the following manner. We first discuss the conceptual framing of the analysis and briefly introduce the Russian historical context relevant for the ensuing analysis. We then present the main discursive strategies and practical means through which national experts root ILSA in the Russian context.

Discursive Institutionalism and the Domestication Framework

Global governance, and we understand ILSA as important instruments thereof, functions through resonance with the positions and norms held by the national actors. As Alasuutari and Qadir write, "national states adopt global standards and policy models not because they are coerced to do so but primarily because governments are convinced that it is good for them, and hence global governance works particularly through knowledge production and consultancy."[15] This means

---

14 See Galina Gurova, Nelli Piattoeva, and Tuomas Takala, "Quality of Education and Its Evaluation: An Analysis of the Russian Academic Discussion," *European Education* 47 (2015), doi: 10.1080/10564934.2015.1107377.

15 Pertti Alasuutari and Ali Qadir, "Epistemic governance: an approach to the politics of policy-making," *European Journal of Cultural and Political Sociology* 1 (2014a), 68,

that local actors are not passive or unquestioning emulators, but play an active role in promoting exogenous ideas or models as domestic policy entrepreneurs who utilize and disseminate the global cultural discourses. Consequently, in order to understand how global governance acts upon or corresponds to people's understandings, we need to interrogate "[a]ctors' deep-seated values and beliefs," in other words, the paradigmatic assumptions that form a fruitful ground for the reception of global norms.[16]

Vivien Schmidt[17] distinguishes discursive institutionalism from the rational choice institutionalism, historical institutionalism and sociological institutionalism in order to highlight the role of ideas and discourse in institutional change. While the four institutionalisms share the belief that "social world and actors' decision-making cannot be properly explained without taking into account the role of institutions in constituting the conditions under which actors make their moves and how they expect others to react,"[18] discursive institutionalism as well as the domestication paradigm explicated below are focused specifically on the local processes through which global ideas are adopted. Local actors translate problems to bridge the gap between local goals and broader policy initiatives. They transform the original model and/or use it for a *problématique* that differs from the original. Such processes of localisation are an important focus of study of global governance because they make globally traveling policies and ideas *experientially domestic*.[19] During such a domestication process, when a global matter becomes part of the local context, politics or other, "local actors retain their sense of agency" and no longer perceive it as imitation of a foreign item.[20]

In this manner domestication refers to a transformation in which exogenous models, ideas or catchwords result in people viewing the outcome as a domestic

doi: 10.1080/23254823.2014.887986; see also Marjaana Rautalin, "Domestication of International Comparisons: The Role of the OECD Programme for International Student Assessment (PISA) in Finnish Education Policy" (Phd diss., Tampere University Press, 2013).

16 Alasuutari and Qadir, "Epistemic governance," 68.

17 Vivien A. Schmidt, "Discursive Institutionalism: The Explanatory Power of Ideas and Discourse," *Annual Review of Political Science* 11 (2008), doi: 10.1146/annurev. polisci.11.060606.135342.

18 Pertti Alasuutari, "The Discursive Side of New Institutionalism," *Cultural Sociology* 9 (2015): 3, doi: 10.1177/1749975514561805.

19 Alasuutari, "Discursive Side," 11, emphasis ours.

20 Ibid.

creation.[21] To achieve this, local actors often play a crucial role in (re)-packaging and constructing the success and appropriateness of the 'global model'. These practices call for analytical attention to the conceptions and actual practices of local actors.[22] A similar line of thinking could be identified in the concepts of "externalisation" and "sociologic" developed by Schriewer and Martinez.[23] They write about the system's internal need for a "supplementary meaning," and emphasise the distinct intrasocietal reflection processes[24] triggered by or occurring in parallel with transnational globalisation. Globalisation, they write, is interlinked with the recurring processes of culture-specific diversification.[25] Transnational globalisation and culture-specific diversification are intertwined and reciprocally enhance or undermine one another.[26] Therefore it is imperative to examine the complex overlap between the transnational diffusion of modern models and rules and the persistence or even revival of culture-specific semantic traditions.[27]

In utilizing the conceptual framework presented above we decentre the power of global governance agents and their instruments, and highlight the reliance of global actors on the epistemic premises and everyday practices of those whom they seek to influence.[28] As has been discussed elsewhere, "a great deal of organisational activity is directed towards editing externally-derived influences" and it is this activity that feeds the circulation of global idea(l)s and models, and thus makes them 'truly' global.[29] Researchers, professionals, leaders, consultants and planners as "carriers of ideas," "merchants of meaning" and cultural translators play a pivotal role in carrying ideas across time and space.[30] At the same time,

---

21　Pertti Alasuutari and Ali Qadir, "Introduction," in *National Policy-Making: Domestication of Global Trends*, eds. Pertti Alasuutari and Ali Qadir (Abingdon, Oxon: Routledge, 2014b), 9.

22　Ibid.

23　Jürgen Schriewer and Carlos Martinez, "Constructions of Internationality in Education," in *The Global Politics of Educational Borrowing and Lending*, ed. Gita Steiner-Khamsi, (New York, NY: Teachers College Press, 2004).

24　Ibid., 32–3.

25　Ibid., 34.

26　Ibid., 36.

27　Ibid., 36–7.

28　See Nelli Piattoeva, "Power as Translation in the Global Governance of Education," in *Shaping of European Education. Interdisciplinary Approaches*, eds. Martin Lawn and Romuald Normand (Oxon: Routledge, 2015b).

29　Suárez and Bromley, "Institutional Theories," 146.

30　Barbara Czarniawska-Joerges, "Merchants of Meaning: Management Consulting in the Swedish Public Sector," in *Organisational Symbolism*, ed. Barry A. Turner (Berlin: de

our research is embedded in the view that policy-making more generally is a complex and messy endeavour that involves and relies upon contributions from a wide range of actors from different scales and sites.[31] From this point of view, and bearing in mind the general context marked by the rise of knowledge societies and evidence-based policy-making,[32] to which Russia is no exception, it is particularly important to understand how those actors who produce potential knowledge and evidence define what counts as knowledge, research, evidence, valid methods etc. in their field of scholarly activity.

Historical Context and International Assessments

Standardized testing in Russia has a distinct history that several of our interviewees narrated in order to account for developments in the field, their personal career trajectories and interest in international assessments. All psychological testing, including standardized tests, came under fire in the 1930s with the decree by the Central Committee of the All-Russia Communist Party, known as the "Decree on Pedology," condemning those psychologists who had engaged in "pedological and/or testological studies on children."[33] The decree practically stopped all forms of testing for more than forty years, while charging a number of prominent scholars, including Lev Vygotsky posthumously, with cosmopolitism (i.e. utilisation and admiration of Western theories), idealism, and being an enemy of the Soviet people.[34]

Gruyter, 1990); David Suárez, "Education Professionals and the Construction of Human Rights Education," *Comparative Education Review* 51 (2007a), quoted in Suárez and Bromley, "Institutional Theories," 147.

31 For an overview, see Radhika Gorur, "Policy as Assemblage," *European Educational Research Journal* 10 (2011), doi: 10.2304/eerj.2011.10.4.611.

32 E.g. Reiner Grundmann and Nico Stehr, *The Power of Scientific Knowledge. From Research to Public Policy* (Cambridge, UK: Cambridge University Press, 2012).

33 Pedology as an empirical study of children behavior and development first developed in Europe and the USA, and was endorsed by a number of prominent Russian and Soviet psychologists particularly in the beginning of the 20th century. For historical accounts, see e.g. Elena Minkova, "Pedology as a Complex Science Devoted to the Study of Children in Russia: The History of Its Origin and Elimination," *Psychological Thought* 5 (2012): 92, doi: 10.5964/psyct.v5i2.23; Ivan Z. Holowinsky, "Vygotsky and the History of Pedology," *School Psychology International* 9 (1988), doi: 10.1177/0143034388092006.

34 Elena L. Grigorenko et al., "Is There a Standard for Standardized Testing? Four Sketches of the Applicability (or Lack Thereof) of Standardized Testing in Different Educational Systems," in *Extending Intelligence. Enhancement and New Constructs*, eds.

Pedology was also criticised within the academic community, echoing the ideologically motivated demolition of the discipline, but also independently of the political context. As one author summed up, the harshest criticism concerned the testing methods applied by the researchers. Pedologists were viewed as crude empiricists and their testing methods as developed to serve "[a]s justification for the inequality of human beings and the human race,"[35] meaning that test results served the purpose of early segregation and negatively affected teacher expectations based on crudely tested learning abilities. In addition, it was argued that "bourgeois pedology" tested "in order to exploit individuals" whilst in Russia "the interests of each individual would come first and it was important to enrich people's knowledge and skills, without which they would not be able to become great communists."[36] Following this historical decoupling, testing was only used in clinical psychology and diagnostic tests of children's intellectual development. Testing reappeared slowly in Soviet/Russian psychology in the 1960s and 1970s, particularly through tests of intelligence. Application of emerging computer technologies in human sciences, together with intensifying competition with the United States, created favourable conditions for this renewed interest in testing.[37] Since then, Soviet/Russian psychologists have adapted and created many psychological tests and testing is widely used in experimental and clinical psychological research.[38] However, this early reappearance of testing occurred outside the system of public education.

With the demolition of the Soviet system in 1991 and the invalidation of the "Decree on Pedology" testing techniques once again drew attention of education researchers and practitioners, who this time received an opportunity to learn from both Russian and international sources. This interest in tests was powered by the new orientation towards diverse, student-centred and individually tailored education which required more nuanced and 'modern' tools of pedagogical

---

Patrick C. Kyllonen, Lazar Stankov and Richard D. Roberts (New York, NY: Lawrence Erlbaum Associates, 2008).

35 A. S. Zaluzhny, *Lzhenauka pedologia v trudah Zalkinda* (Moskwa: Izd, 1937), 38, qtd. in Minkova, Elena, "Pedology as a Complex Science Devoted to the Study of Children in Russia: The History of Its Origin and Elimination," In *Psychological Thought* 5 (2012): 92.

36 Ibid.

37 Valeriy Kadnevskiy, "Genezis testirovaniya v istorii otechestvennogo obrazovaniya" (PhD diss., Ural State Pedagogical University, 2006), 41, accessed September 2, 2016, http://elar.uspu.ru/bitstream/uspu/342/1/aref00077.pdf.

38 Grigorenko et al., "Is There a Standard."

assessment.[39] In 1995, amidst the growing diversity of schooling, the newly established National Testing Centre for School Graduates started the first standardized testing of graduates' educational achievements for university entrance.[40] In 2001 the national school-leaving examination (the Unified State Exam, USE) was introduced. Despite the fact that standardized testing only recently became prominent, the number of standardized tests conducted in schools for selection, attestation, performance measurement, and diagnostic purposes illustrates their steady increase.[41]

The main goals of the Unified State Exam were stated as ensuring greater equality by facilitating the access of all school-leavers to higher education, and making the quality of school education more even across the country. Through encouraging compliance with the official school curricula, the USE facilitated the re-centralisation of school education governance.[42] The State Program for Education Development for 2013–2020 outlined a comprehensive system of education evaluation and quality control, composed of state regulation of education activities, assessment of educational achievement (national examinations after grades 9 and 11 that can utilize different assessment techniques), procedures of independent quality evaluation, and the participation of Russia in international studies.[43] The most recent 'second generation' national curriculum defines educational outcomes primarily in terms of competencies, thus resembling the competence-based approach of PISA in particular.[44] In general, both the academic discussion and policy documents of the 2000s show that the understanding of the quality of education shifted to quality as compliance with state standards and high achievement in international tests.[45]

The IEA's (International Association for the Evaluation of Educational Achievement) TIMSS (Trends in International Mathematics and Science Study) was the first international comparative study of academic achievement in which Russia

---

39 Gurova, Piattoeva, and Takala, "Quality of Education," 353–4; Kadnevskiy, "Genezis testirovaniya."

40 Kadnevskiy, "Genezis testirovaniya," 42.

41 See e.g. Piattoeva, "Elastic Numbers"; Nelli Piattoeva, "The Imperative to Protect Data and the Rise of Surveillance Cameras in Administering National Testing in Russia," *European Educational Research Journal* 15 (2016), doi: 10.1177/1474904115617767; Gurova, Piattoeva, and Takala, "Quality of Education."

42 Yulia Tyumeneva, *Disseminating and Using Student Assessment Information in Russia* (Washington, D.C.: World Bank, 2013); Piattoeva, "Elastic Numbers."

43 Government of Russia, "State Programme," 218.

44 Alla Sidenko, "O modeli podgotovki shkol k realizatsii FGOS vtorogo pokolenia", *Obrazovanie i nauka* no. 1 (2012): 4.

45 Gurova, Piattoeva, and Takala, "Quality of Education."

took part. The study was undertaken in 1995 with relatively high rankings for Russian students. Russia continued to participate in all consecutive cycles of TIMSS (undertaken every four years). Since 2000 Russia has also participated in all the OECD's PISA (Programme for International Student Assessment) studies and since 2001 – in IEA's PIRLS (Progress in International Reading Literacy Study). The results of Russian students in TIMSS and PIRLS have been consistently above the international average scores: in TIMSS Russia was ranked among the ten top-performing countries in both mathematics and science, and in PIRLS 2006 Russia occupied the top-ranking position. This was not the case with PISA, where the results of Russian students were significantly below the OECD average and showed no "improvement dynamics."[46]

The sections below examine the streams of consolidated ideas mapped through our analysis of expert interviews and academic publications, and together constitute a decidedly positive discourse on international assessments among Russian evaluation experts. These ideas are entangled with and materialised in concrete practices that help to root international assessments in the Russian education context at the policy level, and also, importantly, within the academic and expert community. We grouped the results of the study under four broad, inter-related themes with each theme embracing the ideational and practical side of the discourse examined. The expert interviews were based on a semi-structured questionnaire developed for the ongoing comparative research project. The interviewees responded to questions related to the role of international cooperation and international assessments in their work, and they were asked to characterize data circulation and utilisation in academic studies and political decision-making. They also made references to international assessments in relation to other topics. In the analysis of the articles and the interviews, we aimed at reconstructing

---

46 Galina Tsukerman, Galina Kovaleva and Marina Kuznetsova, "Pobeda v PIRLS i po-razhenie v PISA: Sud'Ba chitatel'skoy gramotnosti 10–15-letnikh shkol'nikov", *Voprosy obrazovaniya / Educational Studies* 2 (2011), accessed March 24, 2016, https://vo.hse.ru/2011--2/98041394.html. Russia also took part in the IEA's civic education studies CIVED (Civic Education Study) and ISSC (International Civic and Citizenship Education Study) (e.g. Leonid Bogolubov, Galina V. Klokova, Galina S. Kovalyova and David I. Poltorak, "The Challenge of Civic Education in the New Russia," in *Civic Education Across Countries, Twenty-Four National Case Studies from the IEA Civic Education Project*, eds. Judith Torney-Purta, John Schwille and Jo-Ann Amadeo (Amsterdam: IEA, 1999)). However, most of the articles on international assessments that we examined are concerned with TIMSS, PIRLS, and PISA, and therefore we concentrate primarily on these three.

the interviewees' discourse on international assessments in the Russian context. In adopting the understanding of discourse from discursive institutionalism, we were equally interested in the streams of ideas that constitute the discourse and in "the interactive processes by which ideas are conveyed."[47] In the latter case, we concentrated on how experts legitimize international assessments and re-utilize international data and tools, as the latter practices appeared to constitute an important means by which to root international assessments in the national context through their active adaptation and editing.

Historical Injustice

The historical legacy described above means that the cultural tradition of standardized testing in education is recent and emerging, cultivating criticism of the lack of testing and data culture.[48] In our data, the interviewed experts narrated the history of testing in Russia as one of historical injustice. Such an interpretation helps to explain why they long to reconnect with the worldwide scientific community in order to restore the "natural" evolution of the discipline and consequently to rescue Russia from "the outskirts of the global development in testing sciences."[49] As one interviewee passionately explained:

> "If before that moment [the interviewee refers to the "Decree on Pedology" mentioned above] Russia moved forward together with the rest of the world… we were no different, we had equally stupid tests. They were absolutely out of control and caused more harm than good, this is true. But the situation was similar in other countries. But *here* all was banned. So *there* the development took its natural form, poor quality was gradually washed out, tests became better, they are controlled more than before, people bear responsibility of some sort, this is a kind of evolutionary development. But *here* it was all interrupted, totally stopped, and after that psychology returned to its, so to say, ancestress discipline of philosophy. And again, we started to philosophize about the human being."[50]

As we explore in the forthcoming sections, this interpretation of history as forced decoupling from the general historical trajectory feeds the notions of lagging behind international developments in the field of assessment and curriculum development, contributing greatly to the overall positive appraisal of international assessments by the Russian experts.

---

47 Schmidt, "Discursive Institutionalism," 309.
48 E.g. Alexander Shmelev, "Test kak oruzhie", *Psihologia* 1 (2004).
49 Ibid., 41.
50 All translations from Russian are by the authors.

Embracing Scientism

International assessments concur with the idea of a solid scientific study in view of their Russian proponents, as the quote above also demonstrated. Experts praise assessments for being representative, offering a clear and well-developed methodology, and applying this methodology consistently across all cases. Being well resourced, these studies systematically collect masses of data, including contextual information that is deemed important for a comprehensive interpretation of the results. Some studies (i.e., PIRLS) apply both quantitative and qualitative approaches to data analysis, which lends them additional credibility in the Russian academic world. In other words, national experts seem convinced and impressed by the reliability and validity of international assessments, and perceive them as scientific benchmarks.[51]

Moreover, experts argue that even though USE data as average scores circulates well, it is hard or even impossible to obtain more detailed USE results in comparison to the openness of all the international assessment data. Open access and a large volume of background information make them attractive to national evaluation experts, who are interested in exploring correlations and even causal relationships between achievement and other factors, like family support, school administration or resources available:

> "The PIRLS study makes it possible to accumulate colossal amounts of data related to all the main parameters of primary education: achievements and failures of fourth graders in reading fiction and non-fiction texts; school problems; teachers', students' and parents' attitudes towards reading; pedagogical approaches; social and cultural characteristics of students' families. This body of data has so far been under-utilised in Russia. The potential of in-depth secondary analysis of PIRLS data is hard to overestimate. Analytical work with this data will give educational professionals the basis for detailed comparisons and well-grounded hypotheses, and at the same time enable parents to choose educational strategies for their children wisely. People responsible for education policy will be able to perform their tasks guided not only by good intentions and common sense, but also by scientific data."[52]

---

51 See e.g. Galina Kovaleva and Marina Kuznetsova, "Mezhdunarodnoe issledovanie PIRLS 2006 "Izuchenie kachestva chteniia i ponimaniia teksta"", *Narodnoe Obrazovanie* 4 (2008); Marina Demidova, "Okruzhajuschij mir" v standartah vtorogo pokolenija", *Narodnoe Obrazovanie* 9 (2010); Anatoly Kasprzhak et al., "Rossiiskoe shkol'noe obrazovanie: Vzgliad so storony", *Voprosy obrazovaniia* no. 1 (2004); Yulia Tyumeneva and Yulia Kuzmina, "Chto daiot god obucheniia rossiiskomu shkol'niku", *Voprosy obrazovania* no. 1 (2013).

52 Isak Froumin, "Introduction," in *Neozhidannaia pobeda: Rossiiskie shkol'niki chitaiut luchshe drugikh*, ed. Isak Froumin (Moscow: Izdatel'skii dom GU – Vysshei Shkoly Ekonomiki, 2010), 6.

The tests provide researchers with exciting intellectual puzzles through their diverse and often contradictory findings. These contradictions are taken as food for thought and further investigation without questioning the overall applicability of the studies to the Russian context, or raising concerns over their methodology. Specifically, Russian assessment experts have devoted time to understanding the discrepancy between PIRLS and PISA reading scores in order to fine-tune their understanding of the failures of the Russian education system:

> "The professional significance of the study lies in answering the question that has troubled many in recent years: how to explain the gigantic gap between the results of Russian schoolchildren in two international comparative assessments in reading literacy, PISA and PIRLS [...]. We — the authors of the article — have for several years gotten nowhere on the question as to why there emerges such an impressive gap in reading literacy in the primary and secondary school, as captured by PIRLS and PISA."[53]

The TIMSS and PISA mathematics results have likewise triggered a national debate and created another intellectual puzzle due to a similar discrepancy in their results, as analysed in the article by Carnoy, Khavenson and Ivanova.[54]

In order to address the intellectual puzzles triggered by the controversies of international literacy studies, the experts create new testing tools that recycle international assessment techniques and materials. One example of such a development is the "Pull-and-push" test that is referred to by its creators as a "hybrid of PIRLS and PISA" and was designed to explore the development of reading literacy in time among fourth, sixth and ninth graders.[55] This tool promotes the importance of understanding learning achievements in a comparative way. Its authors argue that this is a common practice elsewhere, but that Russia still lacks such "diagnostic methods of the dynamic side of learning achievements."[56]

The experts approach international assessments in a cohesive, intertwined manner, presenting them as a unified body of research. In addition, they demonstrate how the knowledge encompassed in these assessments carries a general

---

53 Tsukerman, Kovaleva, and Kuznetsova, "Pobeda v PIRLS," 124.

54 Martin Carnoy, Tatiana Khavenson, and Alina Ivanova, "Using TIMSS and PISA Results to Inform Educational Policy: A Study of Russia and Its Neighbours," *Compare: A Journal of Comparative & International Education* 45 (2015), doi: 10.1080/03057925.2013.855002.

55 Galina Tsukerman, Galina Kovaleva, and Marina Kuznetsova, "Stanovlenie chitatel'skoy gramotnosti, ili Novye pokhozhdeniya Tyani-Tolkaya", *Voprosy obrazovaniya / Educational Studies* 1 (2015), accessed March 24, 2016, https://vo.hse.ru/2015--1/147131158.html.

56 Ibid., 284.

socio-economic value, thus endorsing the wider political relevance of the studies. In explaining the benefits of a study such as PIRLS, a group of experts wrote that, among others, the importance of reading literacy assessments stems from the recently verified correlations between PISA scores and the probability that a young person will continue to tertiary education, and that high levels of literacy as measured by PISA are better predictors of individual economic well-being than his/her grade in the school-leaving diploma. They also pointed out that the average level of literacy in the country predicts economic growth better than the general level of learning achievements.[57]

In referring to the literature produced by international assessment agencies and organisations, experts tend to present them as repositories of the most advanced, accumulated international expertise in the field. By excluding alternative sources of knowledge, they seem to take for granted the claim that literacy can and should be measured in a comparative and standardized format:

> "[i]n defining reading literacy as an ability to extract and use information from the text we refer to the understanding of the international expert community whose efforts created the two most known and, more importantly, most reliable measures of reading literacy: the tests of PIRLS and PISA."[58]

As Hamilton, Maddox and Addey[59] remind, the literacy model embedded in the OECD program is based on the information-processing theory of functional literacy. This model tests a broad set of skills mainly through reading comprehension and then establishes the threshold levels of competence. The authors note the existence of an alternative, relational view of literacy as being embedded in the everyday situated practices. According to this theory, a comparative survey for measuring literacy is not feasible since individual performance is always generated in a particular context and its social relations.

National Culture and Values

One the one hand, Russian authors support the general conclusions of international agencies about the correlation between scores in international assessments and various aspects of (economic) well-being. This way, experts apply and

---

57 Tsukerman, Kovaleva, and Kuznetsova, "Pobeda v PIRLS."
58 Tsukerman, Kovaleva, and Kuznetsova, "Stanovlenie chitatel'skoy gramotnosti."
59 Mary Hamilton, Bryan Maddox and Camilla Addey, "Introduction," in *Literacy as Numbers. Researching the Politics and Practices of International Literacy Assessment*, eds. Mary Hamilton, Bryan Maddox and Camilla Addey (Cambridge, UK hinzufügen: Cambridge University Press, 2015), xiv.

legitimize these actors and their outputs within the national community, simultaneously reinforcing their own academic credibility by citing sources deemed authoritative. On the other hand, experts argue that the general conclusions cited in international sources are context-bound as they derive from the countries with developed economies and established democracies. Therefore, the experts find it necessary to complement these arguments with 'culture-friendly' ones, or perhaps, they attempt to convince audiences indifferent or even hostile to the reasoning that values economic logic above all others. For Russia, they say, the link between education and annual economic income is less evident. Therefore,

> "acute interest in the problem of literacy of school graduates is, above all, connected to *our* faith (for "you will not grasp her with your mind,"[60] emphasis ours) in the power of the written word. The people who today decide about the fate of our country grew up with books and for the most part believe that literacy constitutes the cornerstone of past and future civilisation."[61]

In this statement, the researchers clearly link literacy assessments to what they perceive as the shared Russian values, that is, appreciation of reading and being cultured. Interestingly, they implicitly address their statement to the decision-makers, reminding them of their own cultural background and thus obliging them to appreciate international assessments, too.[62] In one article, after referring to a speech by the Russian-American Nobel Prize laureate and dissident, Iosif Brodsky, experts conclude that introducing the new generation of children to written practice is a pedagogical means of maintaining the bond of times and generations,[63] meaning that international assessments help to understand where and how the system of education fails in its socialisation function. Simultaneously, experts connect international assessments to an educational topic that has been high on the Russian political agenda since the end of the 1990s, that is, the political socialisation of future citizens.[64]

---

60 Here the authors make a reference to a famous Russian poem by Fyodor Tyutchev, 1803–1873: "You will not grasp her with your mind or cover with a common label, For Russia is one of a kind — Believe in her, if you are able..."

61 Tsukerman, Kovaleva, and Kuznetsova, "Pobeda v PIRLS," 124.

62 Ibid.

63 Ibid.

64 See Nelli Piattoeva, "Citizenship Education Policies and the State. Russia and Finland in a Comparative Perspective" (PhD diss., Tampere University Press, 2010).

Modernisation Through Comparison

Of all international studies, PISA appeared to present a breakthrough technology for Russian experts because of its perceived ability to test general competencies rather than knowledge of curriculum content. Scrutinizing the test items and assessment criteria, researchers speculate about the underlying education goals and teaching methods that would enable their achievement. Thus, PISA materials serve as a benchmark of how to both teach and assess the "most relevant XXI century skills," and represent a "new paradigm of education" with which the Russian school system needs to catch up.[65] Inspired by the design of the test items, the authors advocate the broad application of the novel approach, from rewriting textbooks to reorganizing teaching process and redefining educational outcomes in the Russian national curriculum.[66]

Even authors taking a critical view of the superiority of context- or problem-based learning over the more traditional science-based instruction characteristic of the Russian school suggest that specialists in teaching methods might draw inspiration from PISA to develop their own problem-based assignments for extracurricular education.[67]

Through diverse interactions between assessment experts, curriculum specialists and national test designers, international assessments can then impact curriculum content and national assessment instruments. The two quotes below, one from a publication and the other from an interview, explain how such reciprocal influences operate in the daily work of Russian international assessment experts:

> "We've been lucky that almost half of the team that develops testing items for the USE takes part in the development of instruments for national surveys and is well acquainted with the experience of international assessments in Russia. This guarantees the comparability of indicators and utilisation of complementary indicators."[68]

> "In the framework on the Russian Academy of Education and its Institute for Content and Methods [...] we have many laboratories [...] when administering PIRLS, reading in primary school, we work with specialists from the Centre for Primary Education. Specialists in TIMSS are the authors of standards and textbooks. So, we go to the eighth grade, and there work together with mathematicians from the Laboratory of Mathematical

---

65 Kasprzhak et al., "Rossiiskoe shkol'noe obrazovanie."

66 Ibid., Galina Kovaleva, "PISA-2003: Rezul'taty mezhdunarodnogo testirovania", *Narodnoe obrazovanie* no. 8 (2005); Demidova, "Okruzhajuschij mir."

67 Natalya Konasova, "Budet li u nas 'russkaia PISA'?", *Narodnoe obrazovanie* no. 2 (2011).

68 Galina Kovaleva, "Mozhno li ispol'zovat' rezul'taty YeGE dlia monitoringa kachestva obrazovania", *Narodnoe obrazovanie* no. 9 (2006): 57.

Education. They are authors of textbooks and standards. So, we work directly with those who determine the content of education in the country."[69]

The development of new testing tools that take advantage of international assessments is rooted in the idea that assessments should serve quality development and management at the national and local levels rather than mere control. National experts value international assessments for belonging to the former orientation and contrast them, as well as their own work with the new testing techniques, to the apparent reorientation in the federal usage of national assessments for purposes of rigid central control and reward and punishment by results without a significant development interest. Related to their interest in assessment as a tool for quality management, experts voice critical comments about international assessments while still capitalizing on them in many aspects. They argue that international assessments are removed from the life of the school. They do not raise interest among the teachers and do not motivate them to change, providing no information that would help the teacher to better understand students' learning in relation to the ongoing pedagogical work. In other words, these critical arguments emphasise a lack of feedback mechanisms; as one respondent described the outcome of international assessments — "you administer the test and then carry off."

What national teams try to do is to develop school-based instruments that would motivate the teacher to organise testing, analyse the results and stimulate his/her thinking process, enabling further adjustments in teaching. Experts want to motivate teachers to engage in greater reflexivity and approach their work in a more systematic, scientific manner. In this regard, the comparative logic is viewed as particularly promising and comparison is described as a means to produce knowledge and better understanding at the individual level but also in aggregate terms. As one expert explained when addressing the interviewer's question about possible resistance on the part of local actors towards assessment tools promoted by national experts:

"We try to explain and say that a specific mechanism is required for the school to develop. A mechanism that combines internal and external evaluation provides stimuli for development. The teacher and his/her assessment are internal regarding the classroom, and ours is external. If the teacher's internal and our external assessment match up, but well, in fact they will diverge in some aspects. It is stimuli for development. Or stimuli to understand that all you are doing is correct and that you should find other objectives. Or to look who is better than you, that is, obtain indicators and reference points."[70]

---

69 Interview conducted by the authors.
70 Ibid.

More generally, throughout the data that we examined, the importance of comparison was stressed from many perspectives. Interestingly, while comparison for internal use and self-evaluation were understood as a new phenomenon, international comparisons and interest in evaluating one's national education system in comparison to other countries were seen as having a long legacy. In response to the interviewer's question as to whether or not a comparative interest is a new phenomenon in the process of understanding the Russian education system as a whole one respondent stated:

> "No, there was always an interest, throughout life, because in our sphere, in education, there are no *talmuds* or objective norms, so the only way to understand where one is heading, whether one is good or bad, is through comparison. There is no other way."[71]

Conclusion

Our study has shown that national experts contribute considerably to circulating the international tests and their data around, and that at the same time their involvement with international assessments is an important factor in the ongoing development of the overall assessment culture. In exploring how Russian experts relate to international assessments we found that their arguments made reference to the development of the field of assessment historically, arguing that learning from, as well as adopting and adapting the tools of international assessments is a way to fill the gap and restore the development of testing expertise interrupted in the early Soviet period. In this manner they narrate the history of testing in Russia as one of historical injustice to be rectified through joining the global expert community, whose competence is distilled into international tests.

The experts perceive the 'science of testing' as a set of consensual, universally applicable knowledge with a uniform development trajectory. In this respect, international assessments and the organisations that administer them appear as repositories of international best practices in testing, and therefore association with these organisations and utilisation of their knowledge present a short-cut in catching-up with the overall scientific development in the field. Our research can be read as confirming the conclusions of Lingard, Sellar and Baroutsis[72] about the shared habitus of international and national actors in the field of assessment. In particular, we, too, detected a strong modernist confidence in science and

---

71 Ibid.

72 Bob Lingard, Sam Sellar, and Aspa Baroutsis, "Researching the Habitus of Global Policy Actors in Education," *Cambridge Journal of Education* 45 (2015), doi: 10.1080/0305764X.2014.988686.

technology and in understanding the social through quantitative methods. In this manner, working with PISA and other international assessment data, testing items and methods is an expression of this shared worldview rather than a manifestation of international borrowing.

The OECD's influence is generally perceived to come from its knowledge production capacities and the perception of the high quality of its information and analysis.[73] The chapter illustrates that prestige is shared at the national level, meaning that the included actors whom we studied appreciate and largely endorse the assessment culture promoted by the international agencies. In voicing their total trust in the assessments and the bodies that produce them, national experts mediate their reputation in their own national setting, acting as agents of these institutions and at the same time ensuring prestige for themselves through borrowing legitimacy from the organisations deemed authoritative. In this manner, our research highlights the reciprocity or interdependence between national experts who utilize international studies and the organisations that produce them.

The researchers make explicit efforts to domesticate and normalize international studies by linking them to the history and the presumed values of the national society in whose name they speak. As we have shown, the importance of reading literacy assessments is connected to the Russian tradition of reading and culture, and high appreciation of the 'written word.' Participation in the assessments, secondary analysis of their results and the development of domestic testing techniques on the basis of these are then presented as a way to cherish and promote the cornerstones of *Russian culture* and to secure the key task of the education system of socializing future generations. We find this strategy very important in the national context that is otherwise portrayed as lacking a tradition of testing and where, due to this historical path, testing may and is often viewed in negative terms.

In referring to particular advantageous aspects of Russian culture experts make Russia's involvement in international assessments seem less of a departure from the national context.[74] In this manner, national experts work as local translators and editors of global models described in the research on domestication, that is, they "draw on worldwide models and blueprints while reinforcing national identity," justify their appreciation of international assessments by "constructing a national interest — and, therefore, national identity — from which a particular

---

73   Morgan and Shahjahan, "Legitimation."

74   C.f. Pertti Alasuutari and Maarit Alasuutari, "The Domestication of Early Childhood Education Plans in Finland," *Global Social Policy* 12 (2012): 135, doi: 10.1177/1468018112443684.

solution or eclectic mix of solutions is considered against its relevance for *us*."[75] They negotiate and weave international assessments into the existing practices and beliefs, making the alien appear familiar. Thus national experts ought to be seen as active and creative agents in constructing the Russian assessment culture at the interface between the national context and global education governance.

Although the comparative aspect of assessments was mostly taken for granted and the experts expressed a clear orientation toward comparison as a mode of governance,[76] they attributed little significance to comparing the achievement of Russian students to their counterparts abroad, simultaneously viewing interest in international comparisons as natural and persistent through time. National experts saw international instruments as valuable and important in understanding the national system of education through nationally framed comparisons (of schools, regions etc.) and were keen to adapt international assessment technologies to more closely scrutinize the national space of education. Finally, the chapter has shown that experts make explicit statements that address policy-makers and include concrete advice for policy-makers by means of pointing to the current failures of the system of education and ways to fix them. Therefore, their interest in international studies as a scientific model to emulate is intertwined with an ambition to contribute to policy-making.

Literature

Alasuutari, Pertti. "The Discursive Side of New Institutionalism." *Cultural Sociology* 9 (2015): 162–84. doi: 10.1177/1749975514561805.

Alasuutari, Pertti, and *Maarit Alasuutari*. "The Domestication of Early Childhood Education Plans in Finland." *Global Social Policy* 12 (2012): 129–48. doi: 10.1177/1468018112443684.

Alasuutari, Pertti, and *Ali Qadir*. "Epistemic Governance: An Approach to the Politics of Policy-making." *European Journal of Cultural and Political Sociology* 1 (2014a): 67–84. doi: 10.1080/23254823.2014.887986.

Alasuutari, Pertti, and *Ali Qadir*. "Introduction." In *National Policy-Making: Domestication of Global Trends*, edited by Pertti Alasuutari, and Ali Qadir, 1–22. Abingdon, Oxon, UK: Routledge, 2014b.

Bogolubov, Leonid, Galina Klokova, Galina Kovalyova, and *David Poltorak*. "The Challenge of Civic Education in the New Russia." In *Civic Education Across Countries, Twenty-Four National Case Studies from the IEA Civic Education*

---

75 Alasuutari and Qadir, "Introduction," 7, emphasis original.
76 C.f. Nóvoa and Yariv-Mashal, "Comparative Research."

Project, edited by Judith Torney-Purta, John Schwille, and Jo-Ann Amadeo, 523–43. Amsterdam: IEA, 1999.

Bolotov, Viktor. "O sozdanii obscherossiiskoi sistemy otsenki kachestva obrazovaniia v Rossiiskoj Federacii". *Vestnik Obrazovaniia* 11 (2005): 10–8.

Carnoy, Martin, Tatiana Khavenson, and *Alina Ivanova.* "Using TIMSS and PISA Results to Inform Educational Policy: A Study of Russia and Its Neighbours." *Compare: A Journal of Comparative & International Education* 45 (2015): 248–71. doi: 10.1080/03057925.2013.855002.

Czarniawska-Joerges, Barbara. "Merchants of Meaning: Management Consulting in the Swedish Public Sector." *Organisational Symbolism*, edited by Barry A. Turner, 139–50. Berlin: de Gruyter, 1990.

Demidova, Marina. "Okruzhajuschij mir" v standartah vtorogo pokolenija". *Narodnoe Obrazovanie* 9 (2010): 193–200.

Froumin, Isak, "Introduction." *Neozhidannaia pobeda: Rossiiskie shkol'niki chitaiut luchshe drugikh*, edited by Isak Froumin, 6–7. Moscow: Izdatel'skii dom GU — Vysshei Shkoly Economiki, 2010.

Gorur, Radhika. "Policy as Assemblage." *European Educational Research Journal* 10 (2011): 611–22. doi: 10.2304/eerj.2011.10.4.611.

Government of Russia. "State Programme of the Russian Federation 'Development of Education' for 2013–2020." 2013. Accessed May 22, 2015. www.минобрнауки.рф/документы/3409.

Grigorenko, Elena L., Linda Jarvin, Weihua Niu, and *David Preiss.* "Is There a Standard for Standardized Testing? Four Sketches of the Applicability (or Lack Thereof) of Standardized Testing in Different Educational Systems." In *Extending Intelligence. Enhancement and New Constructs*, edited by Patrick C. Kyllonen, Richard D. Roberts, and Lazar Stankov, 135–55. New York, NY: Lawrence Erlbaum Associates, 2008.

Grundmann, Reiner, and *Nico Stehr. The Power of Scientific Knowledge. From Research to Public Policy.* Cambridge, UK: Cambridge University Press, 2012.

Gurova, Galina, Nelli Piattoeva, and *Tuomas Takala.* "Quality of Education and Its Evaluation: An Analysis of the Russian Academic Discussion." *European Education* 47 (2015): 346–64. doi: 10.1080/10564934.2015.1107377.

Hamilton, Mary, Bryan Maddox, and *Camilla Addey.* "Introduction." In *Literacy as Numbers. Researching the Politics and Practices of International Literacy Assessment*, edited by Mary Hamilton, Bryan Maddox, and Camilla Addey, xii–xxx. Cambridge, UK: Cambridge University Press, 2015.

Holowinsky, Ivan Z. "Vygotsky and the History of Pedology." *School Psychology International* 9 (1988): 123–8. doi:10.1177/0143034388092006.

Kadnevskiy, Valeriy. "Genezis testirovaniya v istorii otechestvennogo obrazovaniya". PhD diss., Ural State Pedagogical University, 2006. Accessed September 2, 2016. http://elar.uspu.ru/bitstream/uspu/342/1/aref00077.pdf.

Kasprzhak, Anatoly, Katerina Polivanova, Galina Tsukerman, Kirill Mitrofanov, and *Olga Sokolova.* "Rossiiskoe shkol'noe obrazovanie: Vzgliad so storony". *Voprosy obrazovaniia* no. 1 (2004): 190–231.

Konasova, Natalya. "Budet Li u nas 'russkaia PISA'?". *Narodnoe obrazovanie* no. 2 (2011): 182–90.

Kovaleva, Galina. "Mozhno li ispol'zovat' rezul'taty YeGE dlia monitoringa kachestva obrazovania". *Narodnoe obrazovanie* no. 9 (2006): 53–57.

Kovaleva, Galina. "PISA–2003: Rezul'taty mezhdunarodnogo testirovania". *Narodnoe obrazovanie* no. 8 (2005): 37–44.

Kovaleva, Galina, and *Marina Kuznetsova,* "Mezhdunarodnoe issledovanie PIRLS 2006 "Izuchenie kachestva chtenia i ponimania teksta"". *Narodnoe Obrazovanie* no. 4 (2008): 171–180.

Lawn, Martin, and *Sotiria Grek. Europeanizing Education: Governing a New Policy Space.* Oxford, UK: Symposium Books, 2012.

Lingard, Bob, Sam Sellar, and *Aspa Baroutsis.* "Researching the Habitus of Global Policy Actors in Education." *Cambridge Journal of Education* 45 (2015): 25–42. doi: 10.1080/0305764X.2014.988686.

Mau, Vladimir, and *Yaroslav Kuzminov,* ed. *Strategiya-2020: Novaya model' rosta — novaya sotsial'naya politika. Itogovyy doklad o rezul'tatakh ekspertnoy raboty po aktual'nym problemam sotsial'no-ekonomicheskoy strategii Rossii na period do 2020 goda.* Moscow: Delo, RANEPA University Press, 2013.

Miller, Peter, and *Nikolas Rose. Governing the Present: Administering Economic, Social and Personal Life.* Cambridge, UK: Polity Press, 2008.

Minkova, Elena. "Pedology as a Complex Science Devoted to the Study of Children in Russia: The History of Its Origin and Elimination." *Psychological Thought* 5 (2012): 83–98. doi: 10.5964/psyct.v5i2.23.

Morgan, Clara, and *Riyad A. Shahjahan.* "The Legitimation of OECD's Global Educational Governance: Examining PISA and AHELO Test Production." *Comparative Education* 50 (2014): 192–205. doi: 10.1080/03050068.2013.834559.

Nóvoa, Antonio, and *Tali Yariv-Mashal.* "Comparative Research in Education: A Mode of Governance or a Historical Journey?" *Comparative Education* 39 (2003): 423–38. doi: 10.1080/0305006032000162002.

Piattoeva, Nelli. "Citizenship Education Policies and the State. Russia and Finland in a Comparative Perspective." PhD diss., University of Tampere, 2010.

Piattoeva, Nelli. "Elastic Numbers: National Examinations Data as a Technology of Government." *Journal of Education Policy* 30 (2015a): 316–34. doi: 10.1080/02680939.2014.937830.

Piattoeva, Nelli. "Power as Translation in the Global Governance of Education." In *Shaping of European Education. Interdisciplinary Approaches,* edited by Martin Lawn and Romuald Normand, 66–80. Oxon: Routledge, 2015b.

Piattoeva, Nelli. "The Imperative to Protect Data and the Rise of Surveillance Cameras in Administering National Testing in Russia." *European Educational Research Journal* 15 (2016): 82–98. doi: 10.1177/1474904115617767.

Rautalin, Marjaana. "Domestication of International Comparisons: The Role of the OECD Programme for International Student Assessment (PISA) in Finnish Education Policy." Phd diss., University of Tampere, 2013.

Schmidt, Vivien A. "Discursive Institutionalism: The Explanatory Power of Ideas and Discourse." *Annual Review of Political Science* 11 (2008): 303–26. doi: 10.1146/annurev.polisci.11.060606.135342.

Schriewer, Jürgen, and *Carlos Martinez.* "Constructions of Internationality in Education." In *The Global Politics of Educational Borrowing and Lending,* edited by Gita Steiner-Khamsi, 29–53. New York, NY: Teachers College Press, 2004.

Shmelev, Alexander. "Test kak oruzhie." In *Psihologia* 1 (2004): 40–53.

Sidenko, Alla. "O modeli podgotovki shkol k realizatsii FGOS vtorogo pokolenia". *Obrazovanie i nauka* no. 1 (2012): 3–16.

Suárez, David. "Education Professionals and the Construction of Human Rights Education." *Comparative Education Review* 51 (2007a): 48–70. Quoted in Suárez, David and Patricia Bromley. "Institutional Theories and Levels of Analysis: History, Diffusion, and Translation." In *World Culture Re-contextualised,* edited by Jürgen Schriewer, 139–59. London, UK: Taylor and Francis, 2016.

Suárez, David, and *Patricia Bromley.* "Institutional Theories and Levels of Analysis: History, Diffusion, and Translation." In *World Culture Re-contextualised,* edited by Jürgen Schriewer, 139–59. London, UK: Taylor and Francis, 2016.

Tsukerman, Galina, Galina Kovaleva, and *Marina Kuznetsova.* "Pobeda v PIRLS i porazhenie v PISA: Sud'Ba chitatel'skoy gramotnosti 10–15-letnikh shkol'nikov". *Voprosy obrazovaniya / Educational Studies* 2 (2011): 123–50. Accessed March 24, 2016. https://vo.hse.ru/2011--2/98041394.html.

Tsukerman, Galina, Galina Kovaleva, and *Marina Kuznetsova.* "Stanovlenie chitatel'skoy gramotnosti, ili Novye pokhozhdeniya Tyani-Tolkaya". *Voprosy obrazovaniya / Educational Studies* 1 (2015): 284–300. Accessed March 24, 2016. https://vo.hse.ru/2015--1/147131158.html.

Tyumeneva, Yulia. Disseminating and Using Student Assessment Information in Russia. Washington, D.C.: World Bank, 2013.

Tyumeneva, Yulia, and *Yulia Kuzmina.* "Chto daiot god obucheniia rossiiskomu shkol'niku". *Voprosy obrazovania* no. 1 (2013): 107–25.

Zaluzhny, A. S. *Lzhenauka pedologia v trudah Zalkinda.* Moskwa: Izd, 1937. Quoted in Minkova, Elena. "Pedology as a Complex Science Devoted to the Study of Children in Russia: The History of Its Origin and Elimination." *Psychological Thought* 5 (2012): 83–98. doi: 10.5964/psyct.v5i2.23.

Funding

The research for this chapter was supported by the Academy of Finland grant 273874 for the research project "Transnational Dynamics of Quality Assurance Policies and Evaluation in Brazil, China and Russia" 2014–17.

Ángela Adriana Rengifo Correa

From the Experimental Examination to Educational Evaluation in Colombia: A Study in the Perspective of the History of Concepts, 1930-1970

Neither *examen experimental* (experimental examination) nor *evaluación educativa* (educational evaluation) had their origin in educational discourse. These concepts come from disciplinary fields such as medicine, biology, experimental psychology, administration, economics and statistics, that is, of social disciplines that have been considered more or less scientific when linked with the experimental methods of the exact sciences. One could say that this type of discourse helped to consolidate the educational discourse in the late 19th and early 20th century, while giving legitimacy to the task of national states as guarantors and organisers of education systems. At the time, scientific discourse and its premises became an endorsement of unquestionable truths about human behaviour and social relations, among which are the studies on education and school organisation.

It is possible to demonstrate today the power of the *prueba* (test).[1] Its uses spread across the clinical, business and educational spheres. There are collective and individual tests, personality tests (some projective), skills and knowledge tests. They are used to detect possible personality disorders, learning difficulties. They are employed as vocational guidance tests, admission tests in clinics, rehabilitation centres, prisons, schools and companies. All this reveals that the power of measurement and the discourse of objectivity remain fully valid, even if it has been (and still is) harshly criticised. The purpose of this paper is to present how the qualities of validity and reliability that were awarded to psychological tests from the discursive field of medicine, biology and experimental psychology also became part of the semantic component of the concept of evaluation stemming from scientific administration, economics and statistics.

The methodology that this paper intends to follow is the history of the concepts. From the perspective of the School of Bielefeld in Germany, initiated by Reinhart Koselleck, it has constituted itself as a methodology of important expansion in

---

1 Josefina Granja Castro, "Evaluación institucional y procesos de legitimación," *Avances y perspectivas* 10 (1991): 221-225.

political and intellectual history.[2] This approach is anchored in a social perspective, which seeks to review the interaction between the linguistic and the extralinguistic, considering not only the concepts but also the uses given to them by social actors. The notion of *concept* differs, according to Koselleck, from those of *terms* or *words* because they cover a large number of significant contents that are in dispute within a given time-space framework. Like words, concepts can be polysemous and have diachronic variations, but they differ in their aspiration of generality: "a word becomes a concept if the totality of a context of experience and socio-political meaning in which it is used and for which a word is used, becomes globally part of that single word."[3] Although conceptual history is a branch of social history, in a certain sense it overcomes and transcends it because it articulates significant long-term networks "insofar as they serve to significantly articulate the different social experiences that form discursive networks that cross epochs and the transcend spheres of immediate sociability."[4]

Recently, conceptual history has received a special interest in Spanish-language works on history of education, in what could be considered an emerging approach. According to Roldán Vera,[5] the concepts used in the educational field can also be seen with a nuance in the political and social field, in the sense that they have implications beyond school: public instruction, freedom of education, *Estado Docente* (teaching state), etc. The history of concepts is not only rooted in a theory of language, but also in a historical theory of modernity. In Roldan Vera's perspective, conceptual history and history of education are framed within a broader study of the languages in education.

This paper is divided in three parts. The first one presents the practices of *certámenes* (oral examinations), originated in the colonial period and which received other meanings in the organisation of the nascent republics, especially for the organisation of a school system by the state, based on an apparatus of administration, inspection and surveillance that introduces a bureaucracy with new educational actors: inspectors and teachers. The second part refers to the

---

2   Pierre Rosanvallon, *Por una historia conceptual de lo político. Lección inaugural en el Collège de Francia* (México, Fondo de Cultura Económica, 2002).

3   Reinhart Koselleck, *Futuro pasado. Para una semántica de los tiempos históricos* (Barcelona, Paidós, 1993), 117.

4   Elías José Palti, "Ideas, conceptos, metáforas. La tradición alemana de historia intelectual y el complejo entramado del lenguaje," *Res pública* 25 (2011): 231.

5   Eugenia Roldán Vera, "La perspectiva de los lenguajes en la historia de la educación," *Ariadna histórica. Lenguajes, conceptos, metáforas* 3 (2014): 13. Dr. Roldán Vera is a researcher at the Departamento de Investigaciones Educativas, CINVESTAV (México).

way in which discourses of experimental psychology, medicine and pedagogy circulated among the educational actors in Colombia, and allowed the emergence of the concept of experimental examination in the country, which involved the use of psychological tests. The third part refers to the mode in which discourses of economic developmentalism, educational planning and scientific management circulated among the country's educational actors and allowed the emergence of the concept of educational evaluation in Colombia, sometimes in convergence and in other instances, as opposition to practices of examination. In both moments, it is possible to identify the constant of a semantic field of the 'modern', based on the scientific conditions of validity and objectivity.

This paper aims to contribute to the research project that investigates the concept of student assessment culture in different historical moments and different parts of the world. This semantic transition from examination to evaluation implied a change in the Colombian student assessment culture, with modifications during the period under study (1930–1940), considering linguistic and extra-linguistic factors. The transformation went from an assessment culture of oral examinations, which was labelled as 'subjective', to an assessment culture of evaluation in which standardized and objective tests were applied as guarantee of validity and reliability. In this process, new educational actors appeared who relied on discourses that were considered scientific and thus guaranteed the legitimation of that culture.

The concept of *examen* and examination practices in Colombia during the 19ᵗʰ century until 1930

It is important to consider that examination practices have been in place in Colombia since the appearance of the school, but the concept of educational evaluation only emerged between the 1950s and 1970s. Some understand that the advent of the school was much earlier than that of the educational institution as such, thanks to the confluence of teacher and curriculum at the end of the eighteenth century with the Moreno and Escandón reforms. Others argue that it is vitally important to consider the role of the state and the instruction of different social classes in the emergence of the school.[6]

During the 19ᵗʰ century, after the independence period, several educational reform attempts were undertaken: the Santander Plan (1821), the Ospina Plan (1844) and the reform by radical liberals known as the *Decreto Orgánico de*

---

6   Alberto Martínez Boom and Renán Silva, *Dos estudios sobre educación en la Colonia* (Bogotá: Universidad Pedagógica Nacional, 1984).

Instrucción Pública Primaria (DOIP) (Organic Decree of Public Elementary Instruction) of 1870.[7] From this decade, the debates about the function and organisation of schools intensified. One of the characteristics of these discussions is the patent intention to inscribe them in a modern discourse, in a growing tendency towards the secularisation. In 1870, the United States of Colombia consisted of nine states, including Panama, with a federal government headed by radical liberals. After a political and military process of decadence of the liberals, in 1886 a new constitution establishes the present Republic of Colombia as a centralised government under the direction of the conservatives and of the Catholic Church. However, after the reform of 1870 it can be observed that the priest ceased to be the sole custodian of souls, and that the profession of teacher was institutionalised with the strengthening of the *Escuelas Normales* (teachers' colleges) as well as the school inspection as an 'eye' of the state to supervise schools.[8] The DOIP reform of the 1870s was considered the closest attempt to consolidate the beginnings of the school system in Colombia, with the establishment of public officials in charge of education: inspectors, principals and teachers. Around this hierarchy, an apparatus of examination and school inspection was organised that included the so-called *actos literarios* (literary acts) or oral examinations. Then, a series of other reforms aimed at modernizing the apparatus were implemented: The Zerda Plan (1893), the Organic Law on Public Instruction (1903), and the Educational Reform of the Liberal Republic (1930–1946). During the latter, the principles of modern pedagogy, of active school and experimental examination were introduced in the country.[9]

The oral examinations were public events in which the students' progress was presented. These events were held at the end of the school year or an extended period (semester or quarter). The proceedings were known as literary acts, *exámenes anuales* (annual examinations) or *sabatinas*. They were organised in a very ceremonious and solemn way, in some cases in places like churches or the school building itself. Parents and local authorities (governor, mayor, priest, inspectors, examinations committee, etc.) were invited, and constituted themselves as the public, guarantors and judges of the students' knowledge but, above

---

7   Jane Rausch, *La Educación durante el Federalismo. La Reforma Escolar de 1870* (Bogotá: Universidad Nacional, 1993).

8   Gilberto Loaiza Cano, *Sociabilidad, Religión y Política en la definición de Nación. Colombia, 1820–1886* (Bogotá: Universidad Externado de Colombia, 2011).

9   Óscar Saldarriaga, Javier Sáenz Obregón and Armando Ospina, *Mirar la infancia: pedagogía, moral y modernidad en Colombia, 1903–1946*, Vol. 1–2 (Bogotá: Universidad de los Andes-Universidad de Antioquia, 1997).

all, of the good performance of the school and its teachers. The oral examinations were a traditional customary practice with their own rites. Each college or school decreed in its prospects how these events would be held and the dates on which they would take place, usually prior to the holidays. Shortly before oral examinations, an examination program was organised, which contained the subjects and topics to be assessed. Likewise, invitations to prestigious external personalities to take part in the examining board were sent out. At the beginning of the event, the important guest or the schoolmaster pronounced a speech. The oral examinations could take place on weekends or evenings and could last for several days. As a closing of the solemn session, a prize presentation was arranged. The rewards could be a money sum, toys or books and study material. Usually the events were accompanied by other presentations that would account for the skills students were honing in schools (music, recitation, composition, and dance). The proceedings were recorded in examination reports which highlighted the names of the students in each subject. The files were kept in the schools and could be published. Such was the importance of the oral examinations that newspapers and official journals profusely reported on them. This evidenced the importance of these events for instruction: after all, they aimed to show effectiveness and good results. It can be said that this, although with some variations, was the generalised way to carry out these oral examinations. The examination was denominated a "celebration of civilisation."[10]

It is worth mentioning other characteristics of the oral examinations. Priority was given to orality rather than writing. Those who began to write for examination were the *Bachiller, Licenciado, Doctores* university students or *maestros normalistas* (primary teachers) who, in order to graduate, had to present a short-written dissertation or a lecture on a certain subject that was called 'thesis.' But in the schools, with younger students, written examinations only became frequent during the 20th century. In the 19th century, written work was limited to a few sheets that complemented the oral presentation. Another important issue to note is that not always all students were examined. In many oral examinations, students and subjects to be examined were chosen at random. The idea was that if one gave a good exam, it could be assumed that the rest knew the same. Thus, the oral examination was not to examine each student, but rather the school and the

---

10 "Discurso pronunciado por el señor Demetrio Gómez, Secretario General de la Intendencia, en el solemne acto de distribución de premios en el Colegio de niñas de la Presentación de Quibdó, el 30 de noviembre de 1913." *Revista de Instrucción Pública de Quibdó* 6 (1913): 149. Sala de libros raros y manuscritos. Biblioteca Luis Ángel Arango. Banco de la República.

teacher, and so to grant it a social status. This led to the custom that many teachers began selecting beforehand those students who would represent them, knowing their strengths or weaknesses. Likewise, in the daily practice of schools each child was examined orally and individually at least once a week or once a month by his teachers to account for the lessons learnt. At the end of the 19th century, the practice of examining every child in all subjects became more widespread. The truth is that the oral examination was the occasion for a display of the school and its teachers before society. Between the end of the 19th century and the beginning of the 20th century, the oral examinations were questioned as an anachronistic and mistaken practice that had to be replaced by more modern and effective methods. A separation was established between the part called properly examination (individual) and the closing ceremony (collective).[11]

Emergency of the concept of experimental examination in Colombia, 1930–1950

At the beginning of the 20th century, Colombia was essentially a rural economy with very low levels of literacy.[12] In fact, the century began with The Thousand Days War (1899–1902) that left it devastated in several aspects and brought about the loss of Panama. Political power was in the hands of the Conservatives, who had held it since the 1880s and reinforced it with the Constitution of 1886. Public education was dominated by the Catholic Church and various religious communities. The first decades of the 20th century represented a period of incipient modernisation in Colombia with the coffee boom and the growth of the main cities thanks to a process of internal migration, with the appearance of some urban facilities, especially in Bogotá, and the organisation of industries and the labour sector.[13]

During this slow process of modernisation and reorganisation of the different political-administrative branches of the state, certain events were relevant to the educational discourse. The first was the founding of the *Gimnasio Moderno* in 1914 by Agustín Nieto Caballero, who was the first to introduce ideas about the New School and experimental psychology in the country. Nieto Caballero would become inspector of elementary and normal education, and general director

---

11 María M. de Ide. "Exámenes por escrito." *La Escuela Normal. Periódico Oficial de Instrucción Pública* 6, no. 235 (1875): 214–216. Biblioteca Luis Ángel Arango. Microfilm.

12 Aline Helg, *La educación en Colombia, 1918–1957: una historia social, económica y política* (Bogotá: Fondo Editorial Cerec, 1987).

13 Marco Palacios and Frank Safford, *Colombia: país fragmentado, sociedad dividida. Su historia* (Bogotá: Norma, 2002).

of education.[14] The second important event was the First National Pedagogical Congress celebrated in 1917, which was attended by delegations from all over the country and where important topics for an educational reform were discussed, especially physical education. The third event is the second German Pedagogical Mission in 1925 that suggested different proposals for the organisation of a public education system, and that led to the foundation of the Pedagogical Institute for Ladies of Bogotá in 1926, headed by the German Francisca Radke, and the arrival in 1928 of the German Julius Sieber to the *Escuela Normal* in Tunja.[15]

During the 1920s, several intellectuals, among them the physicians Miguel Jiménez López and Luis López de Mesa, promoted the discussion on the "degeneration of the Colombian race" and the discourse of the hygiene.[16] Education was considered as one of the main tools to correct the deficiencies of the Colombian race, caused by alcoholism, venereal diseases and poverty.[17] These debates took shape in the project of educational reform during the so-called Liberal Republic (1930–1946).[18] This reform was modelled on the one carried out in Mexico by Vasconcelos, and sought the diffusion of the New School and hygiene measures such as the improvement of school establishments, the organisation of village libraries as well as restaurants, vacation colonies, savings banks and the school trust.

One of the flagship projects was the training of the teachers in the teachers' colleges and, for in-service teachers, in the new pedagogical discourses, among which was experimental psychology. The *Escuela Normal* of Tunja, the *Escuela Normal* of Medellín and the Pedagogical Institute in Bogotá stand out in this regard. Later, the *Escuela Normal Superior* of Bogotá would be created (1936), directed by the physician Jose Francisco Socarrás. These institutions dealt with experimental psychology as it is evidenced by the chairs of psychology, the books and manuals in

14 Humberto Quiceno Castrillón, *Crónicas históricas de la educación en Colombia* (Bogotá: Ed. Magisterio, 2003).

15 Olga Lucía Zuluaga Garcés and Gabriela Ossenbach Sauter, *Bases para el avance de la historia comparada de la educación en Iberoamérica*, Vol. I centred on the 19th century and vol. II on the 20th (Bogotá: Ed. Magisterio, 2004).

16 María Teresa Gutiérrez, "Proceso de institucionalización de la higiene: Estado, salubridad e higienismo en Colombia en la primera mitad del siglo XX," *Estudio Socio-Jurídicos* 12, no. 1 (2010).

17 Carlos Noguera, *Medicina y política: Discurso médico y prácticas higiénicas durante la primera mitad del siglo XX en Colombia* (Medellín: Universidad EAFIT, 2006).

18 Rubén Sierra Mejía, *República Liberal: sociedad y cultura* (Bogotá: Universidad Nacional de Colombia, 2009).

their archives, and the production of written theses on the subject[19] as well as the application of practical exercises and other works.[20] In the case of the Pedagogical Institute of Bogotá, its library contained copies of "Educational Psychology" and "An Introduction to the Theory of Mental and Social Measurement" by E.L. Thorndike or "The Measurement of Intelligence," by Terman.[21] In the Pedagogical Archive of the *Escuela Normal Superior* of Medellín it is possible to find texts such as: "Abnormal Children" and "Modern Ideas about Children," by Binet; "The school Made to Measure" and "Psychology of the Child and Experimental Pedagogy", by Claparède. These are just some titles from broad collections.

Agustín Nieto Caballero, in his capacity as national inspector of education (1932–1936), organised *Cursos de Información* (information courses for practising teachers). Elements (i.e. teachers) were selected in a representative quantity from each region of the country. The candidates were chosen by the delegated inspectors of each zone who gave reports on their good performance and academic conditions. Many of these teachers took up directive positions in their regions and reformed establishments. Although their impact seemed quite small compared to the overall number of teachers and schools in the country, the information courses became a suitable space for updating in new discourses such as experimental psychology. Among the subjects studied were: psychology, methodology and physiology.[22]

The *Cursos de Información* also included practical exercises aimed at identifying the lag of Colombian students. So it was reported regarding the application of Ballard's test: "in Colombia, the information course of Medellín has been specially adapted for the villages of Antioquia and Caldas in 1933, through a good number of verified experiences in the villages of Jericó, Yarumal, Caldas and Medellín."[23] This test was performed with children between 8 and 14 years of chronological age

---

19 Rafael Ríos Beltrán, *"Compilación Tesis de Grado de los maestros de la Escuela Normal de Varones de Antioquia, 1938–1944,"* Dentro del proyecto: *La apropiación de la Escuela Nueva en el saber pedagógico colombiano: una mirada a las escuelas normales en Colombia*, Escuela Normal Superior de Medellín y Universidad de Antioquia, 2010.

20 *Trabajos de la Escuela Normal Superior: Filosofía y Psicología, 1938–1941.* Universidad Pedagógica y Tecnológica de Colombia.

21 Archivo General de la Nación, *Listado de libros de la biblioteca del Instituto Pedagógico,* Sección Archivo Anexo II. Fondo Ministerio de Educación, Serie Escuelas Normales Informes (1934–1937), Box 4, file 3.

22 Ibid.

23 Camilo Ramírez C., "Pruebas mentales," *La Cátedra. Órgano de la Dirección de Educación Pública* XIV, no. 126 (1934): 220.

who could read and write. For the younger students, the Dearborn test was used, where the drawing plays a relevant role: "this adaptation is verified in Antioquia, through the practices carried out by the students of the pedagogical information course of Medellín in 1933 and 1934."[24]

Ramírez C., author of the quoted article, discusses the importance of applying these tests in schools to determine the mental age of students and thus to organise the centres of interest promoted by the New School. The tests diminish the subjectivity of the teacher, since personal appreciation "is dominated by infinity of circumstantial factors that make it unscientific and often unfair."[25] According to this author, a true test requires two essential characteristics: objectivity and standardisation. Referring to a case cited by Binet:

> "It is concluded that each teacher has a manner (and that is very natural) to appreciate the results of their students, ways that are generally different from teacher to teacher. And it is this subjectivism that is destroyed by the test [...]. When a test has been applied to a large number of children of the appropriate age and level; when the results have been calculated, and expressed as a mean to median for the respective age or grade (and when the addition of more data corresponding to other unselected subjects maintains the results without altering the general trend) a test has been standardized."[26]

During this period (1930–1950), the concept of examination undergoes a process of expansion or specialisation in Colombia, since its semantic field is extended with the circulation of the discourses of experimental psychology in teacher training institutions. The objective of this specialisation was to be able to investigate more thoroughly all the characteristics of the individual, starting from a medical, psychological and pedagogical review. While the random selection of a student in the oral examinations could account for the progress in a given school, with the so-called scientific and objective sciences, based on criteria of reliability and validity, it was possible to individualize the school subjects and determine their degree of personal advancement or retardation. First the school doctor and later the psychologist became the experts in these discourses. That is why teachers were taught different types of examinations to which they had to submit each of their students, as evidenced by their degree theses:

> "*Physical examination*: This examination is the probe into the fitness of the subject [...]. The examination should include: rapidity and dexterity in movements; eye examination;

---

24 Ibid., 220.
25 Ibid., 226.
26 Ibid., 226–227.

examination of the ear; appearance of fatigue; height and weight; respiratory capacity; nervous system.

Medical examination: This must be done by a specialist in school medicine or, in his absence, by a good doctor. It must include, among other things, the following information: prenatal history; birth; age at which he began to speak; hereditary background; diseases suffered in childhood and its consequences; age at which he started walking; etc. Blood examinations and radioscopy should be performed on each child.

Psychological examination: It is undoubtedly the most difficult of examinations [...]. There are tests of global intelligence, memory, attention, skills and many others that, given the current circumstances, would be of great benefit if an exact pattern was given. But unfortunately, the tests, as Cleparede says, are too delicate, their results depend on multiple factors so they should be applied cautiously by very practical individuals, best by psychologists [...]. First of all, it should include at least the following points: global intelligence test, memory test, attention test and observation of judgment and reasoning.

Pedagogical examination: The pedagogical examination is about recognising the degree of knowledge of the child. There are standardized tests for this. The child must solve questionnaires based exclusively on the current programs and the teacher should not only take into account the study certificate but the grades obtained, grade retention, the reason for this non-promotion, social environment, etc."[27]

The application of mental tests and examinations did not have an extensive diffusion in Colombian schools, compared to other Latin American countries,[28] since they were only used for special education and rehabilitation centres as well as for vocational guidance. Although the schools did not have the appropriate instruments or teachers sufficiently trained in the discourses of experimental psychology, it is possible to observe that factors such as mental age and intelligence became the axes of understanding school activity in the educational discourse. These ideas were based on an experimental knowledge, considered scientific and objective, that responded to the qualities of validity and reliability. By the 1950s this scientific knowledge had become an institutionalised discourse. In 1937 the Institute of Experimental Psychology was founded, attached to the *Escuela Normal Superior*. Its creation was promoted by the physician Alfonso Esguerra Gómez and was headed by Leo Walter, with the goal "perform studies on the mental development of the child, to offer courses in psychology and vocational guidance."[29]

---

27 Palacio Moreno, Raúl, "Apuntes sobre clasificación escolar" (Thesis, Escuela Normal de Varones de Antioquia, 1941), 11, 21, 23, 28.

28 Josefina Granja Castro, "Contar y clasificar la infancia. Las categorías de la escolarización en las escuelas primarias de la Ciudad de México 1870–1930". *Revista Mexicana de Investigación Educativa* 14, no. 40 (2009): 217–254.

29 Claudia Figueroa, Ramos Londoño and Carlos Arturo, "La Escuela Normal Superior y los test en Colombia," *Praxis y Saber* 5, no. 10 (2014): 248.

Subsequently, the institute would be overseen by the Spanish psychologist Mercedes Rodrigo, who, in 1940, founded the section of psychology of the Faculty of Medicine of the National University of Colombia, the origin of the Institute of Applied Psychology, created in 1949.[30] The Decree 690 of 1942 (article 4) and Resolution 2401 of 1950 (article 43) referred to the possibility that secondary school students should undergo psychometric tests and vocational guidance before entering the faculties, tests that would be directed by the National University.

Emergence of the concept of *educational evaluation* in Colombia, 1950–1970

In the first half of the 20th century, Colombia faced a slow process of modernisation. Cities like Medellín and Bogotá had a high growth of the industrial sector, as well as a better organisation with urban facilities and transport. These changes went hand in hand with the development of cultural activities and the diffusion of mass media (radio, film, television).[31] Most of the country remained rural, with an emphasis on a booming coffee economy. Likewise, the state was able to strengthen its bureaucratic institutions. This slow process of development contrasted with the so called *La Violencia* (a period of political crisis and bloody violence).[32] The conservative restoration (1946–1957)[33] led to an "educational re-Catholisation," displacing the ideas of the New School. The country experienced a process of bipartisan violence (1945–1974), which was aggravated by the assassination of Gaitán and the *Bogotazo* (April 9, 1948) with a strong repression of the nascent socialist and communist currents. There was also the dictatorship of General Rojas Pinilla (1953–1957) and the National Front (1958–1975) at a time when the world was going through the Cold War. Effects of *La Violencia* on the country endure to this day.

Parallel to these social and political conflicts, the country took part in the policy of Pan-Americanism. It was precisely in the IX Pan American Conference, held

---

30 Jaime E. Jaramillo Jiménez, "La Escuela Normal Superior: un semillero de las ciencias humanas y sociales," in *República Liberal: sociedad y cultura*, ed. Rubén Sierra Mejía (Bogotá: Universidad Nacional de Colombia, 2009), 598.

31 Santiago Castro-Gómez, *Tejidos Oníricos. Movilidad, capitalismo y biopolítica en Bogotá, 1910–1930* (Bogotá: Universidad Javeriana, 2009).

32 Daniel Pécaut, *Orden y Violencia: Colombia, 1930–1953* (Medellín: Fondo Editorial EAFIT, 2012, 1987).

33 Rubén Sierra Mejía. *La restauración conservadora, 1946–1957* (Universidad Nacional de Colombia, 2012).

in Bogotá in 1948, where the Organisation of American States (OAS) was created. Colombia needed foreign resources and technical assistance to boost productive activities. In this context, several economic missions visited the country, among them the mission of Kemmerer (1930), Currie (1950), CEPAL (1954), Lebret (1955), and CEPAL (1958),[34] as well as the German Pedagogical Mission (1968). The economic missions gave a diagnosis of all the sectors of the country, but especially on education. These missions were immersed in the economic discourse of developmentalism,[35] with the firm conviction that scientifically developed planning and evaluation processes would lead to an improvement of living conditions of the population. Their diagnosis was the urgency of reorganising the school system and ensuring greater access to it, especially in technical training for the most vulnerable population. For this purpose, the National Learning Service (*Servicio Nacional de Aprendizaje, SENA*) and the National Institute for Secondary and Diversified Education (*Instituto Nacional de Educación Media Diversificada, INEM*) were created in 1957 and 1969, respectively. This eagerness for educational and instructional planning manifested itself in educational technology and the curricular reform instituted by the Decree 088 of 1976.

These discourses on planning and evaluation come from disciplines such as scientific management and economics, with a high statistical component. In 1911 "Principles of Scientific Management-Industrial and General Administration" by Taylor and Fayol, was published. This book laid the groundwork for industrial planning and control processes, considered to be the parents of scientific administration. With respect to the educational discourse, in 1949 "Basic Principles of the Curriculum" by Tyler was published, who adapted the principles of the administration to the school for the curricular development, and is considered the father of assessment.[36]

Colombia was one of the pioneer countries in institutionalizing planning and evaluation.[37] In 1950, the National Planning Council and the Economic

---

34 Decsi Arévalo Hernández, "Misiones económicas internacionales en Colombia, 1930–1960," *Historia Crítica* 14 (1997): 9.

35 Arturo Escobar, *La invención del Tercer Mundo. Construcción y deconstrucción del desarrollo* (Bogotá: Norma, 1996).

36 It is necessary to point out that evaluation and assessment has experienced various conceptualisations: Tyler, Bloom, Stuffleabeam, Stake, Cronbach, Scriven, MacDonald, Parlett y Hamilton, Guba y Lincoln. This article follows the review of the documentation for the period under study in Colombia.

37 Alberto Martínez Boom, De *la escuela expansiva a la escuela competitiva: dos modos de modernización educativa en América Latina* (Bogotá: Anthropos, 2004).

Development Committee were created, followed by the Planning Office, in 1951, and the National Planning Committee, in 1954. This process was led by several experts and promoted by Gabriel Betancourt Mejía, graduated from the *Escuela Normal* of Medellín and the *Universidad Javeriana*, ambassador to the United States, minister of education, and assistant director-general for education of UNESCO, among many other diplomatic posts. He is considered the creator of the Integral Planning of Education (PIE). According to Betancourt, "planning makes education an effective tool for progress."[38] The author defines PIE as follows:

> "It is the system that organises and coordinates investigative, statistical, pedagogical, administrative and financial techniques, both in the public and in the private sector, to guarantee all or part of the population an adequate education [...] to turn the human factor of a nation to a dynamic subject of its development."[39]

According to Betancourt, PIE should be accompanied by a permanent review and evaluation, since "evaluation is an essential element, because only by applying it periodically it can be determined whether the plan is being executed properly and, if not, to investigate the respective causes to apply a remedy."[40] It should be noted that this concept was encouraged in several seminars and congresses by international organisations dedicated to the field of education, like UNESCO.

Although the discourse of school organisation had circulated in Colombia since the late 19th century with numerous manuals for teachers, scientific management and evaluation were considered modern discourses because they had new nuances, among them the principle of objectivity and the power of measurement. In the *Escuelas Normales* these discourses were disseminated through training plans and *Cursos Piloto,* (Pilot Courses) with the distribution of some books for libraries. At the *Escuela Normal* of Medellín, this streamlining process was led by José María Rodríguez Rojas, graduated from *Escuela Normal* and the University of Antioquia, who was headmaster and inspector in the same department. His educational work is quite prolific;[41] we will highlight his definition of knowledge evaluation:

---

38   Gabriel Betancourt Mejía, "Significado y alcance del planeamiento educativo, ponencia presentada en Washington, 1958," in *Documentos para la historia del Planeamiento Integral de la Educación* (Bogotá: Universidad Pedagógica Nacional, 1984), 23.

39   Ibid., 23.

40   Ibid., 31.

41   *Sicopedagogía: Pruebas mentales y de conocimiento* (1962), *Legislación y organización escolar* (1962), *Panorama de la educación colombiana: texto para el desarrollo del programa oficial de Historia de la Educación en Colombia en el sexto año de las Escuelas*

"Evaluation or examination of the knowledge acquired by children is absolutely essential. But evaluation should not only refer to reviewing learning outcomes, but should be a continuous process of educational activity. Evaluation should be made in relation to the educational objectives without making the mistake of the traditional school of practicing examinations just to see if the children developed the whole school program, reason why the teachers and teachers came to the conviction that they should only teach for examinations."[42]

According to this author, examinations can be classified in oral and written, and in school tests. The purpose of the evaluation is to:

"Adequately and scientifically measure students' work; to select, by means of a good school classification, the children who are normal; in this fashion, to correctly perform the promotion and graduation examinations; to give a guide for the appraisal of teaching methods."[43]

For Rodríguez Rojas, evaluation is part of every program, of all teaching and all learning. Evaluation, objective measurement and review of school performance "are today's practices recommended by modern pedagogy."[44]

During the period studied (1950–1970), it is possible to understand the relationship between the concepts of examination and evaluation in two ways: by contrast or by inclusion. On the one hand, there are the social actors (teachers, state officials, experts in pedagogy) who considered the examination as anachronistic in relation to the modern proposals of evaluation. On the other hand, some argued that evaluation was an integral part of the entire educational process (planning, implementation and evaluation) and that the examinations — whether written or oral — represented one of the possible ways of evaluating, which could include others such as interviews or objective tests. These distinctions are also influenced by the circulation of different discourses and authors related to the field of educational evaluation. Initially, closer to the 1950s, evaluation by objectives in the manner of Tyler was common. Closer to the 1970s, the discussion is centred on process-based evaluation, in the framework of systems theory, considering the definitions advanced by Stuffleabeam.

Normales (1963), *Metodología y didáctica especial de las materias básicas: lenguaje y matemáticas. Desarrollo del programa oficial para Escuelas Normales* (1963), *Administración, organización y legislación escolar* (1969).

42 José María Rodríguez Rojas, *Metodología especial de las materias básicas: Lenguaje* (Medellín, Editorial Bedout, 1964): 23–24.

43 Ibid., 26.

44 Ibid., 27.

During the Pilot Course held in Medellín in 1969, ordered by the Ministry of National Education for the training of teachers in the *Escuelas Normales*, pedagogical encyclopaedias, among others, were used, as work materials. One of them was the Encyclopaedia of Modern Education, written by Harry Rivlin and Herbert Schueler of the Queens College Department of Education, which was translated by the Luzuriaga brothers and published in Argentina in 1956 (second edition). In this encyclopaedia, "evaluation" and "examinations" are listed as differentiated entries: "the term evaluation is often used with reference to the innumerable situations in which one or more persons should estimate the value obtained from some experience."[45] The authors state that evaluation can be developed subjectively through discussions, or objectively, through a series of tests or questionnaires. The authors refer to the works of Ralph Tyler where "the process of evaluation is broadly described in the fullest sense of the word."[46] The evaluation should take into account:

> "1. Definition of the objectives. 2. Use of evaluation tools and techniques to determine what has been done and what changes have occurred. 3. Use of appropriate statistical techniques to interpret the data. 4. Planning of processes by which the action can be improved."[47]

Regarding written examinations, the authors maintain that they are called "traditional or subjective examinations" in contrast to the so–called "modern or objective examinations". According to them, since 1910 (probably referring to the studies of E.L. Thorndike) written examinations were subject to various objections, such as the different grading imposed by equally competent. "The validity of written examinations is reduced by the intervention of so many strange factors in the formulation and classification of responses."[48] Likewise, written examinations are criticised for the wording of questions that may be ambivalent or confusing. The authors suggest that examinations that require students to elaborate essays, outlines, or summaries, serve to identify their abilities in writing, relating topics and interpreting. Choosing this type of examination will depend on the educational objectives posed by the teacher. The authors also suggest accompanying

---

45 Harry Rivlin and Herbert Schueler, *Enciclopedia de Educación Moderna*, traducción de Carlos y Lorenzo Luzuriaga (Buenos Aires, Editorial Losada, 1956), 354.

46 Ibid., 354.

47 Ibid., 355.

48 Ibid., 356.

written examinations with objective tests "that allow knowing in a more complete way the quality of the student's ability."[49]

One of the most important questions during the period under study was the possible use of evaluation in higher education. In this regard, Rómulo Naranjo — a respected university professor of Antioquia — referred to statistical evaluation. According to Naranjo, the term evaluation implies the idea of value; it is about evaluating the results of a process. Evaluation should be considered as an integral part of the whole educational process, closely linked to the teaching method. Naranjo states that:

> "Among the instruments used in the evaluation, the tests called examinations stand out. Examinations generally do not imply a value judgment, and therefore, have a smaller reach than evaluation. Mensuration refers to mathematical measures regarding the individuals, objects or situations measured."[50]

The author summarises the criticisms of traditional examinations: they are harmful to the mental and physical health of students because they cause nervous tension, they only serve to stimulate the exercise of mechanical memory, they become the ultimate object, they lend themselves to foment cheating and bad writing, and "the results of the educational process are not measurable as are the yields in the field of industry, agriculture [...] because in reality they are not tangible."[51] Naranjo proposes objective tests as the best strategy to solve these problems since they can offer validity. To paraphrase Professor Naranjo, a correct evaluation would be one that would allow to validly and reliably measuring the results of the educational process, in order to make the corresponding improvements and corrections.

Initially, the concept of evaluation came to Colombia through the discourses of economic developmentism for planning and evaluation of projects and development plans – which also included the educational field. The discourses of the scientific administration, the school organisation, systems and curriculum theories propelled this concept fully into the school environment. It could be said that the institutionalisation of school evaluation in Colombia was due to the creation of the ICFES (Colombian Institute for the Promotion of Higher Education), by the Decree 3157 of 1968, which was responsible for the development of objective tests for access to higher education and which is maintained until

---

49   Ibid., 357.
50   Rómulo Naranjo, "Naturaleza e importancia de la evaluación," in *Revista de la Universidad de Medellín* 12, no. 13 (1967): 129–136. Biblioteca Luis Ángel Arango. Hemeroteca.
51   Ibid., 130.

today. Likewise, with the creation of institutions such as the ICOLPE (Colombian Institute of Pedagogy), through Decree 3153 of 1968, attached to the National Pedagogical University, which was responsible until 1976, among other functions, for conducting research on all branches of education and provide guidance to all public and private elementary and secondary schools.

Final Considerations

This paper presented the way in which the concepts of *experimental examination* and *educational evaluation* between 1930 and 1970 in Colombia corresponded with a scientific and objective logic, with qualities such as validity and reliability. Neither experimental examination nor evaluation had its origin in the educational discourse. The concept of experimental examination came from the discourses of medicine and psychology, while that of the educational evaluation came from administration and economics. Between 1930 and 1950, the concept of exam in Colombia underwent a process of expansion or specialisation since its semantic field was extended with the circulation of the discourses of experimental psychology. Educational actors referred to the physical, medical, psychological and pedagogical examinations. Between the 1950s and 1970s, the relationship between the concepts of examination and evaluation can be understood in two ways: by opposition or by inclusion. Some social actors considered the examination to be anachronistic and others felt that examinations represented one of various possible ways of evaluating. It is of special importance that the semantic field of both concepts had in common measurement, although the concept of evaluation will be much more extensive when considering other notions such as to value and to compare. These concepts gave legitimacy to the state in its task as organiser of the educational system. The scientific discourse and its premises became an endorsement of unquestionable truths about human behaviour.

This work investigated the Colombian assessment culture in the period under study (1930–1970), giving an account of the semantic change from "examination" to "evaluation." It went from an assessment culture of examination, understood as subjective, towards an assessment culture of evaluation in which objectivity was sought. Likewise, it is possible to suggest other research perspectives like investigating the relation between this type of semantic changes with the organisation of a state apparatus that would account for the creation of the school system, or comparative studies about the circulation of this type of discourse and the appropriation made by the educational actors at the international level.

Sources

Archivo General de la Nación in Bogotá
Biblioteca Luis Ángel Arango in Bogotá

Literature

Arévalo Hernández, Decsi. "Misiones económicas internacionales en Colombia 1930–1960." *Historia Crítica* 14 (1997): 7–24.

Betancourt Mejía, Gabriel. "Significado y alcance del planeamiento educativo, ponencia presentada en Washington, 1958." In *Documentos para la historia del Planeamiento Integral de la Educación*, 21–33. Bogotá: Universidad Pedagógica Nacional, 1984.

Castro-Gómez, Santiago. Tejidos Oníricos. Movilidad, capitalismo y biopolítica en Bogotá 1910–1930. Bogotá: Universidad Javeriana, 2009.

Escobar, Arturo. La invención del Tercer Mundo. Construcción y deconstrucción del desarrollo. Bogotá: Norma, 1996.

Figueroa, Claudia, Ramos Londoño, and *Arturo Carlos.* "La Escuela Normal Superior y los test en Colombia." *Praxis y Saber* 5, no. 10 (2014): 245–265.

Granja Castro, Josefina. "Evaluación institucional y procesos de legitimación." *Avances y Perspectivas* 10 (1991): 221–225.

–. "Contar y clasificar la infancia. Las categorías de la escolarización en las escuelas primarias de la Ciudad de México, 1870–1930." *Revista Mexicana de Investigación Educativa* 14, no. 40 (2009): 217–254.

Gutiérrez, María Teresa. "Proceso de institucionalización de la higiene: Estado, salubridad e higienismo en Colombia en la primera mitad del siglo XX", *Estudio Socio-Jurídicos* 12, no. 1 (2010): 73–97.

Helg, Aline. La educación en Colombia, 1918–1957: una historia social, económica y política. Bogotá: Fondo Editorial Cerec, 1987.

Jaramillo Jiménez, Jaime E. "La Escuela Normal Superior: un semillero de las ciencias humanas y sociales." In *República Liberal: sociedad y cultura*, edited by Rubén Sierra Mejía, 557–603. Bogotá: Universidad Nacional de Colombia, 2009.

Koselleck, Reinhart. Futuro pasado. Para una semántica de los tiempos históricos. Barcelona: Paidós, 1993.

Loaiza Cano, Gilberto. Sociabilidad, Religión y Política en la definición de Nación, Colombia, 1820–1886. Bogotá: Universidad Externado de Colombia, 2011.

Martínez Boom, Alberto, and *Renán Silva. Dos estudios sobre educación en la Colonia.* Bogotá: Universidad Pedagógica Nacional, 1984.

Martínez Boom, Alberto. *De la escuela expansiva a la escuela competitiva: dos modos de modernización educativa en América Latina.* Colombia: Anthropos, 2004.

Naranjo, Rómulo. "Naturaleza e importancia de la evaluación." In *Revista de la Universidad de Medellín* 12, no. 13 (1967): 129–136.

Noguera, Carlos Ernesto. *Medicina y política: Discurso médico y prácticas higiénicas durante la primera mitad del siglo XX en Colombia.* Medellín: Universidad EAFIT, 2006.

Palacio Moreno, Raúl. "Apuntes sobre clasificación escolar". Thesis, Escuela Normal de Varones de Antioquia, 1941.

Palacios, Marco, and Frank Safford. *Colombia: país fragmentado, sociedad dividida. Su historia.* Bogotá: Norma, 2002.

Palti, Elías José. "Ideas, conceptos, metáforas. La tradición alemana de historia intelectual y el complejo entramado del lenguaje." *Res pública* 25 (2011): 227–248.

Pécaut, Daniel. *Orden y Violencia: Colombia 1930–1953.* Medellín: Fondo Editorial EAFIT, 2012.

Quiceno Castrillón, Humberto. *Crónicas históricas de la educación en Colombia.* Bogotá: Ed. Magisterio, 2003.

Rausch, Jane. *La Educación durante el Federalismo. La Reforma Escolar de 1870.* Bogotá: Universidad Nacional, 1993.

Ramírez C., Camilo. "Pruebas mentales." *La Cátedra. Órgano de la Dirección de Educación Pública* XIV, no. 126 (1934): 220–227.

Ríos Beltrán, Rafael. "*Compilación Tesis de Grado de los maestros de la Escuela Normal de Varones de Antioquia, 1938–1944.*" Dentro del proyecto: La apropiación de la Escuela Nueva en el saber pedagógico colombiano: una mirada a las escuelas normales en Colombia, Escuela Normal Superior de Medellín y Universidad de Antioquia, 2010.

Rivlin, Harry, and Herbert Schueler. *Enciclopedia de Educación Moderna.* Traducción de Carlos y Lorenzo Luzuriaga. Buenos Aires: Editorial Losada, 1956.

Rodríguez Rojas, José María. *Metodología especial de las materias básicas: Lenguaje.* Medellín: Editorial Bedout, 1964.

Roldán Vera, Eugenia. "La perspectiva de los lenguajes en la historia de la educación." *Ariadna histórica. Lenguajes, conceptos, metáforas* 3 (2014): 7–14.

Rosanvallon, Pierre. *Por una historia conceptual de lo político. Lección inaugural en el Collège de Francia.* México: Fondo de Cultura Económica, 2002.

Saldarriaga, Óscar, Javier Sáenz Obregón, and Armando Ospina. *Mirar la infancia: pedagogía, moral y modernidad en Colombia, 1903–1946,* Vol. I–II. Bogotá: Universidad de los Andes, Universidad de Antioquia, 1997.

Sierra Mejía, Rubén. República Liberal: sociedad y cultura. Bogotá: Universidad Nacional de Colombia, 2009.

–. *La restauración conservadora 1946–1957. Bogotá:* Universidad Nacional de Colombia, 2012.

Torres Zambrano, Guillermo et al. "El surgimiento del Servicio Nacional de Pruebas del ICFES en las voces de sus protagonistas." Grupo de Investigación sobre Pruebas Masivas en Colombia de la Universidad Santo Tomás, *Magistro. Revista de la Maestría en Educación* 2, no. 3 (2008): 115–134.

Zuluaga Garcés, Lucía Olga, and *Gabriela Ossenbach Sauter. Bases para el avance de la historia comparada de la educación en Iberoamérica.* Vol. I centred on the 19th century and vol. II on the 20th century. Bogotá: Ed. Magisterio, 2004.

Sverre Tveit[1]

(Trans)national Trends and Cultures of Educational Assessment: Reception and Resistance of National Testing in Sweden and Norway during the Twentieth Century

The twentieth century was a time of increasing international relations in education policy and research. Lawn (2013) observes that "the field of education was riven with the problems of the expansion of secondary education, selection processes and school outcomes."[2] Research centres and international projects became central nodes for solving policy problems in national education systems. Educational measurement thus became "a defining element of the governing of education."[3] The growth of intelligence expertise in the United States during the interwar years paved the way for new approaches to educational measurement for multiple purposes that were circulated through new institutions, such as United Nations Educational, Scientific and Cultural Organisation (UNESCO), the International Association for the Evaluation of Educational Achievement (IEA), and the Organisation for Economic Co-operation and Development (OECD).

The objective of this paper is to outline analytical-conceptual frameworks for understanding transnational trends with respect to the various roles of educational assessment emphasised in national assessment instruments, which emerged in concert with the increased international collaboration during the twentieth century described above. The first framework identifies three trends that can be related to transnational research and policy endeavours: First, the *meritocracy* trend, focusing on fair certification and selection procedures for individual

---

1   This chapter reports in-part on archive investigations into Columbia University's Rare Book & Manuscript Libriary, which were undertaken with support from the Ryoichi Sasakawa Yong Leaders Fellowship Fund (Sylff) scholarship provided by the University of Oslo and the Sylff Research Abroad scholarship provided by the Tokyo Foundation. The author is also indebted to Dr. Thomas Hatch at Teachers College, Columbia University, who facilitated the research visit.

2   Martin Lawn, "Voyages of Measurement in Education in the Twentieth Century: Experts, Tools and Centres," *European Educational Research Journal* 12, no. 1 (2013): 109, doi:10.2304/eerj.2013.12.1.108.

3   Ibid.

students, was emphasised in international research projects such as the International Examinations Inquiry (IEI) in the 1930s. Second, the *accountability* trend, which places more emphasis on the governing of education systems and their role in global competition among national states, became more prominent when comparative testing programmes were organised in fixed cycles from the 1990s onwards. Third, the *Assessment for learning* trend, emphasising the role of assessment instruments and procedures in supporting student learning, emerged at the change of the millennium. While researchers and policymakers may emphasise this third trend as a reaction (or in opposition) to the effects associated with the meritocracy and accountability trends, the OECD also embraced it as a key strategy of the accountability policies it advocates. As such, *Assessment for learning* may by some be perceived as a trend that reacts and is in opposition to the accountability trend, while for others it is subordinated to the accountability trend's emphasis on strategies for improving countries' educational outcomes. In sum, these three transnational trends of educational assessment have shaped the roles of educational assessment emphasised in countries' national assessment instruments worldwide.

The second framework utilises Hopmann's (2003) distinction between *process*- and *product*-controlled education systems, and relates it to modes of determining students' level of attainment.[4] It is developed to illustrate how product-controlled education systems were more receptive to the accountability trend's quest for measurable outcomes as the basis for governing education because its meritocratic instruments had already been adapted to new psychometric principles. Process-controlled education systems, on the other hand, resisted psychometric approaches to measure outcomes until the PISA shock paved the way for such tests as the basis for governing education in many countries. These two different cultures of certifying and governing learning and instruction are labelled the (American product-controlled) testing tradition and the (continental European process-controlled) examination tradition respectively.

By analysing Sweden and Norway's participation in large scale international assessments, and investigating second hand literature and archive documents that capture these developments, the paper demonstrates how the three transnational trends of educational assessment shaped the emphasis on roles of educational assessment in the countries' national assessment instruments, and how this can be related to the countries' different testing and examinations cultures. With the

---

4   Stefan T. Hopmann, "On the Evaluation of Curriculum Reforms," *Journal of Curriculum Studies* 35, no. 4 (2003), doi: 10.1080/00220270305520.

examples of Sweden and Norway, the chapter illuminates how different engagement with transnational research projects and trends of educational assessment, and different testing and examination cultures, shaped the accumulation of purposes associated with contemporary national assessment instruments. Conclusively the chapter discusses how the differences between these two Scandinavian countries may be illustrative of wider patterns in European countries' cultures — and their reception and resistance towards transnational trends — of educational assessment.

Analytical Framework: Transnational Trends of Educational Assessment

By integrating theoretical conceptualisations of the purposes of educational assessment in the research literature with an empirical investigation of policy documents in Norway and Sweden, I identify three principal *roles of educational* assessment, that can be associated with the process of determining students' level of attainment in national education systems: Educational assessment used to *certify*, to *govern* and to *support* learning and instruction (Table 1).[i]

However, the roles of assessment instruments cannot be understood through contemporary analyses alone. Contemporary use should be understood in view of how the assessment instruments emerged. While these developments are largely due to domestic factors, they are also a product of transnational influence. Nordin and Sundberg discuss how UNESCO, the World Bank, the OECD and the European Union "have come to play an increasingly important role in the construction of transnational policy arenas, as resourceful actors working together, forming powerful discourse coalitions that influence and to some extent even govern national reforms."[5] Issues that have traditionally been perceived as national in character, such as educational assessment, has also become relevant to the transnational sphere.

To come to terms with what has sparked or influenced changes in the use of national assessment instruments, and with the accumulation of purposes in contemporary policies, I outline the three previously mentioned transnational trends of educational assessment. As will be showed, the *meritocracy, accountability*, and *assessment for learning* trends are related to transnational research projects (IEI), research agencies (IEA) and policy agencies (OECD). Each of these trends are elaborated below.

---

5   *Nordin, Andreas*, and *Daniel Sundberg*, "The Making and Governing of Knowledge in the Education Policy Field," in *Transnational Policy Flows in European Education*, eds. Andreas Nordin, and Daniel Sundberg, (Oxford, UK: Symposium Books, 2014), 14.

Meritocracy, a term initially coined by Michael Young (1958) in the satiric text *The Rise of Meritocracy*, characterises the change from a society in which social status is ascribed by birth (aristocracy) to one in which social status depends on individuals' achievements.[6] Young portrayed the twentieth century as obsessed by a (utopic) vision of developing assessment procedures that would distinguish between candidates based on their achievement rather than their social status. Thus, while meritocracy has come to mean the notion of (objective) merit-based qualification, Young's point was that this was a utopia because the elite control the procedures. Nevertheless, the term meritocracy is now commonly associated with a desired principle for fair distribution of educational opportunities in democratic education systems.[7]

Examinations and tests are key institutions of meritocratic education systems, set up to facilitate fair competition. Concerns over the instruments' effectiveness in this regard increased in the first decades of the twentieth century. The International Examinations Inquiry (IEI) of the 1930s was a notable international project that investigated the validity and comparability problems of the tests used for certification and selection purposes. When established, the IEI study included the United States, Scotland, England, France, Germany and Switzerland. It later grew to include Norway, Sweden, and Finland as well. The researchers dealt with the expansion of secondary education and the determination of "the most effective way of examining pupils for entry into the secondary school."[8] The project served as an arena for exchanging experiences with research on the participating countries' assessment instruments. As elaborated further below, it became a node for the exchange of new psychometric approaches to educational assessment.

Accountability became a key focus of international research projects in the second half of the twentieth century, which saw a large increase in

---

6   Michael Young, *The Rise of Meritocracy* (London, UK: Penguin Books, 1958). The etymological origin is the Latin word 'meritum', which means 'due reward' and is related to the verb 'mereri', 'to earn, deserve'.

7   Gro H. Aas, "Likhet uten solidaritet? Idéhistoriske studier av karakterer I utdanning og meritokrati" (PhD diss., University of Gothenburg, 2006).

8   Martin Lawn, ed., *An Atlantic Crossing? The Work of the International Examination Inquiry, its Researchers, Methods and Influence* (Oxford, UK: Symposium Books, 2008), 7.

performativity-oriented policies[9] and "governing by numbers."[10] Initiatives from global and European actors led to national discussions about what is required of a nation and its inhabitants for excelling in international competition. When national states' human capital takes precedence over products and services as the key factor in economic success, it legitimises external involvement in national education systems.[11] Supranational agencies[12] have therefore made politicians accountable not only to their respective populations but also to European and global standards.[13]

While this development in the contemporary discourse is largely associated with the OECD and the PISA tests, the emphasis on comparing educational outcomes started with studies initiated by UNESCO and the IEA. While the IEA became a legal entity in 1967, the scholarly collaboration dates back to 1958 when a group of scholars, educational psychologists, sociologists, and psychometricians met at the UNESCO Institute of Education. The two first studies undertaken in the 1960s (the Pilot Twelve-Country Study, 1960; the First International Mathematics Study, 1964) included 12 countries. While the emphasis was on a range of subjects in the early 1970s (the Six-Subject Study, 1970–71), the emphasis became more concentrated on mathematics, science, and reading from the 1980s onwards.

The basic idea of the IEA's founders was that different national practices could "lend themselves to comparisons that would yield new insights into the determinants of educational outcomes, servicing as a basis for the improvement of the quality of education."[14] The 1990s saw an increase in global influence on Eastern European and developing countries as well. Following the declaration of the World Conference on Education for All,[15] several less-developed countries

---

9   Stephen J. Ball, "The Teacher's Soul and the Terrors of Performativity," *Journal of Education Policy* 18, no. 2 (2003), doi: 10.1080/0268093022000043065.

10   Sotiria Grek, et al., "National Policy Brokering and the Construction of the European Education Space in England, Sweden, Finland and Scotland," *Comparative Education* 45, no. 1 (2009), doi: 10.1080/03050060802661378.

11   Eva Forsberg, "Utbildningens Bedömningskulturer I Granskningens Tidevarv," *Utbildning & Demokrati* 23, no. 3 (2014): 53–76.

12   Roger Dale, "Globalisation, Knowledge Economy and Comparative Education," *Comparative Education* 41, no. 2 (2005), doi: 10.1080/03050060500150906.

13   Grek et al., "National Policy Brokering."; Tine S. Prøitz, "Uploading, Downloading and Uploading Again — Concepts for Policy Integration in Education Research," *Nordic Journal of Studies in Educational Policy* 1 (2015), doi:10.3402/nstep.v1.27015.

14   Lawn, "Voyages of Measurement," 108.

15   UNESCO, "World Declaration on Education for All: Meeting basic needs" (adopted by the World Conference on Education for All, New York, NY: UNESCO, 1990).

embarked on national testing programmes, using expertise developed from cross-Atlantic research collaborations.[16] Global agencies' increased emphasis on national testing as governing instruments coincided with the IEA launching new testing programmes in mathematics, science, and reading, now known as TIMSS (Trends in International Mathematics and Science Study), in 1995 and PIRLS (Progress in International Reading Literacy Study) in 2001. Both were to be undertaken cyclically (every fourth and fifth year, respectively), with more emphasis on facilitating comparisons measures between countries and over time. In the 1990s, the OECD also began its work on its Programme for International Student Assessment (PISA), with the first tests undertaken in 2000, to follow every third year thereafter. The PISA studies radically changed the premises of policy legitimation and education governance globally,[17] causing a "manic search for best practices."[18] In summary, while the IEA's founders were already concerned with tests' governing role in the 1960s, the cyclic use of IEA tests from the 1990s, followed by the OECD's PISA tests in the new millenium, defined the breakthrough of the accountability trend of educational assessment.

Assessment for learning emerged as a new policy area in tandem with (and partly in opposition to) governments and international agencies' increased focus on accountability measures. Sparked by meta-studies that reported impressive effect sizes and compelling arguments for the effectiveness of *formative assessment*,[19] several countries implemented new policies called *Assessment for learning* or similar.[20] In response to the 'standards crisis', governments saw the potential of

---

16 Thomas Kellaghan, "The Globalisation of Assessment in the 20th Century," *Assessment in Education: Principles* 8, no. 1 (2001), doi: 10.1080/09695940120033270.

17 Heinz-Dieter Meyer and Aaron Benavot, "Introduction," in *PISA, Power, and Policy: The Emergence of Global Educational Governance*, ed. Heinz-Dieter Meyer and Aaron Benavot (Oxford, UK: Symposium Books, 2015).

18 David H. Kamens, "Globalisation and the Emergence of an Audit Culture: PISA and the Search for 'Best Practices' and Magic Bullets," in *PISA, Power, and Policy: The Emergence of Global Educational Governance*, ed. Heinz-Dieter Meyer and Aaron Benavot (Oxford, UK: Symposium Books, 2015), 137.

19 Paul Black and Dylan Wiliam, "Assessment and Classroom Learning," *Assessment in Education* 5, no. 1 (1998), doi:10.1080/0969595980050102; John Hattie, *Visible Learning* (London, UK: Routledge, 2008).

20 For Norway, see Therese N. Hopfenbeck, Maria Teresa Flórez Petour and Astrid Tolo, "Balancing Tensions in Educational Policy Reforms: Large-Scale Implementation of Assessment for Learning in Norway," *Assessment in* Education: Principles 22, no. 1 (2015); for Sweden, see Anders Jonsson, Christian Lundahl and Anders Holmgren, "Evaluating a Large-Scale Implementation of Assessment for Learning in Sweden,"

formative assessment to raise standards through slogans such as "formative use of summative tests."[21] The much-quoted Black and Wiliam review article "Assessment and Classroom Learning"[22] can be perceived as a milestone in the emergence of a greater emphasis on the formative use of tests and teachers role in assessment at the turn of the millennium. In 2002, the OECD's "What Works in Innovation in Education programme" gave emphasis to studies that reported formative assessment to produce educational gains "among the largest ever reported for educational interventions."[23] The book "Formative Assessment: Improving Learning in Secondary Classrooms"[24] featured exemplary cases from secondary schools in eight countries and reviewed research publications in German and French. Assessment for learning and formative assessment policies were key components of OECD's "Review on Evaluation and Assessment Frameworks for Improving School Outcomes" which included 14 countries.[25] The OECD has also taken the role of reviewing countries' "*Assessment for learning*" programmes.[26]

As shown in Table 1, these developments can be viewed as three transnational trends that have influenced countries' use of educational assessment instruments. The years listed do not indicate an exclusive emphasis on the respective purpose but, rather, are the time when countries' policies and associated instruments *accumulated* these educational assessment purposes. The three transnational trends can be linked to three principal roles of educational assessment, and associated

Assessment in Education: Principles, Policy & Practice 22, no. 1 (2015), doi:10.1080/09 69594X.2014.970612.

21 Wynne Harlen, "On the Relationship Between Assessment for Formative and Summative Purposes," in *Assessment and Learning*, ed. John Gardner (London, UK: Sage, 2006), doi: 10.4135/9781446250808.n6.

22 Black and Wiliam, "Assessment and Classroom Learning."

23 "Centre for Educational Research and Innovation (CERI) — What Works," OECD, accessed July 21, 2015. http://www.oecd.org/edu/ceri/centreforeducationalresearch andinnovationceri-whatworks.htm.

24 OECD, *Formative Assessment: Improving Learning in Secondary Classrooms* (OECD, 2005).

25 "OECD Review on Evaluation and Assessment Frameworks for Improving School Outcomes — Country Reviews," OECD, accessed July 22, 2015. http://www.oecd.org/ edu/school/oecdreviewonevaluationandassessmentframeworksforimprovingschool outcomescountryreviews.htm.

26 See, e.g., Therese N. Hopfenbeck, Astrid Tolo, Maria Teresa Florez and Yasmin El Masri, "Balancing Trust and Accountability? The Assessment for Learning Programme in Norway," 2013, accessed May 21, 2015. http://www.oecd.org/edu/ceri/ Norwegian%20GCES%20case%20study%20OECD.pdf.

processes of determining students' level of attainment, that has been identified in a review of research literature and an empirical investigation of contemporary policy documents in Sweden and Norway.[27] As described in Table 1, these are called: to *certify*, to *govern* and to *support* learning and instruction.[ii]

Table 1: Roles and Transnational Trends of Educational Assessment

Process	To determine educational goal (or standard) attainment		
Role	To *certify* learning and instruction	To *govern* learning and instruction	To *support* learning and instruction
Level	Student and teacher level (teachers' grading, exit examinations)	Organisational level (schools, municipalities, national states)	Student and teacher level (classroom assessment)
Institutional practice	To identify and report the final level of attainment (a grade/mark, examination); used for certification and selection for further education and professional life	To evaluate (aggregated) student attainment data; used to (a) inform decision makers' quality development efforts; and (b) to control application of curricula and regulations	To identify and communicate gaps between the current and desired attainment levels; used to inform learning and instruction strategies
Transnational Trends	Meritocracy (1930s→)	Accountability (1990→)	Assessment for learning (2000→)
Transnational research projects	International Examinations Inquiry (IEI), 1933–1938	**IEA TIMSS**: 1995, 1999, 2003, 2007, 2011, 2015, 2019 **IEA PIRLS**: 2001, 2006, 2011, 2016 **OECD PISA**: 2000, 2003, 2006, 2009, 2012, 2015, 2018	OECD, 2005 OECD, 2013

In the next section, I sketch the emergence of examinations and tests as certification and governing instruments in Europe and the United States in the nineteenth and

---

27 Sverre Tveit, "Ambitious and Ambiguous: Sverre Tveit, "Ambitious and Ambiguous: Shifting Purposes of National Testing in the Legitimation of Assessment Policies in Norway and Sweden (2000–2017)," *Assessment in Education: Principles, Policy & Practice* (forthcoming, 2018)

twentieth century. Furthermore, I explain how the roles of Sweden's and Norway's contemporary national assessment instruments reflect the different reception of (American) psychometric approaches to educational assessment, which was mediated both through the meritocracy and accountability trends.

The Emergence of Examinations and Tests in Europe and the United States in the Nineteenth and Twentieth Centuries: Process and Product Control

In the seminal volume *The Measure of Merit*, John Carson[28] describes how the French and American republics responded in different ways to the problem of balancing equality and difference as their education systems expanded from the 1750 to 1940. Combined with Stefan Hopmann's distinction between process- and product-controlled education systems,[29] these perspectives offer a framework for coming to terms with how national assessment instruments (i.e. examinations and tests) emerged as certification and governing instruments in continental Europe[30] and the United States in the nineteenth and twentieth centuries. Hopmann defines *process* and *product control* as two fundamentally different ways of steering the education system through educational assessment,[31] which I contend in part can explain the different emphases on *professional (social) judgement* versus *external (objective) measurement* procedures to facilitate the validity and comparability of assessments. Table 1 envisions the relationship between process- and product-control and the assessment instruments used to govern the education system and its certification procedures.

---

28 John Carson, *The Measure of Merit: Talents Intelligence, and Inequality in the French and American Republics, 1750–1940* (Princeton, NJ: Princeton University Press, 2007).

29 Hopmann, "On the Evaluation of Curriculum Reforms".

30 The qualification 'continental' is used as the premises of process- and product-control in the United Kingdom is more comparable to that of the United States than to e.g. Germany, France and the Scandinavian countries. In contemporary policies, the United Kingdom can be perceived as a blend of the examination and test cultures, by using standardized yet more essay-based tests and the use of external markers, which is different from the largely multiple-choice dominated testing in the United States. This notion of a blended examination and test tradition that mixes the emphasis on external (objective) measurement with professional judgments is not elaborated further in this chapter.

31 Ibid.

Table 2: Relationship between Process- and Product-Control and the Emphasis on professional judgments vs. external measurement[32]

Curriculum steering	Process-control	Product-control
Premises for controlling the curriculum and teachers:	The national curriculum provides guidelines to teachers, who are recognised as qualified through national teacher education.	The school sector is divided between private and public providers, with no unified concept of teacher education. Thus, the emphasis is on external product control instead.

Assessment instruments	EXAMINATIONS	TESTS
Assessment instruments used to govern the education system and its certification procedures rely on:	**Professional (subjective) judgement:** Members of the profession control each other's assessments to facilitate the validity and comparability of assessments.	**External (objective) measurement:** Standardized tests developed by measurement experts facilitate the validity and comparability of assessments.

The (European) Examination Culture

Hopmann (2003) observes that many European countries introduced new ways of controlling and evaluating schools in the nineteenth and twentieth century: teachers were licenced to teach according to their own standards but within centralised guidelines.[33] The teaching profession gained more influence over the centralised guidelines and the definitions of what was considered adequate student attainment, which was reflected in the profession's control over examination procedures. Such *process-control*, Hopmann argues, characterised most of continental Europe. Jarning and Aas note that the *Examen Artium* in Norway and Denmark (legislated in 1809) and the *Studenteksamen* in Sweden and Finland (legislated in 1824) are the functional equivalents of the German *Abitur* and the French

---

32 The distinction between process and product control was developed by Hopmann (2003), while the distinction between concepts of merit was developed drawing on Carson (2007).

33 Hopmann, "On the Evaluation of Curriculum Reforms."

Baccalauréat.[34] They belong to a pattern of key national educational institutions of liberal modernity.[35]

According to Hopmann, the role of examinations in process-controlled education systems has its roots in post-Napoleonic Prussia.[36] From the 1820s onwards, this system of curriculum control "diffused through most of continental Europe."[37] This system is based on the principle of the state providing general curriculum guidelines that outline what to teach, combined with prescriptions for who is qualified to teach (having passed required teaching examinations), but leaves the pedagogical or methodological freedom to the local teaching staff or school.[38] Hopmann continues: "This open system of process control enhanced the independence of the teaching profession, which then turned against all other forms of external school evaluation and control, denouncing them as not being professionally grounded."[39] "Passing the final internal exams of one type of school became enough to gain access to the following stages."[40] During the expansion of the education system in the twentieth century, examinations were a tool for controlling an otherwise largely autonomous teacher profession.[41]

Carson observes that, unlike the American republic (discussed below), the French adopted a national, universal, and comprehensive approach to education with rigorous examinations, relying on expert judgments to determine which students should move up in the system.[42] French psychologists invented the modern intelligence test that the Americans later embraced — the Binet-Simon intelligence scale. However, French administrators were ambivalent about employing the new technology in their meritocratic procedures and preferred to assess individuals on the basis of methods that relied on expert judgement: "Rigorous examinations determined who could move up, with the goal of ensuring that the most talented

---

34 Harald Jarning and Gro H. Aas, "Between Common Schooling and the Academe: The International Examinations Inquiry in Norway, 1935–1961," in *An Atlantic Crossing? The Work of the International Examination Inquiry, its Researchers, Methods and Influence*, ed. Martin Lawn (Oxford, UK: Symposium Books, 2008).

35 Detlef Müller, Fritz K. Ringer and Brian Simon, *The Rise of the Modern Educational System* (Cambridge, UK: Cambridge University Press, 1986).

36 Hopmann, "On the Evaluation of Curriculum Reforms."

37 Ibid., 470.

38 Ibid., 469.

39 Ibid., 470.

40 Ibid.

41 Christian Lundahl and Sverre Tveit, "Att legitimera nationella prov i Sverige och i Norge – en fråga om profession och tradition," *Pedagogisk forskning i Sverige*, no. 4–5 (2014).

42 Carson, *The Measure of Merit*.

received the best education and became the core of the nation's technocratic elite."[43] Although substantial amendments were made during the expansion and modernisation of education throughout the twentieth century, the principle remains in many European countries: the responsibility for certifying education is undertaken by teachers, under modest state control through examination systems.

The (American) Testing Culture

In countries where the public-school sector or the teaching profession "failed to secure the same prominence as it did in much of continental Europe"[44], a tradition of product control emerged instead. The history of schooling in the former British Empire offers many examples of traditions of product control. United States is the most prominent example, as education was a local affair and no national system of teacher education existed.[45] In line with Hopmann's observations, Carson[46] captures how different traditions for determining merit emerged in France and the United States as the education systems expanded over the course of the nineteenth and twentieth centuries. The American republic however, put more weight on personal attributes than on formal education and embraced intelligence tests as a means of social advancement or distinction. By the 1920s and 1930s, distinctly different ways of understanding differences in mental abilities had emerged. The technology of intelligence testing that Binet and Simon initiated was employed by the Americans for military recruitment during World War I. In the interwar period, testing underwent an enormous boom. What we now know of as the American SAT tests were first used for college admission in 1926. The methodological approaches that started with intelligence testing in the early twentieth century emerged to become comprehensive methods for educational measurement over the next decades.

According to Brookhart "almost all summative assessment and grading in schools were based on teacher judgement" in the United States until the minimum competence movement of the 1970s and 1980s.[47] Brookhart contends that studies of teacher judgments undertaken in the early twentieth century nevertheless had,

---

43 Ibid., 4.
44 Hopmann, "On the Evaluation of Curriculum Reforms," 471.
45 Ibid.
46 Carson, The Measure of Merit.
47 Susan M. Brookhart, "The Use of Teacher Judgement for Summative Assessment in the USA," *Assessment in Education: Principles, Policy & Practice* 20, no. 1 (2013): 70, doi:10.1080/0969594X.2012.70317.

"Set the stage for a distrust of teacher judgement of the quality of students' work, a perspective that has been typical of the attitudes towards teacher judgement in the United States ever since [....]. The 'new science' of education swept in with the solution to the problem of unreliable teacher judgement: standardized, objective testing of student achievement."[48]

These increasingly found their way into classrooms as the public trust in the quality of education fell post World War II. Around this time, viewed from the United States, the developments in the Soviet Union represented the anti-thesis to democratic education. A House Committee on "un-American activities'" led by Richard Nixon argued that the Soviet system was set up to give loyal teachers "new and extreme authority over their pupils, who in turn have become cowed, uniformed puppets."[49] A distinction was drawn between 'training' and 'education', where the latter was held to foster independent thinkers as opposed to 'trained puppets'. Tröhler noted that the Soviet Union's 1957 launch of the Sputnik satellite — the first human-made object to orbit the earth — was a shock for the Americans, who had predicted the failure of the education system of the Soviet Union.[50] It "triggered an educational offensive designed to serve both the military and the economic development."[51] In 1958, President Eisenhower introduced the first national law in education, the National Defense Education Act. This was the start of a shift from education viewed as a cultural system to a view of it as a production system.

The American constitution does not allow the federal government to mandate curriculum and teaching reforms. Instead, the states and local school districts were motivated to undertake reform through funding incentives, first introduced by President Lyndon B. Johnson in the 1965 Elementary and Secondary Education Act (ESEA). The federal government could not govern directly, yet it "at least wanted to see what effects its incentives had, and for this purpose a test instrument had to be developed."[52] While the administration of education was and remains a local affair in the United States, this federal involvement marked a shift from input to output steering at the local level that further enhanced the emphasis

---

48 Ibid., 72.
49 House Committee on Un-American Activities, Title, 57, quoted in Daniel Tröhler, "Truffle Pigs, Research Questions, and Histories of Education," in *Rethinking the History of Education: Transnational Perspectives on Its Questions, Methods, and Knowledge*, ed. Thomas S. Popkewitz (New York, NY: Palgrave Macmillan US, 2013), 114.
50 Ibid., 145.
51 Ibid., 145.
52 Ibid., 150.

on measuring education outcomes of both individual students and schools.[53] Thus — in comparison with continental Europe — the American emphasis on product-control was further propelled by output steering related to funding provided via the federal budget through agreements in the national education acts. ESEA has been revised several times since. In the past decade it has been known as No Child Left Behind, with increased emphasis on holding schools and teachers accountable for student outcomes.

Parallel to the developments towards output steering that was enhanced with the federal involvement in education in the United States, American scholars such as Ralph Tyler and Benjamin Bloom were central in the development of new approaches to curriculum programs and instruction methods. Tyler's landmark eight-year study investigating the effects of progressive education methods in high schools in the 1930s produced a set of principles for educational program evaluation. Bloom's theories on behavioural objectives, master learning and measurement-driven instruction "pushed Tyler's principles of evaluating broad learning outcomes at the school and programme level to the level of fine-grained, classroom lesson objectives."[54] Madhaus noted that Ralph Tyler's contributions to testing and to curriculum development and its evaluation "were both a product and a victim of the times," as it coincided with the rise of behaviourism.[55] Theories for 'programmed instruction' emerged drawing on theories of the 'teaching machine' proposed by behavioural psychologist B.F. Skinner in the mid-1950s. "The general idea behind programmed instruction and teaching machines was that knowledge can be split in many easy-to-learn, small, and consecutive steps to be learned individually."[56] Tyler's and Bloom's writings were on hand when large-scale program evaluation was mandated in order to qualify for federal funding. "The adaptation of both Tyler's and Bloom's works to the needs of the time changed the way people understood them over the ensuing four decades."[57]

In the 1970s the minimum competency movement sparked the use of standardized tests. This was a reaction to the dissatisfaction with public education. By

---

53 National Assessment of Educational Progress (NAEP) began with a grant from the Carnegie Corporation in 1964. Administered by a centre of the US Department of Education, the first NAEP tests were administered in 1969.

54 Brookhart, "The Use of Teacher Judgement," 70.

55 George F. Madhaus, "Ralph Tyler's Contribution to Program Evaluation," in *Evaluation Roots. A Wider Perspective of Theorists' Views and Influences*, 2nd edition, ed. Marvin C. Alkin (Los Angeles, CA: Sage, 2013), 162.

56 Tröhler, *Truffle Pigs*, 148.

57 Madhaus, "Ralph Tyler's Contribution," 162.

1980 minimum competency testing for reading and mathematics was required in 29 states. These were external to the classroom and neither made nor scored by teachers. When it became clear that minimum competency testing lowered expectations to meet the minimum requirements it was succeeded by the educational reform movement of the 1980s and 1990s, later known as the 'standards movement'. The national commission report, "A Nation at Risk" (National Commission on Excellence in Education, 1983), advocated "rigorous and measurable standards and high expectations, a commitment to both excellence and equity, and recommended state and local use of standardized achievement tests."[58] This approach was further expanded with the No Child Left Behind Act of 2002, which mandated annual standards-based tests in grades 3–8 and once during high school.

In summary, the developments in the United States started without a national education system and associated teacher profession, which paved the way for a product-controlled education system. In lack of national and state structures for the organisation of schooling and teacher education from the outset, the premises of process control were not present in the United States. As studies showed poor inter-rater reliability of teacher judgements, psychometric tests gained preference as certification instruments as the basis for college admission. Public dissatisfaction with the standard of education from the 1960s onwards, further propelled the product-controlled education system as federal investment in public education was tied with psychometric measures of student outcomes in order to hold schools and teachers accountable.

While there are many reasons for the increased emphasis on standardized testing in the United States in the twentieth century,[59] the above brief outline of the (European) examination and (American) testing cultures establish that they, in part, can be explained by different premises of process- and product-control. The next section discusses how the testing culture that emerged in (product-controlled) American education systems in various ways influenced European countries with a long-standing (process-controlled) examination culture. These developments are analysed using the framework of the three transnational trends of educational assessment and exemplified with the cases of Sweden and Norway,

---

58 Brookhart, "The Use of Teacher Judgement," 71.
59 Race (Carson, 2008) and gender (Lundahl, 2006) issues are important to understanding how psychometric testing became popular; however, this chapter limits its focus on the interrelationship between premises of governing education systems and procedures for certifying and selecting individual students, and how (the magnitude and modes of) participation in transnational research projects may have prompted or reinforced these developments.

which responded in different ways to the (largely American-led) transnational meritocracy and accountability trends.

Transnational Trends Shaping the Assessment Cultures of Sweden and Norway

This section demonstrates that product-controlled education systems are more inclined to be receptive to the accountability trend than process-controlled education systems. When transnational emphasis on accountability increased throughout the twentieth century, these national states already had education systems that where built for independent measures of outcomes. Process controlled education systems, on the other hand, relies on meritocratic procedures that constitutes the teachers' authority (and licence them) to make judgments. Process controlled education systems did not have the capacity to embed the accountability demands in their existing procedures for determining merit. Thus, in these countries one can observe a separation between national assessment instruments used for meritocratic and accountability purposes, whereas in product controlled education system these may be included in the same national assessment instrument.

Sweden Adopts Psychometric Tests in Concert with the Transnational Meritocracy Trend

Norway and Sweden have a long-standing tradition of using national examinations to distinguish between students' levels of attainment. Both countries were later exposed to the progressive movement, where psychometric tests were perceived as an important tool for identifying students of special needs.[60] The use of psychometric tests in general education were, however, received in different ways by the public and the teacher profession in the two countries.

Swedish educators were highly involved in the American-led development of new psychometric instruments after World War II.[61] The Swedish researcher Frits

---

60 Lundahl, "Viljan att veta vad andra vet: Kunskapsbedömning i tidigmodern, modern och senmodern skola" (PhD diss., Uppsala University, Sweden, 2006); Jarning and Aas, "Between Common Schooling and the Academe"; Christian Ydesen, Kari Ludvigsen and Christian Lundahl, "Creating an Educational Testing Profession in Norway, Sweden and Denmark, 1910–1960," *European Educational Research Journal* 12, no. 1 (2013), doi: https://doi.org/10.2304/eerj.2013.12.1.120.

61 Christian Lundahl and Daniel Pettersson, "Den svenska skolens resultat. Från standardprov til PISA," in *Pisa – sannheten om skolen?*, ed. Eyvind Elstad and Kirsten Sivesind (Oslo: Universitetsforlaget, 2010); Florian Waldow, "Undeclared Imports:

Wigforss' contribution to the IEI study formed the beginning of a series of studies identifying low predictive validity of the Swedish examinations. The IEI project offered a basis for criticising the current examination system. Reporting on the influence of the Swedish contribution to the IEI project, Lundahl notes that Wigforss far from implemented 'American tests' in the Swedish education system.[62] Instead — drawing on the psychometric competence he had access to through the IEI project and beyond — Wigforss pushed for a Swedish 'twist' to the use of psychometric tests. Wigforss was convinced that teachers, when equipped with sufficient standardized instruments, were more capable of making comparable judgments than the existing examination system. Wigforss was at the time also involved in a governmental report which was investigating prospects of abolishing the examination entrance tests and instead let elementary school marks serve as instruments for selection. "If standardized marks could show better correlation with school success, then entrance tests would be unnecessary."[63]

As such, the IEI study marked the beginning of a blend of the examination and testing cultures, with larger emphasis given to American approaches to psychometric testing, albeit as a basis for helping teachers taking an even larger responsibility for certifying students' learning. The utilisation of psychometric tests was believed to provide more comparable measures and thus gave legitimacy to a transition where teachers were given more responsibility for grading based on tests developed through psychometric scientific principles. The psychometric expertise in Sweden emerged under large influence from American scholars in the IEI study and beyond, in particular through the State Psychological and Pedagogical Institute (SPPI) that was established in 1942. Lundahl observes that the participation in the IEI study helped Swedish researchers and policymakers to allege the need of a modern institution bringing science and educational practice closer together.[64] SPPI was established to develop psychometric competence in Sweden, and with a specific notion that "one important task for the Institute should be to develop new forms of tests that could substitute the entrance tests."[65]

Silent Borrowing in Educational Policy-making and Research in Sweden," *Comparative Education* 45, no. 4 (2009), URL: http://www.jstor.org/stable/40593191.

62 Christian Lundahl, "Inter/National Assessments as National Curriculum: The Case of Sweden," in *An Atlantic Crossing? The Work of the International Examination Inquiry, its Researchers, Methods and Influence* (London, UK: Symposium Books, 2008).

63 Ibid., 160.

64 Ibid.

65 Ibid., 172.

In the subsequent decades SPPI was a key institution for the termination of the Swedish entrance examinations as part of the reform in the 1960s, when Sweden unified its parallel school system to comprehensive schools.[66] Lundahl and Waldow observe that SPPI played an important role "as a producer and mediator of a standardized language; connecting diverging interests and creating the techniques to sustain an individualised and meritocratic education."[67]

Torsten Husén, professor at the Stockholm Teacher College from 1956 to 1971, was a prominent scholar in Sweden who exercised large influence on the education system for decades. As the chair of the IEA from 1962 to 1979, during which time it embarked on several studies in mathematics and science, Husén was in the position to project new global standards for educational assessment on Sweden's meritocratic procedures.[68] His recognition in Sweden was partly a product of the large international recognition he had being part of international research projects. Sweden participated in all eight IEA studies from 1960 to 1970, including the "Pilot Twelve-Country study" (1960), the "First International Mathematics Study" (1964) and the "First International Science Study" (1970–71) (Appendix 1). During this decade, the Swedish national tests (*standardprov*) gained preference over the traditional examinations, which were ultimately terminated in 1968.

The incremental transition from examinations to test-based certification procedures from the 1930s to the 1960s can be related to two wider features of Swedish society: the emphasis on psychological theories and methods, and the centralised governing tradition during this period. One may argue that Wigforss and Husén's contributions to IEI and IEA, respectively, reinforced these distinct features of Swedish society. Through these collaborative efforts, American psychometric theories and methods for testing student attainment made 'an Atlantic crossing'[69] and were incorporated into the education system in a distinct Swedish fashion. Tests were perceived as principle tools assisting teachers in making comparable judgments and as such they in some respects initially represented a strengthening of teachers' autonomy compared to the previous examination system in which the

---

66 Bo Lindensjö and Ulf P. Lundgren, *Utbildningsreformer och politisk styrning* (Stockholm: Liber, 2014).

67 Christian Lundahl and Florian Waldow, "Standardisation and 'Quick Languages': The Shape-Shifting of Standardized Measurement of Pupil Achievement in Sweden and Germany," *Comparative Education* 45, no. 3 (2009): 368, doi: 10.1080/03050060903184940.

68 Lundahl, "Inter/National Assessments."

69 Lawn, *An Atlantic Crossing.*

state — through higher education institutions — controlled teachers.[70] While the implications of the IEI and IEA studies varied across participating countries, these collaborative efforts can be viewed as milestones in what Lundahl and Waldow describe as the *first cycle of standardisation* in European education systems.[71]

In the 1990s, Sweden embarked on a more decentralised and market-based organisation of the education system.[72] While the national tests also had a role in the governing of the education system at the time of implementation in the 1960s, they became more important tools for controlling the more output-oriented and product-controlled education system that emerged from the 1990s. As the national tests were already based on psychometric principles that increasingly gained preference as a basis for governing education systems, it was not necessary to implement a new testing programme in response to the transnational *accountability* trend. Unlike Norway (discussed below), Sweden could simply expand its existing testing programme.

Recently the Swedish National Agency for Education also put emphasis[73] on formative use of the national tests. Its official webpage expresses certification and governing as key purposes, yet adds that "the national tests can also help specify curricula and subjects plans, and improve student achievement."[74] The recent addition of the emphasis on *supporting* learning and instruction can be perceived in view of the transnational *Assessment for learning* trend, that help the authorities to legitimise the expansion of the testing programme.[75] As such, since it was implemented primarily for *certification* from the 1930s through the 1960s, the national testing programme has accumulated the roles of *governing* and *supporting* learning and instruction in concert with the associated transnational *meritocracy, accountability* and *Assessment for learning* trends respectively.

Norway Adopts Psychometric Tests in Concert with the Transnational Accountability Trend

Norway did not have prominent contributors to the IEI study and IEA, as Sweden did. Norway's relatively limited contribution to the IEI study can be observed

---

70 Lundahl and Tveit, "Att legitimera nationella prov."
71 Lundahl and Waldow, "Standardisation and 'Quick Languages.'"
72 Johanna Ringarp, *Professionens problematik* (Stockholm: Makadam, 2011).
73 Swedish National Agency for Education, "*National tests*," accessed June 30, 2015, http://www.skolverket.se/bedomning/nationella-prov.
74 Ibid.
75 Sverre Tveit, "Ambitious and Ambiguous."

when comparing the Swedish and Norwegian delegations' project reports.[76] Furthermore, reporting of the IEI study and further collaboration were constrained by the German occupation (1940–45) during World War II.[77] While Swedish members in the research team belonged to the progressive movement in primary education, Norwegian members of the research team were based in higher education and affiliated with secondary education.[78] As opposed to their fellow Swedish IEI members, they were not in a good position to influence the use of assessments in general education. The main institution where they could exercise influence was the University of Oslo, where the Department of Educational Research (*Pedagogisk forskningsinstitutt*) had been established in 1938. The head of the department, Johs Sandven — 'Norway's Husén' — had been visiting Edward Thorndike and colleagues at Teachers College in New York and was committed to developing psychometric tests for use in general education in Norway. He was, however, not as successful in establishing an institutional environment of psychometric testing as his Swedish counterpart. In the late 1960s controversies over the establishment of educational measurement as an academic discipline occurred in concert with the democratisation and increased student influence on university policies.[79] Sandven had to step down in 1972.

As shown in Appendix 1, unlike Sweden, Norway did not participate in the IEA studies until the Second International Science Study (1983–84) and the Reading Literacy Study (1990–91). Therefore, despite Norway modelled its education system on its Swedish neighbour after World War II,[80] weaker engagement with (and less implications of) the IEI and IEA studies from the 1930s to the 1960s may be one of the explanations as to why Norway did not follow Sweden in tak-

---

76 Archive Observations, the Carnegie Collections, the Rare Book and Manuscript Library, Columbia University, April 15th 2016. International Examinations Enquiry Committee, Norway, 1929–1937; International Examinations Enquiry Committee, Sweden, 1929–1937.

77 Kay Piene, *Eksamenskarakterer og forhåndskarakterer* (Oslo: Cappelen, 1961); Jarning and Aas, "Between Common Schooling."

78 Jarning and Aas, "Between Common Schooling."

79 Kim G. Helsvig, "Pedagogikkens grenser. Kampen om norsk pedagogikk ved Pedagogisk forskningsinstitutt 1938–1980" (Oslo: Abstract forlag, 2005).

80 Francis Sejersted, *Sosialdemokratiets tidsalder. Norge og Sverige i det 20. århundre* (Oslo: Pax forlag, 2005); Alfred Telhaug Oftedal, Odd Asbjørn *Mediås* and Petter Aasen, "From Collectivism to Individualism? Education as Nation Building in a Scandinavian Perspective." *Scandinavian Journal of Educational Research* 48, no. 2 (2004), doi: 10.1080/0031383042000198558.

ing on psychometric approaches to educational assessment in general education in the 1950s and 1960s.

At the time Norway attempted to introduce psychometric testing, in the late 1960s, resistance towards American psychometric approaches to determining merit flourished in Scandinavia. Seen from a Scandinavian progressivist educator of the 1960's perspective, it was too late for the Swedes to reject American standardized tests, while in Norway there was still time. Due to protests from the teacher profession and left-wing intellectuals, initial attempts to implement national testing in Norway in 1968 failed.[81]

It would take another three decades until standardized tests were implemented in full in Norwegian schools. As part of what Lundahl and Waldow calls the *second cycle of standardisation*, which I have called the *transnational accountability trend*, emphasis was put on holding schools and teachers accountable for student outcomes.[82] Norway's outcomes on the TIMSS 1995 study had raised some concerns, but it did not cause the same public outcry that followed the publication of the first PISA tests in 2001. What is often labelled the 'PISA shock' prompted several European countries that had taken a reluctant attitude towards standardized testing (Denmark and Germany are other notable examples) to implement new national testing programmes.[83]

In Norway an OECD report of 1988 had expressed criticism for the country's lack of a system for monitoring student performance as a way to hold municipalities accountable for learning outcomes.[84] Government committees and the Ministry and Parliament discussed a system for national evaluation of schooling throughout the 1990s.[85] However, it was not until after the PISA shock that a national system for quality assessment was implemented. The PISA and OECD influence is illustrated well by the words of the Norwegian minister of education,

---

81 Forsøksrådet for skoleverket, *Standardiserte prøver i skolen. Forsøk og reform i skolen – Nr. 16* (Oslo: Universitetsforlaget, 1969).

82 Lundahl and Waldow, "Standardisation and 'Quick Languages.'"

83 Aaron Benavot and Erin Tanner, "The Growth of National Learning Assessments in the World, 1995–2006" (Background paper for the EFA global monitoring report: Education For All by 2015: Will We Make It?. Paris: UNESCO, 2007).

84 OECD, *OECD-vurdering av norsk utdanningspolitikk* (Oslo: Kirke- og undervisnings-departementet, 1988).

85 Marit K. Granheim, Ulf P. Lundgren and Tom Tiller, *Målstyring og evaluering i norsk skole. Sluttrapport EMIL-prosjektet, NORAS/LOS,* LOS-notat nr. 7 (Oslo: Norges råd for anvendt samfunnsforskning, 1990); OECD, *OECD-vurdering av norsk utdannings-politikk; Stortingsmelding nr. 47; Stortingsmelding nr. 28.*

who, due to the disappointing results of the first PISA tests, stated that it was "almost like coming home from a winter Olympics without one Norwegian medal."[86] This power of the league tables that the PISA studies[87] produce can be related to the tests' close connection with the role of the OECD as a global policy agency[88] and how this information is used by governments to legitimise reforms.[89] A new national testing program was implemented in Norway in 2004, initially motivated by the need for information to be used in the governing of education.[90]

Table 3: The National Assessment Instruments in Sweden and Norway

Country	SWEDEN	NORWAY	
Instrument	National tests (prov)	National examinations	National tests (prøver)
Year and subject/skill	Year 3: Mathematics, Swedish, and Swedish as a second language. Year 6: Mathematics, Swedish, Swedish as a second language, and English. Year 9: Mathematics, Swedish, Swedish as a second language, and English. Additionally, one natural science-oriented test (biology, physics, or chemistry) and one social science-oriented test (geography, history, religion, or social science).	Year 10: One examination in either Norwegian, English, or mathematics	Year 5: English, reading, and numeracy. Year 8: English, reading, and numeracy. Year 9: Reading and numeracy.

86 Helge O. Bergesen, *Kampen om Kunnskapsskolen* (Oslo: Universitetsforlaget, 2006), 41.
87 Meyer and Benavot, "Introduction."
88 Daniel Pettersson, "Internationell kunskapsbedömning som inslag i nationell styrning av skolan" (PhD diss., Uppsala University, 2008).
89 Sverre Tveit, "Educational Assessment in Norway," *Assessment in Education: Principles, Policy & Practice* 21, no. 2 (2014), doi: 10.1080/0969594X.2013.830079.
90 Tveit, "Educational Assessment in Norway."

Country	SWEDEN	NORWAY	
Instrument	National tests (prov)	National examinations	National tests (prøver)
Instrument developer	Developed by expert groups at universities commissioned by the Swedish National Agency for Education.	Developed by expert groups of teachers and scholars, commissioned by the Norwegian Directorate for Education and Training	Developed by expert groups at universities, commissioned by the Norwegian Directorate for Education and Training.
Marking procedures	The teachers mark the responses themselves, based on guidelines from the Swedish National Agency for Education	Two external and trained examiners mark the responses based on guidelines from the Norwegian Directorate for Education and Training.	Auto-computerised marking of most items. For open questions in the reading tests, teachers assign scores, based on guidelines from the Norwegian Directorate for Education and Training.
Subject or skill orientation	The instruments are constructed based on disciplinary goals stated in the curriculum for the respective subjects.	The instruments are constructed based on disciplinary goals (competence aims) stated in the curriculum for the respective subjects.	The instruments are constructed based on the basic skills, which are integrated in the competence aims for all subjects' curriculum.
Implemented	1930–1960s	Emerged in the 1800s	2004
Certification role	1960s	1800s	
Governing role	1960s (increased from the 1990s)	1800s	2004
Support role	2004		2006

Due to alleged overemphasis on school accountability, including student boycotts that jeopardised the validity of the assessment data,[91] the policy discourse changed in 2005. A one-year moratorium was held due to substantial problems

---

91   Halvard Hølleland, "Nasjonale prøver og kvalitetsutvikling i skolen," in *Elevvurdering i skolen – grunnlag for kulturendring*, ed. Sverre Tveit (Oslo: Universitetsforlaget, 2007).

with the testing programme and controversies over the publication of league tables,[92] and, following a change of government, radical changes were undertaken to ensure the legitimacy of the testing programme. Upper secondary education tests were terminated, and compulsory education tests were moved from the conclusion of Year 4 and 7 to the beginning of the subsequent years (Year 5 and Year 8). This change reflected a shift of purposes where new emphasis was put on the tests' role in supporting, along with governing, learning and instruction.

This change can be interpreted in view of the increased transnational emphasis on the *Assessment for learning*, and resistance to the *accountability* trend that was perceived to have dominated the new education reform and associated national testing programme. Despite less emphasis on the publication of league tables, *governing* remained the key purpose of the national tests, although the government and its executive agency also stressed their role in *supporting* learning and instruction.

Concluding Discussion: National Assessment Instruments' Accumulation of Roles in Concert with Transnational Trends of Educational Assessment

In this chapter I have demonstrated that different premises of process- and product-control partly explain the emergence of two distinctly different approaches to educational assessment in the continental European countries and the United States: The emphasis on professional (subjective) judgments and external (objective) measurement respectively. I have explained how both the increased emphasis on the *certification* and *governing* roles of educational assessment prompted the psychometric testing technology in the United States, and I further addressed how other countries took up the potential of using national tests for these purposes through the transnational *meritocracy* and *accountability* trends in the second half of the twentieth century. With the examples of Sweden and Norway, I have demonstrated how countries that began with an examination culture developed in different directions, which is, in part, related to level of engagement with the transnational *meritocracy* and *accountability* trends throughout the twentieth century.

Whereas the *meritocracy* trend from the 1930s brought psychometric approaches to educational assessment to Sweden (and ultimately the replacement of examinations with psychometric tests by the 1960s), it was through the *accountability* trend

---

92 Eyvind Elstad, "Schools Which Are Named, Shamed and Blamed by the Media: School Accountability in Norway," *Educational Assessment, Evaluation and Accountability* 21, no. 2 (2009), doi:10.1007/s11092009-9076-0; Svein Lie et al., *Nasjonale prøver på ny prøve* (Oslo: Department of Teacher Education and School Research, University of Oslo, 2005).

from the 1990s onwards that psychometric approaches to educational assessment broke through in Norway. As shown in Table 3, the result of this is that Norway currently has two national assessment instruments, one with a *certification* role and one with a *governing* role. When the *accountability* trend brought increased emphasis on psychometric testing, Sweden could instead simply strengthen its existing national testing programme. At the turn of the millennium, the transnational emphasis on *Assessment for learning* contributed to a new emphasis on assessment instruments' role in *supporting* learning and instruction. Both countries have 'added' this purpose to its respective national tests. As such, contemporary uses of national examinations and tests should be understood in view of the accumulation of educational assessment roles in concert with the transnational emphasis on *meritocracy, accountability* and, *Assessment for learning.*

It is essential to acknowledge the different timings of the implementation of national tests if different cultures of educational assessment are to be understood. As demonstrated in Table 3, the national tests in Sweden are subject and disciplinary based in accordance with the IEI research project that shaped the meritocracy trend. This reflects how they are used to *certify* (subject) learning. In Norway the national tests are interdisciplinary and skills based, which reflects the emphasis on skills in PISA, the most influential comparative testing programme associated with the *accountability* trend.

Thus, while they are called 'national tests' in both Norway and Sweden, these assessment instruments underwent completely different transnational influences characteristic to the transnational trend at the time of implementation. These differences may be illustrative of wider patterns in European countries' cultures of educational assessment. Similar to Norway, Denmark and Germany opposed implementation of psychometric tests during the *meritocracy* trend that emerged from the 1930s. In these countries such tests did not break through until the *accountability* trend that took firm root in the 1990s and was further propelled by PISA shocks at the turn of the millennium. Other countries' developments may have been more similar to that of Sweden, which replaced its existing national examination programme. Being already based on psychometric principles, only strengthening and expansion of existing testing programmes were needed to respond to the *accountability* trend.

Conclusively, as observed in both Norway and Sweden, all countries are likely to be affected by the *Assessment for learning* trend. The recent emphasis on formative assessment can both be associated with a genuine change of focus from 'summative' to 'formative' assessment, as advocated by many scholars and policymakers. It may however also reflect a legitimation strategy intended to make sure that teachers accept national tests in which *governing* learning and instruction remains the principal purpose albeit in a more attractive wrapping. The promulgation of the three roles and the three transnational trends of educational assessment undertaken in this chapter help envision how national assessment instruments have come to accumulate multiple purposes in response to different transnational developments at the time of implementation, revision and legitimation.

Literature

Aas, Gro H. "Likhet uten solidaritet? Idéhistoriske studier av karakterer I utdanning og meritokrati." PhD diss., University of Gothenburg, 2006.

Ball, Stephen J. "The Teacher's Soul and the Terrors of Performativity." *Journal of Education Policy* 18, no. 2 (2003): 215–28. doi:10.1080/0268093022000043065.

Benavot, Aaron, and *Erin Tanner.* "The Growth of National Learning Assessments in the World, 1995–2006." Background paper for the EFA global monitoring report: Education For All by 2015: Will We Make It? Paris: UNESCO, 2007.

Bergesen, Helge O. Kampen om Kunnskapsskolen. Oslo: Universitetsforlaget, 2006.

Black, Paul, and *Dylan Wiliam.* "Assessment and Classroom Learning." *Assessment in Education* 5, no. 1 (1998): 7–74. doi:10.1080/0969595980050102.

Brookhart, Susan M. "The Use of Teacher Judgement for Summative Assessment in the USA." *Assessment in Education: Principles, Policy & Practice* 20, no. 1 (January 30, 2013): 69–90. doi:10.1080/0969594X.2012.703170.

Carson, John. The Measure of Merit: Talents Intelligence, and Inequality in the French and American Republics, 1750–1940. Princeton, NJ: Princeton University Press, 2007.

Dale, Roger. "Globalisation, Knowledge Economy and Comparative Education." *Comparative Education* 41, no. 2 (2005): 117–49. doi:10.1080/0305006050015 0906.

Elstad, Eyvind. "Schools Which Are Named, Shamed and Blamed by the Media: School Accountability in Norway." *Educational Assessment, Evaluation and Accountability* 21, no. 2 (2009): 173–89. doi:10.1007/s11092-009-9076-0.

Forsberg, Eva. "Utbildningens Bedömningskulturer i Granskningens Tidevarv." *Utbildning & Demokrati* 23, no. 3 (2014): 53–76.

Forsøksrådet for skoleverket. Standardiserte prøver i skolen. Forsøk og reform i skolen – nr 16. Oslo: Universitetsforlaget, 1969.

Granheim, Marit K., Ulf P. Lundgren, and *Tom Tiller. Målstyring og evaluering i norsk skole. Sluttrapport EMIL-prosjektet NORAS/LOS-i-utdanning.* LOS-notat nr. 7. Oslo: Norges råd for anvendt samfunnsforskning, 1990.

Grek, Sotiria, Martin Lawn, Bob Lingard, Jenny Ozga, and *Risto Rinne.* "National Policy Brokering and the Construction of the European Education Space in

England, Sweden, Finland and Scotland." *Comparative Education* 45, no. 1 (2009): 5–21. doi:10.1080/03050060802661378.

Harlen, Wynne. "On the Relationship Between Assessment for Formative and Summative Purposes." In *Assessment and Learning*, edited by John Gardner, 87–102. London, UK: Sage, 2006. doi: 10.4135/9781446250808.n6.

Hattie, John. *Visible Learning*. London, UK: Routledge, 2008.

Hayward, E. Louise. "Curriculum, Pedagogies and Assessment in Scotland: The Quest for Social Justice. 'Ah Kent Yir Faither'." *Assessment in Education: Principles, Policy & Practice* 14, no. 2 (July 2007): 251–68. doi:10.1080/09695940701480178.

Helsvig, Kim G. *Pedagogikkens grenser. Kampen om norsk pedagogikk ved Pedagogisk forskningsinstitutt 1938–1980*. Oslo: Abstract forlag, 2005.

Hopfenbeck, Therese N., Maria Teresa Flórez Petour, and Astrid Tolo. "Balancing Tensions in Educational Policy Reforms: Large-Scale Implementation of Assessment for Learning in Norway." *Assessment in Education: Principles* 22, no. 1 (2015): 44–60.

Hopfenbeck, Therese N., Astrid Tolo, Maria Teresa Florez, and Yasmine El Masri. "Balancing Trust and Accountability? the Assessment for Learning Programme in Norway." 2013. Accessed May 21t, 2015. http://www.oecd.org/edu/ceri/Norwegian%20GCES%20case%20study%20OECD.pdf.

Hopmann, Stefan T. "On the Evaluation of Curriculum Reforms." *Journal of Curriculum Studies* 35, no. 4 (2003): 459–478. doi: 10.1080/00220270305520.

Hølleland, Halvard. "Nasjonale prøver og kvalitetsutvikling i skolen." In *Elevvurdering i skolen – grunnlag for kulturendring*, edited by S. Tveit, 29–44. Oslo: Universitetsforlaget, 2007.

IEA. "Completed Studies." *IEA*. Accessed May 30, 2015. http://www.iea.nl/completed_studies.html.

Jarning, Harald, and Gro H. Aas. "Between Common Schooling and the Academe: The International Examinations Inquiry in Norway, 1935–1961." In *An Atlantic Crossing? The Work of the International Examination Inquiry, its Researchers, Methods and Influence*, 181–204, edited by M. Lawn. Oxford, UK: Symposium Books, 2008.

Jonsson, Anders, Christian Lundahl, and Anders Holmgren. "Evaluating a Large-Scale Implementation of Assessment for Learning in Sweden." *Assessment in Education: Principles, Policy & Practice* 22, no. 1 (2015): 104–21. doi:10.1080/0969594X.2014.970612.

Kamens, David H. "Globalisation and the Emergence of an Audit Culture: PISA and the Search for 'Best Practices' and Magic Bullets." In *PISA, Power, and Policy: The Emergence of Global Educational Governance*, edited by Heinz-Dieter Meyer, and Aaron Benavot, 117–139. Oxford, UK: Symposium Books, 2015.

Kellaghan, Thomas. "The Globalisation of Assessment in the 20th Century." *Assessment in Education: Principles* 8, no. 1 (2001): 87–102. doi: 10.1080/0969 5940120033270.

Lawn, Martin. ed. *An Atlantic Crossing? The Work of the International Examination Inquiry, its Researchers, Methods and Influence.* London, UK: Symposium Books, 2008.

Lawn, Martin. "Voyages of Measurement in Education in the Twentieth Century: Experts, Tools and Centres." *European Educational Research Journal* 12, no. 1 (2013): 108–119. doi:10.2304/eerj.2013.12.1.108.

Lie, Svein, Therese N. Hopfenbeck, Elisabeth Ibsen, and Are Turmo. *Nasjonale prøver på ny prøve.* Oslo: Department of Teacher Education and School Research, University of Oslo, 2005.

Lindensjö, Bo, and Lundgren, Ulf P. *Utbildningsreformer och politisk styrning.* Stockholm: Liber, 2014.

Lundahl, Christian. *"Viljan att veta vad andra vet: Kunskapsbedömning i tidigmodern, modern och senmodern skola."* PhD diss., Uppsala University, Sweden, 2006.

–. "Inter/National Assessments as National Curriculum: The Case of Sweden." In *An Atlantic Crossing? The Work of the International Examination Inquiry, its Researchers, Methods and Influence,* edited by Martin Lawn, 157–180. Oxford, UK: Symposium Books, 2008.

Lundahl, Christian, and Daniel Petterson. "Den svenska skolens resultat. Från standardprov til PISA, in *PISA: sannheten om skolen?,* edited by Eyvind Elstad and Kirsten Sivesind, 222–239. Oslo: Universitetsforlaget, 2010.

Lundahl, Christian, and Florian Waldow. "Standardisation and 'Quick Languages': The Shape-Shifting of Standardized Measurement of Pupil Achievement in Sweden and Germany." *Comparative Education* 45, no. 3 (2009): 365–385. doi: 10.1080/03050060903184940.

Madhaus, George F. "Ralph Tyler's Contribution to Program Evaluation." In *Evaluation Roots. A Wider Perspective of Theorists' Views and Influences,* 2nd edition, edited by Marvin C. Alkin, 157–164. Los Angeles, CA: Sage, 2013.

Meyer, Heinz-Dieter, and Aaron Benavot. "Introduction." In: *PISA, Power, and Policy: The Emergence of Global Educational Governance,* edited by Heinz-Dieter Meyer and A. Benavot, 9–26. Oxford, UK: Symposium Books, 2015.

Müller Detlef, Fritz K. Ringer, and Brian Simon. *The Rise of the Modern Educational System.* Cambridge, UK: Cambridge University Press, 1986.

Nordin, Andreas, and Daniel Sundberg. "The Making and Governing of Knowledge in the Education Policy Field." In *Transnational Policy Flows in European Education,* edited by Andreas Nordin, and Daniel Sundberg, 9–20. Oxford, UK: Symposium Books, 2014.

Organisation for Economic Co-operation and Development [OECD]. OECD-vurdering av norsk utdanningspolitikk. Oslo: Kirke-og undervisningsdepartementet, 1988.

–. *Formative Assessment: Improving Learning in Secondary Classrooms.* OECD, 2005.

–. "Centre for Educational Research and Innovation (CERI) – What Works." Accessed July 21, 2015. https://www.oecd.org/edu/ceri/centreforeducational researchandinnovationceri-whatworks.htm.

–. *Synergies for Better Learning: An International Perspective on Evaluation and Assessment,* OECD, 2013. Accessed July 22, 2015. http://www.oecd.org/edu/school/oecdreviewonevaluationandassessmentframeworksforimproving schooloutcomescountryreviews.htm.

Pettersson, Daniel. "Internationell kunskapsbedömning som inslag i nationell styrning av skolan." PhD diss., Uppsala: Uppsala University, 2008.

Piene, Kay. *Eksamenskarakterer og forhåndskarakterer.* Oslo: Cappelen, 1961.

Prøitz, Tine S. "Uploading, Downloading and Uploading Again – Concepts for Policy Integration in Education Research." *Nordic Journal of Studies in Educational Policy* 1 (2015): 70–80. doi:10.3402/nstep.v1.27015.

Ringarp, Johanna. *Professionens problematic.* Stockholm: Makadam, 2011.

Sejersted, Francis. *Sosialdemokratiets tidsalder. Norge og Sverige i det 20. århundre.* Oslo: Pax forlag, 2005.

Swedish National Agency for Education. *National tests.* Accessed June 30, 2015. http://www.skolverket.se/bedomning/nationella-prov.

Telhaug, Alfred Oftedal, Odd Asbjørn Mediås, and Petter Aasen. "From Collectivism to Individualism? Education as Nation Building in a Scandinavian Perspective." *Scandinavian Journal of Educational Research* 48, no. 2 (2004): 141–158. doi: 10.1080/0031383042000198558.

Tröhler, Daniel. "Truffle Pigs, Research Questions, and Histories of Education." In *Rethinking the History of Education: Transnational Perspectives on Its Questions, Methods, and Knowledge,* edited by Thomas S. Popkewitz, 75–92. New York, NY: Palgrave Macmillan US, 2013.

Tveit, Sverre. "Ambitious and Ambiguous: Shifting Purposes of National Testing in the Legitimation of Assessment Policies in Norway and Sweden (2000–2017)." *Assessment in Education: Principles, Policy & Practice* (forthcoming, 2018).

Tveit, Sverre and Christian Lundahl. "New Modes of Policy Legitimation in Education: (Mis)using Comparative Data to Effectuate Assessment Reform". *European Educational Research Journal* (2017). doi: https://doi.org/10.1177/1474904117728846»

Tveit, Sverre. "Educational Assessment in Norway." *Assessment in Education: Principles, Policy & Practice* 21 no. 2 (2014): 221–237.

UNESCO. "World Declaration on Education for All: Meeting basic needs." Adopted by the World Conference on Education for All. New York, NY: UNESCO, 1990.

Ydesen, Christian, Kari Ludvigsen, and *Christian Lundahl.* "Creating an Educational Testing Profession in Norway, Sweden and Denmark, 1910–1960." *European Educational Research Journal* 12, no. 1 (2013): 120. doi: https://doi.org/10.2304/eerj.2013.12.1.120.

Young, Michael. The Rise of Meritocracy. London, UK: Penguin Books, 1958.

Waldow, Florian. "Undeclared Imports: Silent Borrowing in Educational Policymaking and Research in Sweden." *Comparative Education* 45, no. 4 (2009): 477–494. URL: http://www.jstor.org/stable/40593191.

Appendix 1: Participation in IEA and PISA studies[93]

Year	Test	Content	Age	Provider	NO	SE
1960	Pilot Twelve-Country Study	Mathematics, reading comprehension, geography, science, and non-verbal ability	13	IEA	-	X
1964	FIMS (First International Mathematics Study)	Mathematics	13	IEA	-	X
1970–71	FISS (First International Science Study)	Science	10, 14, final SE	IEA	-	X
1970–71	Six Subject Survey: Reading comprehension	Reading	10, 14, final SE	IEA	-	X
1970–71	Six Subject Survey: Literature Education	Literature	14, final SE	IEA	-	X
1970–71	Six Subject Survey: English as a Foreign language	English as a foreign language	14, final SE	IEA	-	X
1970–71	Six Subject Survey: French as a Foreign language	French as a foreign language	14, final SE	IEA	-	X

93 Information gathered from http://www.iea.nl/brief_history.html on April 17th 2016. Not included: Classroom Environment Study (1981–83); Computers in Education Study (COMPED) (1989, 1992); Preprimary project (PPP), 1987–89, 1992, 1995–97; Second Information Technology in Education Study Modul 1 (SITES-M1).

Year	Test	Content	Age	Provider	NO	SE
1970–71	Six Subject Survey: Civic Education	Civic Education	10, 14, final SE	IEA	-	X
1980–82	SIMS (Second International Mathematics Study)	Mathematics	13	IEA	-	X
1983–84	SISS (Second International Science Study)	Science	10, 14, final SE	IEA	X	X
1984–85	Written Composition Study	Writing	10–12; 15–17; 17–19	IEA	-	X
1990–91	Reading Literacy Study	Reading	9, 14	IEA	X	X
1994–95	TIMSS (The Third International Mathematics and Science Study)	Mathematics and Science	9, 13, final SE,	IEA	X	X
1995	Language Education Study	English, French, German, and Spanish.	15–16; 17–18	IEA	X	X
1998–99	TIMSS 1999	Mathematics and Science	Grade 8	IEA	X	X
2000	PISA 2000	Reading, Mathematics, Science	15	OECD	X	X
2001	PIRLS 2001	Reading	Grade 4	IEA	X	X
2003	TIMSS 2003	Mathematics and Science	Grade 4, 8	IEA	X	X
2003	PISA 2003	Reading, Mathematics, Science	15	OECD	X	X
2006	PIRLS 2006	Reading	Grade 4	IEA	X	X
2006	PISA 2006	Reading, Mathematics, Science	15	OECD	X	X
2007	TIMSS 2007	Mathematics and Science	Grade 4, 8	IEA	X	X
2009	PISA 2009	Reading, Mathematics, Science	15	OECD	X	X
2011	TIMSS 2011	Mathematics and Science	Grade 4, 8	IEA	X	X
2011	PIRLS 2011	Reading	Grade 4, 8	IEA	X	X
2012	PISA 2012	Reading, Mathematics, Science	15	OECD	X	X
2015	PISA 2015	Reading, Mathematics, Science	15	OECD	X	X

Assessment and the Construction of 'Deviance'

Mette Buchardt and Christian Ydesen

Testing the Culturally Deviant of the Welfare State: Greenlandic Children and the Children of Labour Migrants in Danish Minority Education, 1960–1970

A Cultural History of Educational Practices Testing the Culturally Deviant

This chapter investigates the testing and assessment of children and families rendered culturally deviant by the established Danish welfare state in general and the national public school system (*Folkeskolen*) in particular.[1] The method is to put together two distinct historical cases from the heyday of the Nordic welfare state model in the 1960s and 1970s, when educational testing was used to handle pupils on the periphery of the welfare state.[2] As our first case, we focus on the testing of schoolchildren in Greenland, today a self-governed country in the Danish Realm, but a Danish colony up until 1953, when its status was changed into a Danish county, something which lasted until the introduction of home rule in 1979. Following the change from Danish colony to Danish county a distinct modernisation and Danification project unfolded from the 1950s till the 1970s, during which time education was a central arena. Secondly, we focus on the children of labour migrants who started arriving in metropolitan Denmark in the 1960s and became the object of municipal school authorities' attention since the beginning

---

1 Public primary and lower secondary schooling.
2 We draw from the welfare state historian Heidi Vad Jønsson's framing of integration politics as a so-called peripheral area of the welfare state. Heidi Vad Jønsson, "I velfærdsstatens randområde. Socialdemokratiets integrationspolitik 1960'erne til 2000'erne (PhD diss., Department of History and Centre for Welfare State Research, University of Southern Denmark, 2013). See also Mette Buchardt, Pirjo Markkola, and Heli Valtonen, "Education and the Making of the Nordic Welfare States," in *Education, State and Citizenship. A Perspective in the Nordic Welfare State History*, ed. Mette Buchardt et al. (Helsinki: NordWel Studies in Historical Welfare State Research 2013), and Marta Padovan-Özdemir and Christian Ydesen, "Professional Encounters with the Post-WWII Immigrant: A Privileged Prism for Studying the Shaping of European Welfare Nation-States," *Paedagogica Historica* 52, no. 5: 423–37.

of the 1970s. Especially migrants from Turkey, Pakistan and Yugoslavia caught the attention.

The former case concerns the selection of Greenlandic children between 1961 and 1971 in connection with the so-called preparation scheme (*præparandar-rangementet*).[3] This scheme was designed to boost Greenlandic children's Danish language skills by sending them on a one-year school trip to Denmark. In the period covered, the children were selected based on test results, teachers' evaluations, and the final recommendation of the school director in Nuuk (formerly *Godthåb*).

The latter case concerns examples of the testing of foreign language pupils — often the newly arrived children of labour migrants — in so-called reception classes (*modtagelsesklasser*) and special needs education in the municipalities of Copenhagen and Aarhus, respectively.[4] Testing this group of pupils was a practice that became common during the 1970s and included language as well as intelligence testing in addition to and in combination with teachers' evaluations.

Both cases illustrate how standardized assessment was used for the purpose of categorisation, selection and distribution of children considered 'culturally deviant.' Its use was legitimated through the argument of objectivity and universality (culture neutral). However, in the process of implementing the tests the notion of objectivity was questioned not least by teachers. Also, both cases display the distinctions between assessment cultures, for instance the non-verbal intelligence test, a test that claimed to be objective and culturally neutral because it required no reading skills and the use of the subjective teachers' evaluation, used in daily school practice with pupils as well as in selection processes. It is, nevertheless, significant that both types of assessment were utilised in relation to one another and thus that the forms of knowledge these assessment cultures draw on intertwined.

Using Stake's terminology, the case study design in this chapter amounts to a 'collective case' aiming to disclose a particular phenomenon from a number of

---

3   The empirical material of this case was gathered for the purpose of writing Christian Ydesen's PhD dissertation between 2007 and 2010, which dealt with the selection and testing of Greenlandic children. To present a fresh inquiry for this analysis, the dissertation's original analysis of and the empirical data have been reread and analysed anew, with a specific focus on the culture surrounding the testing practices.

4   The part of the case that concerns Aarhus municipality has been analysed as part of Mette Buchardt and Liv Fabrin, "PISA Etnisk i lyset af tosprogede elevers skole- og testhistorie", in *Test og prøvelser. Oprindelse, udvikling, aktualitet*, ed. Karen Egedal Andreasen et al. (Aalborg: Aalborg Universitetsforlag, 2015), 154–156. In this chapter, the source material has been reread in light of the practice in Copenhagen municipality earlier in the 1970s and given the focus of this chapter, as mentioned above.

different cases.[5] At the same time, however, the two historical cases selected also fit under Stake's definition of instrumental cases because of their suitability in throwing light on a 'particular issue, redraw[ing] generalisations, or build[ing] theory.'[6] The cases build on broader studies we have conducted respectively, but the key sources in our case studies are material municipal reports, test and teaching manuals, professional debates, education system accounts, and school authority correspondence.[7]

Read in relation to each other, the two cases of testing practices exemplify a double and contradictory scheme of welfare state schooling: On the one hand, the whole population was to be included in school by means of the principle of equity, a central part of the educational policy in the Nordic welfare states, but on the other hand, the population was seen as neither identical nor equal.[8] Testing and describing children and allowing for compensatory precautions by means of testing thus became a strategy in welfare state education in Denmark during the 20th century along with the growth of educational psychology as a means of optimizing education.[9] In this respect, the chapter aims at contributing to our understanding of schooling and education as the key domains where the state is crafted by impacting, ordering, and organizing the population. This amounts to a focus on the welfare state strategies of modernisation, where the aim of homogenisation and differentiation were mixed in complex ways.

Both cases clearly indicate that the notion of culture played a distinct role in the complex balance between homogenisation and differentiation in education. The Greenlandic and labour migrant children exemplify groups of the Danish populace marked by differences in 'race' and 'culture'. The two cases also show attempts to handle the changing world order under decolonisation, where labour migrants from the southern hemisphere increasingly travelled to the former metropolises of

---

5   Robert E. Stake, *The Art of Case Study Research* (Thousand Oaks, CA: Sage Publications, 1995).

6   Gina Grandy, "Instrumental Case Study," in *Encyclopedia of Case Study Research*, eds. A. J. Mills, G. Durepos, and E. Wiebe (Thousand Oaks, CA: Sage Publications, 2010), 474–476.

7   Buchardt and Fabrin, "PISA Etnisk"; Mette Buchardt, *Kulturforklaring: Uddannelseshistorier om muslimskhed* (Copenhagen: Tiderne Skifter, 2016); Christian Ydesen, *The Rise of High-Stakes Educational Testing in Denmark, 1920–1970* (Frankfurt am Main: Peter Lang Verlag, 2011).

8   Buchardt, Markkola, and Valtonen, "Nordic Welfare States."

9   Bjørn Hamre and Christian Ydesen, "The Ascent of Educational Psychology in Denmark in the Interwar Years," *Nordic Journal of Educational History* 1, no. 2 (2014): 87–111.

the colonial sphere, and where the former colonies were often integrated in new ways, whether in a commonwealth, as was the case of the United Kingdom, or as in Denmark, which sought to integrate Greenland as an administrative county under the Danish state from 1953 until its home rule in 1979.[10] Thus, the testing practices investigated also exemplify two cases of cultural deviance, both intersecting with decolonisation and the renewed and changing globalisation process characterised by intensified questions of belonging and economic optimisation.[11]

The sense in reading these two cases in continuation can also be articulated at a more specific level. In the 1970s, very little research and practical experience were available regarding the education of what was dubbed "foreign language children" in Denmark, who, since a circular in 1970, had been covered by the school system and its obligation to offer instruction.[12] In this context, the teaching of children in Greenland and thus the 'bilingual problem' served as an example — as well as a bogey — and thus as negative as well as positive inspiration.[13] Furthermore, the test batteries employed in Greenland as well as in metropolitan Denmark were, to a wide extent, developed through the same methodology and by the same actors.[14]

Based on an unfolding of the two examples of testing practices as part of schooling on the periphery of the Danish welfare state during the 1960s and 1970s, we seek to explore which processes unfolded in the tensions between bureaucrats and school teachers and different forms of academic knowledge applied in schooling.

These practices simultaneously sought to resolve dilemmas of homogenisation and differentiation in light of colonialism undergoing change and thus different conditions and a new meaning of borders within what would later be called globalisation and, here, an understanding of culture and the notions of tradition and modernisation in different ways were brought to the fore. This chapter aims to elucidate these components to create knowledge about the production of meaning

---

10 Dansk Institut for Internationale Studier, *Afvikling af Grønlands kolonistatus, 1945-54 - en historisk udredning* (Copenhagen: Dansk Institut For Internationale Studier, 2007).

11 Fazal Rizvi and Bob Lingard, *Globalizing Education Policy* (London, New York: Routledge, 2010).

12 Undervisningsministeriet [Ministry of Education], *Cirkulære om undervisning i folkeskolen af udenlandske børn*, Circular no. 293, 30 November 1970.

13 For example Inger Kleivan, "Tosprogsproblematikken", in *Fremmedarbejderpolitik - en bog om fremmedarbejderproblematikken*, eds. Jan Hjarnø, Torben Lundbæk, and Sven Skovmand (Copenhagen: Mellemfolkeligt Samvirke, 1973), 176-179.

14 For example Kaj Spelling, *Miljøets indflydelse på intelligensudviklingen — specielt med henblik på 'racemæssige' forskelle* (Copenhagen: Nyt Nordisk Forlag Arnold Busck, 1963).

on the ground – including the ambiguities and paradoxes of the Danish welfare state in general and the national public-school system in particular. The theme of this chapter is, in other words, which meanings were ascribed to the children through testing and to the reach of testing. Hence, the chapter contributes to the history of assessment cultures through approaching the cultural history of testing the culturally deviant as seen from the outskirts of a Nordic welfare state.

Testing Greenlandic Minority Children: The Paradoxes of Social Engineering

In 1950, when Greenland was still a colony under Danish rule, a new education act for Greenland was passed in Danish Parliament.[15] The act actively promoted the use of the Danish language in Greenland and, in a wider sense, reflected a new Danish policy in relation to Greenland. At the call of Greenlandic politicians — eager to obtain a status equal to that of the Danes — this new policy line heralded initiatives of social engineering that were often launched with reference to modernisation initiatives.[16]

In the field of education, the new policy line promoted and facilitated reforms and initiatives to lay out the direction for the modernisation of Greenlandic society. This case focuses on a high-stakes testing practice entailed by one of the key initiatives at the time that was aimed at the screening and selection of Greenlandic children, namely the so-called preparation program which had an active testing component between 1961 and 1971. The aim of the preparation program was to select talented Greenlandic children and send them on a one-year school trip to Denmark to improve their Danish language skills and thus enhance their chances of passing the Danish lower secondary exam (*realeksamen*). Between 1967 and 1971, the only way a Greenlandic child could obtain a secondary education was to be admitted in the program and go to Denmark.

The selection process of the preparation program involved distinctly cultural components heavily accentuated by the post-colonial setting, more specifically

---

15 The revision of the Danish constitution in 1953, when Greenland ceased to be a colony and was granted formal status as a Danish county, with two representatives in the Danish parliament, also meant that Greenland was governed by the newly established Ministry for Greenland in Copenhagen.

16 Christian Ydesen, *Rise of High-Stakes Educational Testing*, 168ff.

the decolonisation strategy in which a central feature was the Danification of Greenlandic society.[17]

Context of the Preparation Program: Clash of the Forms of Knowledge

The post-colonial project of modernizing Greenland as part of the decolonisation basically a reintegration strategy, clearly shaped the imaginations of decision makers as they devised solutions to problems and laid out the direction for the future. In the 1950s and 1960s, the Greenlandic education system witnessed a boom in the number of pupils.[18] This created severe logistical problems aggravated by the fact that many school buildings were dilapidated and inadequate and there was a shortage of teachers.[19] An easily recognizable solution was to launch a program of sending Greenlandic children to Denmark.

The preparation program sprung from a streamed education system based on Danish language skills. The 1950 Education Act had introduced a scheme of division into A and B classes after the second grade. Children with an aptitude for learning Danish entered the so-called B classes, in which a growing number of subjects would be taught in Danish, whereas children in the A classes would be taught in Greenlandic, with Danish only offered as a foreign language in the curriculum.[20] Being in a B class was a condition for obtaining a secondary education.[21] The launch and sustenance of this elitist system combined with scarce resources was associated with the need to carefully select the appropriate children. To meet this need, the School Directorate in Nuuk and the Ministry for Greenland in Copenhagen saw tests as a useful component in the selection process, able to secure fairness and efficiency.

---

17 Tupaarnaq Rosing Olsen, *I skyggen af kajakkerne: Grønlands politiske historie 1939–79* (Nuuk: Atuagkat, 2005); Axel Kjær Sørensen, *Danmark-Grønland i det 20. århundrede. En historisk oversigt* (Copenhagen: Nyt Nordisk Forlag, Arnold Busck, 1983).

18 As of 31 December 1951, there were 4,328 pupils in compulsory education in Greenland. As of 31 December 1969, the number had risen to 10,502. Christian Berthelsen, *Den grønlandske skole gennem 20 år* (Skoledirektøren for Grønland, Nuuk 1972).

19 Ernst Jensen, "Langt hjemmefra – grønlandske skolebørn i Danmark i 1960'erne og 1970'erne," *Grønland* 4 (1997): 150–154.

20 Ernst Jensen, *Langt hjemmefra – grønlandske børn på skoleophold i Danmark i 1960'erne og 1970'erne* (Nuuk: Atuagkat, 2001).

21 The 1950 Education Act clearly stated that candidates for lower secondary school were to be recruited from among children in the B classes.

The school director in Nuuk, Christian Berthelsen, a central member of the educated Greenlandic elite, viewed the tests of the preparation program as a useful technology to counteract the inflation of teacher evaluations and to strengthen his own position and preserve his latitude regarding both local schools and the Ministry for Greenland.[22] Teachers and schools referring children to the preparation program were generally keen to have as many as possible enrolled in the program because they knew it could pave the way to secondary education. These demands created a mismatch between the number of spots available and the number of children referred. One example dates back to 1970, when the Paamiut (formerly *Frederikshåb*) school referred 20 pupils to the program but only received four spots. The school then wrote a very angry complaint to the school director, calling into question the validity of the test results overruling the 'pedagogical work and knowledge' of the teachers.[23]

It is important to note that the number of Greenlandic children sent to Denmark was not just decided upon on the basis of academic achievement and the child's psychological 'robustness'; budgetary considerations, along with the number of available Danish foster homes, their wishes in terms of gender, and the increasing exclusion of children attending the seventh grade also played a role.[24] Against this tense background, the school director could use the test results to argue that the right pupils had been selected, and the test results could also be used to request an expansion or modification of the program — or the Greenlandic education system at large — with the Ministry for Greenland. The argument would be that the test results indicated the presence of many promising pupils and, therefore, the education system is obliged to provide them with appropriate opportunities.

This use of test results as an objective tool of measurement clearly reveals tension between what could be termed a psychometric form of knowledge aiming at objectivity (i.e. the objective results of measurement), a political-pragmatic form of knowledge (i.e. what is feasible and realistic), and pedagogical knowledge emphasising the importance of context and background (what our experiences and knowledge tell us about an individual child). The tension, ambiguity, and entanglements

---

22 Ydesen, *Rise of High-Stakes Educational Testing*, 188ff.
23 Ydesen, *Rise of High-Stakes Educational Testing*, 210ff.
24 The teachers supervising the program in Denmark raised concerns about the Greenlandic seventh graders having reached puberty whereas most Danish pupils in the sixth grade had not. The 1966 school leader meeting discussed the issue and concluded that primarily sixth graders were to be selected together with the best of the best from the fifth grade. *Beretning om det grønlandske skolevæsen, 1966–67* (Nuuk, 1968), 9.

between these forms of knowledge become particularly apparent when looking more closely at the selection process of the preparation program itself.

The Selection: The Paradoxes of a Fair and Efficient Selection

As already indicated, the use of tests in the preparation program was not always well received among teachers, who frequently criticised the weight ascribed to test results compared to the schools' prioritised lists of recommendations based on teachers' holistic evaluations. Such an example can be found in a 1967 letter from the teachers' council of Aasiaat (formerly *Egedesminde*) to the School Directorate. Regarding the selection process of the preparation scheme, it was stated:

> "This might indicate that the Danish language test results have been attributed more weight in the selection process. The Greenlandic language and arithmetic and not least the evaluation seem to have been of secondary importance. [...] Finally, we cannot help mentioning that we feel our work overruled. When we have evaluated a pupil and worked out a priority list, it is done with our best conviction and our knowledge about the individual child. [...] School recommendations must be held as based on such a knowledge of the abilities and talent of the individual child as can only be obtained through day-to-day work with them and should only be deviated from in exceptional cases – and then always with a clear motivation."[25]

However, although the teachers would criticize the cultural and geographical biases of the tests, it is also clear that their evaluations often contained perceptions of the children that were themselves rooted in cultural differences and ideas about deviance.

This trend was particularly widespread among Danish teachers in Greenland, i.e. teachers who had moved to Greenland, or who came from families that had lived in Greenland for more than one generation.[26] The group of Danish teachers often described Greenlandic children as shy, modest, and reluctant although usually happy. An example stems from a 1962 teacher's evaluation of a pupil in Qaqortoq (formerly Julianehåb): "Might at times seem a bit dull and absent-minded and like most Greenlanders a little shy but always smiling and easy to make contact with." Head teacher Henriksen, a Dane working in Greenland, even wrote that it was not rare for Danish teachers to view Greenlandic children as

25   Kultureqarnermut, Ilinniartitaanermut, Ilisimatusarnermut, Ilageeqarnermullu Naa-lakkersuisoqarfik [Department for Culture, Education, Research, and Church] KIIIN Archive, j.nr. 0670-05-01, 67/68.

26   In 1952 there were approximately 33 Danish teachers in Greenland and 182 Greenlandic teachers. In 1970 the teacher composition was 459 Danish teachers and 119 Greenlandic teachers. Christian Berthelsen, *Den grønlandske skole.*

mentally handicapped.[27] This indicates that a colonial mindset also played into questions revolving around the category of race most explicitly present in teachers' expectations and evaluations.

The entire selection question of the preparation program was the object of critical discussion at a language conference in 1967. Professor Jesper Florander of the Danish Educational Research Institute (*Danmarks Pædagogiske Institut*) criticised that the selection process would preclude a number of potentially suitable candidates whose abilities were just as strong as those of the ones selected, but whose home environment had not been as conducive to learning the Danish language as for those selected. Thus, the selection process overlooked a number of potentially academically minded children. Second, Florander spurned the teacher evaluations, since these would be aimed at the same type of selection based on specific Danish language abilities. Third, he criticised the use of obsolete tests that had been found to have an error margin of 10–20%. Florander concluded that the selection process in general and the identification of academic aptitude in particular prevented a number of pupils from receiving the appropriate higher education.[28]

Florander's severe criticism intensified efforts to select the right children and, acceding to the criticism, the Greenlandic Non-Verbal Test Battery (*GNVTB*) intelligence test was added to the test battery in 1969, although it was only used in cases of doubt. The Non-Verbal Test Battery test was a so-called culture-neutral test developed by the Danish educational psychologist and later professor at the Royal Danish School of Education (*Danmarks Lærerhøjskole*) Kaj Spelling in Malaysia in the late 1950s.[29] In developing the test Spelling divided the Malaysian population into distinct race groups and listed their respective test scores. For the purpose of implementing the test in Greenland it was subsequently standardized on 375 Greenlandic children from 10 towns and eight villages in Western Greenland, which gave cause to adding G to the name of the test.

Looking specifically at the selection process and the criticisms surrounding it has indicated at least two main paradoxes. The first stems from the canonisation of the Danish language itself, because it was tied to the modernisation project, partly defined by ideas about a cultural taxonomy placing Greenlandic culture in an inferior position. The paradoxical question that arises is on what terms and conditions could a Greenlandic child be included in the Danish welfare state community,

27 Holger Henriksen, "Skole og kulturmøde i Grønland II," *Grønland* 3 (1970): 85–96.
28 Ydesen, *Rise of High-Stakes Educational Testing*, 192ff.
29 Spelling, *Miljøets indflydelse på intelligensudviklingen*.

and was it even possible? In other words, was the homongenisation agenda too salient to handle differentiation? Second, there was the paradox emerging from the political ambition to secure equity via a fair and efficient selection capable of identifying the brightest and most promising Greenlandic pupils in light of the biases resulting from the unevenly distributed presence of the Danish language. The Danish language, Florander argued, was disproportionately present in the children's home environment, in the teachers' evaluations, and in the language tests used. In other words, children's frames of reference had significant importance in terms of their test results and in terms of equity and differentiation. Florander's solution was to circumvent these paradoxes by adding an allegedly neutral and objective IQ test to the selection process, the GNVTB test; that is, he subscribed to what we term the psychometric form of knowledge of objectivity. This makes a closer look at the test battery relevant.

Culturalised Test Batteries

Analysing a test battery in relation to the understandings of culture at stake makes it useful to focus on the fact that testing subscribes to the idea of objective and well-defined domains — for example, reading comprehension and mathematics problem-solving ability — as particular and well-defined areas of knowledge.[30] This underlying assumption structures the test design and forces a division between skills such as language skills, mathematical skills, and logical reasoning skills. In this case, the test battery clearly reflected this division, encompassing language tests, arithmetic tests, and the GNVTB test.

The notion of knowledge domains permeating the test battery of the preparation program refers to the societal division of labour modelled on the Danish industrialised society. This was not culturally neutral and is certainly in stark contrast with the habits of Greenlandic society, where the need for skills did not necessarily follow the same lines of division. This point is reflected in a 1963 letter from a Western Greenland settlement: "Please observe that the tests are very difficult for a pupil from a remote settlement."[31] The quotation points to the fact that knowledge domains are historically and socially constructed. One historic example of such a dimension can be found in a late-1960s memorandum on Greenlandic education concerning the eighth and ninth grades issued by the

---

30 George Madaus, Michael Russell and Jennifer Higgins, *The Paradoxes of High-Stakes Testing* (Charlotte, NC: Information Age Publishing, 2009).

31 KIIIN Archive, j.nr. 943.3, 1963/64, læg 3, Letter from Qoornoq school to the deputy school inspector in Nuuk, dated 23 May 1963.

Ministry for Greenland, which reads, "The aim is to provide teaching which will enable the pupil to live up to the demands of the test and thus the demands of society."[32] The quotation testifies to a direct link between an educational test and external societal demands.

Certainly, educational testing has special importance in a bilingual context because the different test takers often do not have the same frames of reference.[33] It is striking that the GNVTB test claims to be able to transcend exactly these cultural biases in knowledge domains by probing the IQ of the children, which is inherently another constructed domain.

The Greenlandic case indicates that the workings of the Danish welfare state were characterised by continuous efforts to manage an extremely complex area featuring struggles between professional groups, forms of knowledge, organisational structures, cultural positions, and geographical locations. It was in this vortex that testing appeared as a tool aiming to secure the functionality of the Danish welfare state.

Testing the Children of Labour Migrants

In the early 1970s, testing was used to handle an allegedly new group of pupils: The children of labour migrants and refugees who had arrived since the 1960s. These children had started to attend the Danish education system, more precisely the *Folkeskole*. This was especially the case in the bigger cities. In 1970, a Ministry of Education circular stipulated that mandatory instruction officially also included 'foreign children' and, in the first years of the 1970s, pedagogical attention gravitated towards this group of children at the municipal and local school levels.[34] At the parliamentary-political level and regarding the Ministry of Education, not much attention was yet directed towards the children of labour migrants and refugees, and no further legislation was issued until 1976. Then, a ministerial order provided additional guidelines, for instance, about so-called reception classes (*modtagelsesklasser*) for newly arrived pupils with no or little knowledge

32 Ydesen, *Rise of High-Stakes Educational Testing*, 199.
33 Jagdish Gundara, *Interculturalism, Education and Inclusion* (London, UK: Sage, 2004); Elana Shohamy, "Assessment in Multicultural Societies: Applying Democratic Principles and Practices to Language Testing," in *Critical Pedagogies and Language Learning*, eds. Bonny Norton and Kelleen Toohey (Cambridge, UK: Cambridge University Press, 2004), 72–92.
34 Undervisningsministeriet 1970, *Cirkulære om undervisning*. Mandatory instruction covered seven years and was extended to nine years in 1972.

of the Danish language, which became a central national strategy.[35] This model for integrating what were now called foreign language pupils originated in the municipality of Copenhagen which had practiced such a model since 1972.

In the autumn of 1971, 314 foreign language pupils were registered in the municipality, 96 of which received special needs education (*støtteundervisning*), to which pupils were normally referred due to poor academic achievement. Such special instruction was indicated, for instance, through intelligence testing by an educational psychologist.[36] The reception class model created an alternative to special needs education, due to growing acknowledgement in the municipal schools of the fact that this specific group of children could not be expected to receive instruction with Danish as the medium language without previous Danish language instruction, since they had only recently arrived in the country. In addition, this type of schooling used testing as a measurement tool, for instance, to determine if the pupil was ready to be partly or fully integrated in the home class – i.e. the regular class at the pupil's home district school. Testing was also used to general knowledge production about this newly discovered part of the school population.

Testing as an Instructional Tool

The first two classes of its kind opened at the School of Sjællandsgade (*Sjæl-landsgades Skole*) in the central Copenhagen district of Nørrebro. At the time, this district was a working-class neighbourhood where, since the late 19th century, many migrants had settled, such as Russian Jews, Swedes, and migrants from the Danish provinces.[37] Migration was therefore not a new phenomenon to the district or its schools, but the situation around 1970 was clearly perceived as new by the municipal and local school authorities, as well as the teaching staff. It was especially the children of Chinese labour migrants and Macedonian labour migrants from Yugoslavia who were brought to the fore by the instructional and pedagogical publications until the mid-1970s. Among the central authors of such materials

---

35 Undervisningsministeriet 1976. *Bekendtgørelse om folkeskolens undervisning af frem-medsprogede elever*, Undervisningsministeriets bekendtgørelse, no. 179, 8 March 1976.
36 Niels Bøgsted-Møller, *Kulturmøde i folkeskolen. En undersøgelse over fremmed-sprogede elever i det københavnske skolesystem* (Copenhagen: Københavns Kommunale Skolevæsen, Forsøgsafdelingen, January 1976), Erik Odde's introduction, 6.
37 Garbi Schmidt, *Nørrebros indvandringshistorie 1885–2010* (Copenhagen: Museum Tusculanums Forlag, 2015), 95f and 108f. In 1919–1940, migrants from the Danish provinces counted as emigrants in the statistics of the Copenhagen municipality (ibid. 82).

were members of the teaching staff at this particular school. One of the head teachers at the school, Erik Odde, also became the head of the Office for Foreign Language Pupils (*Kontoret for Fremmedsprogede Elever*) which the municipality created and placed at the school in November 1971. Odde was also a consultant with the UNESCO school project of the Ministry of Education. The UNESCO school project cofounded several projects emanating from the Office for Foreign Language Pupils, for instance, an instructional manual and a textbook system in Danish for foreign language pupils, consisting of reading and writing exercises that simultaneously served as testing material, published in January 1972. When this material was revised in 1973, similar material in arithmetic (*Regning*) was published as well. This new textbook system emphasised the testing portion.[38] The purpose of the test sheets was to determine the level of the pupils, whereas the exercise sheets were to be used if the test results were unsatisfactory. Hence, instruction and testing were inseparable tools.

As was the case in the Danish instruction system, the arithmetic instruction system was primarily directed towards teaching language skills. The pupil's goal was to learn "a small-language-based, correct Danish and adapt it to Danish school conditions."[39] The term "a small-language-based correct Danish" was used by teachers and municipal consultants in Copenhagen working with foreign language pupils to mean a simple but correct first-step alternative to what was called "baby talk" and "circus language", suggesting that this was the way the pupils spoke Danish.[40]

The textbook and test systems were developed based on practical experience, as was the case with other pedagogical writings concerning the group of pupils at the time. The forms of instruction were strongly regulated: The teacher was to use so-called sentence patterns (*sætningsmønstre*) from the system when asking questions. Improvised questions to which the pupils had not already learned the answer were strongly discouraged.[41] Since the system was used in the reception classes, it aimed at testing the new pupils' Danish language skills as well as measuring when a

38 Susannah-Marie Hill et al., *Dansk for fremmedsprogede* (Copenhagen: Lærerforeningernes Materialeudvalg, 1973 [1972]); Birgit Odde, Mogens Jakobsen and Kjeld Kjeldsen, *Regning for fremmedsprogede elever* (Copenhagen: Lærerforeningernes Materialeudvalg, 1973).

39 Odde, Jakobsen, and Kjeldsen, *Regning for fremmedsprogede elever*, Vol. I, III ("[…]et lillesproget korrekt dansk samt tilpasse dem til danske skoleforhold").

40 Hill et al., *Dansk*, 1. The term "*the small language*" (*Det lille sprog*) had been derived from the Danish English teacher and linguist Aage Salling.

41 Hill et al., *Dansk*, 4.

pupil could be considered to have sufficient Danish language skills to be placed in regular classes, where Danish language was the medium of instruction. Nevertheless, Danish was also the instructional language in the reception classes and, there, the language of the test and exercise material aimed at training subject matter, as well as the language for daily life situations such as doctor's appointments. The examples used mainly Danish names, geographical locations, and so forth, but a few attempts were also made to include examples that were supposed to be more familiar to the pupils, such as calculations involving Yugoslavian dinars.[42] While translation into the pupil's mother tongue was strongly advised against, since it was deemed "outright harmful", the teachers were encouraged to use examples from "the pupil's area of experience" when having freer conversations: for example,

"(a city: Beograd, an island: Taiwan, a river: Wisla)."[43]

On the one hand, the main approach of the test- and exercise-based instruction system was monolingual (Danish) and strictly aimed at socializing the pupils into Danish society and its school system; on the other hand, what was perceived to be the pupils' experience and reference frame was tentatively integrated as well.

Testing Miming at the Knowledge Production of the Pupils and their Families and 'Cultural Norms'

In 1976, the same year as the reception class model was implemented nationwide, a report was published on what was called the integration of foreign language pupils in the municipality of Copenhagen, written by psychology student Niels Bøgsted-Møller, who had himself taught reception classes. The report was issued by the experimental division (*Forsøgsafdelingen*) of the Copenhagen school authorities, but was clearly developed with the Office for Foreign Language Pupils, since Erik Odde wrote the introduction as its representative. As was the case in Odde's writings about foreign language pupils, the question of cultural encounters and cultural clashes was central in the framing of the report, as revealed by the title, *"Cultural Encounters in the Folkeskole. An examination of the Integration of Foreign Language Pupils in the Copenhagen School System."*[44]

The report consisted of 13 anonymised case studies of pupils and their families, especially Turkish and Pakistani families. A Yugoslavian family was also represented, but no Chinese families. The families were all described as labour migrants.

---

42 Odde, Jakobsen, and Kjeldsen, *Regning for fremmedsprogede elever*, Vol. II, 57.

43 Hill et al., *Dansk*, 3.

44 Bøgsted-Møller, *Kulturmøde*, Erik Odde's introduction, 6.

It was underlined that 10 of the families "belonged to Islam."[45] Besides interviews with parents, the case studies were based on a language test, a non-verbal intelligence test, and the teacher's description and assessment of each pupil. When the interviews (conducted through an interpreter) and language testing were conducted by the author, the intelligence test was conducted by a psychologist from the Municipal Office of Educational Psychology (*Skolepsykologisk Kontor*).

In the methodological chapter of the report, the use of the non-verbal intelligence test was problematised:

> "Unfortunately, the results of the standardized non-verbal intelligence test do not, even though the language factor was eliminated, have the usual validity due to the fact that the temporal factor in the task solution situation affects the calculation of the results, since the test is standardized according to a Western pace. Thus the pupils in this inquiry were not able to assert themselves."[46]

Nevertheless, the results of the intelligence testing were considered useful in concert with the teachers' impression-based assessment of the pupils' intelligence levels. Forms of assessment that aimed at methodological objectivity, an objectivity which was simultaneously questioned, thus mixed with the classical forms of subjective but professional authority-based school assessment: the teacher's statement about the pupil.

The report described many pupils as uncomfortable as well as slow in the testing situation. In a speaking skills test, in which the pupils were asked to describe a drawing of a kitchen scene with a nuclear family, the child "f" from an "Arab family" was described as "very shy and stuffy in the testing situation. She did not say anything unless asked directly, and therefore it was actually impossible to complete the test."[47] The teacher described her as "just below average", something that "corresponds well with the non-verbal intelligence test."[48]

In the description of the pupils, the different types of test results and impressions of the teacher assessments were mixed with explanations pointing to different "norms" and different "cultural patterns" and the parents as the central bearers of this problem. An example is the description of the pupil called "c" with Turkish parents and the second-lowest intelligence score among the case study's pupils, who was also described by her teachers as "below average" in intelligence. The report concluded that

---

45 Bøgsted-Møller, *Kulturmøde*, 14.
46 Bøgsted-Møller, *Kulturmøde*, 15.
47 Bøgsted-Møller, *Kulturmøde*, 67.
48 Bøgsted-Møller, *Kulturmøde*, 33.

"c's difficulties coping subject matter-wise as well as socially should be described as an interplay between 'mental capacities', difficulties dealing with the sets of norms that apply here, the negative attitude and lack of support from the home, as well as the burden of domestic work and child care. This has not provided her with the incentive or the resources to open up to the world."[49]

The pupil 'I' from a "Pakistani family" was described as "a slightly tense, very industrious boy, of mediocre intelligence, who is strongly influenced by the cultural pattern of his homeland."[50]

As implied in the report title, cultural differences were considered central to understanding foreign language pupils. The report argued that whether the family came from a rural or an urban area was important. The former was associated with "strong religiosity in a more traditional sense", while the latter was assumed to be "more in harmony with a modern society."[51] "Cultural patterns," more specifically what was seen as traditional "life rules" associated with strong and thus non-modern religiosity, thus served as a central explanatory parameter. This was also the case in the critique of the non-verbal intelligence test, where culture served to explain what was perceived as a general slowness among the pupils: As non-Westerners, they had a different and slower pace and thus could not score high in the test. A critique of the norms of what was seen as Western and Danish culture and of modernity was thus mixed with a perception of traditional cultural patterns as below average subject matter-wise. Psychological as well as cultural assumptions ("traditional," non-modern) thus mixed in the professional language of classification produced in and surrounding the test practice.

Testing of Culture – Testing as a Cultural Problem

This entanglement between the psychological (psychometric) categories of assessment and cultural valuations is also mirrored in a case from the municipality of Aarhus, the second-largest city in Denmark after Copenhagen. In the fall of 1978, 26 Turkish girls between 12 and 14 years allegedly did not receive any education in the municipality.[52] Hence, in 1979, a specific education was offered to the girls and

49 Bøgsted-Møller, *Kulturmøde*, 26.
50 Bøgsted-Møller, *Kulturmøde*, 40; Buchardt 2016.
51 Bøgsted-Møller, *Kulturmøde*, 55. See also Mette Buchardt, "How did 'the Muslim Pupil' Become Muslim? Danish State Schooling and 'the Migrant Pupils' since the 1970s," in *Islam in Denmark. The Challenge of Diversity*, ed. Jørgen S. Nielsen (New York, NY: Lexington Books, 2011), 125f.
52 Inger Johansen, "En tyrkisk pigeklasse," *Unge indvandrere. LUFE-Tema*, no. 1 (Copenhagen: LUFE – Landsforeningen for Undervisere af Fremmedsprogede Elever, 1981), 24.

their parents. The special class that was then formed was, however, institutionally outside the *Folkeskole* and the municipal school administration, at the Foreign Worker Centre, and thus under the municipality's social and health administration. The curriculum was also different, since sewing and weaving were taught in addition to school subjects included in the national curriculum.[53]

According to an article in the journal *LUFE-Tema* published a couple of years later by the Association for Teachers of Foreign Language Pupils (LUFE),[54] the girls were "kept at home for traditional and religious reasons." They were, for example, not allowed to be in contact with boys, and they had to do household chores.[55] However, it turned out that "not only traditional and religious reasons, but also social" reasons formed part of why the girls had given up the Danish school system, e.g. the experience of defeat.[56]

Since there was no legal basis and thus no financing for the girls' form (*pigeklasse*) within the school system, cooperation with the municipal administration for social and health matters was crucial for the program's success. To secure an economic basis for the girls' form, a legal basis was found by combining the Act for Social Security and the so-called Observation Circular, concerning special needs education.[57] It also meant, however, that the form was organised as a special needs form, and that admission was granted through visitation by an educational psychologist, and thus through intelligence testing.

In LUFE-Tema, this procedure was criticised as transforming the pupil into "a psychological phenomenon" "simply for being a traditionally raised Turkish girl," but also because "the psychologists find it very difficult to test these children, because they come from a different culture than ours."[58] Among teachers of foreign language children, the perception of cultural difference was thus consolidated by means of testing, while the testing practice was criticised for its shortcomings when it came to sensitivity toward what was perceived as cultural difference.

---

53 *Aarhus Kommunes beretning 1979* (Viby J.: Marselis Tryk A/S, 1979), 233.
54 Landsforening for Undervisere af Fremmedsprogede Elever, also founded in 1979.
55 Johansen, "En tyrkisk pigeklasse," 24.
56 Johansen, "En tyrkisk pigeklasse," 25.
57 This also paved the way for moving the project into the school for voluntary youth educa-
    tion a couple of years later, Ungdomsskolenævnet, Beslutningsprotokol, referat [Coun-
    cil for Voluntary Youth Education, Protocol, minutes], 9 December 1982, 1970–1995,
    Århus Kommunale Skolevæsen, Århus Stadsarkiv [Aarhus Municipal School Depart-
    ment, Aarhus City Archive].
58 Johansen, "En tyrkisk pigeklasse," 24.

Simultaneously, a distinction between cultural problems (which were ascribed to the girls) and psychological problems was established.[59]

The examples from testing practices in respectively Copenhagen and Aarhus municipality during the 1970s show on the one hand that testing, not least non-verbal intelligence testing, was used and simultaneously problematised in relation to children of labour migrants. Objectivity-aiming test forms were in educational and administrative practices used intertwined with classical evaluation forms known from classroom practices, consultation with parents and staff meetings. Across these forms of assessment, a stable pattern was, however, that the perceived cultural difference of the children served as a parameter of explanation.

Concluding Remarks: Juxtaposing The Two Cases

Examining the two cases, we can make a number of observations about the educational testing of culturally deviant children in a welfare state setting. It has become clear that educational testing was used as a cultural marker in both cases. In the Greenlandic case, testing was conducted according to the canonisation of Danish culture in a post-colonial setting, where decolonisation meant Danification, and culture became a tool able to set the standards of educational proficiency. In the labour migrant case, testing was a central tool in the locally based pedagogical strategies that had started to develop towards the "new" group of pupils from the 1970s onwards. Here, the test-based classification language was mixed with perceptions of foreign language pupils as being culturally different across forms of assessment: in the classical subjective forms of evaluation statements as well as in the — critical — use of for instance non-verbal intelligence tests.

Looking specifically at the production of meaning surrounding the use of tests — or the culturality of the selection and differentiation process — it is clear that the allure of objectivity associated with the tests was a central component of their use. Although the use of testing was contested in both cases because of doubts whether the test batteries could actually capture the culturally different children, the psychometric form of knowledge represented by the test results carried a high level of currency, especially in the Greenlandic case, but also in relation to the pedagogical knowledge base represented by the local schools and teacher evaluations. In the labour migrant case, the severe criticism of objective testing raised since the 1960s seems to have sedimented in the practices, causing ambiguities that gave rise to a clash between categories of assessment and cultural

---

59   Buchardt and Fabrin, "PISA Etnisk," 156.

valuations. The core issue under debate was the explanatory power of the concept of intelligence versus the concept of culture; it was in many ways a clash between an ideal of objectivity versus an ideal of holistic contextual understandings drawing distinctions between modernity and tradition inspired by cultural sociology.

Nevertheless, in reality, these ideals were not clear-cut but, rather, entangled. Even though language difference was the specific obstacle and problem for the Danish school authorities, psychological and cultural explanations seemed just as central. In addition, the critique of the non-verbal intelligence test as being culturally biased in the labour migrant case seems to have consolidated the perception of cultural difference as a main explanatory factor, but it did not seem to have prevented its use when describing and creating pedagogical interventions directed towards the target group.

These entanglements reached an even higher level of complexity when used in relation to the political-pragmatic knowledge in evidence in both cases and that had another type of currency, namely, the practical functionality of the education system as well as the political goal-setting in light of the resources available. This was for instance the case with regard to the use of testing in relation to the preparation program, the reception classes, and special needs education. Hence, what seems to have fuelled the use of testing in both cases was also the question of the distribution and prioritisation of economic resources, where science-based descriptions of the population had been a central tool in the Danish welfare state project since the 1950s.[60] The testing practices can thus also be understood as science-based social engineering and economical micromanagement.

Although the cultural taxonomy of the post-colonial modernisation project was ubiquitous in the preparation program, its organisational and geographical structure — with remote local schools, a central school directorate, and a ministry for Greenland in Copenhagen — sometimes created conflicts of interest. These conditions created entanglements and ambiguities united under the umbrella of Danification and modernisation project that created a distinct assessment culture underpinning the call for social engineering in terms of the Greenlandic child, but which also involved paradoxes centred on social inequality and the issue of belonging to the Danish welfare state.

A different but comparable type of paradox was at stake concerning the children of the labour migrants. Here, municipal and local school authorities needed to act since, on the one hand, the children of migrants had the same right to education

---

60   Else Hansen and Leon Jespersen, eds., *Samfundsplanlægning i 1950'erne. Tradition eller tilløb?* (Copenhagen: Museum Tusculanums Forlag, 2009).

as other children but, on the other hand, the medium language of the welfare state school for all was not fully spoken or understood by all the children. Reception classes and the use of special needs education legislation thus became part of the local solution to a dilemma that was not fully resolved through state policy at the central administrative level. In this local context, intelligence testing and evaluation with regard to (traditional) culture seem to have become parameters just as central to the measurement of progress as Danish language skills and, thus, to the measurement of the capacity of the deviant child in its integration into the normal welfare state school, that is, with Danish language as the medium of instruction. The question of language was thus bound up with and sometimes seems to have been overshadowed by the question of cultural norms and intelligence.

The main issue in terms of schooling on the periphery of the Danish welfare state as it emerges from the analysis is thus, in both cases, the construction of cultural differentiation versus homogenisation in light of decolonisation and the handling of 'the global'. These two strands became entangled in a way that gave rise to an assessment culture created not least by the assessment of cultural difference and which served the wider purpose of shoring up the functionality of the Danish welfare state.

Sources

Aarhus Stadsarkiv
[Aarhus City Archive]
Kultureqarnermut, Ilinniartitaanermut, Ilisimatusarnermut, Ilageeqarnermullu Naalakkersuisoqarfik
[Department for Culture, Education, Research, and Church] KIIIN Archive

Literature

Aarhus Kommunes beretning 1979. Viby J.: Marselis Tryk A/S, 1979.

Berthelsen, Christian. *Den grønlandske skole gennem 20 år*. Skoledirektøren for Grønland, 1972.

Buchardt, Mette. "Schooling the Muslim family. The Danish school system, foreign worker children and their parents from the 1970s to the early 1990s." *The Finnish Centre of Excellence in Historical Research: History of Society: Re-thinking Finland 1400–2000* (2018 in press).

–. *Kulturforklaring: Uddannelseshistorier om muslimskhed*. Copenhagen: Tiderne Skifter, 2016.

–. "How did 'the Muslim Pupil' Become Muslim? Danish State Schooling and 'the Migrant Pupils' since the 1970s." In *Islam in Denmark. The Challenge of Diversity*, edited by Jørgen S. Nielsen, 115–42. New York, NY: Lexington Books, 2011.

–. "'The Immigrant Pupil' between 'Cultural Difference' and Division of Labour in the Danish Curriculum since the 1970s," paper presented at the annual meeting of the American Educational Research Association, San Francisco, California, 28 April–1 May 2013.

–. *Pedagogised Muslimness. Religion and Culture as Identity Politics in the Classroom*. Münster/New York: Waxmann, 2014.

Buchardt, Mette, and Liv Fabrin. "PISA Etnisk i lyset af tosprogede elevers skoleog testhistorie." In *Test og prøvelser. Oprindelse, udvikling, aktualitet*, edited by Karen Egedal Andreasen et al., 141–65. Aalborg: Aalborg Universitetsforlag, 2015.

Buchardt, Mette, Pirjo Markkola, and Heli Valtonen. "Education and the Making of the Nordic Welfare States." In *Education, State and Citizenship. A Perspective in the Nordic Welfare State History*, edited by Mette Buchardt, Pirjo Markkola, and Heli Valtonen, 7–30. Helsinki: NordWel Studies in Historical Welfare State Research, 2013.

Bøgsted-Møller, Niels. *Kulturmøde i folkeskolen. En undersøgelse over fremmedsprogede elever i det københavnske skolesystem*. Copenhagen: Københavns Kommunale Skolevæsen, Forsøgsafdelingen, January 1976.

Dansk Institut for Internationale Studier. *Afvikling af Grønlands kolonistatus, 1945–54 — en historisk udredning*. Copenhagen: Dansk Institut for Internationale Studier, 2007.

Grandy, Gina. "Instrumental Case Study." In *Encyclopedia of Case Study Research*, edited by A. J. Mills, G. Durepos, and E. Wiebe, 474–76. Thousand Oaks, CA: Sage Publications, 2010.

Gundara, Jagdish. *Interculturalism, Education and Inclusion*. London, UK: Sage, 2004.

Hamre, Bjørn, and Christian Ydesen. "The Ascent of Educational Psychology in Denmark in the Interwar Years." *Nordic Journal of Educational History* 1, no. 2 (2014): 87–111.

Hansen, Else, and Leon Jespersen, eds. *Samfundsplanlægning i 1950'erne. Tradition eller tilløb?* Copenhagen: Museum Tusculanums Forlag, 2009.

Henriksen, Holger. "Skole og kulturmøde i Grønland II." *Grønland* 3 (1970): 85–96.

Hill, Susannah-Marie et al. *Dansk for fremmedsprogede*. Volumes: Lærerens bog; Læseblade; Øvelsesblade. Copenhagen: Lærerforeningernes Materialeudvalg, 1973 [1972].

Jensen, Ernst. "Langt hjemmefra — grønlandske skolebørn i Danmark i 1960'erne og 1970'erne." *Grønland* 4 (1997): 150–54.

–. *Langt hjemmefra – grønlandske børn på skoleophold i Danmark i 1960'erne og 1970'erne*. Nuuk: Atuagkat, 2001.

Johansen, Inger. "En tyrkisk pigeklasse." *Unge indvandrere. LUFE-Tema* no. 1 Copenhagen: LUFE — Landsforeningen for Undervisere af Fremmedsprogede Elever (1981): 24–26.

Jønsson, Heidi Vad. "I velfærdsstatens randområde. Socialdemokratiets integrationspolitik 1960'erne til 2000'erne". PhD diss., Department of History and Centre for Welfare State Research, University of Southern Denmark, 2013.

Kleivan, Inger. "Tosprogsproblematikken." In *Fremmedarbejderpolitik – en bog om fremmedarbejderproblematikken*, edited by Jan Hjarnø, Torben Lundbæk, and Sven Skovmand, 176–79. Copenhagen: Mellemfolkeligt Samvirke, 1973.

Madaus, George, Michael Russell, and Jennifer Higgins. *The Paradoxes of High-Stakes Testing*. Charlotte, NC: Information Age Publishing, 2009.

Odde, Birgit, Mogens Jakobsen, and Kjeld Kjeldsen. *Regning for fremmedsprogede elever*. Vol. I, Regnebogen; Vol. II, Test og øvelsesblade; Vol. III, Facitliste. Copenhagen: Lærerforeningernes Materialeudvalg, 1973.

Olsen, Tupaarnaq Rosing. *I Skyggen Af Kajakkerne: Grønlands Politiske Historie 1939-79*. Nuuk: Atuagkat, 2005.

Padovan-Özdemir, Marta and Christian Ydesen. "Professional Encounters with the Post-WWII Immigrant: A Privileged Prism for Studying the Shaping of European Welfare Nation-States." *Paedagogica Historica* 52, no. 5: 423–37.

Rizvi, Fazal, and Bob Lingard. *Globalizing Education Policy*. London, New York: Routledge, 2010.

Schmidt, Garbi. *Nørrebros indvandringshistorie 1885–2010*. Copenhagen: Museum Tusculanums Forlag, 2015.

Shohamy, Elana. "Assessment in Multicultural Societies: Applying Democratic Principles and Practices to Language Testing." In *Critical Pedagogies and Language Learning*, edited by Bonny Norton and Kelleen Toohey. Cambridge, UK: Cambridge University Press, 2004.

Spelling, Kaj. *Miljøets indflydelse på intelligensudviklingen — specielt med henblik på 'racemæssige' forskelle*. Copenhagen: Nyt Nordisk Forlag, Arnold Busck, 1963.

Stake, Robert E. *The Art of Case Study Research*. Thousand Oaks, CA: Sage Publications, 1995.

Sørensen, Axel Kjær. *Danmark-Grønland i det 20. århundrede. En historisk oversigt*. Copenhagen: Nyt Nordisk Forlag, Arnold Busck, 1983.

Undervisningsministeriet [Ministry of Education]. *Cirkulære om undervisning i folkeskolen af udenlandske børn*, Circular no. 293, 30 November 1970.

Undervisningsministeriet. Bekendtgørelse om folkeskolens undervisning af fremmed-sprogede elever, Undervisningsministeriets bekendtgørelse, no. 179, 8 March 1976.

Ydesen, Christian. The Rise of High-Stakes Educational Testing in Denmark, 1920–1970. Frankfurt am Main: Peter Lang Verlag, 2011.

Michaela Vogt

Primary School Attendance or Special Education: Historical Comparative Analysis of Student Files from the German Democratic Republic and the Federal Republic of Germany

Practices of assessing students are as old as schools themselves, and have always been present within schooling systems in a rich diversity of forms. Assessment practices serve a variety of ends and can reveal cultural and historical specificities. The suitability of one form of assessment, long-established in Germany, has in recent years come indirectly into question in connection with debates on inclusion: the assessment designed to determine whether a student is suited to the regular school system, or whether he or she should instead attend a special education school.[1] Referred to as a special education intake procedure (SEIP, *Hilfsschulaufnahmeverfahren*), this form of assessment comprises the process by which various professionals evaluate the student before a final decision is reached regarding his or her ability to attend a regular school versus his or her need for special education. By entering information into a form, every professional involved in this procedure produces an evaluation, all of which proceed the final decision in the course of the SEIP. Both these professional evaluations (*Professionelle Gutachten*) as well as the final schooling decision are entered into the personal student file (*Schülerpersonalbogen*) compiled for each assessed student.

Whether the SEIP provides access to learning opportunities that adequately address the needs of individual students, thus constituting a justifiable alternative to inclusive schooling, or whether it above all stands for a process of arbitrary exclusion from regular schooling, hinges on the degree to which it leads to reliable and consistent final schooling decisions. This question can only be answered retrospectively, and with reference to adequate sources. From a historical perspective, it takes on a special interest in light of the divided history of Germany between 1945 and 1990 based on the contrasting social systems and socially conditioned

---

1   In Germany, these represent two institutionally and professionally distinct school systems. Thus special education is offered in the special education school system. A transfer from the regular school system into the system of special education schools is rather negatively connoted in the public perception.

specifics of the SEIP between East Germany (GDR) and West Germany (FRG). An inter-German comparison can reveal specific features of the assessment of students during the SEIP in each German state, and can shed light on connections between wider societal influences and the outcomes of the SEIP. To date, the SEIP has not been investigated from this perspective for either the GDR or the FRG.[2] In general, studies have tended to ignore this specific feature of the German context, restricting instead their focus to the formal course of the procedure.[3]

Thus, this article addresses the SEIP by way of an inter-German comparative perspective between the FRG and the GDR focusing primary schools[4] as a variant of the regular schooling system and assistance schools as a variant of the special education schools. The basis for this are findings derived from an ongoing investigation of the SEIP during the period 1958 to 1978.[5] The professional evaluations from the FRG and the GDR used here as source material (see point 3) are analysed with a view to determining whether the schooling decisions about the ability to attend primary school, or the need for special education, reached in the SEIP and documented in students' personal files were made consistently, or whether they instead reveal the existence of a diachronically shifting 'border zone', characterised by ambiguity and inconsistency in reaching the decision (see point 4 and 5). Before engaging in depth with the student files, however, a brief introduction to the historical context to the SEIP in the FRG and the GDR will be provided (see point 2).

---

2   See e.g. Mechthild Gomolla and Frank-Olaf Radtke, *Institutionelle Diskriminierung: Die Herstellung ethnischer Differenz in der Grundschule* (Wiesbaden: Verlag für Sozialwissenschaften, 2009).

3   See e.g. Thomas R. Hofsäss, *Die Überweisung von Schülern auf die Hilfsschule und Schule für Lernbehinderte: Eine historisch-vergleichende Untersuchung* (Berlin: Edition Marhold im Wissenschaftsverlag Volker Spiess, 1993); Birgit Werner, *Sonderpädagogik im Spannungsfeld zwischen Ideologie und Tradition: Zur Geschichte der Sonderpädagogik unter Berücksichtigung der Hilfsschulpädagogik in der SBZ und der DDR zwischen 1945 und 1952* (Hamburg: Kovac, 1999).

4   In both the FRG and the GDR, the primary school is the first stage of the regular school system. During the period being studied, it included the first three to four years of a child's schooling. In both German states, attendance was mandatory for all children from the age of six. Since the majority of assessments in the SEIP are documented for these grades, the study focuses on these first years of schooling.

5   The timeframe chosen seemed appropriate in the context of historical developments in both German states (see point 2) and derived from the density of files on hand in the source basis for this study (see point 3).

The SEIP in the Historical Context of the FRG and the GDR

For both the FRG and the GDR, the period under investigation falls into two phases. While these phases exhibit different key features and diverge in terms of the central developments in both the German states, they parallel each other in that the transition between phases in both cases occurs in the early 1970s.

In West Germany the period under investigation 1958 to 1978 falls into two phases, one based on new guidelines for the organisation of the system of special schools and one dominated by a shift of focus within educational policy. Therefore the years 1958 to 1971 as the first phase were marked by efforts within educational policy to further expand the system of special schools and to standardize its legally fragmented situation with central guidelines.[6] In 1960 the Education Ministers Conference (KMK)[7] published a set of "guidelines for the organisation of special schools,"[8] representing the first set of uniform recommendations for the West German special school system, ratified by all of West Germany's federal states, in the post-war period. These recommendations also defined specific groups of students for whom distinct types of special schools[9] would be responsible. In general, according to the KMK guidelines, twelve types of special schools were to be responsible for those children or young people exhibiting a physical or intellectual disability and who, because of learning difficulties or disruptive behaviour, hindered or endangered the development of their fellow students. As one of the types of special schools, the assistance school was explicitly intended to take in children for whom, on the specific basis of intellectual disability[10], the regular primary school, with its pedagogical and educational methods, was not suitable.[11] Orienting itself towards the "memorandum on legislation for a system of special schools,"[12] which the Association of German Special Schools (VDS), a professional

6 The cause of this legally fragmented situation is the federal system in the FRG, in which authority over educational policy rests with the individual states.

7 Institutions that operate across the states, such as the KMK, cannot issue policy, but merely provide recommendations that the individual states may choose to follow.

8 See KMK, *Gutachten zur Ordnung des Sonderschulwesens* (Bonn: J.F. Carthaus, 1960).

9 The KMK guidelines enumerate a total of twelve different types of special schools (see KMK, *Gutachten zur Ordnung des Sonderschulwesens*, 9).

10 This could take the form of disability in the following areas: psychic, kinesthetic and motor, attention and concentration, and task completion and design (see KMK, *Gutachten zur Ordnung des Sonderschulwesens*, 27).

11 See KMK, *Gutachten zur Ordnung des Sonderschulwesens*.

12 See VDS, "Denkschrift zu einem Gesetz über das heilpädagogische Sonderschulwesen," *Zeitschrift für Heilpädagogik* 6 (1955): 44–55.

association of special educators, had already provided to all West German state education ministries in 1954, the KMK guidelines also dealt with rules regarding the individual types of special schools, concentrating particularly on the formal course of intake procedures into these various types of special schools. In line with the recommendations of the VDS memorandum, the intake procedure for assistance schools were to be initiated by the primary school[13] being attended by the student deemed potentially in need for special education.[14] The assessment itself was to be carried out by the assistance school, while the binding, final schooling decision was to be reached by the lowest local educational oversight authority.[15] The KMK guidelines supplemented the VDS memorandum on several points: the VDS proposals regarding the course of the SEIP were expanded by including the binding participation of the school doctor as well as the child's legal guardians. Legal guardians were, however, not given a decision-making role in the intake procedure, but were merely entitled to receive advice from the professional evaluators participating in the SEIP, as well as having the opportunity to make a personal statement.[16] The KMK guidelines furthermore established the areas to be assessed: performance in school to date, projected performance capacity, intellectual ability, and social behaviour. They also required that all observation, examination, and assessment results were documented and recorded in writing by the professional evaluators taking part.[17] The KMK guidelines did not, however, regulate entirely the question of assessment design. Hesse, the federal state from which the professional evaluations being examined in this study originate (see point pint 3), adopted the recommendations of the KMK without modifications to the Hessian mandatory school attendance law of 1961 and the supplementary

---

13 The formal procedure of a SEIP was the basis for admitting students into other forms of special education. However, in the cases of children with sensory disabilities, the process would be initiated by the parents or family doctor, not the school (see KMK, *Gutachten zur Ordnung des Sonderschulwesens.*).

14 See VDS, "Gesetz über das heilpädagogische Sonderschulwesen."; KMK, *Gutachten zur Ordnung des Sonderschulwesens.*

15 See Ibid.

16 See KMK, *Gutachten zur Ordnung des Sonderschulwesens.*

17 See Ibid.

procedural regulations for the SEIP.[18] The KMK recommendations were again found in the new version of that law passed in 1969.[19]

The years following 1972 and thus the second phase included a reform of the West German educational system and were marked by a rethinking of educational policy regarding the separate system of special schools. As a result, in 1972, the KMK published a set of "recommendations for the organisation of special schools."[20] The recommendations did not expand on the content of the 1960 guidelines regarding the SEIP and its implementation, but rather dealt thoroughly with the question of integrative schooling within the system of regular schools.[21] This issue was also taken up by the German Educational Council[22] in its 1973 recommendations on the "pedagogical support for children and young people with disabilities or at risk of disability,"[23] again, without affecting the formal structure of the SEIP. Because of a shift of focus within educational policy, the SEIP would not be subject to any further structural reform. In the case of Hesse, this ultimately resulted in the fact that the mandatory school attendance law of 1969, with its attendant procedural regulations regarding the SEIP, remained the sole basis and reference point for the implementation of the SEIP across the entire remainder of the time period under investigation.[24] Nonetheless, the recommendations for integrative schooling produced by the KMK and the German Educational Council

---

18 See Kultusministerium Hessen, "Hessisches Schulpflichtgesetz 17.5.1961," in *Gesetz und Verordnungsblatt für das Land Hessen (GVBL)*, ed. Hessische Staatskanzlei (Wiesbaden: Wiesbadener Kurier, 1961), 69–72; Karl-Heinz Hevekerl, *Die Einweisung in die Hilfsschule: Rechtsvorschriften und Grundsatzentscheidungen der Gerichte* (Berlin-Charlottenburg: Marhold, 1965).

19 See Kultusministerium Hessen, "Hessisches Schulpflichtgesetz 30.05.1969," in *Gesetz und Verordnungsblatt für das Land Hessen (GVBL)*, ed. Hessische Staatskanzlei (Wiesbaden: Wiesbadener Kurier, 1961), 104–108.

20 See KMK, *Empfehlung zur Ordnung des Sonderschulwesens* (Nienburg, Weser: Schulze, 1972).

21 See Ibid.

22 The German Educational Council is a panel that existed from 1965 to 1975, made up of scientists who advised the FRG in educational matters and who suggested numerous changes to the school system, its curricula and institutional structure (see Klaus Hüfner and Jens Naumann, *Konjunkturen der Bildungspolitik in der Bundesrepublik Deutschland, Bd. I: Der Aufschwung (1960–1967)* (Stuttgart: Klett, 1977).

23 See Deutscher Bildungsrat, *Empfehlungen der Bildungskommission: Zur pädagogischen Förderung behinderter und von Behinderung bedrohter Kinder und Jugendlicher* (Bonn: Deutscher Bildungsrat, 1973).

24 See Kultusministerium Hessen, "Schulpflichtgesetz 30.05.1969."

could have had the effect in Hesse of increasing the number of students deemed able to attend primary school in SEIPs from the early 1970s on. The sources examined in this study demonstrate this to have been the case (see fig. 1).[25]

In the GDR, the diachronic changes undergone by the SEIP over the period under investigation can also be traced in two phases, one lasting until 1972 with primarily school-structural and ideological changes and another from 1973 to 1978 with a general upheaval in the practice of referring children for intake into the system of special schools: The first legislation in the GDR regarding the referral of individual students to certain types of special schools – and thus to assistance schools as a type of special schools – was issued in the early 1950s. The SEIP was also regulated by this legislation for the first time following the founding of the East German state[26] in 1949. These regulations were contained within the 1951 "directive regarding the schooling of children and young people with considerable physical and psychic deficiencies," which defined the existence of physical and psychic shortcomings, as well as deficient thinking processes, as the necessary prerequisites for transfer into an assistance school. In addition, the 1953 "regulation regarding the implementation of intake procedures for assistance schools" played an important role, defining the concrete implementation of the SEIP and the use of student personal files as the standardized documentation.[27] Both of these provisions were issued in the period before the fundamental structural and curricular reorganisation of the East German school system. This took place in the context of the so-called "antifascist, democratic construction"[28] of the GDR state according to the Soviet model and brought about a restructuring and reorientation of

---

25 See Michaela Vogt, Margarete Götz and Lisa Sauer, "Professionelle Gutachten und schuladministrative Entscheidung im Hilfsschulaufnahmeverfahren in der BRD," *Vierteljahresschrift für Heilpädagogik und ihre Nachbargebiete (VHN)* 85 (2016): 78–80.

26 From 1952, the GDR was structured as a centralised state with 14 administrative precincts. In contrast to federally-organised West Germany, authority over the entire school system rested in the hands of the People's Ministry of Education, the head of which also sat on the central committee of the SED, the ruling party in the GDR (see Gert Geißler, *Geschichte des Schulwesens in der Sowjetischen Besatzungszone und in der Deutschen Demokratischen Republik 1945 bis 1962* (Frankfurt am Main: Peter Lang, 2000).

27 See MfV, "Verordnung über die Beschulung und Erziehung von Kindern und Jugendlichen mit wesentlichen physischen oder psychischen Mängeln. Vom 5. Oktober 1951," GBl.Nr.122/51, in BBF/DIPF DPZI 2978 (Bibliothek für Bildungsgeschichtliche Forschung des Deutschen Instituts für Internationale Pädagogische Forschung). Hofsäss, *Überweisung von Schülern auf die Hilfsschule und Schule für Lernbehinderte.*

28 Winfried Baudisch, Bodo Bröse and Chananin S. Samski, *Hilfsschulpädagogik* (Berlin: Volk und Wissen Volkseigener Verlag, 1987), 17.

the regular school system alongside a quantitative expansion of the special school system. The basis for these changes was the "law on the socialist development of schooling in the German Democratic Republic"[29] of 1959.[30] As soon as 1965, the entire educational system of the GDR was again fundamentally reorganised[31]; however, the special school system would not be significantly altered until the passage in 1968 of the "fifth provision for the implementation of the law on the unitary socialist education system." The principal result of this new legislation was the expansion of assistance schools by means of its reorganisation into a tripartite system, which nonetheless remained part of the larger system of special schools. Also connected to this implementation provision was a more thorough engagement with the task of matching certain groups of students to various types of special schools, which had only been roughly formalised in the early 1950s.[32]

The second phase of the period under investigation, beginning in 1973, was shaped by new regulations laid out in the "guidelines for the intake of children into assistance schools."[33] The tripartite structure into which assistance schools

29 See MfV, "Über die sozialistische Entwicklung des Schulwesens in der Deutschen Demokratischen Republik. Thesen des Zentralkomitees. Vom 17. Januar 1959 (Auszüge)," in *Dokumente zur Geschichte des Schulwesens in der Deutschen Demokratischen Republik, Teil 2: 1956 1967/68, 1. Halbband, Reihe: Monumenta Paedagogica,* ed. Kommission für deutsche Erziehungs- und Schulgeschichte der Deutschen Akademie der Wissenschaften zu Berlin (Berlin: Volk und Wissen Volkseigener Verlag, 1969), 180–193.

30 The law of 1959 brought about the structural differentiation among the nine various types of special schools that had been in place since 1952. It also effected adaptations within teacher training (see MfV, "Anordnung über den organisatorischen Aufbau des Sonderschulwesens. Vom 5. Juli 1952," Mbl. 52/102, in BBF/DIPF DPZI 2978; Sieglind Ellger-Rüttgardt, *Geschichte der Sonderpädagogik* (München: Reinhardt, 2008).

31 APW, *Das Bildungswesen der Deutschen Demokratischen Republik* (Berlin: Volk und Wissen Volkseigener Verlag, 1987).

32 See MfV, "Fünfte Durchführungsbestimmung zum Gesetz über das einheitliche sozialistische Bildungssystem – Sonderschulwesen – Vom 20. Dezember 1968," in *Dokumente zur Geschichte des Schulwesens in der Deutschen Demokratischen Republik, Teil 3: 1968–1972/73, 1. Halbband, Reihe: Monumenta Paedagogica, Bd. XVI/1,* ed. Kommission für deutsche Erziehungsund Schulgeschichte der Deutsche Akademie der Wissenschaften zu Berlin (Berlin: Volk und Wissen Volkseigner Verlag, 1974), 110–117.

33 MfV, "Richtlinie zur Aufnahme von Kindern in die Hilfsschule. Vom 2. Februar 1973," in *Dokumente zur Geschichte des Schulwesens in der Deutschen Demokratischen Republik, Teil 3: 1968–1972/73, 2. Halbband, Reihe: Monumenta Paedagogica, Bd. XVI/2,* ed. Kommission für deutsche Erziehungs- und Schulgeschichte der Deutschen Akademie

had been divided was replaced with a dual system. Furthermore, the position of the assistance school within the system of special schools was further consolidated. Concerning the SEIP, the new guidelines on the one hand brought about an increasing centralisation of the SEIP and a growing influence of state organs. Thus, a so-called "intake commission" was introduced, which would issue its own recommendation about the further schooling placement preceding the final schooling decision.[34] On the other hand, the new guidelines formulated explicit criteria for children subject to assessment in an SEIP, based on Soviet developmental and pedagogical models.[35] In addition, the guidelines legally defined which diagnostic instruments were to be used in the SEIP, the main purpose of which was to make possible extended observations designed to produce a total personality assessment. Prior to 1973, primary and assistance school teachers had enjoyed considerable freedom in choosing which diagnostic tools to employ.[36] Thus, the 1973 guidelines formed the central framework for aspects of policy dealing with school structure, for the implementation of the SEIP and for the definition of student groups deemed in need for transfer into assistance schools. Despite another regulation issued in 1984, they remained essentially unchanged until the end of the GDR.[37]

---

der Wissenschaften zu Berlin (Berlin: Volk und Wissen Volkseigener Verlag, 1975), 667–671.

34   This intake commission, to which both teachers and representatives of the education administration belong, would determine whether sufficient efforts were undertaken to support the student in the regular school prior to the opening of the SEIP. In addition, they would compile all the professional evaluations submitted and add to their schooling recommendations. Schooling decisions were thus substantially influenced by educational policy actors (see e.g. Ute Geiling, "Schulfähigkeit und Einschulungspraxis in der DDR: Ein Rückblick im Spannungsfeld von Förderung und Ausgrenzung," in *Vielfalt durch gute Ordnung im Anfangsunterricht*, ed. Annedore Prengel (Opladen: Leske und Budrich, 1999), 161–219.

35   See e.g. MfV, "Richtlinie zur Aufnahme von Kindern in die Hilfsschule. Vom 2. Februar 1973."; Autorenkollektiv, *Beiträge zur Verhinderung des Zurückbleibens* (Berlin: Volk und Wissen Volkseigener Verlag, 1975).

36   See MfV, "Richtlinie zur Aufnahme von Kindern in die Hilfsschule. Vom 2. Februar 1973."; Baudisch, Bröse and Samski, *Hilfsschulpädagogik*.

37   See e.g. Hofsäss, *Überweisung von Schülern auf die Hilfsschule und Schule für Lernbehinderte*. See Michaela Vogt, Margarete Götz and Agneta Floth, "Professionelle Gutachten und schuladministrative Entscheidung in Hilfsschulanahmeverfahren in der DDR," *Vierteljahresschrift für Heilpädagogik und ihre Nachbargebiete (VHN)* 85 (2016): 78–80.

Archival Sources in the FRG and the GDR

The personal student files from the FRG and the GDR used as archival sources in the investigation exhibit overwhelming convergences and can be regarded as comparable. Besides educational biographical data about the children and their school career they also contain all results of the SEIP documented in several professional evaluations as well as the final schooling decision about the need for special education or the ability to attend primary school. Regarding the involved professionals in the SEIP, there are also high similarities between the two countries. In the FRG as well as in the GDR there were always one primary school teacher, one of the assistance school and one medical evaluating the children during the SEIP.[38] In the FRG, also the primary school principal and since 1964 the assistance school principle wrote down their own additional statement. In the GDR, a psychological evaluation and a politically influenced recommendation on the further school attendance were added since 1974. The documentation of the SEIP in the student files always ends with the final decision whether the child was able to attend the regular school or needed to visit a special education school.

Concerning the FRG, the archived student files originate from an assistance school in Frankfurt am Main. This collection of files is well suited to serve as a source base for investigation, particularly owing to its density and continuity. It encompasses 910 student files from yearly assessments in the period 1958 to 1978, referring both to primary school students who were placed in assistance schools as well as to students allowed to remain in primary schools by means of a SEIP. Student files on students in need for special education exist for all of the assessment years under investigation. These furthermore outnumber the files on students allowed to remain in primary school, especially for the years 1958 to 1971. Files for students considered able to continue to attend primary school are available for nearly all of the assessment years while the number of such files increases somewhat over the period 1970 to 1978 relative to the preceding 12 years (see fig. 1).

---

38 The primary school teacher was asked to assess basic scholastic knowledge (i.a. reading and writing), intellectual abilities, somatic-psychic development, and the child's social surroundings. This information would also be compiled in the evaluations provided by the assistance school teacher, but would be supplemented with judgements of the child's thinking capacities, attention, and concentration. The medical evaluation focused largely on the child's physical condition.

Fig. 1: Number of student files (Y-Axis) per assessment year (X-Axis) differentiated according to the final schooling decision for the FRG-project

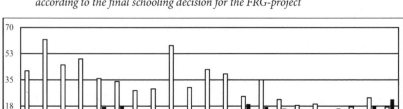

The East German student files come from a local school and are archived in Görlitz, a city with 54.000 inhabitants close to the border to Poland. The data evaluation has revealed that 615 of these student files are relevant for the purposes of this study. The number of files conducted in the SEIP per assessment year varies widely. In an overview, you can see the changing frequency at which files appear over the course of the period under investigation. There are consistently more cases deemed in need for special education than capable of attending primary school over the period studied. In some years, the existing gaps regarding the cases retained in primary education are obvious but will hopefully be filled by further archival investigations (see fig. 2).

Fig. 2: Number of student files (Y-Axis) per assessment year (X-Axis) differentiated according to the final schooling decision for the GDR-project

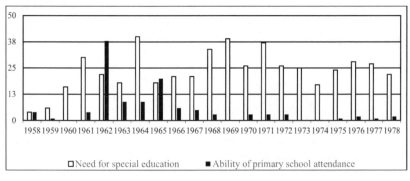

Theoretical Basis of a 'Border Zone' between Primary School Attendance and Special Education

Both source bases are well-suited for analysing the consistency of the schooling decisions made in the FRG and the GDR. To this end, however, certain basic theoretical assumptions are necessary that can serve as a reference for measuring consistencies or inconsistencies that may be present. The idea of the 'border zone' stands at the heart of the theory of objects being employed.

The definition of this key term is oriented towards Link's (1997) theory of 'normalism' (in German: *Normalismustheorie*), while his idea of a 'border of normality' has only been adopted partially. Because of the differences here vis-à-vis Link, the term 'border of normality' is replaced for the purposes of this study with the term 'border zone'. The following assumptions are determining for this term:

- The 'border zone' spans on the one hand the definable space in which decisions regarding students' ability to attend primary school versus their need for special education accumulate and cannot be consistently differentiated.
- This 'border zone' on the other hand is itself defined by boundary lines that shift over time, expanding or contracting.

The professional evaluations, which are part of the proclaimed 'border zone', can be characterised by the use of Wittgenstein's idea of "family resemblances" (in German: *Familienähnlichkeiten*) (1958).[39] According to Wittgenstein, members of a family are not characterised by identical features, but rather exhibit similar traits or combinations thereof. In other words, family members can differ from one another on the basis of individual characteristics. As a result, the professional evaluations produced with reference to a single student under assessment belong to the same "family," when they comprise similar traits or clusters of traits, which here are understood as attributions or combinations of attributions. On the basis of these professional evaluations student files belonging to the same family become part of the 'border zone' itself, as soon as the assessed students within that family are not constantly classified as able to attend primary school or as in need for special education. Hence, similar traits or clusters of traits lead to variable schooling decisions.

To link the research results about the 'border zone' with the social and cultural content and its changings over time, the 'border zone' can be seen as socially constructed. According to the assumptions of social constructivism in the sense of

---

39 See Ludwig Wittgenstein, *Philosophische Untersuchungen* (Oxford: Basil Blackwell, 1958).

Berger and Luckmann (1969),[40] the attributions contained in the students' reports and therefore the 'border zone' identified is regarded as knowledge produced and shared by a defined group of people, which act in a specific social and cultural content. Furthermore, the students' reports were not publicly accessible but only to the persons involved in the SEIP.

Toward the possible Characterisation of a 'Border Zone' by way of Individual Case Analysis

In the following section, one example each of a student deemed in need for special education and a student deemed able to attend regular primary school will be presented for both the FRG and the GDR, in the sense of an analysis of their personal student files. These cases will be compared separately for the FRG and the GDR and then together as a set of four. The cases selected here, for both the FRG and the GDR, indicate that they, after Wittgenstein (1958),[41] belong to a family and can thus provide insights into the form of the established 'border zone' as well as the shifts that it may undergo. After introducing the cases, they will be first discussed in terms of their ability to shed light on the theoretically established 'border zone'; further questions that are raised by the case analysis will then be addressed.

Individual Case Analysis from the FRG

In the FRG, Karl-Heinz, who despite the SEIP was ultimately deemed able to attend primary school and Günther, who was judged as in need for special education, both underwent the SEIP — in the former case in 1968[42] and in the latter in 1973.[43] Karl-Heinz is described by his primary school teacher as exhibiting weakness in verbal expression and in his ability to fluidly read words.[44] His knowledge of arithmetic is considered sufficient. In principle he is agreeable and willed, but is also easily distracted and exhibits a certain poverty of motivation to work. This behavioural and psychological underdevelopment stands in contrast to his strong physical stature. His parents are disappointed in his performance and are

---

40 See Peter L. Berger and Thomas Luckmann, *Die gesellschaftliche Konstruktion der Wirklichkeit: Eine Theorie der Wissenssoziologie* (Frankfurt am Main: Fischer Taschenbuch Verlag, 1969).

41 See Wittgenstein, *Philosophische Untersuchungen*.

42 See m_1960/58_Fra. (Schularchiv in Frankfurt am Main).

43 See m_1965/54_Fra.

44 See m_1960/58_Fra.

very concerned to encourage his progress in school. The assistance school teacher also notes that Karl-Heinz exhibits a slow working style and a lack of motivation to work, combined with a low intelligence, issuing a recommendation for transfer into an assistance school. Karl-Heinz's mother, however, objects. The school principal supports the assistance school teacher's evaluation, as Karl-Heinz has already repeated a grade in the regular school, his performance especially in writing remains deficient (while sufficient in arithmetic and reading), his work behaviour is slow and short-lived, and the child could experience frustration at home resulting from the immense pressure. He determines an intellectual retardation corresponding to 1.5 years and an IQ of 84. Similarly, the doctor diagnoses a childish and awkward style of behaviour and, against the wishes of the family, repeats the recommendation made by the assistance school teacher that Karl-Heinz should be transferred into an assistance school. Ultimately, however, Karl-Heinz is deemed able to remain in a regular primary school. The second case, Günther, has already attended extra lessons in his first year of primary school in order to compensate for having fallen behind the curriculum. His primary school teacher nonetheless ranks him as a student with a minimal vocabulary, difficulties in expressing himself, and difficulty in fluidly reading words.[45] He is however sufficient in arithmetic and is a quick writer. He is often passive during lessons and exhibits low motivation to accomplish tasks. Occasionally he disrupts the class during relaxed lessons. He is spoiled by his parents. The assistance school teacher confirms Günther's deficient performance as well as his notably deficient motivation and thus recommends transfer into an assistance school. Günther's mother objects to the transfer, however, because of the attendant stigma. The assistance school principal also notes infantile, unsettled behaviour, a lack of motivation and willingness to perform, combined with low intelligence (IQ of 88). He supports the assistance school teacher's recommendation that Günther should be transferred into an assistance school, again contradicting the wishes of Günther's mother. The school doctor attests Günther normal, age-appropriate physical development, accompanied by infantile behaviour and potentially lower boundary intellectual ability. He also recommends, against the parental appeal, a school transfer. As a result, Günther is designated in need for special education.

Looking beyond the single professional evaluations provided for each of these students, it is evident that both Karl-Heinz and Günther are similarly physically well-developed. They are both nonetheless seen by their primary school teachers as exhibiting a clearly low level of learning performance, particularly in the

---

45 See m_1965/54_Fra.

domain of reading. Neither one is directly and notably disruptive during lessons — Günther only being disruptive in relaxed lesson settings — but their behaviour is characterised by an obvious poverty of motivation and passivity and is deemed to be age-inappropriate. In addition, both have a similar IQ score — although Günther's is somewhat higher — and are therefore at the lower boundary of the spectrum of intellectual ability. Consequently, both Karl-Heinz and Günther are unambiguously classified in the single professional evaluations as in need for special education. Another parallel lies in the fact that in both cases the family objects to this recommendation. The only clear difference between the two cases is Günther's occasional disruption of certain lessons and the involvement of the grandmother as an additional family member in the case of Karl-Heinz. In light of these clear parallels, both in terms of the result of the assessment and the agreement among the professional recommendations during the SEIP regarding a school transfer, the fact that Karl-Heinz, the child with the lower IQ score, is ultimately able to remain in the primary school is thus surprising.

The results of the comparison of these two examples is very significant in terms of the 'border zone' this study seeks to locate. Two cases are presented here that, despite numerous parallels in terms of their content, result in differing schooling decisions. In addition, the time elapsed between these two cases is short enough to rule out the possibility that this discrepancy was caused by a significant general shift in the manner in which such schooling decisions were made. Such a shift could have been caused, for example, by new legislations that would have been taken into account in the SEIP. Thus the comparison of these examples raises especially the question of the family's engagement of family members in the face of the two students' largely similar situations. Only the study of further examples can clarify the question as to whether the family's engagement was taken into account in SEIPs in accordance with a certain, durable pattern, or whether this difference was largely a result of arbitrariness without meaningful contours.[46] The

---

46 A preliminary view of contextual documents in the FRG has revealed that, while parents were involved in the SEIP insofar as they were brought into discuss the matter and were advised on the procedure, they were legally unable to exert any influence on the final schooling decision. The decision-making authority lay solely with the school administrative bodies. Administrators were thus asked to exercise a certain degree of discretion with respect to the circumstances of each case. In terms of the 'border zone' concept, these guidelines could well have brought about inconsistencies (see e.g. KMK, *Gutachten zur Ordnung des Sonderschulwesens.*; Hevekerl, *Die Einweisung in die Hilfsschule*).

grandmother's involvement cannot tentatively be considered a meaningful factor, although the comparison of the above cases would suggest otherwise.

Individual Case Analysis from the GDR

Turning now to the examples selected from the GDR source material, Helmut underwent the SEIP in 1972, and was ultimately able to attend primary school.[47] Richard, on the other hand, was subjected to an SEIP in 1961 and found to be in need for special education.[48] According to the judgment of his primary school teacher, Helmut is deficient in his performance – in both verbal and writing tasks: he cannot compile phonetic units into words, he only recognises certain words by their shape, and cannot recount events in a logical order.[49] He can count forwards and backwards, but is unable to perform calculations with the numbers 1–10 without visual aids. Despite his deficient attention span and easily distracted nature, he can recite poems and songs he has learned, but cannot carry out tasks assigned to him by teachers, despite being in principle willing to do so. In certain situations, he will become ill-tempered or behave defiantly, which is often accompanied by physical confrontations with his fellow students. The assistance school teacher sees Helmut as a lively and open-minded student and notes that he is often happy to take on tasks, attributing his uncontrolled style of behaviour, and his tendency to overestimate himself, to his compensating for his low level of performance. The special educator, however, does not find reason to believe that Helmut's deficiencies as a student can be directly attributed to debility. Instead, the special educator sees in Helmut a deficient willingness to learn, accompanied by inadequate parental support and influence and therefore recommends that Helmut remains in primary school while being referred to a youth home.[50] The school doctor notes no physical or developmental irregularities in Helmut's case. To this is added the opinion of the psychologist, provided outside of the standard structure of the evaluation form. He regards Helmut as a poorly motivated, slow,

---

47 See VAGÖ (Verwaltungsarchiv der Stadt Görlitz) /SU 2047.

48 See VAGÖ/ SU 567.

49 See VAGÖ/SU 2047.

50 Youth and children's homes of various kinds existed in the GDR, set up according to age group, social setting and/or schooling opportunities, in both the regular and special school systems. In Helmut's case, it would have been a so-called "normal school home" (*Normalschulheim*) (Autorenkollektiv, *Das Bildungswesen der Deutschen Demokratischen Republik* (Berlin: Volk und Wissen Volkseigener Verlag, 1989), 85.), which was meant to take in children without parents or at risk of developmental setbacks and teach them according to the regular school system curriculum.

and easily distracted boy in whose case debility cannot be completely ruled out, recommends nonetheless that Helmut remains in primary school. Ultimately, Helmut is deemed as able to attend primary school. Richard, the second case, underwent the SEIP in 1961.[51] His primary school teacher notes that Richard has very little knowledge of letters, cannot read, is unable to commit speech to writing, and records his experiences in incomplete sentences. He is able to count, but can barely visualize or conceptualize numbers. Furthermore, he cannot accurately recite text from songs or poems. Although he has had trouble obeying the rules at school and in the classroom, he is a good-natured boy. This ambivalent behaviour is confirmed by the assistance school teacher, who attests Richard good-naturedness as well as impulsive and uncontrolled need for physical movement. Richard's deficient learning performance and major attention-span deficit is noted, as is his poor performance in intelligence testing. Thus, the assistance school teacher recommends transfer to an assistance school. The school doctor judges Richard to be, for the most part, physically healthy and normal — despite a mutation of the thorax — but is convinced that Richard is affected by debility and a damaging environment and should therefore be transferred into an assistance school. In line with these professional evaluations, the ultimate decision is for Richard to be placed in an assistance school.

Comparing the two cases from the GDR they exhibit important parallels, even if the characterisations of the students within them came from different evaluators. Thus, Helmut's inability to pay attention was noted by his primary school teacher, while in Richard's case this observation was made by an assistance school teacher. In Helmut's case, the psychologist suspects debility, while in Richard's it is the school doctor. In both cases, the assistance school teacher is more cautious in his or her evaluation. Because his SEIP took place eleven years before Helmut's, Richard was not subjected to psychological evaluation; nonetheless, the evaluations that make up his case file contain the same range of information. Apart from their divergent abilities in memorizing or reciting poems or songs, the biggest difference between the two students are their social surroundings: Richard already attends school at a children's home, while Helmut is subject to insufficient parental care. Despite the consistencies between the two boys on a number of individual points, the evaluations in Helmut's case consistently recommend that he remains in primary school, while those in Richard's case consistently recommend a transfer into an assistance school. The final schooling decisions were in line with these recommendations.

---

51 See VAGÖ/SU 567.

Looking at the files from the GDR, similar combinations of characteristics often lead to different recommendations in the professional evaluations, which ultimately translate into matching schooling decisions. Despite their similarities, these two cases could also have had divergent schooling decisions because of historical changes. With eleven years between them, this seems a more plausible explanation than in the case of the files from the FRG. However, should no significant historical contextual shifts be identifiable, these two cases, similarly to those examined from the FRG, indicate the importance influence exercised by support systems on the outcome of the SEIP. For Helmut, the option of transfer into a youth home to better himself is raised, but not for Richard. That this possibility was available could have influenced the recommendations within the evaluations; at least the opinion of the assistance school teacher in Helmut's SEIP suggests this to have been the case. An alternative hypothesis, which can only be tested by examining a sufficient number of student files, is that the source of opinions on students played a significant role in the final schooling decision. Thus, the psychologist believes Helmut to be a case of debility, while it is the doctor who issues this opinion in Richard's case. Similarly, the boys' inability to pay attention is noted by different professionals.

A brief Comparison of the Analysis of Individual Cases from the FRG and the GDR

Looking at all four discussed cases in comparison, they can no longer be seen as bearing a family resemblance, but they nonetheless reveal noteworthy parallels between the two German states. Apart from gender and the attended grade at the time of the SEIP, they refer principally to a general low level of learning performance. This goes constantly in hand with a general level of intellectual ability judged as crossing into the domain of deficiency. This judgment was expressed in the FRG in the form of an IQ score, while in the GDR it could be articulated through the category of debility. In either case, the same information underlies a variety of terminological uses, a fact that should be noted in the further course of the study. Social behaviour varies among the cases examined and appears, both in the four examples used and beyond, not to be the decisive factor in reaching a final schooling decision. The same cannot be said of the influence of the social environment, which indeed seemed to be of particular relevance, though not in a consistent manner — at least not in the case of the examples from the FRG. This factor is of special interest, as the parents' will was decidedly to be documented only within the assessment forms of the FRG.

Conclusion

The four examples selected from the FRG and the GDR stand for several other similar cases from both German states, which received different schooling decisions despite of their similar clusters of attributions. It consequently appears that the 'border zone' the study seeks to uncover does in fact exist in both the FRG and the GDR. Nonetheless, on the basis of the examples discussed, it is not yet possible to draw reliable conclusions regarding its diachronic durability or changes in its characteristics that may have occurred over the period under investigation. For this, further examination of the sources is needed.

In terms of the thematic orientation of this edited volume, our findings above all raise the question as to whether the SEIP, in both German states, really represented a "student assessment", and thus a testing of the learning behaviour and performance of the student him — or herself. Rather, the SEIP emerges from the research results of the present state as more of an "assessment of social surroundings," in which especially the social setting and the conditions within it are of central relevance to the final schooling decisions made in the SEIP. Thus, the SEIP appears to have fallen short of its own claim to being a method whereby an individually tailored supportive learning environment can be identified for each student. Rather it would perpetuate, by means of sophisticated diagnostic instruments and procedures, precisely that which both German states sought to overcome in their educational systems: the dependence of a student's degree of success in school upon his or her social background. In light of the current debate in Germany on the issue of inclusive schooling, this potential dysfunction of the SEIP would provide a valuable argument in favour of finding solutions within the school system that would ultimately make such procedures superfluous.

Archives

Bibliothek für Bildungsgeschichtliche Forschung des Deutschen Instituts für Internationale Pädagogische Forschung
Schularchiv in Frankfurt am Main
Verwaltungsarchiv der Stadt Görlitz

Literature

Autorenkollektiv. *Beiträge zur Verhinderung des Zurückbleibens*. Berlin: Volk und Wissen Volkseigener Verlag, 1975.

–. *Das Bildungswesen der Deutschen Demokratischen Republik*. Berlin: Volk und Wissen Volkseigener Verlag, 1989.

APW (Akademie der Pädagogischen Wissenschaften der Deutschen Demokratischen Republik). *Das Bildungswesen der Deutschen Demokratischen Republik.* Berlin: Volk und Wissen Volkseigener Verlag, 1983.

Baudisch, Winfried, Bodo Bröse, and Chananin S. Samski. *Hilfsschulpädagogik.* Berlin: Volk und Wissen Volkseigener Verlag, 1987.

Berger, Peter L., and Thomas Luckmann. *Die gesellschaftliche Konstruktion der Wirklichkeit: Eine Theorie der Wissenssoziologie.* Frankfurt am Main: Fischer Taschenbuch Verlag, 1969.

Bernart, Emanuel. "Das psychologisch-heilpädagogische Kurzgutachten." *Zeitschrift für Heilpädagogik* 8 (1957): 173–176.

Deutscher Bildungsrat. *Empfehlungen der Bildungskommission: Zur pädagogischen Förderung behinderter und von Behinderung bedrohter Kinder und Jugendlicher.* Bonn: Deutscher Bildungsrat, 1973.

Ellger-Rüttgardt, Sieglind. *Geschichte der Sonderpädagogik.* München: Reinhardt, 2008.

Geiling, Ute. "Schulfähigkeit und Einschulungspraxis in der DDR: Ein Rückblick — im Spannungsfeld von Förderung und Ausgrenzung." In *Vielfalt durch gute Ordnung im Anfangsunterricht*, edited by Annedore Prengel, 161–219. Opladen: Leske and Budrich, 1999.

Geißler, Gert. *Geschichte des Schulwesens in der Sowjetischen Besatzungszone und in der Deutschen Demokratischen Republik 1945 bis 1962.* Frankfurt am Main: Peter Lang, 2000.

Gomolla, Mechthild, and Frank-Olaf Radtke. *Institutionelle Diskriminierung: Die Herstellung ethnischer Differenz in der Grundschule.* Wiesbaden: Verlag für Sozialwissenschaften, 2009.

Hevekerl, Karl-Heinz. *Die Einweisung in die Hilfsschule: Rechtsvorschriften und Grundsatzentscheidungen der Gerichte.* Berlin-Charlottenburg: Marhold, 1965.

Hofsäss, Thomas R. *Die Überweisung von Schülern auf die Hilfsschule und Schule für Lernbehinderte: Eine historisch-vergleichende Untersuchung.* Berlin: Edition Marhold im Wissenschaftsverlag Volker Spiess, 1993.

Hüfner, Klaus, and Jens Naumann. *Konjunkturen der Bildungspolitik in der Bundesrepublik Deutschland. Bd. I: Der Aufschwung (1960–1967).* Stuttgart: Klett, 1977.

Kätner, Erwin, and Hermann Wegener. *Das Umschulungsverfahren in die Sonderschule (Hilfsschule): Eine einführende Darstellung der rechtlichen, schulorganisatorischen, psychologischen und heilpädagogischen Seiten des Verfahrens.* Kiel: Hirt, 1961.

KMK (Ständige Kultusministerkonferenz der Länder in der Bundesrepublik Deutschland). *Gutachten zur Ordnung des Sonderschulwesens.* Bonn: J.F. Carthaus, 1960.

–. *Empfehlung zur Ordnung des Sonderschulwesens.* Nienburg, Weser: Schulze, 1972.

Kossakowski, Adolf, Horst Kühn, Joachim Lompscher, and *Gerhard Rosenfeld. Psychologische Grundlagen der Persönlichkeitsentwicklung im pädagogischen Prozeß.* Berlin: Volk und Wissen Volkseigener Verlag, 1977.

Kultusministerium Hessen. "Hessisches Schulpflichtgesetz 17.5.1961." In *Gesetz und Verordnungsblatt für das Land Hessen (GVBL),* edited by Hessische Staatskanzlei, 69–72. Wiesbaden: Wiesbadener Kurier, 1961.

–. "Hessisches Schulpflichtgesetz 30.05.1969." In *Gesetz und Verordnungsblatt für das Land Hessen (GVBL),* edited by Hessische Staatskanzlei, 104–108. Wiesbaden: Wiesbadener Kurier, 1969.

Link, Jürgen. Versuch über den Normalismus: Wie Normalität produziert wird. Göttingen: Westdeutscher Verlag, 1997.

MfV (Ministerium für Volksbildung). "Über die sozialistische Entwicklung des Schulwesens in der Deutschen Demokratischen Republik. Thesen des Zentralkomitees. Vom 17. Januar 1959 (Auszüge)." In *Dokumente zur Geschichte des Schulwesens in der Deutschen Demokratischen Republik. Teil 2: 1956–1967/68. 1. Halbband. Reihe: Monumenta Paedagogica,* edited by Kommission für deutsche Erziehungs- und Schulgeschichte der Deutschen Akademie der Wissenschaften zu Berlin, 180–193. Berlin: Volk und Wissen Volkseigener Verlag, 1969.

–. "Fünfte Durchführungsbestimmung zum Gesetz über das einheitliche sozialistische Bildungssystem — Sonderschulwesen — Vom 20. Dezember 1968." In *Dokumente zur Geschichte des Schulwesens in der Deutschen Demokratischen Republik. Teil 3: 1968–1972/73. 1. Halbband. Reihe: Monumenta Paedagogica. Bd. XVI/1,* edited by Kommission für deutsche Erziehungs- und Schulgeschichte der Deutschen Akademie der Wissenschaften zu Berlin, 110–117. Berlin: Volk und Wissen Volkseigener Verlag, 1974.

–. "Richtlinie zur Aufnahme von Kindern in die Hilfsschule. Vom 2. Februar 1973." In *Dokumente zur Geschichte des Schulwesens in der Deutschen Demokratischen Republik. Teil 3: 1968–1972/73. 2. Halbband. Reihe: Monumenta Paedagogica. Bd. XVI/2,* edited by Kommission für deutsche Erziehungs- und Schulgeschichte der Deutschen Akademie der Wissenschaften zu Berlin, 667–671. Berlin: Volk und Wissen Volkseigener Verlag, 1975.

Roth, Heinrich. Begabung und Lernen: Ergebnisse und Folgerungen neuer Forschungen. Stuttgart: Klett, 1969.

Scholz-Ehrsam, Elfriede. Die Psychopathologie des Hilfsschulkindes. Berlin: Volk und Gesundheit Volkseigener Verlag, 1967.

VDS (Verband deutscher Sonderschulen). "Denkschrift zu einem Gesetz über das heilpädagogische Sonderschulwesen." *Zeitschrift für Heilpädagogik* 6 (1955): 44–55.

Vogt, Michaela, Margarete Götz, and *Agneta Floth.* "Professionelle Gutachten und schuladministrative Entscheidung im Hilfsschulaufnahmeverfahren in der DDR." *Vierteljahresschrift für Heilpädagogik und ihre Nachbargebiete (VHN)* 85 (2016): 76–78.

Vogt, Michaela, Margarete Götz, and *Lisa Sauer.* "Professionelle Gutachten und schuladministrative Entscheidung im Hilfsschulaufnahmeverfahren in der BRD." *Vierteljahresschrift für Heilpädagogik und ihre Nachbargebiete (VHN)* 85 (2016): 78–80.

Werner, Birgit. Sonderpädagogik im Spannungsfeld zwischen Ideologie und Tradition: Zur Geschichte der Sonderpädagogik unter Berücksichtigung der Hilfsschulpädagogik in der SBZ und der DDR zwischen 1945 und 1952. Hamburg: Kovac, 1999.

Wittgenstein, Ludwig. Philosophische Untersuchungen. Oxford: Basil Blackwell, 1958.

National Perspectives

María Teresa Flórez Petour

High-stakes Assessment Systems as a Historical Barrier in the Struggle for Change in Education: The Case of Chile

In the current context of expansion of neo-liberal models of education both at a European and international level, high-stakes assessment systems as a technology of power have become particularly salient. In the absence of a strong centralised state to govern education, neo-liberal ideologies have transformed these assessment systems into a means of steering the system at a distance and governing by numbers.[1] The actors of the education system move towards a specific direction in connection to the requirements of high-stakes assessment systems, which therefore play a significant role in shaping the goals of education. Literature generally refers to these mechanisms as located in the context of current trends towards *polycentric governance*[2], which emerges after the overcoming of the welfare state.

However, as early as in the 1870s, a Chilean Conservative politician stated in the context of a controversy around the examinations system for secondary schools that "in this matter it is an axiom that the one who owns the examinations is the owner of education."[3] This quotation sounds extraordinarily contemporary for those who are familiar with the literature around the use of high-stakes assessment systems as a governance tool. Contrary to this literature, the excerpt reveals there was an early political awareness among elites in connection to the role of these assessment systems in maintaining or changing the educational status quo. These systems, however, are seldom studied in historical perspective in terms of its use as a lever that moves the education system in a particular direction. This chapter suggests that high-stakes assessment systems have had a long-standing role as a lever in the education system and have historically constituted a power

---

1   Sotiria Grek, "From Symbols to Numbers: The Shifting Technologies of Education Governance in Europe," *European Educational Research Journal* 7, no. 2 (2008): 208–218, doi: 10.2304/eerj.2008.7.2.208.

2   Stephen Ball and Carolina Junemann, *Networks, New governance and Education* (Bristol, UK: The Policy Press, 2012).

3   Rolando Mellafe, Antonia Rebolledo and Mario Cárdenas, *Historia de la Universidad de Chile* (Santiago: Universidad de Chile, 2001), 94.

device that has hindered change towards more holistic, child-centred, emancipatory and transformational ideas in education.

Literature on assessment as a social practice highlights how this technology can be understood as a way of structuring modern societies, as a means of promoting certain types of hegemonic knowledge, and as mechanisms that shape our views about ourselves.[4] As Foucault indicated in 1975,[5] examinations are among the strongest technologies of discipline, which allow for controlling societies and individuals. The chapter argues that high-stakes assessment systems in Chile both historically and in the present have favoured an assessment culture that responds to a functional view of society. In the context of a predominance of the certification and social purposes of assessment, to the detriment of its pedagogical aims, individuals are distributed in a pre-defined social order by means of this technology. This assessment culture has been in tension with more emancipatory and egalitarian models of society and education, which have been promoted in different periods and with different names but advocating similar principles, although not always with a clear alternative assessment culture that is consistent with these values. As the high-stakes have been on the side of traditional memory-based and mechanistic assessment systems, actors in education (teachers, students and parents among them) have tended to follow this direction rather than that of change and reform, generating a vicious cycle where more critical and emancipatory discourses have been kept as marginal.

The historical development of assessment policies in Chile has been studied by different authors both in terms of chronological historical accounts[6] and in connection to networks of power around testing technologies in specific historical periods[7] as well as in terms of analysing the interaction between the state

---

4   Ann Filer, ed., *Assessment. Social Practice and Social Product* (London, UK: Routledge, 2000).

5   Michel Foucault, *Vigilar y castigar* (Buenos Aires: Siglo XXI Editores, 2005).

6   Iván Núñez Prieto, *La producción de conocimiento acerca de la educación escolar chilena, 1907–1957* (Santiago: CPEIP, 2002); Leonora Reyes, "Profesorado y trabajadores: Movimiento educacional, crisis educativa y reforma de 1928," *Docencia* 40 (2010): 40–49.

7   Cristina Alarcón, "Governing by Testing: Circulation, Psychometric Knowledge, Experts and the "Alliance for Progress" in Latin America During the 1960s and 1970s," *European Education* 47, no. 3 (2015): 199–214, doi: 10.1080/10564934.2015.1065396; Javier Campos, Francisca Corbalán and Javier Inzunza, "Mapping Neoliberal Reform in Chile: Following the Development and Legitimation of the Chilean System of School Quality Measurement (SIMCE)," in *Mapping Corporate Education Reform*, eds. Wayne Au and Joseph J. Ferrare, 106–125 (New York, NY: Routledge, 2015).

and the private sector around assessment regimes.[8] The chapter contributes to this literature by offering an overarching account of long-standing discursive struggles in the field of education in Chile, highlighting the role that high-stakes assessment systems have historically held in hindering the expansion of alternative repertoires, embedded in more egalitarian and emancipatory ideas of education and society. It does so by including a wide range of actors and systems in the historical reconstruction of attempts at reform in education in the country, and by ideologically situating their discourses in the context of recursive struggles around common principles that have been advocated for by different groups (not restricted to policy elites) in different periods. The assessment field is thus portrayed as a dynamic and complex discursive arena both synchronically and diachronically. The chapter examines these processes of discursive struggle by analysing four waves of reform in Chilean history of education, which in many ways resemble those that emerged in European countries. Findings are presented in relation to four periods (1860–1900; 1920–1940; 1965–1985; 1990–2010), each starting with a reform process and allowing enough time for the intended change to take place. On the basis of an analysis of 166 historical documents of diverse nature (legal documents, examinations and supervision reports, teacher journal articles, expert documents, samples of tests, public controversies, among others) and 24 interviews[9] with policymakers and practitioners, it describes and interprets the interaction between high-stakes assessment systems and different attempts at changing curriculum and pedagogy in Chile.[10]

---

8   Jacqueline Gysling, "The Historical Development of Educational Assessment in Chile, 1810–2014," *Assessment in Education: Principles, Policy & Practice* 23, no. 1 (2016): 8–25, doi: 10.1080/0969594X.2015.1046812.

9   These interviews were carried out in the Metropolitan Region of Chile between July and September 2011. They included 20 teachers who were selected considering a high variety in connection to experience, type of initial teacher education, location of the school (urban, rural), gender, school administration, disciplines and levels in which they taught. Four policy authorities that were involved in assessment policies during the 2000s were also interviewed.

10   More details about the methodology of the study on which this chapter draws can be found in María Teresa Flórez Petour, "Systems, Ideologies and History: A Three-dimensional Absence in the Study of Assessment Reform Processes," *Assessment in Education: Principles, Policy & Practice* 22, no. 1 (2015): 3–26, doi: 10.1080/0969594X.2014.943153.

1860–1900: The struggle between colonial and modern pedagogies

Chile had recently become independent from Spain after centuries of colonial domination. The *First Organic Law for Primary Instruction*[11] was published in 1860 as an initial attempt organise a national education system. Two high-stakes assessment systems emerged in this period. One was the system of examinations in public primary schools, which were oriented towards the education of students from lower socioeconomic backgrounds. Public oral examinations (*exámenes públicos*) were carried out by external examiners designated by the state (*comisiones examinadoras*). The high-stakes were given by the judgement of teachers' quality in relation to students' results, as supervision reports of the time reveal (e.g. by establishing promotion and recognition systems in connection to results). Additionally, students' promotion was decided on the basis of the outcome of these examinations, which turned them into high-stakes for this actor as well.

A second system was that of examinations in secondary schools. These schools were aimed at educating the elite of the country and their functioning was almost completely separated from public primary schools. They had their own system for the first levels of primary education called *preparatorias*. In secondary schools, both public and private, the high-stakes were related to the use of examinations for university entrance. These were also oral public examinations controlled by the state. They consisted of annual examinations (*exámenes anuales*) in different subjects throughout the years of secondary schooling, which were a prerequisite to take the *bachillerato* examination, the final hurdle before access to higher education was granted.

In this context, two pedagogical repertoires began to struggle. During the 1880s, Liberal and Radical politicians as well as some teacher educators started criticising the persistence of the colonial model of teaching in school practice, a model that was disseminated in Chile through Catholic private schools, mostly attended by children of the Conservative elite. José Abelardo Núñez, a Liberal intellectual, criticised traditional education in the following terms:

> "The great mistake in which we have remained for a long time is our idea around what we think constitutes man's true education. Our efforts have constantly (if not exclusively) been directed to provide the child with a certain number of facts and to store in

---

11 Manuel Montt and Rafael Sotomayor, "Primera Ley Orgánica de la Instrucción Primaria," in "'*I el silencio comenzó a reinar.' Documentos para la historia de la instrucción primaria, 1840–1920*, ed. Mario Monsalve Bórquez, (Santiago: DIBAM, Centro de Investigaciones Barros Arana, 1998).

his memory what we considered necessary to that end. With this aim, all we demanded from the teacher was that he knew the subject he taught. Given that the textbook was the deposit of rules, definitions and information related to each subject, the teacher was considered as a supplement of the book. To fix the historical date in the students' memory; to make him retain a mathematical formula so he could apply it with certain mechanical precision in the resolution of an arithmetic problem [...] such was the old idea of education, an idea that unfortunately persists in the majority of this country. [...] But to think of the human mind as a living force, as a thinking, reasoning and judging being; that possesses in itself all possible and necessary faculties, and (to think) that the ultimate end of what we call education is to develop and discipline these forces [...] (this) idea of education is a novelty for many people, for many teachers [...]."[12]

The traditional memory and repetition-based approach is characterised by Núñez as lacking in the development of thinking and critical judgement among students. In contrast to this approach, Liberal intellectuals and politicians advocated for the import of the German model of education. Its concern for the education of all the people and its practical approach to teaching were some of the features that attracted the interest of Chilean Liberal and Radical politicians as well as teacher educators of the time. José Abelardo Núñez was among the Liberal intellectuals who travelled in the 1880s around Western countries, commissioned by the government, to study trends in international education systems. In this context, he also favoured German pedagogy. In the following quotation, which is representative of the positive view of various actors in relation to this model, Núñez highlights some features of Mathematics teaching in Germany:

"There is a very important principle in education which consists of using exercises and problems as a means for the student to incidentally acquire many interesting and useful notions. Instead of meaningless abstract cyphers, in adding, subtracting or multiplying it is convenient that every problem or exercise contains some numeric data related to nature and daily life uses, anticipating as much as possible the use that students will have to make of this knowledge throughout the course of their lives."[13]

Alarcón[14] characterises the adoption of the German model in Chile in terms of changes to teaching methodologies that aimed at overcoming the monotonous memory-based colonial *catecismo* and promoted instead a practice-centred and

---

12 José Abelardo Núñez, *Estudios sobre educación moderna. Organización de las Escuelas Normales. Informe presentado al Señor Ministro de Instrucción Pública* (Santiago: Impr. de la Librería Americana, 1883), 109–110.

13 Ibid., 218.

14 Cristina Alarcón, *El discurso pedagógico fundacional de docentes secundarios. Sobre la transferencia educativa alemana en Chile, 1889–1910* (Buenos Aires: Editorial Nuevas Ideas, FLACSO, 2010).

scientific approach to teaching and learning, which had Herbart's pedagogical principles as a fundamental reference. This new repertoire was mainly promoted through teacher education and school supervision but very little is found of this orientation in the legislation of the time. Only a few fragments in this type of documents after 1883 offered a moderate idea of practice-based education. The main strategies of traditional education were maintained, that is, repetition of canonical knowledge as transmitted by the teacher and without consideration of the interest and involvement of the student. The diagnosis of change in practice was also pessimistic. Reports and public discourses of visitors and teacher educators were consistent from 1861 to 1896 in stating the continuity of the memorising practices of colonial times and highlighting the need for teachers to learn and use modern pedagogy. The few cases where the adoption of modern methods was seen in some teachers, mostly by the end of the century, received the praise of visitors. It can be inferred from some of the documents that the lack of change and the persistence in traditional pedagogical approaches was related to an important blind spot in the policy of the time: examinations.

Legislation on examinations and examination reports of the period were mainly focused on the ritual conditions in which interrogations had to take place as well as on the consequences derived from their results. Virtually nothing was said in relation to the pedagogical approach underlying these assessment practices. On the one hand, this reveals the priority given at the time to the social use of assessment in terms of promotion and certification. On the other hand, it shows the lack of awareness among progressive politicians and intellectuals in relation to the importance of changing high-stakes assessment systems if a transformation in pedagogy was expected. The following excerpt from a school visitor illustrates how the clash between modern pedagogy and examinations occurred in the classroom:

> "Religion is taught, with very few exceptions, in a mechanical way, because almost all teachers follow the old programme. Nothing that speaks to the heart, that awakens and encourages feelings of faith, confidence in God or fear of him. Everything is directed towards memory, which is loaded with non-comprehended words for the 'examinations.' [...] The cold and indifferent tone that has shocked me in teaching in general, becomes more perceptible in this subject in which the teacher is the girls' main educator."[15]

---

15 Teresa Adametz, "Informe sobre las escuelas de niñas de Santiago presentado al señor Inspector Jeneral de Instrucción Primaria, por la visitadora estraordinaria de las mismas doña Teresa Adametz; Santiago, en febrero de 1896," in '… I el silencio comenzó a reinar'. Documentos para la historia de la instrucción primaria, 1840–1920, Vol. IX, ed. Mario Monsalve Bórquez (Santiago: DIBAM, Centro de Investigaciones Barros Arana, 1998), 36.

This was a general report about all primary schools for girls in Santiago. The author diagnosed the predominance in them of a mechanical practice oriented towards examinations, which she observed as being present in all subjects and more perceptibly in Religion. However, if examinations were high-stakes for teachers and students, it is understandable that they persisted in the pedagogy that underpinned these practices, as they had too much to lose by following the innovative repertoire offered by modern pedagogy.

Documents around a controversy that occurred in the 1870s, in relation to the control over examinations exerted by the state, reveal how high-stakes examinations were also the ones that ruled practice in secondary schools.[16] Authors such as the Liberal intellectual and politician Miguel Luis Amunátegui referred repeatedly to the motivation of students as being exclusively focused on examinations, exemplifying this phenomenon through the tendency of pupils to study only during the examinations period or to attend only those courses whose results were relevant to university entrance.[17] This author also referred critically to the idea promoted by Catholic private schools of a single examination at the end of secondary school as the only means to regulate university entrance. This new mechanism was proposed instead of the predominant system at the time, which consisted of examinations for each subject, whose results were considered as a whole in order to gain access to higher education. In the following excerpt Amunátegui quotes the thoughts of a French bishop in relation to the idea of a single examination, given that France had already adopted this system. Amunátegui's words on this controversy reveal the discursive struggle of the time in relation to curriculum, pedagogy and high-stakes assessment systems:

"The *bachillerato* examination (the single test), says the wise bishop, is extraordinarily overloaded, and includes all together the subjects of almost all the literary, historical and scientific studies, and this becomes a universal science, both impossible and inefficient [...] which does not teach any substance, terror of youth and despair of parents and, because of these reasons, a fatal dejection for French youth. Understood like this, *bachillerato* is not, and cannot be, but an immature and confusing mixture of mnemonic notions with which the spirit is overloaded for a specific day, to then forget them at the following day and never ever remember them. [...]. Such a preparation (the one that leads to the single test), so fictitious and so hasty, devours everything. Thenceforth, the

---

16 Gysling, *Historical development*.
17 Miguel Luis Amunátegui, "La cuestión de exámenes," in *Estudios sobre instrucción pública*, Vol. I, 39–78 (Santiago de Chile: Imprenta Nacional, 1897).

handbook replaces all books; the trainer replaces all teachers. [...]. We ask for men, and we are given bachelors."[18]

As can be inferred from the analysis of documents of this period, the role of high-stakes assessment systems in hindering the entrance of innovative repertoires in curriculum and pedagogy was already apparent in the 1800s. Phenomena such as curriculum reduction and *teaching to the test* do not seem to be as new as research on assessment has generally suggested. Ideas of teaching and learning that promoted the value of experience, meaning, thoughtfulness, criticality and participation were at odds with the underpinning principles of examinations, namely certification, competition, individualism, and mechanistic short-term responses aimed at obtaining social rewards. The establishment of a single examinations system for university entrance by the end of the 1800s as well as the persistence of criticisms around traditional memory-based methodologies in the next period under scrutiny tell us who eventually triumphed in this first attempt at change.

1920–1940: Teachers' struggle for change towards progressive education

This period began with the publication of the *Ley N° 3654 sobre Educación Primaria Obligatoria* (Law for Compulsory Primary Education),[19] which according to Reyes,[20] emerged from a political consensus between Conservative and Liberal/Radical forces. In relation to high-stakes assessment systems, this law proposed a change in the social scenario of education in terms of its historical functioning in two separated paths, one for lower classes and one for the elite. In the context of its aim at generating a single education system for the country, it proposed the abolition of *preparatorias* and the elimination of the examination that was required to gain access to secondary schools. Article 99 of this law states:

> "Art. 99. Within 6 years from the 1ˢᵗ of January 1920, preparatory courses that currently function in public secondary schools will be abolished and to enter these (secondary schools) a certificate of attendance (*certificado de asistencia*) to all the courses of a higher primary school will suffice."[21]

---

18 Ibid., 49–50.
19 Dirección General de Educación Primaria (DGEP), *Lei N° 3.654 sobre educación primaria obligatoria: publicada en el diario oficial Nª12,755 de 26 de agosto de 1920* (Santiago: Imprenta Lagunas, 1921).
20 Reyes, *Profesorado y trabajadores*.
21 DGEP, *Lei N° 3.654 sobre educación primaria obligatoria*, 37.

This small paragraph meant a significant shift in terms of the functional role of examinations in the distribution of individuals in the social order, as it opened the gate for lower classes to enter elite schools without the barrier historically sustained though a high-stakes assessment system. As addressed later in the chapter, however, this legal change was hindered before it could be implemented in practice.

A second attempt for change at the time was led by teachers. As part of a context of increasing strength of social movements during the first years of the 20th century, teachers acquired a strong voice during the 1920s and became an actor capable of promoting new repertoires in education. They identified themselves with the international movement of New Education, as can be derived from the visit of foreign members of this pedagogical current to Chile and from multiple publications in teacher-led journals during the decade, where names such as Pestalozzi, Fröbel, Montessori, Decroly, Freinet and Dewey frequently circulated. The Chilean education historian, Iván Núñez Prieto,[22] refers to the new scenario of the time as very lively and characterised by a thirst for knowledge about scientific pedagogy, where teachers acquired books and met to discuss about them and to debate on the conditions of education. Teachers were critical of the persistence of traditional pedagogy, in terms that resemble the words of Liberal politicians and intellectuals of the previous period, as the following excerpt from the teachers' journal *Nuevos Rumbos* illustrates:

> "[...] in many schools the class with 'taking notes' (*la clase con apuntes*) still exists as well as the 'lesson from here to there' marked on textbooks. Working-centred teaching is barely tried in an isolated way by some teachers who feel the weariness and inefficiency of their methods. Some years ago a system called 'of lectures' (*de cátedras*) was established with the aim of making studies more active and personal; but its results were negative due to the absence of the spontaneous work of the student and because the activity was something imposed by the teacher. For the activity to be healthy and efficient it must emerge as a need, as a consequence of a frame of mind. This is what active school tends to, and its methods are not presented as catecismo, are not a priori ways of acting, but ways of doing, flexible in relation to each work, to each initiative. [...]. We must stop cramming students with textbook tasks, with memory-based lessons. Is time for the *normalista*[23] to stop being the individual without initiative, without an eagerness for research, with no horizon."[24]

---

22 Núñez Prieto, *La producción de conocimiento*.
23 Name given to primary school teachers who studied in the *Escuelas Normales*.
24 Salvador Fuentes Vega, "Nuestras Escuelas Normales," *Nuevos Rumbos* 6 (1927): 109.

The quotation reveals how this discursive struggle repeats the principles of the dispute from the previous period: teachers were against mechanistic and memory-based approaches to teaching and learning, which they regarded as cramming students with meaningless contents, and advocated for more active pedagogies that were able to engage pupils in their learning in a more natural and flexible way. The difference between periods, however, lies in teachers' awareness about the role of traditional examinations in hindering the enactment of this approach to pedagogy in practice. Adolphe Fèrriere a Swiss educator invited to Chile to report on the development of New Education in the country, states:

> "It is clear that while examinations based on reciting by memory occupy the foreground, it will not be possible for teachers to make the most of their personal talents, because the obligation to finish passing the programme monopolises their entire attention. That will have to be deeply reformed one day [...]."[25]

Given the strength that the teachers' movement acquired in Chile, they were invited in 1927 by the authoritarian government of Carlos Ibáñez del Campo to take responsibility for the design of the education reform. Two teachers were appointed to occupy positions in the Ministry of Education with the aim of formulating the new legal framework for education. In this context, teachers demonstrated their awareness about the role of high-stakes examinations in the hindrance of change. In the *Regulation for Primary Schools* derived from the main document of the reform (Decree N° 7500), they proposed the abolition of examinations (*exámenes*):

> "Art. 68. Examinations are cancelled in primary school and promotions will be made annually taking students' work and attendance during the school period into account; which does not exclude the exhibitions of students (work) that teachers make as a demonstration of the efficiency of their labour."[26]

This period, therefore, witnessed two important attempts at change in education that required the elimination of high-stakes assessment systems, both as a social barrier and as an obstacle for curriculum and pedagogical transformation.[27] However, given the consequences of the proposed changes, the discussion

---

25 Adolfo Ferriere, *La Educación Nueva en Chile, 1928–1930* (Madrid, 1932), 234.
26 Ibid., 53.
27 To these attempts at reforming high-stakes assessment systems in Chile at the time, one could also add the temporary suppression of the *Bachillerato* examination in 1928 during the government of Ibáñez del Campo. Decree N° 4096 established the abolition of this system and proposed instead that the only requirement for university entrance was the *licencia secundaria* (secondary leaving certificate). This decree, however, was promulgated in the context of a long-standing controversy between the government of

became an arena of political struggle that reached the government. The failure of the intended reform was experienced again. The government of Ibáñez, as could be expected given its authoritarian nature, after a few months of teachers' participation in the design of education policy, decided to expel them from the Ministry and initiated a process known as the *contra reforma* (counter-reform). This process involved the persecution of teachers in the context of a teacher evaluation system, which was implemented through the figure of the local inspector (*inspectores locales*). Among her duties, the inspector had to denounce any kind of political propaganda that circulated among teachers and head teachers or in their interaction with students and parents, to the central authorities.[28] This indicator was used to raise suspicion and fear among teachers, and became a (very effective) disempowering device. Only a few aspects of their ideas remained in the final version of the *Law for Compulsory Primary Education* in 1929.[29]

As part of this counter-reform process, the idea of abolishing entrance examinations for secondary schools also eventually vanished. Decree N° 5486 (published in 1929) established the following requirement:

> "Students who have satisfactorily completed the 6th year of the Annexe School[30] will have the right to be admitted to the first year of Secondary School without previous examination. Students from the 6th year coming from any Primary School will also be admitted, provided that they evidence the corresponding knowledge through their examination."[31]

Ibáñez and the University of Chile and of a general educational crisis. *Bachillerato* was, therefore, reinstated shortly after the government of Ibáñez ended. Carlos Ibáñez del Campo and Eduardo Barrios, "Decreto 4096. Supresión del Bachillerato en Filosofía y Humanidades. Crea la licencia secundaria", in *Recopilación de leyes, reglamentos y decretos relativos al servicio de la enseñanza pública*, ed. Ricardo Donoso, (Santiago de Chile: Dirección de Prisiones, 1937), 332.

28 Carlos Ibáñez del Campo and Bartolomé Blanche, "Decreto 4669. Organiza servicio de Inspección de Educación Primaria", in *Recopilación de leyes, reglamentos y decretos relativos al servicio de la enseñanza pública*, ed. Ricardo Donoso (Santiago de Chile: Dirección de Prisiones, 1937).

29 Carlos Ibáñez del Campo and Mariano Navarrete, "Ley 5291 de Instrucción Primaria Obligatoria," in *Recopilación de leyes, reglamentos y decretos relativos al servicio de la enseñanza pública*, ed. Ricardo Donoso (Santiago de Chile: Dirección de Prisiones, 1937).

30 Another name for *preparatorias*.

31 Carlos Ibáñez del Campo and Mariano Navarrete, "Decreto 5486. Escuelas Primarias Anexas a Liceos pasan a depender de la Dirección General de Educación Secundaria", in *Recopilación de leyes, reglamentos y decretos relativos al servicio de la enseñanza pública*, ed. Ricardo Donoso (Santiago de Chile: Dirección de Prisiones, 1937), 354–355.

The social function of examinations was re-established, as elite students were still allowed to attend their own primary schools (*preparatorias*) with guaranteed access to secondary school. Lower socioeconomic groups, on the contrary, were kept out of the education system for the elite through the reinstatement of examinations as a barrier for their entrance.

The lack of political willingness to undertake the changes proposed in this period reveals the extent to which power elites were aware of the role of high-stakes assessment systems in keeping the status quo. On the other hand, the struggle in this historical phase also shows how other actors, such as teachers and teacher educators, became aware of this role and argued for the need to overcome traditional high-stakes assessment systems. However, this awareness was not accompanied by an alternative view of assessment, one that was more consistent with the principles of the new repertoire, a gap that persists until the present.

1965–1985: the struggle between socialist and neo-liberal assessment

This period began with the government of the Christian Democrat Eduardo Frei Montalva and his *Revolución en libertad* (Revolution in Liberty). This slogan involved, on the one hand, a promise of significant changes in Chilean society. On the other hand, it used the idea of *liberty* as a means of establishing a difference in relation to Marxist governments of the period, which were seen by these politicians as authoritarian regimes. In the area of education, reforms involved not only increased access for students but also the entrance of managerial and behaviourist approaches through goal-oriented pedagogy and standardized testing regimes. These repertoires became increasingly hegemonic and later stood alongside colonial pedagogy as part of what is understood as 'traditional pedagogy' until nowadays.

It must be noted, however, that despite some common aspects between colonial and behaviourist pedagogical approaches, such as the passive role of the student and the authoritarian relationship between students and teachers, there are significant differences between them, both in terms of their general features and the way they understood assessment. Colonial pedagogy was focused on the transmission of moral models and canonical knowledge through memorisation and repetition. Consistently, examinations were based on the judgement of the teacher or the external examiner understood as an authority in the subject.[32] Behaviourist

---

32   Rafael Flórez Ochoa, *Evaluación Pedagógica y Cognición* (Bogotá: Mc-Graw-Hill, 1999).

pedagogy, in turn, concentrated on observable behaviours, thus eliminating the moral dimension and any other aspect considered as non-objective. These behaviours, unlike the colonial model, are explicitly stated and their learning occurs through processes of automatisation and constant exercising. In terms of assessment practices, these behaviours are controlled through the use of objective and standardized testing.[33]

With the introduction of the Scholastic Aptitude Test (*Prueba de Aptitud Académica*, PAA) as the main means for university selection during Frei's administration, the type of assessment promoted through standardized testing became the hegemonic model both in Chile and other countries Latin America.[34] Alarcón distinguishes in this change the starting point of a process of disempowerment of teachers, who were no longer understood as "mediators of knowledge" and, therefore, "lost their function as evaluators due to the mechanisation of the evaluation process."[35] Despite these differences, it can be stated that both colonial examinations and behaviourist testing regimes share a mechanistic and repetition-based approach to learning and assessment, as well as a focus on the selection, promotion and certification aspect of assessment, that its, on its social function.

However, managerial and behaviouristic ideas promoted in Frei's educational reform were also intertwined in the legal documents of the time with some of the principles advocated in previous periods by progressive educators. It was precisely this hybrid approach to policy that led to a perception of disappointment among citizens. As Haslam indicates: "By 1968 it was clear to everyone that Frei's 'Revolution in Liberty' was going nowhere', as changes were occurring 'at a pace insufficiently rapid for the disadvantaged whose expectations had risen to Frei's bellicose rhetoric."[36]

Unsatisfied with this moderate approach, citizens voted in the next period for the first democratically elected Marxist president, Salvador Allende. The intervention of the government of the United States through the CIA in connection with local elites, as well as the internal divisions of the Chilean Left, led to the well-known sudden ending of this government though Pinochet's coup d'état, followed by 17 years of dictatorship.[37]

---

33 Ibid.
34 Alarcón, *Governing by Testing*.
35 Ibid., 208.
36 Jonathan Haslam, *The Nixon Administration and the death of Allende's Chile* (London, UK: Verso, 2005), 18.
37 Haslam, *The Nixon Administration*.

Despite this violent interruption, the government of Allende developed a proposal for change in education known as the Unified National School (*Escuela Nacional Unificada*, ENU), which reinstated the idea of a single education system for the country, although with a more radical approach that was closer to the ideas of critical pedagogy. The innovative repertoire promoted here, nonetheless, resembled in many ways that of previous periods, as the following excerpt from the document that summarised the project of the new government illustrates:

"To make a new education effective, the application of new methods is required, methods that emphasise an active and critical participation of students in their education, instead of the passive and receptive position they have to hold today."[38]

On the one hand, the persistence of traditional pedagogical approaches where the student is understood as a passive recipient is apparent in the text, which confirms the failure of previous attempts at change. On the other hand, the new repertoire emphasised values that had been repeatedly advocated for in earlier periods: the active and critical engagement of the student in her learning process.

With regards to high-stakes assessment systems, the government of Allende was clearly aware of their function in the maintenance of the social order. The quotation below from the 1973 brochure *The Education Crisis*, where the government enumerates a series of aspects that need to be modified in education, illustrates their perspective on the matter:

"9. Individualistic value system in education: school, primary, secondary and higher education are a reflection of the social, political and economic structure of the country to which they belong. Until now in Chilean society, dominated by capitalist values, patterns of behaviour such as egoism, individualism, competition and the search for profit have predominated. School constitutes a basic instrument to reinforce them. Hence, school has contributed to the competitive environment by stimulating, through the marking system, the performance of each student and not of the group. The Chilean system of education does not link the student to the country's reality neither does it imprint in him/her a consciousness of the collective responsibility towards society."[39]

Predominant approaches at the time emphasised norm-referenced assessment, that is, a method where results were derived from ranking students' scores in order to transform them into a marking scale. The use of the Gauss curve as a means to calculate grades in the Chilean system became widespread among teachers, a method still used in practice nowadays, according to some teachers and policy authorities

---

38 Gobierno de la Unidad Popular, *Programa Básico de Gobierno de la Unidad Popular* (Santiago, 1969), 29–30.
39 Gobierno de la Unidad Popular, *La crisis educacional* (Santiago: Quimantú, 1973), 10.

interviewed in this study.[40] Strangely, although his name was used as one of the main references in Frei's reform, it was Benjamin Bloom[41] himself who criticised this approach as early as in the 1970s, as it promoted competition rather than solidarity among students, damaging their self-esteem and self-concept. The brochure quoted above enriches this criticism by contextualising the political underpinnings and social consequences of these practices, embedded in an assessment culture that promoted the reproduction of the predominant social order.

Given the interruption of this government, their developments around an alternative model of assessment were only exploratory and incipient. One idea was that of group assessment (*evaluación del trabajo en relación al grupo*), that is, to assess the performance of the whole group towards common goals rather than the individual in comparison to others. Another development was the exploration of some of Bloom's ideas on formative assessment through the introduction of continuous, process-centred and skills-based assessment, although this is found in documents only as an initial suggestion at the level of higher education.[42]

The ideas around assessment promoted by the government of Allende were counter-argued in the period through a document written by a group of members of the student union of the Catholic University of Chile, with the support of a group of academics, some of which later had an important role in the dictatorship of Pinochet. A couple of them still hold important positions as right-wing politicians. Their arguments offer some interesting features in terms of the way in which they anticipate some of the strategies that will later be understood as characteristic of neo-liberal policy:

> "It attracts the attention the use of absolutely Marxist terms through which we see the student is taken as a mass, as a group and not an individual, making apparent a clear intention towards depersonalisation. In concrete terms, in the Programme for the First Integrated Year (*Primer Año Integrado*) (PAI) we see they are assessed in relation to the work of the group and not in relation to the individual. The assessment process, among all the elements that compose the pedagogical activity, constitutes one of the more complex and more important. We find that the multitude of aspects that mastering it involves (assessment schemes, group referencing, objectivity) are not properly considered from the technical-pedagogical perspective neither from the practical perspective in the ENU report. Concretely, the PAI report states: 'Assessment will be carried out in relation to

---

40 Flórez, "*Systems, Ideologies and History.*"
41 Benjamin Bloom, Thomas Hastings and George Madaus, *Evaluación del aprendizaje* (Ed. Troquel: Buenos Aires, 1977).
42 Alfredo Jadresic, *La reforma de 1968 en la Universidad de Chile* (Santiago: Editorial Universitaria, 2002).

the work of the group and not the individual and production, productive efficiency and time employed are to be considered in comparison with the normal performance of the zone [...]. This assessment system involves destroying everything pedagogical science has advanced on the subject. [...]. And what is worse, the idea that assessment has to be predominantly individual is ignored."[43]

What later becomes the well-known strategy of *depoliticisation* in neo-liberal models of education is apparent in the excerpt. In this strategy, *social* problems become equivalent to *economic* problems and the ideological aspect is erased by a managerial and technical discourse.[44] The strategy is enacted here through the authors' references to 'pedagogical science', 'technical-pedagogical perspective' and technical aspects that have to be taken into account, as opposed to what they denounce as an ideological use of assessment through its adjustment to Marxist ideas. What is hidden through this strategy is that the use of assessment as a tool to promote individualism, competition, segregation and meritocracy is not inherent to assessment as a pedagogical practice but is also connected to certain ideologies and models of society. These ideas can be portrayed by the authors as more "normal" or "natural" only because they correspond to the ideas of society and education (and to its corresponding assessment culture) that had predominated throughout history. This also allows them to depict the socialist model as a completely marginal discourse.

The sad ending of this period opens the path for the imposition of an extreme version of a neo-liberal and market-oriented model of education in Chile. High-stakes assessment systems gradually gain importance as a mechanism to regulate the market by labelling the quality of education offered to parents and students, who are understood as clients of an educational service. These attempts begin early in the 1980s with the Performance Assessment Test (PER) and later consolidate through the creation in 1988 of the System for the Measurement of Quality in Education (*Sistema de Medición de la Calidad de la Educación*, SIMCE), which

---

43 FEUC (The Catholic University of Chile Student Federation), *ENU: El control de las conciencias (informe crítico preparado por FEUC)* (Santiago: Departamento de Estudios FEUC, 1973), 51–52.

44 Tatiana Suspitsyna, "Accountability in American education as a Rhetoric and a Technology of Governmentality," *Journal of Education Policy* 25, no. 5 (2010): 567–586, doi: 10.1080/02680930903548411; Donald Gillies, "Developing Governmentality: Conduct and Education Policy," *Journal of Education Policy* 23, no. 4 (2008): 415–427, doi: 10.1080/02680930802054388.

continues until nowadays as a fundamental pillar in the Chilean market-oriented education system.[45]

1990–2010: Neo-liberal education and the embodied struggle

The return to democracy initiated the period, with the election of the Christian Democrat Patricio Aylwin as the president of the centre-left parties coalition known as *Concertación*. In the field of education, policy discourses were permeated by the slogans of 'quality' and 'equity', provided that access had been reached by most of the population and now the focus had to be in providing everyone with an education of good quality. However, all efforts had to be made in a landscape where most of Pinochet's legislation was still in force. Policy documents of the period reflect this tension through the presence of multiple contradictory ideas in a single text.

As in several countries, a constructivist reform of the curriculum was promoted during the 1990s, in which many of the principles of previous attempts for change persisted: an active involvement of the student, an experience-based approach to teaching, the need to develop critical thinking, a learner-centred perspective on classroom activity, among others. However, discourses on how assessment had to be understood in this reform were mixed and confusing and co-existed with the national high-stakes assessment system aimed at measuring the quality of education in the context of a market oriented model.

The *Organic Constitutional Law for Education* (LOCE) was one of the legal bodies designed by the government of Pinochet a few months before he left office. Article 19 of this law established:

> "19[th]Article. It is the responsibility of the Ministry of Education to design instruments that allow for the establishment of a system of periodic assessment, both in primary and secondary school, of the accomplishment of the fundamental aims and the minimum contents for those levels. [...]. The Ministry of Education will elaborate statistics of its results, by region and by school, which must be published in one of the national or regional circulation newspapers and, additionally, be fixed in visible places of each of the assessed schools. In any case will the publication individualise students' results."[46]

This article consolidated the continuity of SIMCE after the dictatorship and, more importantly, it emphasised the need for publishing the results of each school.

---

45 Campos, Corbalán and Inzunza, "Mapping Neoliberal Reform in Chile."
46 Ministerio de Educación Pública, "Ley Orgánica Constitucional de Enseñanza (LOCE) Nº 18962," accessed July 28, 2017, http://www.leychile.cl/Navegar?idNorma=30330&t ipoVersion=0.

Public exposure of results, along with a series of policies that linked SIMCE results to economic incentives as well as to negative consequences, turned this system into increasingly high-stakes.

Throughout the period, advocates of SIMCE (International Organisations among them) referred to its recognised long-standing tradition in Latin America and praised its technical quality and contributions. However, interviews with practitioners in this study reveal a contrast in terms of the way they experience SIMCE in schools, as the following representative excerpts illustrate:

> "[…] Sciences cover a plan and programme which is very long, and with two hours (a week) […] it gets too short. Then, many times we don't get to see the whole programme. However, the whole programme is assessed in SIMCE […], thus, the main difficulty is that we have to accommodate […] contents to be able to pass those that are more relevant or the types of questions that are repeated more often in SIMCE […] the main () difficulty I have and that we have as a Department is that many topics that are relevant to us […], we have to pass them very quickly." (Secondary teacher, State school, Biology)

> "So, I think it's too much pressure and that has me very, now overwhelmed, it turns into, into an overwhelming thing. And () that all the school, because then everything begins to revolve around SIMCE, it is so much pressure that () the only thing that matters to you are contents, contents and that distorts a bit what is the, what the holistic teaching of children should be." (Primary teacher, State school, History)

> "Today I have to… reconcile this, the way of teaching that I like, that I love and through which I have proved that children are different when they work like that, but I have had to reconcile this with the demands that (emerge when) SIMCE is coming […]. I prepare handouts, I look for more entertaining readings in which some content is introduced but it is not the same, I mean, it's a bit more paper, a bit more speed, […] we analyse, we read, we talk, but what should happen, which is the other way around, does not happen, that the child discovers it, because for the child to discover things in Sciences, it requires time […]; there comes a time when you want to homogenise everything. You know that doesn't work but you do it anyway." (Primary teacher, State school, Natural Sciences)

In terms of assessment cultures, these quotations show that in this period there is not a clash of perspectives advocated by different actors; it is rather the same actor who experiences this struggle in herself. High-stakes assessment systems have become so pervasive that the discursive struggles of previous periods are now embodied in teachers' experience, which is characterised by a permanent conflict in their professional identities and their daily practice. The quotations illustrate how the predominant assessment culture, which is focused on models promoted in standardized high-stakes testing systems, is at odds with teachers' principles in terms of what they understand as valuable learning and as a more holistic approach to education. Their views resemble in many senses the principles of progressive educators and other actors of previous historical periods.

Attempts at promoting alternative views of assessment in policy during this period repeatedly faced the wall of a long-standing culture of traditional approaches to assessment, where marking, certification, administrative requirements of the school, selection, comparison and competition had been the predominant practices and values. Such is the case of Assessment for Learning in Chile, an attempt in policy that was initially absorbed by a parallel standards agenda and later disappeared when a right-wing government came to office in 2010.[47]

Concluding remarks

The presence of high-stakes assessment systems has been in the landscape of education for longer than is commonly acknowledged. Its role in shaping the direction of education systems has been crucial and long-standing, as this historical account shows. This role goes beyond the realm of pedagogy and is connected to general views of education and society. The assessment culture that has predominated throughout Chilean history of education, represented in oral and written examinations and later in standardized tests, is connected to more functional views of society. From this perspective, individuals need to be distributed in a pre-defined social order and more emancipatory discourses are neutralised by memory-based and mechanistic approaches to teaching and learning, whose aim is to provide future workers with basic skills and knowledge. In this context, discourses that promote principles such as equality, participation, criticality, engagement, solidarity, citizenship, and the development of a more well-rounded human being that is capable of questioning and changing her reality have remained marginal. Among the reasons that can be hypothesised for this marginal condition, on the basis of the findings presented in this chapter, one could mention: 1) the lack of political willingness for a deep change among policy/political/social elites, which in its extreme versions has been manifested through authoritarian responses; 2) assessment as a 'blind spot' in the programme of progressive educators; 3) the gradual historical disempowerment of some of the actors that are more likely to promote innovative repertoires. These three factors seem to constitute the perfect formula for a never-ending vicious cycle, where attempts at change run the risk of becoming a fruitless (and often discouraging) endeavour.

---

47 Flórez, "Systems, Ideologies and History."

The field of assessment has not been successful in developing an approach that is consistent with the principles of more innovative and emancipatory repertoires in pedagogy and education. Attempts at more formative and authentic approaches have been easily adapted to predominant assessment cultures. Given this long-standing vicious cycle characterised by several waves of attempts at change, one can legitimately ask whether there is hope for transformation in the future. The development of an approach to assessment that is explicitly committed to a different idea of education and society could be a starting point. For that to occur, however, the field of assessment needs first to acknowledge the undeniable political side of its activity and, more importantly, to take responsibility for it.

Literature

Adametz, Teresa. "Informe sobre las escuelas de niñas de Santiago presentado al señor Inspector Jeneral de Instrucción Primaria, por la visitadora estraordinaria de las mismas doña Teresa Adametz; Santiago, en febrero de 1896." In *'… I el silencio comenzó a reinar.' Documentos para la historia de la instrucción primaria, 1840–1920*, Vol. IX, edited by Mario Monsalve Bórquez, 36–37. Santiago: DIBAM, Centro de Investigaciones Barros Arana, 1998.

Alarcón, Cristina. *El discurso pedagógico fundacional de docentes secundarios. Sobre la transferencia educativa alemana en Chile, 1889–1910*. Buenos Aires: Editorial Nuevas Ideas, FLACSO, 2010.

Alarcón, Cristina. "Governing by Testing: Circulation, Psychometric Knowledge, Experts and the "Alliance for Progress" in Latin America during the 1960s and 1970s." *European Education* 47, no. 3 (2015): 199–214, doi: 10.1080/10564934.2015.1065396.

Amunátegui, Miguel Luis. "La cuestión de exámenes," in *Estudios sobre instrucción pública*, Vol. I, 39–78. Santiago de Chile: Imprenta Nacional, 1897.

Ball, Stephen and *Carolina Junemann*. *Networks, New governance and Education*. Bristol, UK: The Policy Press, 2012.

Bloom, Benjamin, Thomas Hastings, and *George Madaus*. *Evaluación del aprendizaje*. Ed. Troquel: Buenos Aires, 1977.

Campos, Javier, Francisca Corbalán, and *Javier Inzunza*. "Mapping Neoliberal Reform in Chile: Following the Development and Legitimation of the Chilean System of School Quality Measurement (SIMCE)." In *Mapping Corporate Education Reform*, edited by Wayne Au, and Joseph J. Ferrare, 106–125. New York, NY: Routledge, 2015.

Dirección General de Educación Primaria (DGEP), Lei N° 3.654 sobre educación primaria obligatoria: publicada en el diario oficial Nª12,755 de 26 de agosto de 1920. Santiago: Imprenta Lagunas, 1921).

Ferriere, Adolfo. La Educación Nueva en Chile, 1928–1930. Madrid, 1932.

FEUC. ENU: El control de las conciencias (informe crítico preparado por FEUC). Santiago: Departamento de Estudios FEUC, 1973.

Filer, Ann, ed. *Assessment. Social Practice and Social Product.* London, UK: Routledge, 2000.

Foucault, Michel. Vigilar y castigar. Buenos Aires: Siglo XXI Editores, 2005.

Flórez Ochoa, Rafael. Evaluación Pedagógica y Cognición. Bogotá: Mc-Graw-Hill, 1999.

Flórez Petour, María Teresa. "Systems, Ideologies and History: A three-dimensional Absence in the Study of Assessment Reform Processes." *Assessment in Education: Principles, Policy & Practice* 22, no. 1 (2015): 3–26. doi: 10.1080/0969594X.2014.943153.

Fuentes Vega, Salvador. "Nuestras Escuelas Normales." *Nuevos Rumbos* 6 (1927): 108–109.

Gillies, Donald. "Developing Governmentality: Conduct and Education Policy." *Journal of Education Policy* 23, no. 4 (2008): 415–427. doi: 10.1080/02680930802054388.

Gobierno de la Unidad Popular. Programa Básico de Gobierno de la Unidad Popular. Santiago, 1969.

–. *La crisis educacional.* Santiago: Quimantú, 1973.

Grek, Sotiria. "From Symbols to Numbers: The Shifting Technologies of Education Governance in Europe." *European Educational Research Journal* 7, no. 2 (2008): 208–218. doi: 10.2304/eerj.2008.7.2.208.

Gysling, Jacqueline. "The Historical Development of Educational Assessment in Chile, 1810–2014." *Assessment in Education: Principles, Policy & Practice*, 23. No. 1 (2016), 8–25. doi: 10.1080/0969594X.2015.1046812.

Haslam, Jonathan. The Nixon Administration and the Death of Allende's Chile. London, UK: Verso, 2005.

Ibáñez del Campo, Carlos, and Mariano Navarrete. "Ley 5291 de Instrucción Primaria Obligatoria." In *Recopilación de leyes, reglamentos y decretos relativos al servicio de la enseñanza pública,* edited by Ricardo Donoso, 557–571. Santiago de Chile: Dirección de Prisiones, 1937.

–. "Decreto 5486. Escuelas Primarias Anexas a Liceos pasan a depender de la Dirección General de Instrucción Secundaria." In Recopilación de leyes, reglamentos y decretos relativos al servicio de la enseñanza pública, edited by Ricardo Donoso, 354–355. Santiago de Chile: Dirección de Prisiones, 1937.

Ibáñez del Campo, Carlos, and *Eduardo Barrios.* "Decreto 4096. Supresión del Bachillerato en Filosofía y Humanidades. Crea la licencia secundaria." In *Recopilación de leyes, reglamentos y decretos relativos al servicio de la enseñanza pública,* edited by Ricardo Donoso, 332. Santiago de Chile: Dirección de Prisiones, 1937

Ibáñez del Campo, Carlos, and *Bartolomé Blanche.* "Decreto 4669. Organiza servicio de Inspección de Educación Primaria." In *Recopilación de leyes, reglamentos y decretos relativos al servicio de la enseñanza pública,* edited by Ricardo Donoso, 581–588. Santiago de Chile: Dirección de Prisiones, 1937.

Jadresic, Alfredo. La reforma de 1968 en la Universidad de Chile. Santiago: Editorial Universitaria, 2002.

Mellafe, Rolando, Antonia Rebolledo, and *Mario Cárdenas. Historia de la Universidad de Chile.* Santiago: Universidad de Chile, 2001.

Ministerio de Educación Pública, "Ley Orgánica Constitucional de Enseñanza (LOCE) Nº 18962." Accessed July 28, 2017. http://www.leychile.cl/Navegar?id Norma=30330&tipoVersion=0.

Montt, Manuel, and *Rafael Sotomayor.* "Primera Ley Orgánica de la Instrucción Primaria." In *"'I el silencio comenzó a reinar': documentos para la historia de la instrucción primaria 1840-1920. Documentos para la historia de la instrucción primaria 1840-1920,* edited by Mario Monsalve Bórquez, 213–217. Santiago: DIBAM, Centro de Investigaciones Barros Arana, 1998.

Núñez, José Abelardo. Estudios sobre educación moderna. Organización de las Escuelas Normales. Informe presentado al Señor Ministro de Instrucción Pública. Santiago: Impr. de la Librería Americana, 1883.

Núñez Prieto, Iván. La producción de conocimiento acerca de la educación escolar chilena, 1907-1957. Santiago: CPEIP, 2002.

Reyes, Leonora. "Profesorado y trabajadores: Movimiento educacional, crisis educativa y reforma de 1928." *Docencia* 40 (2010): 40–49.

Suspitsyna, Tatiana. "Accountability in American education as a rhetoric and a technology of governmentality." *Journal of Education Policy* 25, no. 5 (2010): 567–586. doi: 10.1080/02680930903548411.

Ethan Hutt and Jack Schneider

A Thin Line Between Love and Hate: Educational Assessment in the United States

Educational assessment in the United States is characterised by a number of seeming contradictions. It is viewed as a valid measure of learning, but often seen as an inaccurate gauge of student ability. It is regularly the key variable in high-stakes decisions, but is widely considered to be unfair. It is used to motivate students, teachers, and schools, yet is thought to distort the learning process.

Assessment, in short, is deeply accepted and widely reviled.

How did this come to pass? Why is it that Americans are drawn to educational assessment just as strongly as they are repelled by it? What accounts for this love/hate relationship?

Our chapter seeks to unravel this seemingly contradictory stance by viewing it as the manifestation of a distinct culture — a culture with deep and particular historical roots. We believe that in order to understand educational assessment in the U.S., one must first understand the context from which views of assessment spring. What are the systems that give the American educational system its essential character? What are the core beliefs and ideologies that shape the way Americans see schooling?

Asking these questions is akin to asking about soil and the climate in one's quest to understand the plant life of a particular place. Certainly it would be possible to leap directly into a description of the plants themselves — to describe the palm trees so characteristic of Southern California, for instance, or the birch trees emblematic of the New England woods. But detailed descriptions, though they might paint a clear picture, would fail to address the basic question of why each tree grows where it does. In order to answer that, one must examine the demands of a desert environment or the qualities of a broadleaf forest.

Metaphorically, then, this chapter begins with a discussion of soil and climate – examining the cultural context of educational assessment in the United States. Only then, after establishing this basic groundwork, do we look at educational assessment itself, specifically, at the two dominant forms it has taken in the U.S.: A-F grading and standardized testing. Rather than providing a detailed history of each, we move fairly swiftly across long stretches of time, stopping to highlight particular features of grading and testing practice that evolved in response to the American context. We then conclude by outlining several common, and seemingly contradictory, beliefs about assessment in the U.S. — beliefs that, by the end of this chapter, should be entirely understandable.

The Cultural Context of Educational Assessment

Attitudes toward educational assessment in the United States cannot be traced back to a single origin. They are the product of thousands of different factors, just as a tree is the product of its entire ecosystem.

Still, several contextual factors stand out as particularly influential. Thus, despite the fact that they represent only an incomplete subset, these systems, beliefs, and ideologies do have substantial explanatory power.

Local Control

The first essential contextual factor to consider in the American educational system is the tradition of local control, which constitutes both a structure of governance and an ideology of power.

Local control is an old tradition. States have constitutional authority over education, but from the origin of the system, power truly resided at the local level. Initially, all school funding came from local sources; and even as late as 1930, roughly 80 percent of funding came from the local level.[1] Even today, nearly half of school funding comes from cities and towns, and the laypeople elected to schoolboards exert real power over the districts they govern.

Local control is not just a structure; it is also an ideology. Consequently, there is a staunch tradition of resisting efforts — or perceived efforts — by state or federal agencies to exert control over schools in the United States.[2] Local discretion is fiercely guarded and fosters the belief that schools should reflect the values and concerns of their communities in everything from their approach to science curricula to their selection of common assessments.

Of course, communities are not self-governing. In the American system, state and federal authorities exert significant power, and there is general acceptance that children within each state, as well as within the nation as a whole, should be learning more or less the same thing. Even if an American educational system — a system

---

1   U.S. Department of Education, National Center for Education Statistics, *Digest of Educational Statistics, 2012*, accessed August 15, 2016, http://nces.ed.gov/pubsearch/pubsinfo.asp?pubid=2014015.

2   John W. Meyer and Brian Rowan, "The Structure of Educational Organisations: Environments and Organisations," in *Environments and Organisations,* ed. Marshall W. Meyer (New York, NY: John Wiley and Sons, 1978).

that is relatively the same for all students — does not actually exist in practice, it does exist as an idea.[3]

Nevertheless, centralisation is strongly resisted by the whole breadth of the political spectrum, from the radical left to the conservative right. Consequently, the educational system has always had a comparatively weak infrastructure by design.[4] When policy elites have wanted to build national systems, centralize governance, and increase efficiency, they have been largely thwarted. Instead, they have had to repurpose existing infrastructure or make common cause with private and quasi-governmental organisations to bring about change. In this context, educational assessment has often been used as a mechanism to bring an appearance of cohesion and provide more leverage for change.

Open-Access Egalitarianism

The next essential contextual factor worth considering is the idea of open-access egalitarianism.

Prior to the advent of widespread tax-supported public schools in the mid-nineteenth century, education in the U.S. was characterised by a motley assortment of private academies, dame schools, co-operative efforts, and pauper schools. No guiding ethos regarding equal access, at least beyond access to basic literacy, can be said to have existed.[5]

Funding schools through local property taxes, and later through local and state taxes, changed this.[6] By the late 1800s, almost all students were attending tax-funded public schools. Taxpayer funding provided a structure that, in theory, ensured equal access and equal opportunity. Reality, of course, has been much more complicated. Parents angle for advantage for their children and there are wide discrepancies in funding across states, districts, and schools. Still, the vast majority of students in American schools do attend public schools.[7]

---

3   See, for example, works like Diane Ravitch, *The Death and Life of the Great American School System: How Testing and Choice are Undermining Education* (New York, NY: Basic Books, 2011).

4   David F. Labaree, *Someone Has to Fail: The Zero-Sum Game of Public Schooling* (Cambridge, MA: Harvard University Press, 2012).

5   See, for example, Carl Kaestle, *Pillars of the Republic: Common Schools and American Society* (New York, NY: Hill and Wang, 1983).

6   See, for example, Tracy Steffes, *School, Society, and State: A New Education to Govern Modern America, 1890–1940* (Chicago, IL: University of Chicago Press, 2011).

7   U.S. Department of Education, National Center for Education Statistics, *Private School Universe Survey (PSS), 2011–12*, accessed August 15, 2016, https://nces.ed.gov/surveys/

As with local control, open-access egalitarianism is an ideology as much as it is an organisational feature. Critics of charter schools, for instance, often draw a false dichotomy between charters and 'public schools' — a rhetorical move presumably designed to impugn charters by likening them to private schools, despite the fact that they are public institutions. And in higher education, critics of public schools like the University of Michigan often disparage them as 'private publics', indicating disdain for the institution's relatively high levels of selectivity and cost, which violate the open access principle. In short, the idea of open access is not an instrumental good that produces particular outcomes; it is valued in its own right.

The belief that all students should have the same kind of educational experiences has consequences for educational assessment. On the one hand, it creates a climate conducive to testing as a means of ensuring some level of equivalence and equity across the system — a crucial concern given America's history of segregation and discrimination. As a 2015 press release from 12 civil rights organisations put it: "Data obtained through some standardized tests are particularly important to the civil rights community because they are the only available, consistent, and objective source of data about disparities in education outcomes."[8] Such data, they continued, "are used to advocate for greater resource equity in schools and more fair treatment for students of colour, low-income students, students with disabilities, and English learners."[9]

On the other hand, Americans are uncomfortable with the notion that assessment systems would lead to different kinds of educational experiences for children. If assessment creates different kinds of schools — schools dominated by teaching-to-the-test, for instance, as opposed to schools where teachers exercise greater autonomy — it runs the risk of inciting backlash. Consequently, another 2015 press release — this time from the American Federation of Teachers — argued that "Testing should help inform instruction, not drive instruction [...]. We need to celebrate improvement and the joy of learning, not sanction based on high-stakes standardized tests."[10]

---

pss/tableswhi.asp. U.S. Department of Education, National Center of Statistics, *Digest of Education Statistics 2012*, <u>Table 205.20</u>, accessed August 15, 2016, https://nces.ed.gov/programs/digest/d14/tables/dt14_205.20.asp.

8   The Leadership Conference on Civil and Human Rights, "Civil Rights Groups: 'We Oppose Anti-Testing Efforts,'" Press release, May 5, 2015, accessed June 5, 2015, http://www.civilrights.org/press/2015/anti-testing-efforts.html.

9   Ibid.

10 American Federation of Teachers, "AFT's Weingarten on the U.S. Education Department's 'Testing Action Plan,'" Press release, October 24, 2014, accessed January 3, 2015,

Merit and Social Mobility

The idea that education leads to social mobility is certainly stronger today than it was 200 years ago; yet the system, from its origins, was framed as a "great equalizer."[11]

The idea that schools might promote social mobility is inextricably linked to the distinctly American obsession with merit. Though not an American invention, the notion of a meritocracy took fast hold in the Early Republic, and the nation's founders frequently and eagerly referred to themselves as 'Men of Merit.' Early Americans prided themselves on their freedom from inherited ranks and titles and constructed a popular mythology about "self-made men" and an "aristocracy of talent."[12]

If social and economic prizes are to be allocated by merit, however, there must be some means for determining the degree to which people possess it. Schools were quite convenient for this purpose. A few generations after the American Revolution, more than half of white school-age children were enrolled in school. By 1900, most young people in the northern United States, and most whites in the southern U.S. were enrolled in school. In short, for those recognised as citizens, schooling was a common experience. And schools were a natural stage for displaying merit, as a majority of young people attended, were asked to complete relatively similar tasks, and engaged in work across physical, intellectual, and moral dimensions — ostensibly a full view of a young person's worth.[13]

Though currently debated by social scientists, the idea that schooling could lift a person up from the lowest socioeconomic ranks into the highest became a widely accepted belief by the twentieth century.[14] Lawsuits across the second half of the twentieth century, for instance, and even into the twenty-first, argued for more equal educational experiences by positioning schools as a central factor in

---

http://www.aft.org/press-release/afts-weingarten-us-education-departments-testing-action-plan.

11 Lawrence Cremin, *The Republic and the School: Horace Mann on the Education of Free Men* (New York, NY: Teachers College Press, 1957).

12 Joseph F. Kett, *Merit: The History of a Founding Ideal from the American Revolution to the Twenty-First Century* (Ithaca, NY: Cornell University Press, 2012); James Bryant Conant, *Thomas Jefferson and the Development of American Public Education* (Berkeley, CA: University of California Press, 1962).

13 Kaestle, *Pillars of the Republic*.

14 David F. Labaree, "Public Goods, Private Goods: The American Struggle over Educational Goals," *American Educational Research Journal* 34, no. 1 (1997): 39–81, doi: 10.3102/00028312034001039.

determining individual social and economic outcomes. Put simply, the idea was that a level educational playing field would allow talent to shake out, and that it would create a more equal and just society — a society aligned with the founding ideals of equal opportunity and the pursuit of rational self-interest.

In order for schools to recognise merit, though, there would need to be assessments of young people, as well as a set of relatively standard measures. Whether through athletic contests, spelling bees, written examinations, or other acts of performance, young people would need to be evaluated, consistently across their peer group, in order to determine merit. And as the boundaries of such 'peer groups' expanded ever wider — as the nation became more connected, and as Americans became more mobile — there would be even more need for standard evaluations that would allow for comparison of students who might never actually meet face-to-face.

If assessment is to be used as a sorting mechanism — for providing differential access to rewards — it must be accepted as both fair and uniform. Yet those two demands are in conflict with each other in a massive and decentralised system characterised by high levels of student diversity. Consequently, assessment is both widely accepted and vulnerable to criticism.

Consumerism and Entrepreneurialism

The United States is a nation of hustlers — one referred to by *The Economist* as "a beacon of entrepreneurialism."[15] To use Louis Hartz's phrase, the U.S. is an "acquisitive democracy" — a nation in which manipulating the market system for the purpose of securing material rewards is the stuff of heroism.[16]

This entrepreneurial spirit is not confined to the marketplace. Long before *U.S. News and World Report* began ranking high schools and colleges, parents recognised that some schools opened more doors than others and, in turn, began angling for advantage.[17] Parents, for generations, have considered schooling options in the selection of towns to move to and neighbourhoods to settle in. And in more extreme cases, the power of the entrepreneurial spirit drives those with

---

15 "The United States of Entrepreneurs," *The Economist*, March 12, 2009, accessed May 24, 2015, http://www.economist.com/node/13216037; see also Labaree, *Someone Has to Fail*.

16 Louis Hartz, *The Liberal Tradition in America* (New York, NY: Harcourt Brace and Co. 1955), 138.

17 David F. Labaree, *The Making of an American High School: The Credentials Market and the Central High School of Philadelphia, 1838–1939* (New Haven, CT: Yale University Press. 1988).

means to venture *outside* the public system — to private schools that maintain strong connections with prestigious colleges and elite firms.[18]

On its face, the ethos of consumerist entrepreneurialism seems directly to contradict the ideology of open-access egalitarianism. Yet it is often the case that those working the system to provide their children with a presumed advantage still believe strongly in open access. They are not acting in accordance with what they wish the system would become. Rather, in the words of David Labaree, "consumers are simply pursuing their own interests through the medium of education [...] they're just trying to get ahead or at least not fall behind."[19]

This duality can be further explained by dividing the utility of education into public goods and private goods. As a public good, the content of education matters a great deal. All members of society benefit from an education system that serves all students equally well — preparing citizens for the republic and employees for the capitalist economy. As a private good, however, the content of education matters much less. "Front and centre in the consumer agenda for gaining the greatest benefit from schooling," writes Labaree, "is to acquire its marketable tokens of accomplishment. These include gold stars, test scores, grades, track placements, academic credits, and — most of all — diplomas."[20]

Educational assessment, then, matters a great deal to entrepreneurial consumers of education. If grades and test scores are a currency, then savvy parents will seek to acquire the currency of greatest value and to get as much of it as possible. They will make calculated investments, negotiate whenever possible, and leverage any advantage.

Populism and Common Sense

The United States is a nation infatuated with common sense solutions to knotty problems. From the country's origins, a kind of anti-intellectualism has been deeply ingrained in national culture. Popular beliefs, as evidenced through long-standing deference to leaders of business and evangelical religion, often hold greater sway — at least in the public realm — than the theories of experts. In fact, Americans have a distinctly derisive word for experts. As Richard Hofstadter wrote in 1963, "the greater part of the public...has an ingrained distrust

18 See, for instance, Shamus Rahman Khan, *Privilege: The Making of an Adolescent Elite at St. Paul's School* (Princeton, NJ: Princeton University Press, 2012).

19 Labaree, *Someone Has to Fail*, 236.

20 Ibid., 237.

of eggheads."[21] Divorced from reality, isolated in ivory towers, and wedded to unwieldy theories, eggheads cannot see the forest for the trees. They overlook the simple solution obvious to the attentive layman.

This is not to say that Americans reject expertise. Far from it. There is a great deal of deference to experts. But expertise is always open to challenge, and common sense is an accepted evidence base for even the most complicated policy proposals.

In schooling, particularly, this has long been the case.[22] Consider teachers, who are the experts within classrooms, but who have notoriously low levels of prestige given the common assumption that anyone with common sense can teach.[23] Consider, too, how school districts are governed — by boards of elected laypeople, often with little expertise beyond their own school experiences. Or consider the sway that local communities have maintained over the curriculum — rejecting the teaching of particular subjects, like evolution or sex education, or rejecting particular curricular narratives, like those related to historically-rooted inequality.

Americans, thus, feel qualified to weigh in on nearly any issue in social and political life. But perhaps particularly so in education, which they have all experienced for often well over a decade. When allied with politicians who favour populist approaches to policy — as evident in the recent push to roll back the Common Core State Standards — or with deep-pocketed foundations who favour common sense over evidence, the ideology of anti-intellectualism can exert a powerful influence.

With particular regard to educational assessment, populist common sense has been notably evident. Over the decades, assessment has transformed into highly complex work, often impenetrable to laypeople. Consequently, the pushback against ever more opaque assessment practices has often taken the explicit form not only of popular outrage at particular assessment devices, but, increasingly, at the very practice of assessment itself. In short, Americans are willing to defer to testing experts; but the increasingly inscrutable practices of these experts also makes them suspect in the eyes of populists.

---

21 Richard Hofstadter, *Anti-Intellectualism in American Life* (New York, NY: Knopf, 1963).

22 The value of common sense on school matters remains an important concern for contemporary reformers. See, Jack Schneider, *Excellence For All: How a New Breed of Reformers Is Transforming America's Public Schools* (Nashville, TN: Vanderbilt University Press, 2011); David Labaree, *The Trouble with Ed Schools* (New Haven, CT: Yale University Press, 2004).

23 Dan Lortie, *Schoolteacher: A Sociological Study* (Chicago, IL: University of Chicago Press, 1975).

American Culture and Practice of Assessment

Having laid out the climatic conditions that give rise to a particular culture of assessment, we think it instructive to examine the development of the two most common assessment practices in the United States. Though space does not permit a full historical accounting, we have selected key developments in the evolution of these practices that illustrate the interaction between cultural context and assessment practice.[24]

A Brief History of Grading

There are few more central practices in American schooling than grading. Assignments are graded, participation is graded, projects are graded, tests are graded. So central are grades to students' schooling experience, in fact, that they frequently become a part of students' personal identity. 'She's a straight A student' is a phrase intended to convey not only a general description of a student's academic record, but also a more general statement about the *kind* of person the student is: conscientious and hard-working — a striver. And yet, as much as grades have become a ubiquitous part of American schooling, society, and student identity, they have long been reviled as, at best, incomplete and, at worst, corrosive to educational aims. Their evolution and steady spread despite these critiques, then, offers an instructive example for thinking about the dynamics of assessment in the U.S.

At the core of the history of American grading are two sets of tensions. The first is between the internal and external organisational demands of grading — the need for grading to communicate clearly within a school versus the need for grading to communicate something beyond and across schools. The second tension, interwoven with the first, is between the particularistic, local meaning of grades and the standardized, universal meaning of grades.

These tensions can usefully be thought of as reflecting various combinations of the contextual factors identified at the outset of this chapter. For example, the demand for particularised meanings of grades, comporting with both family and teacher notions of local control and discretion, run directly counter to the desires of students seeking wider recognition of their academic merit, as well as to the desires of policymakers seeking egalitarianism through standardisation. Efforts

---

24 For a full history of the development of American grading practices see Jack Schneider and Ethan Hutt "Making the grade: a history of the A–F marking scheme," *Journal of Curriculum Studies* 46, 2 (2014): 201–24, doi: 10.1080/00220272.2013.790480.

to balance such tensions, as this section will demonstrate, have led to constantly shifting practices within a more broadly stable culture of assessment.

The early days of grading were characterised by local control. Idiosyncratic practices reflected the nominally professional vision of individual teachers and the communities that banded together to hire them. These practices were inherently ephemeral, as early evaluation in American common schools usually took the form of oral examinations and public performances.[25] Far from being recorded as part of the permanent record, the assessment was intended to be both instantaneous and dynamic: students received instant praise (or rebuke) and often saw their physical location in the class reflect this regular assessment. Students who did well were moved toward the front of the class, while other students found themselves moving figuratively and literally behind their peers. These kinds of assessment practices were well suited to the early 19th century model of American schooling — one characterised by irregular student attendance, varied curricula, and the one-room school house.

As the 19th century progressed, American educators, influenced by the practices of their colleagues abroad, increasingly began to worry about the messages these grading practices sent to students — placing an emphasis as they did on the immediate goal of 'winning' the competition rather than on the long-term goal of educational self-improvement. As famed educational reformer Horace Mann observed, "if superior rank at recitation be the object, then, as soon as that superiority is obtained, the spring of desire and effort for that occasion relaxes."[26] Policy leaders like Mann believed that replacing daily, ephemeral, performative competition with periodic written, private records of student achievement — like the report card — would turn student attention back to the intrinsic, long-term goals of education and the persistent effort their achievement required. Yet though the report card invited students to take a longer-view of their education, it did not prevent them from bending these practices to their own entrepreneurial ends.

After the introduction of innovations like the report card for recording grades and formally communicating them to students and parents, the form and substance of written grading practices developed substantially over the last decades of the 19th century, reflecting the shifting organisational forms of American schooling. Beginning first with American colleges and disseminating downward through the system, American educators increasingly marked school progress not in years

---

25 William J. Reese, *Testing Wars in the Public Schools: A Forgotten History* (Cambridge, MA: Harvard University Press, 2013).

26 Horace Mann, *Ninth Annual Report* (Boston, MA: Dutton and Wentworth, State Printer, 1846), 504.

but in grade levels and course credit — reflecting the increasing number of curricular options and tracks available to students. One upshot of this was that it was no longer possible for schools to rank students directly with each other because they were not taking the same courses. This created pressure to recognise students as belonging to *categories* defined by their grades and, in higher education, by their graduation honours (e.g. cum laude, summa cum laude). Here again, reformers hoped that these categories would displace competition for individual honours in favour of groups of men with equal distinction. But the value to individuals in achieving these ranks could only reduce competition so much — it left plenty of room for ambitious strivers to make calculated choices for the purpose of achieving the marks that would allow them to get ahead.

Concurrently, schools at all levels began to narrow the meaning of grades in order to communicate more clearly their academic distinction. For much of the 19th century, grades reflected both a moral and behavioural dimension, as well as an academic one; but in the second half of the century, grades came to reflect only a student's academic performance.[27] This move reflected the increasing academic focus of schools, and the increasing importance of academic grades as legitimate markers of distinction beyond the confines of the school. As the president of Philadelphia's celebrated Central High School explained, "the best scholars are not always the most decorous;" consequently, combining behaviour and achievement only served to "depriv[e] the student of those honours which he had fairly won by diligence and industry."[28]

It is only a slight simplification to say that the increasing association of grades with academic merit, and of academic merit with social distinction, created increasing pressure to standardize grades. After all, if grades were to work for the purpose of open access egalitarianism, they needed to have uniform meaning across levels of the school system and throughout the nation. And though this ran against the tradition of local control, only so much local variation could be tolerated in an increasingly national competition for academic merit and social mobility.

Greater uniformity in grading would place serious constraints on the use of grades as contextualised communication tools — as a way of indicating a student's standing within the class. And there was strong pressure for greater uniformity. As one early 20th century commentator put it:

---

27 Labaree, *The Making of an American High School*; Frederick Rudolph, *The American College and University: A History* (Athens, GA: University of Georgia Press, 1962).
28 Labaree, *The Making of an American High School*, 141.

"the one common language in which the scholarly attainments of pupils are expressed is a scalar one [...] if we, who live in the Middle West, read in a New York Magazine that a certain man entered college with an average grade of 95 [...] we know pretty well what that means; and so it is in the country over."[29]

Yet despite the universalistic meaning of these grades, there was no obvious method "whereby grades assigned by one teacher can be intelligently compared with those assigned by another, and all brought to a common standard."[30] Another contemporary commentator put the matter — and stakes attached — even more plainly: "the grade has in more than one sense a cash value and if there is no uniformity of grading in an institution, this means directly that values are stolen from some and undeservedly presented to others."[31]

These calls to shore up faith in grades as the uniform currency of academic exchange resonated well with the ascendant system-building push of Progressive Era educators. This new generation of school reformers was actively interested in using the tools of government and emerging educational science to bring more coherence, higher standards, and greater efficiency to America's sprawling education system.[32] With this systemisation came greater attention and a policy push to standardize teacher grading practices — to ensure that an "A" in Portland, Maine, for instance, would have the same meaning as an "A" in Portland, Oregon. A number of studies published in this period made a great deal about the unreliability and subjectivity of teacher grading and the frequent failure of teacher grades to adhere to characteristics of the normal curve, which had become such a touchstone for psychologists and others working within the mental testing movement.[33]

While the majority of school officials by the mid-20th century accepted the A-F format for grading, as well as the premise of a standardized grade distribution, progress was uneven and contested. Many educators wondered openly about the role of the teacher's own professional discretion in the face of these constraints, pleading for the legitimation of an alternative to the normal curve — a format

---

29 Leroy D. Weld, "A Standard of Interpretation of Numerical Grades," The School Review 25, no. 6 (1917), 412.

30 Ibid.

31 Max Meyer, "Experiences with the Grading System of the University of Missouri," Science 33, no. 852 (1911), 661.

32 David Tyack, The One Best System: A History of American Urban Education (Cambridge, MA: Harvard University Press, 1974); Raymond Callahan, Education and the Cult of Efficiency (Chicago, IL: University of Chicago Press, 1964).

33 See, for instance, Isador E. Finkelstein, The Marking System in Theory and Practice (Baltimore, MD: Warwick and York, 1913).

that might give individual teachers more discretion.[34] Others rejected the premise of reducing student work to a single grade by opting to substitute the report card for a letter home or attempting to efface their meaning and power by reducing the number of categories to Pass/Fail or High Pass/Pass/Fail. Still, these efforts never amounted to much more than rear guard actions against the continued spread and use of grades.

Indeed, the reasons that these practices were rejected provide important insight into the American culture of grading. While many educators and parents complained, as they had in the 19th century, that competition around academic distinction encouraged students to seek grades rather than knowledge, the increasing embeddedness of grades beyond the school environment made it difficult to get out from under their use.

Even when taken on purely academic terms, those who critiqued grades often chose to operate within their basic framework, even as they sought greater distinction, and social mobility, through grades. Concerned that students could have identical grade point averages despite very different academic course selections, the parents of high achieving students, and the colleges that sought their enrolments, pushed for 'weighted-GPAs', with students receiving extra credit for harder courses. Likewise, even students at schools with alternative grading practices worried that these practices might limit their prospects in subsequent academic and labour market settings. For example, the University of California Santa Cruz, founded as a radical alternative to existing state institutions, recently abandoned its three decade-old practice of giving students "narrative evaluations" in lieu of letter grades, citing concerns about student graduate school competitiveness and the inefficiency of narrative grades when done at large-scale.[35] The value of long-form communication between teacher and student, it seems, had to give way to the practical considerations of mass higher education and international labour markets.

As this brief history of grading should make clear, the set of considerations shaping assessment practices extend far beyond those of the teacher in the classroom or the family of the student. Rather, these practices, like schools themselves, are embedded in a much larger context that establishes both demands and constraints.

---

34 Norman E. Rutt, "Grades and Distributions," *National Mathematics Magazine* 18, no. 3 (1943): 120–26.

35 Tanya Schevitz, "UC Santa Cruz Faculty to Vote on Ending Narrative Evaluations," *San Francisco Chronicle*, November 26, 2000, accessed July 15, 2014, http://www.sfgate.com/education/article/UC-Santa-Cruz-Faculty-to-Vote-on-Ending-Narrative-2726032.php.

Grades, then, were transformed into a source of academic distinction for students — trophies of their success in open academic competition — and a currency with a reasonably stable, if not entirely certain, external value. The failure to fulfil both of these roles served as a persistent spur to move in the direction of greater standardisation, competition, and distinction. Moreover, such tensions led to a further elaboration of grading practice, rather than to a rejection of the underlying culture of assessment.

A Brief History of Standardized Testing

As with the history of grading, the history of standardized testing has been shaped by the interplay between cultural factors and the specific ends to which standardized testing has been put. Yet though both are clearly part of the assessment culture of American schooling, there are inherent differences between grading and testing practices — differences instructive for showing how the same dynamic can drive the development of a very different set of practices.

Specifically, while the history of grading represents an attempt to make a personal communication between teacher and student more durable and intelligible to people at increasingly greater remove — both spatially and temporally — standardized testing was always fundamentally about creating standardized comparisons and the creation of larger 'communities.' As with grading, standardisation of testing practice provided both an opportunity and a threat. In drawing larger numbers of students together from across real communities, standardized tests offered students a chance to garner greater distinction in an even larger academic competition. In doing so, however, they threatened existing hierarchies, conventional wisdom, and other ways of knowing about schools. Thus, if the challenge of developing grading practices was to maintain the personal dimension of grades as they became increasingly standardized, the challenge of standardized testing was to maintain the simplicity of common metrics amid a blizzard of competing and conflicting test scores.

The first written standardized test was introduced into American public schools in Boston in 1845. Even in this very first instance, the dynamics that would animate the future use and proliferation of standardized tests were easy to see. As with the introduction of recorded grades, standardized tests were ushered into schools in an effort to replace impressionistic evaluations of students with 'hard facts.' Unlike recorded grades, however, the introduction of tests was done with the explicit intention of engaging the larger public in a debate about school quality. The men responsible for introducing standardized tests to Boston, including none other than Horace Mann, believed that the (low) test scores would provide evidence of the need to adopt their favoured school reforms.[36]

While reformers succeeded in calling into question the presumed superiority of Boston schools and pushing through some of their desired reforms, they did not count on the extent to which these new tools would be taken up by others. It did not take long, for instance, before publishing companies produced an avalanche of test materials for educators and test preparation books for students. And though rote teaching was an explicit target of the reformers who introduced standardized testing, future generations agreed that tests had done as much to solidify such teaching practice as they had to displace it. These consequences reflect the tensions between merit and entrepreneurialism, on the one hand, and between merit and equal access egalitarianism on the other. Reformers seeking to inform the public about undesirable variation and leverage their civic pride in having widely renowned schools were increasingly surprised, then, as they encountered an entrepreneurial perspective that cast testing not an opportunity for reform, but as a chance to get ahead.

Over the next half century, tests would come to occupy an increasingly prominent place in the organisation and operation of schools. Individual schools utilised tests and norm tables to determine student placement; districts used standardized tests to allocate the limited number of seats in high schools; and states like New York introduced a state-wide examination — the Regents Examination — intended to standardize achievement norms and direct competitive energies toward higher academic standards.[37]

The entrepreneurial and meritocratic dimensions of schooling were well-served by the introduction of standardized tests. But so was open-access egalitarianism. As in the case of grades and grading, those who had a vested interest in academic achievement had an interest in making academic merit universally recognizable. By allowing more direct and far-flung comparisons, standardized tests were, from the beginning, enlisted in this cause. As a New York educator explaining the value of a diploma backed by the faith and credit of a statewide standardized test observed to his students, "we may think, and you may believe that what you do here is recognised throughout the state, but outside of our village we are not

---

36 Reese, *Testing Wars in the Public Schools.*

37 Stephen Jay Gould, *The Mismeasure of Man* (WW Norton & Company, 1996); Labaree, *The Making of an American High School*; Nancy Beadie, "From Student Markets to Credential Markets: The Creation of the Regents Examination System in New York State, 1864–1890," *History of Education Quarterly* 39, no. 1 (1999): 1–30. doi: 10.2307/369330.

known; your papers simply show that you have got a certificate somewhere."[38] Such sentiments became increasingly common among the self-styled professional educators and purveyors of the educational sciences during the Progressive Era. As one commentator explained: "Test scores furnish the common language, for anyone can understand what is meant by saying that our schools in Smithville are a year ahead of most schools of America in, say, arithmetic, and a year or two years behind others in music or French or manual training."[39]

Such comparisons could form the basis for arguments to improve schools. As one set of Progressive Educators advised superintendents: "Test results constitute incontrovertible facts, so often needed by the superintendent in a campaign of education of public opinion."[40] But they could also provide an unwelcome entanglement for those who fared poorly. As another commentator of the period observed: "If one could read all the small-town papers of any given state for one year, he would probably find three-fourths of them claiming that their home town had the best schools in the state."[41] Put simply, the tradition of local control, particularly when combined with civic pride, militated against the uncomplicated acceptance of test results.

American educators may have embraced standardized testing but, true to form, they did not do so in any uniform way. The sprawling American education system begat a standardized testing industry that was every bit as eclectic and varied as the system it served and helped to create. By one estimate, there were at least 250 commercially available standardised tests in 1922. The sheer variety of tests ensured that there would be no definitive answer to the best school district, best instructor, or the best method of math instruction because competing claims could easily be supported by their own respective set of standardized test scores.

Unlike Europe, where the responsibility to commission and oversee high stakes qualifying examinations fell to the state, these responsibilities were outsourced to independent entities in the U.S. — sometimes to non-profit organisations, but just as often to for-profit companies. Thus, even in college admissions — an area of comparatively strong standardisation — two separate organisations and tests were allowed to develop and serve an indispensable role in college access.

38　Beadie, "From Student Markets to Credential Markets," 24.
39　Denton L. Geyer, *Introduction to the Use of Standardized Tests* (Chicago, IL: Plymouth Press), 11–12.
40　Sidney L. Pressey and Luella Cole, *Introduction to the Use of Standard Tests: A Brief Manual in the Use of Tests of Both Ability and Achievement in the School Subjects* (New York, NY: World Book Company, 1922), 34–35.
41　Carter Alexander, *School Statistics and Publicity* (Boston, MA: Silver, Burdett), 52–53.

To this day, both the Scholastic Assessment Test (SAT)[42] and American College Test (ACT), emphasise their different approaches to measuring college readiness, and enterprising students are routinely given the advice to take both and submit their highest score.

There was also rarely any incentive for any of the parties involved to commensurate the values or scores produced by the multitude of tests. It was better to leave these self-contained standardized visions to coexist: testing companies had market share to protect; students had records to burnish; and districts (and cities) had political, economic, and civic interests to project an image of scholastic excellence and efficiency. In many cases this permissiveness was a double-edged sword. On the one hand, it allowed those without privilege to move up through the system. On the other hand, however, it allowed their more privileged peers to modify or abandon those metrics which no longer served their interests.

This struggle to enlist standardized test in non-uniform aims has reached its fullest expression in the era of federally-mandated high-stakes testing, which began when No Child Left Behind was signed into law by George W. Bush in 2002. Despite the explicit attempt to use standardized test scores to promote equity and allow for easier comparison of schools, districts, and states, the result produced not one clear fact sheet, but rather, a 50-hued tie-dye of competing tests, standards, and definitions of proficiency. Though many lament this development as the unfortunate byproduct of federalism, we think it is better understood as the logical result of the competing ends that Americans seek to reach through standardized testing. Such a system accommodates the contradictory aims of egalitarianism and advantage, localism and universality.

Just as importantly, for those who reject the premise of quantifying learning — a line of critique that runs uninterrupted through American educational history — the lack of clarity produced by the blizzard of test scores only provides further evidence that the experts and their tests misapprehend what is *really* going on in schools. This is the basis of the current movement by parents to 'opt-out' of state and federal mandated testing. The message from parents could not be clearer: test results dissemble; they have nothing to offer a parent in the know. And yet, despite the outcry against the 'over-testing' of students, the U.S. Congress balked at the chance to remove testing requirements from the latest version of federal law, now rechristened the 'Every Student Succeeds Act'. Instead, they offered states more flexibility, more discretion in the design, use, and

---

42   Originally called Scholastic Aptitude Test.

oversight of tests — ensuring that tests would continue to balance the multiple demands to which they have always been put.

Contradictory Beliefs about Assessment

In the United States, educational assessment is characterised by deep acceptance and persistent complaining. It is remarkably stable, but constantly in a process of churn.

This is the result of contradictory beliefs about assessment — beliefs rooted in a particular cultural context — that simultaneously pull American schools in different directions. And given this rooting, assessment can never be exactly what Americans want it to be. Their feelings must always be mixed.

In this section, we will take a closer look at several examples of seemingly contradictory notions about assessment that are common in the U.S. These are not intended to be comprehensive; they do not sum up all that Americans believe about assessment. However, these examples are representative of a distinct ethos. And, collectively, they constitute a long stretch of the thin line this paper seeks to map out – the line between love and hate that describes the American culture of educational assessment.

Notion 1: Assessment systems should be uniform and coherent, but not national.

Open-access egalitarianism requires a single system that treats all people fairly. And the impulses of merit and social mobility demand that all students take the same tests, opening the same opportunities to receive rewards in exchange for their talent and hard work. The result has been the creation and utilisation of a variety of national assessment systems like the SAT, the ACT, the AP (Advanced Placement Program), the NAEP (National Assessment of Educational Progress), and the PARCC (Partnership for Assessment of Readiness for College and Careers).

Yet there is pushback against these assessment systems because each, in some way, erodes local control. Additionally, any national assessment threatens consumer autonomy in a free market by limiting available choices. Consequently, national assessment systems in the United States are always something short of national. In the case of assessments, the SAT, ACT, and AP tests (Advanced Placement tests), for instance, students can opt-in and opt-out of the exams at will. And in the case of the federally-mandated NAEP exam, the test may be national, but it is also toothless. With no stakes attached to the test, students have nothing to lose by taking it. And without results aggregated at the state level, rather than the student or school level, it is not exactly clear what, exactly, NAEP assessing.

When no compromise is evident, as was the case with the PARCC exam — a test tied to the Common Core State Standards project that sought to unify the nation's 50 different curricular and assessment systems — hostility can build up quickly. Despite the fact that the PARCC exam represented only a tweak to the system, the perception that it was forcing standardisation at the national level produced a surprising coalition of opponents. Overwhelming support in favour of PARCC quickly reversed.

Notion 2: Assessments should create winners, but not losers.

Because of the pressure for open-access egalitarianism, there is consistent demand for assessments that produce comparable information. All students, for instance, should be given grades that have relatively equal meaning and should all sit for the same exams. Additionally, information gathered from such assessments should provide the basis for assuring that students have equal opportunities to advance in a meritocratic system.

Yet the forces of consumerism and entrepreneurism mean that individual families, seeing education as a private good, are generally unwilling to accept that their children have lost in a meritocratic competition. In a system with a single high-stakes national test — as in Korea or Japan — this could be problematic. But in the permissive American assessment culture, these impulses are channelled into the cultivation of new and different forms of distinction. AP tests, for instance, award college credit, but are optional, and students do not suffer for earning low marks on them — they can choose, as with SAT scores, whether and which scores to report colleges. And students often shop for the easiest AP tests to take. In this light, standardized assessment becomes a means not of selection and exclusion, but of building an argument and making a case for one's individual merit.

Grade inflation is perhaps the clearest example of the contradictory desire to produce winners but not losers. While students are graded on a uniform A-F scale, parents and students exert strong pressure on teachers to give good grades. And even if pressure is not applied directly, teachers know that grades can seriously impact a student's advancement through the system. Not surprisingly, then, the modal grade at Harvard University is an A- and the second most frequently issued grade is an A. This compression of grades at the top end of the scale is indicative of the desire to keep as many students in the game as possible.

Notion 3: Assessment results are objective, but not always valid.

The default position in the United States is that the use of educational assessments is a fair and objective way to measure student ability. This is particularly true for winners in the system, who have a vested interest in showing that their advancement is due to merit rather than chance or privilege. The numbers don't lie.

But when the drive for merit-based social mobility is thwarted, it tends to engender populist pushback against assessment developers who, detractors argue, do not understand what really goes on in schools or what it really means to be educated. One clear example of this can be seen in the history of the AP program. Elite high schools championed the AP program, which gave their students an admissions edge. But when the program expanded more broadly, elite schools, which no longer enjoyed an admissions advantage from AP, began dropping the program. They criticised AP as out-of-date and out of touch — an invalid measure of advanced work. Subsequently, many of these schools entrepreneurially crafted alternatives that they branded "post AP" curricula.[43]

Another clear example can be seen in the pushback against state assessment systems adopted under No Child Left Behind. As long as test results did not adversely affect students and their schools, the law garnered widespread support. But when schools began closing, and when researchers began documenting unintended consequences like narrowing of the curriculum and teaching-to-the-test, critics began arguing that the tests were invalid and not worth the costs associated with them.

Notion 4: Assessments should have stakes, but should not distort the process of learning.

Because K-12 education is taxpayer funded, Americans tend to support the idea that public schools should produce results. As they see it, students should not simply drift through the system, learning or not learning according to chance or desire. From this perspective, assessments should be tied to accountability mechanisms as a way of promoting effective management at the local and state level.

Additionally, parents want information about their children's progress, and support mechanisms that help them encourage effort. Given belief in the relatively meritocratic nature of an open-access system, parents believe that grades and test

---

43 Jack Schneider, "Privilege, Equity, and the Advanced Placement Program: Tug of War," *Journal of Curriculum Studies* 41, no. 6 (2009): 813–31; Jack Schneider, *Excellence For All*.

scores provide tools that will help them guide their children toward social mobility. Assessment results are useful carrots and sticks.

Yet Americans do not want assessments to serve as ends in and of themselves. Assessment, they generally believe, should not distort the learning process. And it should especially not do so in a differential way — affecting some schools and students, but not others.

State accountability tests, adopted in the wake of No Child Left Behind, were designed to motivate teachers and students to focus more on the acquisition of content. But the strongest criticism has been that such tests have distorted the learning process — turning too much curricular attention to tested subjects, and orienting schools too strongly toward test results. Consequently, a growing 'opt-out' movement has sprung up, with parents exempting their children from the standardized tests that continue to be mandated by federal policy — a federal policy with widespread support.

Conclusion

In this chapter we have tried to sketch out an answer to a fundamental question: How is it that Americans both embrace and revile educational assessment?

As we suggest, the answer lies deep below what is immediately visible in present practices. Thus, any attempt to unravel this mystery must begin with an examination of the conditions that have given shape to the way Americans approach assessment.

At the outset of this chapter, we used the metaphor of soil and climate, making the case for the importance of context. In the specific case of educational assessment in the United States, however, a better metaphor may be that of tectonic plates. Invisible above the surface, the forces of consumerism and entrepreneurialism, merit and social mobility, open-access egalitarianism, and local control grind constantly against each other. Exerting pressure in different directions, they continue to shape the landscape above.

At various times, different combinations of these values have inspired the pursuit of seemingly contradictory aims. Yet contradictory as they may seem, these aims are consistent with the cultural forces that continue to shape both belief and action. Activity above ground, in other words, aligns with action below.

The resulting picture of assessment in the United States, then, is one of a fault line under intense pressure. This pressure is frequently relieved in small adjustments — the removal of a contested metric, for instance, or the development of a new test. And occasionally, it manifests in disruptive ground-shaking. But the fault line itself never dissolves. Below ground, the forces of love and hate grind on. They do so in equal measure.

Literature

Alexander, Carter. *School Statistics and Publicity*. Boston, MA: Silver, Burdett, 1919.

American Federation of Teachers. "AFT's Weingarten on the U.S. Education Department's 'Testing Action Plan.'" Press release, October 24, 2014. Accessed January 3, 2015. http://www.aft.org/press-release/afts-weingarten-us-education-departments-testing-action-plan.

Beadie, Nancy. "From Student Markets to Credential Markets: The Creation of the Regents Examination System in New York State, 1864–1890." *History of Education Quarterly* 39, no. 1 (1999): 1–30. doi: 10.2307/369330.

Callahan, Raymond. *Education and the Cult of Efficiency*. Chicago, IL: University of Chicago Press, 1964.

Conant, James Bryant. *Thomas Jefferson and the Development of American Public Education*. Berkeley, CA: University of California Press, 1962.

Cremin, Lawrence. *The Republic and the School: Horace Mann on the Education of Free Men*. New York, NY: Teachers College Press, 1957.

Finkelstein, Isador E. *The Marking System in Theory and Practice*. Baltimore, MD: Warwick and York, 1913.

Geyer, Denton L. *Introduction to the Use of Standardized Tests*. Chicago, IL: Plymouth Press, 1922.

Gould, Stephen Jay. *The Mismeasure of Man*. New York, London: WW Norton & Company, 1996.

Hartz, Louis. *The Liberal Tradition in America*. New York, NY: Harcourt Brace and Co. 1955.

Hofstadter, Richard. *Anti-Intellectualism in American Life*. New York, NY: Knopf, 1963.

Kaestle, Carl. *Pillars of the Republic: Common Schools and American Society*. New York, NY: Hill and Wang, 1983.

Karabel, Jerome. *The Chosen: The Hidden History of Admission and Exclusion at Harvard, Yale, and Princeton*. New York, NY: Houghton Mifflin Harcourt, 2006.

Khan, Shamus Rahman. *Privilege: The Making of an Adolescent Elite at St. Paul's School*. Princeton, NJ: Princeton University Press, 2012.

Kett, Joseph F. *Merit. The History of a Founding Ideal from the American Revolution to the Twenty-First Century*. Ithaca, NY: Cornell University Press, 2012.

Labaree, David F. *The Making of an American High School: The Credentials Market and the Central High School of Philadelphia, 1838–1939*. New Haven, CT: Yale University Press, 1988.

–. "Public Goods, Private Goods: The American Struggle over Educational Goals." *American Educational Research Journal* 34, no. 1 (1997): 39–81. doi: 10.3102/00028312034001039.

–. *The Trouble with Ed Schools*. New Haven, CT: Yale University Press, 2004.

–. *Someone Has to Fail: The Zero-Sum Game of Public Schooling*. Cambridge, MA: Harvard University Press, 2012.

Lortie, Dan. *Schoolteacher: A Sociological Study*. Chicago, IL: University of Chicago Press, 1975.

Mann, Horace. *Ninth Annual Report*. Boston, MA: Dutton and Wentworth, State Printer, 1846.

Meyer, Max. "Experiences with the Grading System of the University of Missouri." *Science* 33, no. 852 (1911): 661–67.

Meyer, John W., and Brian Rowan. "The Structure of Educational Organisations: Environments and Organisations." In *Environments and Organisations*, edited by Marshall W. Meyer, 78–109. New York, NY: John Wiley and Sons, 1978.

Pressey, Sidney L., and Luella Cole. *Introduction to the Use of Standard Tests: A Brief Manual in the Use of Tests of Both Ability and Achievement in the School Subjects*. New York, NY: World Book Company, 1922.

Ravitch, Diane. *The Death and Life of the Great American School System: How Testing and Choice are Undermining Education*. New York, NY: Basic Books, 2011.

Reese, William J. *Testing Wars in the Public Schools: A Forgotten History*. Cambridge, MA: Harvard University Press, 2013.

Rudolph, Frederick. *The American College and University: A History*. Athens, GA: University of Georgia Press, 1962.

Rutt, Norman E. "Grades and Distributions." *National Mathematics Magazine* 18, no. 3 (1943): 120–26.

Schevitz, Tanya. "UC Santa Cruz Faculty to Vote on Ending Narrative Evaluations." *San Francisco Chronicle*. November 26, 2000. Accessed July 15, 2014. http://www.sfgate.com/education/article/UC-Santa-Cruz-Faculty-to-Vote-on-Ending-Narrative-2726032.php.

Schneider, Jack. "Privilege, Equity, and the Advanced Placement Program: Tug of War." *Journal of Curriculum Studies* 41, no. 6 (2009): 813–31. doi: 10.1080/00220270802713613.

–. *Excellence For All: How a New Breed of Reformers Is Transforming America's Public Schools*. Nashville, TN: Vanderbilt University Press, 2011.

Schneider, Jack, and *Ethan Hutt*. "Making the grade: a history of the A-F marking scheme." *Journal of Curriculum Studies* 46, 2 (2014): 201–24. doi: 10.1080/00220272.2013.790480.

Steffes, Tracy. *School, Society, and State: A New Education to Govern Modern America, 1890–1940*. Chicago, IL: University of Chicago Press, 2011.

The Leadership Conference on Civil and Human Rights. "Civil Rights Groups: 'We Oppose Anti-Testing Efforts.'" Press release, May 5, 2015. Accessed June 5, 2015. http://www.civilrights.org/press/2015/anti-testing-efforts.html.

"The United States of Entrepreneurs." *The Economist*, March 12, 2009. Accessed May 24, 2015. http://www.economist.com/node/13216037.

Tyack, David. *The One Best System: A History of American Urban Education*. Cambridge, MA: Harvard University Press, 1974.

U.S. *Department of Education, National Center for Education Statistics, Digest of Educational Statistics, 2012*. Accessed August 15, 2016. http://nces.ed.gov/pubsearch/pubsinfo.asp?pubid=2014015.

–. *Digest of Education Statistics 2012, Table 205.20*. Accessed August 15, 2016. https://nces.ed.gov/programs/digest/d14/tables/dt14_205.20.asp.

–. *Private School Universe Survey (PSS), 2011–12*. Accessed August 15, 2016. https://nces.ed.gov/surveys/pss/tableswhi.asp.

Weld, Leroy D. "A Standard of Interpretation of Numerical Grades." *The School Review* 25, no. 6 (1917): 412–21.

Cristina Alarcón

The *Grundschulgutachten* as part of an Assessment Culture: A German Story?

"L. is a gifted pupil and belongs to the best of the class. The production of essays, in which she commits to paper the results of lessons, experiences and reflections, does not pose any difficulties for her, but she writes fleetingly. She is very lively and can be unruly here and there. Apprehension and intellectual capacity are present. Joy of pleasure would increase her performance. Suitable."[1]

This quotation is the example of a so-called *Grundschulgutachten*, a primary school report, regarding a female pupil of the mid-1960's in Tübingen, Germany. As the example shows, this assessment instrument, written by the class teacher, aimed not only at assessing cognitive abilities and the knowledge acquired by the pupil, but would also describe character traits ("lively," "unruly," "fleeting"). Unlike other assessment tools, such as grading or certifications, the report should draw a picture of the child's personality. Another characteristic of the report was its decisive selection function in the vertically structured German school system. Within the framework of a selection process, the children should be assigned to different secondary school types after the end of primary school, i.e. from 5th or 6th grade. This selection followed a so-called 'negative' process, i.e. unsuitable schoolchildren should be kept away from school types such as the *Gymnasium*, which gave the right to study at university levels and therefore grants access to academic professions. As can be seen in the example cited above, all reports ended with a decisive judgment: suitable/ perhaps suitable/ unsuitable. This selection process thus functioned as the most important transitional point of the German school system: not only school careers were determined, but also future social status.

Certainly, written descriptions of pupils such as the *Gutachten* are not a special feature of Germany. There are even similar verbal forms of assessment within the English *report cards* and *scholars leaving certificates,* or the so-called *recommendation letters* in university admission procedures in Britain and the

---

1   Studie des Pädagogischen Seminars Universität Tübingen: Analyse von 300 Grund-schulgutachten. Andreas Flitner and Helmut Kamm, "Das Grundschulgutachten. Seine Voraussetzungen und seine Bedeutung für die Schülerauslese," *Pädagogische Arbeits-blätter* 20, no. 6/7 (1968): 82.

USA.[2] Nevertheless, the dissemination, historical persistence, and decisive selection function which is attributed to assessment instruments such as the *Gutachten* in Germany, is characteristic or, at least, noteworthy.

But when and why did the assessment practice of the pupil description, in particular the *Gutachten,* emerge in Germany? To which educational traditions is it to be linked? What functions should the *Gutachten* serve in the context of school? How can the historical persistence of this assessment instrument be explained?

Several empirical studies have already dealt with the objectivity, validity and prognostic quality of primary school reports,[3] or with the role of the teacher as an expert assessment.[4] Despite the abundance of research literature, a study on the *Grundschulgutachten* from the perspective of history of education research has not been yet undertaken.

---

2   See Heiner Ullrich, "Exzellenz und Elitenbildung in Gymnasien. Traditionen und Innovationen," in *Elite und Exzellenz im Bildungssystem. Nationale und internationale Perspektiven,* ed. Heinz-Hermann Krüger and Werner Helsper (Wiesbaden: Springer VS, 2014).

3   See e.g. Walter Schultze, Werner Knoche and Elisabeth Thomas, *Über den Voraussagewert der Auslesekriterien für den Schulerfolg am Gymnasium* (Frankfurt am Main: Max-Traeger-Stiftung, 1964); Karlheinz Ingenkamp, *Untersuchungen zur Übergangsauslese* (Weinheim: Beltz, 1968); Lothar Tent, *Die Auslese von Schülern für weiterführende Schulen: Möglichkeiten und Grenzen. Beiträge zur Theorie und Praxis der Leistungsbeurteilung in der Schule* (Göttingen: Hogrefe, 1969); Wolfgang Schulte Ladbeck, "Grundschulgutachten und Schulerfolg im Gymnasium: Längsschnittstudie dreier Schülerjahrgänge vom Übertritt ins Gymnasium bis zum Abitur" (PhD diss., Universität Münster, 1989).

4   See e.g. Karl Heinrich Burbach, *Schülergutachten: Eine Untersuchung über Schülerbeobachtung und Schülerbeurteilung* (Frankfurt am Main: Hirschgraben-Verl, 1955); Fritz Latscha, "Der Einfluss des Primarlehrers," in *Die Ungleichheit der Bildungschancen: Soziale Schranken im Zugang zur höheren Schule,* ed. Franz Hess, Fritz Latscha and Willi Schneider (Olten: Walter-Verlag, 1966); Günter Steinkamp, "Die Rolle des Volksschullehrers im schulischen Selektionsprozess: Ergebnisse einer empirisch-soziologischen Untersuchung," *Hamburger Jahrbuch für Wirtschafts- und Gesellschaftspolitik* 12 (1967): 302–324; Helmut Kamm, "Beurteilungskategorien und Perspektiven des Lehrers in Schülercharakteristiken" (PhD diss., Eberhard-Karls-Universität zu Tübingen, 1972); Ruth Gresser-Spitzmüller, *Lehrerurteil und Bildungschancen: Eine Untersuchung über den Einfluss des Grundschullehrers auf die Wahl weiterführender Schulen* (Weinheim: Beltz, 1973); Sanna Pohlmann, *Der Übergang am Ende der Grundschulzeit: Zur Formation der Übergangsempfehlung aus der Sicht der Lehrkräfte* (Münster: Waxmann, 2009); Peggy Richert, *Elternentscheidung versus Lehrerdiagnose: Der Übergang von der Grundschule zur Sekundarschule* (Bad Heilbrunn: Klinkhardt, 2012).

This article analyses the function attributed to the primary school report during the Weimar Republic (1918–1933), the Third Reich (1933–1945) and the Federal Republic of Germany until the reunification (1949–1989). For this purpose, developments in individual (federal) states (*Länder*) are included in the analysis, but no systematic overview of all *Länder* can be provided. From 1949 onwards, only the developments in the Federal Republic of Germany are considered.

I will first analyse the *Gutachten* as a peculiar assessment instrument and professional knowledge, and then undertake a historical examination about its underlying assessment culture, which leads into of the 18th century. After that, I reconstruct the founding context of the primary school report and try a diachronic analysis on the pupil selection procedures as well on the defined objective of the report. The main sources are general legal regulations and guides for teacher's (*Lehreranleitungen*). Then I will discuss the factors that might explain the historical continuity of the *Grundschulgutachten*. The chapter concludes with a summary and discussion on the specificity of the primary school report and its related assessment culture.

About the Specificity of the *Grundschul(gutachten)*

The term *"Gutachten"* has a long history in the German language, which goes back to the 16th century. The term was derived from the combination of the words *gut* (good) and *achten* (estimate), and generally referred to: "opinion, conviction, endorsement" and, in particular, to an "expert judgment."[5] The current definition of the canonical *Duden* dictionary shows further indications on the term and defines it as a "(written) statement of an expert that is to be evaluated in a certain form for a particular undertaking."[6] This definition shows the basic elements of the report. Firstly, it is an assessment of a fact. Secondly, this assessment must be made by a person with a special expertise or an above-average professional competence. Thirdly, it is a written statement.

The *Gutachten* has been used in Germany for a long time and in a relatively wide range of areas, which is probably also linked to a pronounced written culture: expert reports can be found in the judicial, medical, academic, political and school

---

5   Jacob Grimm and Wilhelm Grimm, *Deutsches Wörterbuch. Vol. IV* (Leipzig: S. Hirzel, 1935), 1370.

6   Duden, *Duden. Das große Wörterbuch der deutschen Sprachen. Vol. 3* (Mannheim: Dudenverlag, 1977), 1107.

sectors.[7] As already mentioned, the primary school report is a (written) statement on the suitability of the schoolchild for the secondary school, which is basically a "pass"[8] in the context of a vertically structured school system.

The *Grundschulgutachten* is to be assigned to assessment practices of a subjective type. What distinguishes these practices is that they do not meet the conditions of objectivity and reliability, as opposed to standardized tests procedures, and that they put the assessment in the hands of the teacher. In Germany, this type of assessment practice, unlike the United States or England, enjoys not only a current pre-eminence but also a long tradition. In addition to the primary school report, which has been used for more than 95 years, *Gutachten* were used between 1920 and 1940 in the context of the maturity examination procedure (*Reifeprüfungsverfahren*) at the end of the *Gymnasium*,[9] as well as for transfers to special-needs schools.[10]

The peculiar character of the *Grundschulgutachten* was based, among other reasons, in the fact that the assessment, unlike grading and examination, does indeed provide knowledge about the child, but not *for* the child. As it is directed at internal and external instances of the school system (parents and education authorities), the assessment implies a summative, final judgment. It, therefore, does not serve to optimize and support the learning processes in the sense of a formative assessment. It is also significant that the *Gutachten* is a document independent from the school certificate or report card.

---

7   See Alexa Geisthövel and Volker Hess, eds., *Medizinisches Gutachten: Geschichte einer neuzeitlichen Praxis* (Göttingen: Wallstein Verlag, 2017).

8   Nele McElvany, "Die Übergangsempfehlung von der Grundschule auf die weiterführende Schule im Erleben der Lehrkräfte," in *Der Übergang von der Grundschule in die weiterführende Schule. Leistungsgerechtigkeit und regionale, soziale und ethnischkulturelle Disparitäten. Zusammenfassung der zentralen Befunde.*, ed. Jürgen Baumert et al. (Berlin: Max-Planck-Institut für Bildungsforschung, 2010), 296.

9   Hans-Jürgen Apel, "'Der Leitung des Jungen fehlte die starke Hand des Vaters.' Beurteilungsvorschriften und Beurteilungspraxis: Gutachtliche Bewertungen zum Abitur zwischen 1925 und 1936 in Westpreußen," in Schülerbeurteilungen und Schulzeugnisse: Historische und systematische Aspekte, ed. Johann Georg von Hohenzollern (Bad Heilbrunn: Klinkhardt, 1991); Bernhard Stelmaszyk, "Rekonstruktionen von Bildungsgängen preußischer Gymnasiasten sowie der zugehörigen Lehrergutachten aus Reifeprüfungsverfahren der Jahre 1926–1946" (Habilitation, Johannes Gutenberg-Universität Mainz, 2002).

10 See Thomas Hofsäss, Die Überweisung von Schülern auf die Hilfsschule und die Schule für Lernbehinderte: Eine historisch-vergleichende Untersuchung (Berlin: Spiess, 1993); as well the chapter of Michaela Vogt in this volume.

A further peculiarity is that it concerns different knowledge areas on the child that the teacher should generate and systematize. As already mentioned, unlike other assessment tools, these not only relate to cognitive performance, but rather to the person as such. If one considers the already mentioned functions and knowledge areas of the primary school report, it becomes clear that an "epistemic" expert status is assigned to the primary school teacher, in particular, to the class teacher.[11] Due to his or her long-term personalised contact with the schoolchild, the teacher is recognised as having a specialised and exclusive knowledge, and thus competence to issue an expert judgment.

This sort of assessment as pedagogical professional knowledge comprises diagnostic skills, including "informal"[12] observation and description skills. In other words, they are based on estimations, experiences, beliefs, and intuitions that can be influenced by unrecognised factors like for example social, ethnic or gender stereotypes. In addition, it supposes prognostic skills, i.e. the ability to predict the prospects for the child's development or success with regard to the needs of the secondary school. On closer examination of these skills, it becomes clear that knowledge areas involved are fundamental features of *other* professions (such as psychology and medicine). All the more interesting is that this assessment practice was not trained in a systematic way — seminars or workshops on the subject as part of teacher training were a rarity. The fact that there are these already mentioned teacher's guides for the confection of *Gutachten* suggests that this type of assessment was viewed as part of the teacher's self-formation process. For this reason, this assessment practice can be understood as a "non-explicit" and untested practice that is passed on informally from one generation to another.[13]

The analyses of the *Grundschulgutachten* thus opens up the way to reconstruct standardized and differential images of pupils (i.e. ethnicity, class, gender, etc.), normality and subjectivation processes. It provides information about the child, but also about the teacher, thereby providing insight into different and similar modalities of professions knowledge and practices.

---

11 Achim Volkers, *Wissen und Bildung bei Foucault: Aufklärung zwischen Wissenschaft und ethisch-ästhetischen Bildungsprozessen* (Wiesbaden: VS Verlag, 2008),74.

12 Ewald Terhart, "Die Beurteilung von Schülern als Aufgabe des Lehrers: Forschungslinien und Forschungsergebnisse," in *Handbuch der Forschung zum Lehrerberuf*, ed. Ewald Terhart, Hedda Bennewitz and Martin Rothland (Münster: Waxmann, 2011), 702.

13 Ewald Terhart, "Zensurengebung und innerschulisches Selektionsklima – die Rolle der Schulleitung," *Zeitschrift für Soziologie der Erziehung und Sozialisation* 19, no. 3 (1999): 281.

The *Grundschulgutachten* as part of a traditional Assessment Culture

In this chapter, I understand the *Grundschulgutachten* as part of an assessment culture, located in the German context and connected with educational traditions such as pietism, philanthropism, and classical idealism.[14] This culture gave a decisive value to the consideration of subjectivity, individuality and the idea of holistic (*ganzheitlich*) assessment.[15]

Pietism (from Latin *pietas:* piety) was a religious renewal movement within Protestantism. Its main representative, August Hermann Francke (1663–1727), founded in the end of the 17th century an orphanage (*Waisenhaus*), a latin school (*Lateinschule*) and the exclusive *Pädagogium Regium* for upper classes and nobility. In the Franckian orphanage, pupil descriptions were conducted in the form of a *Waisenalbum* or orphan's album.[16] In this, each child should be judged in terms of three categories: *ingenium* (ability), *mores* (moral), and *pietas* (piety), mostly in tabular and keyword-like form.[17] The same criteria were followed in the pupil descriptions of the *Pädagogium Regium*.[18] Kathrin Berdelmann points out, that what marked these practices was that the individualising gaze at each child followed a strict moral and religious reference frame.[19]

Written pupil assessment practices are also to be found in the educational movement of the philanthropists.[20] In the context of the *Philantropin*, a model

---

14 See E. Brinkmann, *Über Individualitätsbilder: Schülercharakteristiken* (Gotha: Behrend, 1892).

15 To be mentioned, however, are also previous practices of written pupil description attributable to the history of the school report. These are the so-called *Benefizien-zeugnisse* or letters of recommendation, which were written to children of destitute parents or orphans as early as 1550 to apply for scholarship. Masashi Urabe, *Funktion und Geschichte des deutschen Schulzeugnisses* (Bad Heilbrunn: Klinkhardt, 2009), 25.

16 Juliane Jacobi, "Der Blick auf das Kind. Zur Entstehung der Pädagogik in den Schulen des Halleschen Waisenhauses," in Das Kind in Pietismus und Aufklärung. Beiträge des internationalen Symposions vom 12. - 15. November 1997 in den Franckeschen Stiftungen zu Halle, ed. Josef N. Neumann (Tübingen: Verl. der Franckeschen Stiftungen Halle im Max-Niemeyer-Verl., 2000), 49–50.

17 Ibid., 50–52.

18 Kathrin Berdelmann, "'Sein Inneres kennen wir nicht, denn es ist uns verschlossen' – Schulische Beobachtung und Beurteilung von Kindern im 18. Jahrhundert," *Zeitschrift für Grundschulforschung* 9, no. 2 (2017), 21.

19 Ibid., 21.

20 See Sabine Reh, Kathrin Berdelmann, and Joachim Scholz, "Der Ehrbetrieb und unterrichtliche Honorierungspraktiken im Schulwesen um 1800. Die Entstehung des

school located in Dessau, Johann Friedrich Basedow (1724–1790) recommended teachers to keep "two different books,"[21] In the first book should be listed the good and the second the bad acts of the child.[22] In the *Philantropin* of Heidesheim, headed by Karl Friedrich Bahrdt (1740–1792), a "journal" was to be kept for the formation of "manners and virtues" of the children, in which the teacher would "write down immediately everything he observed of the children — be it good or faulty […]."[23]

Despite the differences between the pietistic and the philanthropic tradition, there is a common denominator: Protestantism. The focus on the individual and on strict ethical prescriptions, which comprised the assessment instruments of both currents, can also be found, following Max Weber, in the principles of Protestant ethics (e.g. abstinence, self-discipline, diligence, achievement, hard work, reliability, frugality).[24]

A further root of the *Gutachten* refers to practices of written pupil description which, in the spirit of classical idealism of the 19th century, were developed by Johann Heinrich Pestalozzi (1746–1827), Johann Friedrich Herbart (1776–1841) and Wilhelm von Humboldt (1767–1835). These practices also were based on the principle of individualisation and the holistic assessment of the child. The holistic principle came from the German idea of the universal human inner formation (*Bildung*), which pointed to the harmonious unfolding of all the forces of the individual.[25] This concept of education sought the balanced development of spiritual, sensuous, and moral forces, and thus postulated the unity between mind, body, and soul. Through self-cultivation, every "unique individuality" should be transformed into a "harmonious totality."[26]

Leistungs-Dispositivs," in *Leistung*, ed. Alfred Schäfer and Christiane Thompson (Paderborn: Schöningh, 2015).

21 Dušan Rajičić, *Berücksichtigung der Individualität in der Massenerziehung: Geschichte und Darstellung* (Belgrad: Neue Handelsdruckerei, 1899), 57.

22 Ibid., 57.

23 Jakob Anton Leyser, *Karl Friedrich Bahrdt, der Zeitgenosse Pestalozzis, sein Verhältniß zum Philanthropinismus und zur neuern Pädagogik: Ein Beitrag zur Geschichte der Erziehung und des Unterrichts*. (Neustadt: Gottschick-Witter, 1870), 47–48.

24 Karl-Heinz Hillmann, *Wertwandel: Zur Frage soziokultureller Voraussetzungen alternativer Lebensformen* (Darmstadt: Wiss. Buchges, 1989), 206.

25 Albert Reble, *Geschichte der Pädagogik* (Stuttgart: Klett, 1992), 174–250.

26 Fritz K. Ringer, *Felder des Wissens: Bildung, Wissenschaft und sozialer Aufstieg in Frankreich und Deutschland um 1900* (Weinheim: Beltz, 2003), 115.

Pestalozzi's focus was on this individualisation principle. Comparative pupil assessments, in the form of grades and certificates, should be strictly avoided.[27] In this way, he tended to what is currently known as an individual-referenced assessment, i.e. an assessment designed to capture intra-individual changes in learning development over time.[28] For example, in the educational institution for poor children in Neuhof Birr (1769–1798) and in the educational institute of the castle of Yverdon-les-Bains (1804–1825) teachers had to record their observations of the children.[29] Their comments should be entered into books and the reports would be exchanged in weekly teacher meetings.[30] The profound knowledge of the child as a result of the observation and assessment was to serve, first of all, the teachers themselves, namely for reflection and optimisation of their educational measures.

Herbartianism also had a decisive influence on written description and assessment of pupils. Herbart had pointed out that it would only be possible to "get to know the educability (*Bildsamkeit*) of each individual" by means of "observation."[31] According to this, the pupil's assessment had to be guided by the principle of learning ability. Particularly, the Herbartian Karl Volkmar Stoy (1815–1885) was to follow these principles. Stoy had founded the pedagogical university seminar (*Pädagogische Universitätsseminar*) in Jena with an attached practice school in 1844. By means of his pedagogical seminar, he strived to achieve a theoretical and practical "pedagogical education" of aspiring *Gymnasium* teachers.[32] What was novel was that practices of pupil observation and description were a systematic part of this teacher training concept. Each seminar participant had to choose a "pupil for characterisation" and to write a description, a so-called *Kinderbild* or

---

27 Silvia-Iris Lübke, *Schule ohne Noten: Lernberichte in der Praxis der Laborschule*, (Opladen: Leske + Budrich, 1996), 41.

28 Ibid., 41.

29 Emil Brinkmann, *Individualitäts- oder Schülerbilder (Schülercharakteristiken)* (Bad Sachsa im Harz: H. Haacke, 1908), 9–11.

30 Ibid.

31 Johann Friedrich Herbart, *Umriss pädagogischer Vorlesungen* (Göttingen: Dieterich, 1841), 19.

32 Rotraud Coriand, "Karl Volkmar Stoy (1815–1885) und Otto Willmann (1839–1920). Herbartianer und die Reform der Lehrerbildung," in *Klassiker der Pädagogik. Die Bildung der modernen Gesellschaft.*, ed. Bernd Dollinger (Wiesbaden: VS Verlag, 2008), 158.

children's portrait, for this child.[33] These portraits were subject of discussion in the *"Pädagogikum,"* a weekly course that accompanied regular lectures.[34]

Stoy's successor, Wilhelm Rein (1847–1929), continued the practice of the pupil descriptions within the framework of the university seminar in Jena. The handling of these descriptions, now called *Schülerbilder* (pupil's portraits), was the same as Stoy's *Kinderbilder*.[35] An example of such a portrait is from 1890:

> "N.N. is a boy who has good talents but is only weak in interest. His appearance seems to be neglected, his whole attitude is reminiscent of the phlegmatic. An excellent feature which hinders the approach to the goal of education, and the formation of a condition corresponding to the object of instruction, is the conspicuous obstinacy of the boy, which finds its explanation: 1. In a false, namely, too high, self-esteem, and 2. In the lacking authority of the father. His honest truthfulness and frugality is endearing."[36]

Four principles are clear in this example. First, the necessary attention to individuality. Secondly, that the holistic diagnosis of the child, including his moral qualities ("truthfulness" and "obstinacy") and his family context, had to serve primarily the achievement of educational goals (the ideal of *Bildsamkeit*). The assessment, therefore, attended to more formative objectives. As a new element emerged, thirdly, the need to comply with psychological principles which should help to classify children's individuality (here the reference to the category of the "phlegmatic").

Similar pupil descriptions, which were called *Individualitätenbücher* or "individuality books", were also held at the pedagogical university seminar in Leipzig, under the direction of the Herbartian Tuiskon Ziller (1817–1882).[37]

A further root of the *Grundschulgutachten* leads to the so-called *Schülercharakteristik* or pupil characterisation. In the 17th century, the term "characteristic" was taken from the French, *caractéristique*. It referred to "distinctive features" and from the 18th century onwards, to "a description of the essential traits of a person or thing, 'characterisation.'"[38] In fact, the practice of characterisation of persons

---

33 Friedrich Bartholomäi and Carl Volkmar Stoy, *Das pädagogische Seminar zu Jena: Historische Bilder aus den Akten desselben; Denkschrift zum 300-jährigen Jubiläum der Universität Jena* (Leipzig: Engelmann, 1858), 208–209.

34 Coriand, "Karl Volkmar Stoy (1815–1885)," 161.

35 Paul Henschel, "Ein Schülerbild," *Aus dem Pädagogischen Universitätsseminar Jena* 2 (1890), 145.

36 Brinkmann, *Individualitäts- oder Schülerbilder (Schülercharakteristiken)*, 17–18.

37 Ibid., 18.

38 Wolfgang Pfeifer, *Etymologisches Wörterbuch des Deutschen* (Berlin: Akademie-Verlag, 1989).

during the 19th century was widespread among scholars such as Humboldt, Rousseau, Gall, Lavater.[39] The so-called *Schülercharakeristik* is to be found as a term from the beginning of the 19th century in guidelines for primary school teachers.[40] Interestingly, the term would also be used as a synonym for the *Grundschulgutachten* until the 1950s. The *Schülercharakeristik* was linked to the principles of the classical concept of *Bildung* and also aimed at an individualising, holistic assessment of the schoolchild. A teacher's manual from 1830 stated, for example, that the teacher "judges the talent, the direction of the spirit, the temperament, the development of the mind's forces," i.e. the "whole inner human being."[41]

In summary, it can be said that these early practices of written pupil description shared with the *Grundschulgutachten* their subjective, individualising and holistic features. But in contrast to the *Gutachten* their served primarily *formative*, not summative purposes.

On the legal Persistence of the *Grundschulgutachten*

In the previous remarks I have dealt with the pioneers of the *Grundschulgutachten*, i.e. with assessment practices and their associated pedagogical traditions, which existed *before* the genesis of the *Gutachten*. The question that now arises is: in which context emerged the primary school report as such? Under which legal conditions could it continue to live on for decades?

The *Grundschulgutachten* is to be interpreted as a 'child' of the Weimar Republic and is, therefore, to be understood as part of a radical political transformation process. With the dissolution of the imperial Reich and the constitution of the Weimar Republic, the idea of a common compulsory primary school (*Grundschule*) came into being with the abolition of private and elite preschools (*Vorschulen*). In 1920, the Weimar Constitution laid down, in Article 146, the establishment of this primary school, on which the higher forms of school should

---

39 Hans Krüger, "Wilhelm von Humboldts Charakterschilderungen im Rahmen seiner Persönlichkeitsforschung," *Zeitschrift für angewandte Psychologie und Charakterkunde* 66, 1, 2 (1943), 43.

40 Johann Wolfgang Wörlein, *Bibliologisches Lehrbuch der deutschen Volks-Pädagogik* (Sulzbach: Seidel, 1830), 292; Gustav Friedrich Dinter, *Die vorzüglichsten Regeln der Pädagogik, Methodik und Schulmeisterklugheit: Als Leitfaden bei'm Unterrichte künftiger Lehrer in Bürger- und Landschulen bestimmt,* (Neustadt: Wagner, 1846), 66. Franz Wiedemann, *Der Lehrer der Kleinen: Ein praktischer Rathgeber für junge Elementarlehrer; überhaupt aber ein Buch für alle, welche sich für die Erziehung der Kleinen interessieren* (Leipzig: Oehmigke, 1880), 404–10.

41 Wörlein, *Bibliologisches Lehrbuch der deutschen Volks-Pädagogik*, 292.

be built.[42] With this regulation, the procedure of pupil selection, also called *Schülerauslese* was established, and thus the primary school report as such. Within the framework of the new democratic societal understanding, the decisive criteria for the selection of a child for a secondary school were the "aptitude (*Begabung*) and tendency (*Neigung*)"[43] of the child, and not, as the in imperial Reich, the "economic and social position or religious beliefs of the parents."[44]

The already quoted article of the Weimar Constitution is only to be regarded as the first basic rule for the transitional selection; its details were left to decrees and regulations of the individual states. A glance at the various regulations on the pupil selection procedure of the Weimar Republic shows that the *Gutachten*, together with grades and entrance examinations, was used as a selection instrument.[45] Despite the tendency towards subjective procedures, however, the 'test-friendly' regulations of Prussia, Saxony, Lübeck, Braunschweig, and Hamburg must be pointed out.[46] In these states, standardized or exact methods of examination were expressly permitted, in the first case only as a "supplement" to the conventional examination and only as far as teachers were able to "master the method."[47] In the final phase of the Weimar Republic, the "decree on pupil selection" of 10 February 1931 abolished entrance examinations and thus standardized test procedures.[48] The child's aptitude, in addition to *Gutachten* and grades, would now be the basis for the determination of pupil's suitability for a secondary school.

The Third Reich implied a fundamental system change. With regard to the pupil selection procedure, the removal of the federal organisation meant that the new regime was to apply uniformly to the entire Reich. The "new regulation of pupil selection at secondary schools" (*Neuregelung der Schülerauslese an höheren Schulen*) of 27 March 1935, however, did not break so much with the selection instruments defined in the Weimar Republic.[49] Instead the break concerned

---

42 Margarete Götz and Uwe Sandfuchs, "Geschichte der Grundschule," in *Handbuch Grundschulpädagogik und Grundschuldidaktik*, ed. Wolfgang Einsiedler (Bad Heilbrunn: Klinkhardt, 2011).

43 Karlheinz Ingenkamp, *Pädagogische Diagnostik in Deutschland, 1885–1932. Geschichte der pädagogischen Diagnostik, Volume 1* (Weinheim: Dt. Studienverl, 1990), 174.

44 Ibid.

45 Erich Hylla, *Der Übergang von der Grundschule zu weiterführenden Schulen: Bestimmungen, Erfahrungen, Vorschläge* (Leipzig: Klinkhardt, 1925), 49–61.

46 Ibid.

47 Ibid., 50.

48 See Ingenkamp, *Pädagogische Diagnostik in Deutschland 1885–1932.*

49 "Neuregelung der Schülerauslese an höheren Schulen," *Die Mittelschule* 49, no. 12 (1935).

criteria based on social Darwinism and racial hygiene, which now defined suitability and, above all, assigned radical importance to the so-called "selection (*Auslese*) of the fit" and "eradication (*Ausmerze*) of the unfit"[50] as normative principles of society.[51]

After the Second World War, the Federal Republic of Germany maintained the vertical school system structure and thus the selection procedure, despite the recommendations of the US occupation force. Due to the restoration of the federal system in 1949, various selection procedures were established in the federal states. In spite of certain differences, grades, entrance examinations and/or *Gutachten* were the basic elements of selection in the majority of the *Länder* until the end of the 1960s.[52] The fact that entrance examinations should not be based on standardized test methods, except for some individual cases, strengthens the thesis of the continuity of primarily subjective selection instruments in the German assessment culture.

Interestingly, however, the *Gutachten* should gain in importance from the 1960s onwards. The consequences of the Sputnik shock and its reverberations on the US educational agencies would also strengthen the diagnosis of a general educational crisis in the Federal Republic of Germany. An urgent need for democratisation and an expansion of the education system was to promote not only social justice but also economic performance. Various empirical studies on the pupil selection procedures also confirmed a low predictive quality and objectivity of the existing selection mechanisms and strong social discrimination effects.[53] In the end, the reform led to

---

50 This "eradication" strategy implied ultimately the prohibition for Jewish and Sinti and Roma children to visit public schools, and few years later the deportation to extermination camps, as well as the organised murder of mentally and physically handicapped children.

51 See Hermann Laux, *Pädagogische Diagnostik im Nationalsozialismus, 1933–1945. Geschichte der pädagogischen Diagnostik, Volume 2* (Weinheim: Dt. Studienverl, 1990); Hartmut Titze and Corinna M. Dartenne, "Lernfähigkeit und Geschlecht," in 'Bildung' *jenseits pädagogischer Theoriebildung? Fragen zu Sinn, Zweck und Funktion der allgemeinen Pädagogik; Festschrift für Reinhard Uhle zum 65. Geburtstag*, ed. Detlef Gaus and Elmar Drieschner (Wiesbaden: VS Verl. für Sozialwiss, 2010).

52 See Schultze, Knoche and Thomas, *Über den Voraussagewert der Auslesekriterien*; Marcel Helbig and Rita Nikolai, *Die Unvergleichbaren. Der Wandel der Schulsysteme in den deutschen Bundesländern seit 1949* (Bad Heilbrunn: Klinkhardt, 2015).

53 See Hans J. Hagel, "Der prognostische Wert unserer heutigen Eignungsprüfungen und die Förderstufe des Rahmenplanes" (PhD diss., Universität Münster, 1964); Walter Schultze, "Die Begabtenförderung in ihrer Abhängigkeit vom Schulaufbau: Eine internationale Umschau," *Paedagogica Europea* 3 (1967); Ingenkamp, *Untersuchungen*

the fact that entrance examinations were replaced by a probationary period (*Probe-zeit*) and to establishment of integrated or comprehensive schools (*Gesamtschulen*) and/or orientation-levels (*Orientierungsstufen*) in various federal states.[54]

The *Gutachten* as an image of the child's overall personality

A diachronic analysis of the regulations and teacher's guides reveals that the de-fined objective of the *Gutachten* remained virtually unchanged. Thus, from the 1920s of the Weimar Republic to the 1980s of the Federal Republic of Germany, though with a divergent terminology, the objective of the *Gutachten* was the as-sessment of 'the whole person'. A good example of this is the already quoted article 146 of the Weimar Constitution, in which suitability was associated with "aptitude and tendency." Both "aptitude," understood as innate psychological and physical developmental tendencies, as well as "tendency," i.e. motivation and in-terest, also refer to affective, emotional, and social dimensions. Strictly speaking, it was expected that primary school teachers should provide information about the peculiarities of the schoolchildren. In 1952, the psychologist Max Simoneit defined two basic questions which each teacher had to ask themselves: "What child stands before us today?" and "What kind of human being will become of this child?"[55] The objective of the *Gutachten* differentiated it, so the argument went, basically from other selection instruments such as entrance examinations and the intelligence tests, which would only provide an *intellectual* assessment.[56]

This objective is also to be found in the discussions on pupil selection during the Weimar Republic. One example of this are the guidelines for *Gutachten* of the Psychological Institute of the Leipzig Teacher's Society of 1925. In these, it was advised that the teacher was to consider in his *Gutachten* not only "giftedness

zur Übergangsauslese; Tent, *Die Auslese von Schülern für weiterführende Schulen*; Un-deutsch, "Zum Problem der begabungsgerechten Auslese beim Eintritt in die Höhere Schule während der Schulzeit", in *Begabung und Lernen: Ergebnisse und Folgerungen neuer Forschungen*, ed. Heinrich Roth and Hans Aebli (Stuttgart: Klett, 1971).

54 See Deutscher Bildungsrat, *Empfehlungen der Bildungskommission: Strukturplan für das Bildungswesen* (Stuttgart: Klett, 1970); Christoph Führ, "Das Bildungssystem in der Bundesrepublik Deutschland," in *Deutschland: Porträt einer Nation. Bildung. Wis-senschaft. Technik*, ed. Gert Richter (Gütersloh: Bertelsmann-Lexikothek-Verl, 1987).

55 Max Simoneit, *Über Kindercharaktere: Bewertung und Schülerauslese* (Berlin: Bernard & Graefe, 1952), 56.

56 Otto Engelmayer, *Beobachtung und Beurteilung des Schulkindes: Gegenwartsfragen der pädagogischen Auslese* (Nürnberg: Verl. Die Egge, 1949), 37.

and inclination" but also "character" (the dimensions of "emotion" and "will" —
Gefühlsleben, Willensleben), and, in particular, character typologies.[57] Likewise,
the well-known psychologist, William Stern, recommended teachers to take into
consideration the "individuality" of the pupil in order to convey an "image of
the soul."[58]

Also in the Third Reich, the basic objective of the assessment defined that the
teacher was to "comprehend" the schoolchild as a "person"[59] and to represent the
"living wholeness of the character."[60] New, however, was the centrality of purely
ethnic criteria, expressed in terms such as *"völkisch"* and *"rassisch"* in the regulations as well as in teacher instructions.[61] New was also the assigned centrality of
the physical and character in opposition to mental qualities.[62]

The recognition of the "whole person" should also play a cardinal role in the
teachers' guides, which were published during the young Federal Republic of
Germany. In 1949 the psychologist Otto Engelmayer appreciated the assessment of
the child's whole personality. Nevertheless, he openly criticised the "overvaluation
of the body and certain forms of rearing"[63] which had been promoted during the
Third Reich. Likewise, Richard Kienzle (1951) recommended a "holistic", i.e. a
judgement on the qualities of "the bodily soul, spirit, and character" of the pupil's
being.[64] According to the guidelines for teachers, the information on the child
contained in the *Gutachten* should cover the following areas: physical appearance, family relations, work attitude, performance, social behaviour, and aptitude.

The regulations of the Federal Republic of Germany also differed from those
of the Third Reich. Thus, in the young Federal Republic of Germany, in particular
in the decisions of the Conference of Ministers of Education and Cultural Affairs (KMK), it was stipulated that "the child's suitability, inclination and will for

---

57 Hylla, *Der Übergang von der Grundschule zu weiterführenden Schulen*, 59.
58 William Stern, *Die Intelligenz der Kinder und Jugendlichen und die Methoden ihrer
    Untersuchung* (Leipzig: Barth, 1920), 257.
59 Wilhelm Julius Ruttmann, *Die Begutachtung des Schülers im Dienste der Auslese: Ergeb-
    nisse der Schülerkunde und Wegweisungen der Praxis* (Nürnberg: Korn, 1936), 56.
60 Karl Zietz, "Das Gutachten für die Schülerauslese. (Vorschläge zur Abfassung der
    Schülercharakteristik)," *Die deutsche Schule* 41, no. 2 (1937): 72.
61 "Neuregelung der Schülerauslese an höheren Schulen", 138. See also Alfred Tobias,
    "Berücksichtigt bei der Schülerauslese die Eigenart der nordischen Rasse!" *Reichszei-
    tung der deutschen Erzieher. Nationalsozialistische Lehrerzeitung* 2, no. 3 (1934): 12–13.
62 "Neuregelung der Schülerauslese an höheren Schulen," 138.
63 Engelmayer, *Beobachtung und Beurteilung des Schulkindes*, 37.
64 Richard Kienzle, *Schülerbeobachtung und Schülerbeurteilung: Eine praktische Anleitung
    für Lehrer und Erzieher* (Eßlingen: Burg-Bücherei, 1951), 6.

intellectual work as a whole" should be considered.[65] In other words, emotional and volitive qualities should always be judged in relation to spiritual qualities.[66] However, the assessment of extra cognitive performance was also important in the 1970s, according to the Bavarian regulation of 1972. According to this, the "overall personality" of the schoolchild was to be assessed within the framework of the "pedagogical *Gutachten*."[67]

Interestingly, the concept of aptitude *(Begabung)* would make a protracted career in the regulations. It appears at least explicitly in the regulations of the Weimar Republic and the Federal Republic of Germany.[68] Despite different definitions, the transformation of the concept of aptitude can be traced between the 1920s and 1980s from a more static (nature optimistic) to a more dynamic (environmentally-optimistic) meaning.[69]

On the Historical Persistence of the *Grundschulgutachten*

The fundamental question that now arises is: how can the tenacity of the *Grundschulgutachten* be explained? A persistence that could even survive the transitions from a dictatorial (Third Reich) to a democratic system (Federal Republic of Germany). How can it be explained that even vehement advocates of standardized testing methods defended the irreplaceability of the *Gutachten*? In fact, during the Weimar Republic, a group of psychologists had actively promoted the use of standardized tests, but at the same time pleaded for the continuity of the *Gutachten*. This group argued that the selection could not only be limited to the assessment of "higher

---

65 Sekretariat der Ständigen Konferenz der Kultusminister der Länder in der Bundesrepublik Deutschland (KSK), "Übergang von der Grundschule in Schulen des Sekundarbereichs I und Förderung, Beobachtung und Orientierung in den Jahrgangsstufen 5 und 6 (sog. Orientierungsstufe): Informationsschrift des Sekretariats der Kultusministerkonferenz Stand: 18.10.2010," accessed November 19, 2014, http://www.kmk.org/fileadmin/veroeffentlichungen_beschluesse/2010/2010_10_18-Uebergang-Grundschule-S_eI1-Orientierungsstufe.pdf.

66 Ibid.

67 Gerd Gigerenzer, "Das Portrait des Schülers im Übertrittsgutachten," *Zeitschrift für Sozialpsychologie* 18, no. 3 (1987): 191.

68 See Hylla, *Der Übergang von der Grundschule zu weiterführenden Schulen*; Burbach, *Schülergutachten*; Flitner and Kamm, "Das Grundschulgutachten."

69 Gabriele Weigand, "Geschichte und Herleitung eines pädagogischen Begabungsbegriffs," in *Werte schulischer Begabtenförderung. Begabungsbegriff und Werteorientierung*, ed. Armin Hackl, Olaf Steenbuck and Gabriele Weigand (Frankfurt am Main: Karg-Stiftung, 2011).

intelligence,"[70] which is why the primary school report should complement the test procedure. Thus, the Hamburg psychologist Martha Muchow argued in 1919:

> "The struggle for the leading position requires individuals of a very definite disposition to the life of the mind and will, of a firm character; it demands perseverance, endurance, independence, initiative, organisational and leadership talents. However, all these properties cannot be determined experimentally. The deepest, best, most precious of the human personality does not reveal itself to technically exact procedures."[71]

The psychologist Stern also adhered to the principle of a holistic assessment of the schoolchild since only this form of assessment would make justice to its definition as a *"unitas multiplex,"* i.e. as an "indivisible being set up for the unity of inner determination of purpose."[72] These arguments refer to the firm and broad rootedness of a subjective, individualising and holistic assessment culture in Germany, which can be regarded as a motive for the historical persistence of the *Grundschulgutachten.* However, this group of psychologists warned against the dangers of the *Gutachten.* Stern argued that most teachers could fall into "naive personalism," "aprioristic constructions," and "under-controlled intuition"[73] in their assessment practice — a case that, remarkably, would revive during the 1960s in the Federal Republic of Germany concerning the primary school report: several studies criticised the questionable validity and objectivity as well as the low prognostic quality of the *Grundschulgutachten.*[74]

Another reason can be found in the "test-aversion" or *Testiritis,* defined by the German psychologist Karlheinz Ingenkamp, which he viewed as widespread illness among German intellectuals.[75] This aversion has to be linked to the assessment culture, discussed in this chapter, and to concept of *Bildung,* from which this culture emerges. The individualistic understanding of this concept of education correlates with a social model that assumes that society is not composed of equal individuals. Rather, an organic community model, similar to a symphony

---

70 Martha Muchow, "Notwendigkeit und Möglichkeit der Heranziehung des Lehrerurteils bei der Begabtenauslese," *Zeitschrift für Pädagogische Psychologie und Experimentelle Pädagogik* 20, no. 5 (1919): 304.

71 Ibid., 304.

72 Stern, *Die Intelligenz der Kinder und Jugendlichen und die Methoden ihrer Untersuchung,* 258.

73 Ibid.

74 See Steinkamp, "Die Rolle des Volksschullehrers im schulischen Selektionsprozess."

75 Karlheinz Ingenkamp, "Die Testaversion der deutschen Intellektuellen," in *Diagnostik in der Schule: Beiträge zu Schlüsselfragen der Schülerbeurteilung,* ed. Karlheinz Ingenkamp (Weinheim: Beltz, 1989), 153–54.

orchestra, is proposed: each instrument contributes to the whole because of its uniqueness.[76] The fact that Germany still maintains the vertical structure of the education system and its corresponding selection procedure can also be attributed to this educational tradition. Thus, the *Gymnasium,* as a humanist model institution, has survived all structural reforms and transformations, which can also be regarded as another reason for the 'necessity' of the *Grundschulgutachten.*[77]

The question of the motive of persistence is even more interesting when the international, and specifically English context, is taken into account, in which the objectification of the forms of assessment was fundamental. Thus, in the framework of the Tripartite System, the arrangement of state-funded secondary education between 1945 and the 1970s in England and Wales into a structure containing three types of school, namely: grammar schools, secondary technical schools and secondary modern schools, pupils were allocated according to their performance in the 11-plus examination, which consisted of standardized intelligence, English and math tests.[78] Remarkably, these test instruments have also been expanded with additional components (primary heads' assessments or judgments).[79] However, in contrast to the German context, these teachers' judgments would always be scaled and quantified due to their "subjective" character and "lack of comparability of standards."[80]

A third factor, however, is the development path followed by the pedagogical discipline during the Weimar Republic. The majority of pedagogy professorships were awarded to representatives of the humanities pedagogy.[81] As a successor

---

76 Florian Waldow, "Die internationale Konjunktur standardisierter Messungen von Schülerleistung in der ersten Hälfte des 20. Jahrhunderts und ihr Niederschlag in Deutschland und Schweden," in *"Der vermessene Mensch": Ein kritischer Blick auf Messbarkeit, Normierung und Standardisierung,* ed. Martin Dust and Johanna Mierendorff, Jahrbuch für Pädagogik 2010 (Frankfurt am Main: Lang, 2010).

77 See Marcelo Caruso and Patrick Ressler, "Themenheft: Zweigliedrigkeit: Strukturwandel der deutschen Schullandschaft? *Zeitschrift für Pädagogik* 59, no. 4 (2013).

78 Wilfried Rudloff, "Ungleiche Bildungschancen: Bildungsforschung, öffentlicher Diskurs und Bildungsreform in England und der Bundesrepublik in den Jahren des Bildungsbooms," in *Bildung und Differenz: Historische Analysen zu einem aktuellen Problem,* ed. Carola Groppe, Gerhard Kluchert and Eva Matthes (Wiesbaden: Springer, 2016), 371.

79 Ibid., 371.

80 Alfred Yates and D. A. Pidgeon, *Admission to Grammar Schools: Third interim Report on the Allocation of Primary School Leavers to Courses of Secondary Education* (London, UK: Newnes, 1957), 93.

81 See Peter Drewek, "Defensive Disziplinbildung. Die Akademisierung der deutschen Pädagogik im Kontext der Modernisierungsprobleme des Bildungssystems und der

to the humanist educational tradition, this group of educators blocked the use of standardized measurement methods, and not just for philosophical reasons. Their motives were also of a political nature: because of their social-conservative attitudes, they intended to protect the exclusivity of the gymnasia from the influx of other social groups.[82]

Another reason must be sought in the influence of psychological currents such as holistic psychology (*Ganzheitspsychologie*) and characterology (*Charakterologie*) during the Weimarer Republik and the Third Reich.[83] Both currents preferred "interpreting" to "measuring" and thus favoured subjective assessment instruments.[84] The basic assumption of holistic psychology was to interpret human life in its development as part of a cultural context and to consider emotion as the person's life-determining goal.[85] In addition, a mystical holistic idea (of body, soul, and spirit) aimed at the complete apprehension of the "whole personality" of the schoolchild was proposed.[86] Wilhelm Julius Ruttmann, who had authored an assessment guide for teachers in 1936, criticised the application of exact assessment methods, since "unique essential traits" of the person were not detectable by these methods.[87] Instead, he pleaded for a "holistic" and "true-to-life" assessment practice, in which the teacher had to perform "acts of insight into human nature" to represent the organic structure of "body, spirit, and mind."[88]

Characterology was concerned with the appearances of the human character, the demonstration of various character types and their development, and was aimed at describing humans being, especially their respective *"Sosein"* or "being-thus."[89] In

---

Erziehungswissenschaft am Beginn des 20. Jahrhunderts," in *Zur Geschichte der Erziehungswissenschaften in der Schweiz. Vom Ende des 19. bis zur Mitte des 20. Jahrhunderts*, ed. Rita Hofstetter and Bernard Schneuwly (Bern: Hep, 2011).

82 See Waldow, "Die internationale Konjunktur."

83 See Cristina Alarcón, "Das Kind 'gut-achten'? Zum Grundschulgutachten als 'implizites' Professionswissen von Lehrern (1919–1989)," in *Schulwissen für und über Kinder. Beiträge zur historischen Primarschulforschung.*, ed. Margarete Götz and Michaela Vogt (Bad Heilbrunn: Klinkhardt Verlag, 2016).

84 Laux, *Pädagogische Diagnostik im Nationalsozialismus, 1933–1945*, 92.

85 Ulfried Geuter, "Die Zerstörung wissenschaftlicher Vernunft. Felix Krueger und die Leipziger Schule der Ganzheitspsychologie," *Psychologie heute* 80, April (1980).

86 Ulfried Geuter, *Die Professionalisierung der deutschen Psychologie im Nationalsozialismus* (Frankfurt am Main: Suhrkamp, 1984), 152.

87 Ruttmann, *Die Begutachtung des Schülers im Dienste der Auslese*, 6.

88 Ibid., 6–10.

89 Peter Mattes, "Zur Kontinuität in der deutschen Psychologie über die Zeit des Nationalsozialismus hinaus," *Psychologie und Geschichte* 1, no. 3 (1989), 5.

1933, Johannes Burkersrode and Kurt Ille stated that assessment so far, performed by the "exact recording of the intellectual" had been "one-sided".[90] On the contrary, it was necessary, they stated, to comprehend the "child's soul" through the teacher's appraisal of the schoolchild.[91] Interestingly the principles of these psychological currents are still to be found in the teacher's guides of the young Federal Republic for the assessment of schoolchildren.

Summary and Discussion

In this chapter, I have analysed, from a historical perspective, the function of the primary school report or *Grundschulgutachten* in the context of the primary–secondary school transition and its related pupil selection procedures. Based on the analysis of regulations, it became clear that despite regional divergences and political upheavals, including fundamental ruptures of the political system, the *Grundschulgutachten* remained in use as a selection instrument. The chapter also showed that for decades, regulations and teachers' guides provided almost the same objective for assessment: the primary teacher should always generate knowledge about the 'whole child.' This aim and its historical persistence were linked both to the influence of holistic psychology and characterology as well as to the German tradition of classical humanism.

The prehistory of the *Gutachten* points to the practices of schoolchildren's descriptions which were practiced within the framework of pietism, philanthropism and the spirit of classical idealism. These practices refer to an assessment culture, which, as in the case of the *Gutachten*, placed an emphasis on the ideals of subjectivity, individuality, and holism. In spite of the differences between the pietistic, the philanthropic, and the idealistic-classical tradition, the objective was to assess the 'inner,' the soul, in other words, the essence of the schoolchild on the part of the teacher. These principles as well as moral categories, which were central in the three currents, are also connected with Protestant ethics.

Furthermore, the interpersonal relationship between teachers and schoolchild is significant in the context of this assessment culture. The teacher, especially the class teacher, was recognised as the 'best' expert on the child. Therefore, a special authority and exclusive expert function were attributed to him. This development

---

90   Johannes Burkersrode and Kurt Ille, *Charakterbeurteilung von Kindern und Jugendlichen auf Grund typologischer Betrachtungsweise*, Pädagogisch-Psychologische Arbeiten aus dem Institut des Leipziger Lehrervereins XX. 1. Teil (Leipzig: Verlag der Dürr'schen Buchhandlung, 1933), 4.

91   Ibid., 3.

shows a certain reluctance of the German education and assessment tradition against international, especially Anglo-Saxon, developments.

Finally, the historical tenacity and the 'resistance' to the establishment of standardized tests also point to the survival of the mentioned assessment culture. The extent to which this assessment culture, in particular, the *Grundschulgutachten*, is actually a German specificity, should be investigated within the framework of future, historical-comparative research.

Literature

Alarcón, Cristina. "'Das Kind 'gut-achten'? Zum Grundschulgutachten als 'implizites' Professionswissen von Lehrern (1919–1989)." In *Schulwissen für und über Kinder. Beiträge zur historischen Primarschulforschung*. Edited by Margarete Götz and Michaela Vogt, 76–97. Bad Heilbrunn: Klinkhardt Verlag, 2016.

Apel, Hans-Jürgen. "'Der Leitung des Jungen fehlte die starke Hand des Vaters.' Beurteilungsvorschriften und Beurteilungspraxis: Gutachtliche Bewertungen zum Abitur zwischen 1925 und 1936 in Westpreußen." In *Schülerbeurteilungen und Schulzeugnisse: Historische und systematische Aspekte*. Edited by Johann Georg von Hohenzollern, 148–59. Bad Heilbrunn: Klinkhardt, 1991.

Bartholomäi, Friedrich, and Carl V. Stoy. *Das pädagogische Seminar zu Jena: Historische Bilder aus den Akten desselben; Denkschrift zum 300-jährigen Jubiläum der Universität Jena*. Monographien zur historischen Pädagogik. Leipzig: Engelmann, 1858.

Berdelmann, Kathrin. "'Sein Inneres kennen wir nicht, denn es ist uns verschlossen' – Schulische Beobachtung und Beurteilung von Kindern im 18. Jahrhundert." *Zeitschrift für Grundschulforschung* 9, no. 2 (2017): 9–23.

Brinkmann, E. *Über Individualitätsbilder: Schülercharakteristiken*. Gotha: Behrend, 1892.

Brinkmann, Emil. *Individualitäts- oder Schülerbilder (Schülercharakteristiken)*. Bad Sachsa im Harz: H. Haacke, 1908.

Burbach, Karl H. *Schülergutachten: Eine Untersuchung über Schülerbeobachtung und Schülerbeurteilung*. Frankfurt am Main: Hirschgraben-Verl, 1955.

Burkersrode, Johannes, and Kurt Ille. *Charakterbeurteilung von Kindern und Jugendlichen auf Grund typologischer Betrachtungsweise*. Leipzig: Verlag der Dürr'schen Buchhandlung, 1933.

Caruso, Marcelo, and Patrick Ressler. "Themenheft: Zweigliedrigkeit: Strukturwandel der deutschen Schullandschaft?" *Zeitschrift für Pädagogik* 59, no. 4 (2013).

Coriand, Rotraud. "Karl Volkmar Stoy (1815–1885) und Otto Willmann (1839–1920). Herbartianer und die Reform der Lehrerbildung." In *Klassiker der Pädagogik. Die Bildung der modernen Gesellschaft.* Edited by Bernd Dollinger, 151–77. Wiesbaden: VS Verlag, 2008.

Deutscher Bildungsrat. *Empfehlungen der Bildungskommission: Strukturplan für das Bildungswesen.* Stuttgart: Klett, 1970.

Dinter, Gustav F. *Die vorzüglichsten Regeln der Pädagogik, Methodik und Schulmeisterklugheit: Als Leitfaden bei'm Unterrichte künftiger Lehrer in Bürger- und Landschulen bestimmt.* Neustadt: Wagner, 1846.

Drewek, Peter. "Defensive Disziplinbildung. Defensive Disziplinbildung. Die Akademisierung der deutschen Pädagogik im Kontext der Modernisierungsprobleme des Bildungssystems und der Erziehungswissenschaft am Beginn des 20. Jahrhunderts." In *Zur Geschichte der Erziehungswissenschaften in der Schweiz. Vom Ende des 19.bis zur Mitte des 20. Jahrhunderts.* Edited by Rita Hofstetter and Bernard Schneuwly, 113–39. Bern: Hep, 2011.

Duden. *Duden. Das große Wörterbuch der deutschen Sprachen. Vol. 3.* Mannheim: Dudenverlag, 1977.

Engelmayer, Otto. *Beobachtung und Beurteilung des Schulkindes: Gegenwartsfragen der pädagogischen Auslese.* Nürnberg: Verl. Die Egge, 1949.

Flitner, Andreas, and Helmut Kamm. "Das Grundschulgutachten. Seine Voraussetzungen und seine Bedeutung für die Schülerauslese." *Pädagogische Arbeitsblätter* 20, 6/7 (1968): 81–109.

Führ, Christoph. "Das Bildungssystem in der Bundesrepublik Deutschland." In *Deutschland: Porträt einer Nation. Bildung. Wissenschaft. Technik.* Edited by Gert Richter, 126–40. Gütersloh: Bertelsmann-Lexikothek-Verl, 1987.

Geisthövel, Alexa and Volker Hess, eds. *Medizinisches Gutachten: Geschichte einer neuzeitlichen Praxis.* Göttingen: Wallstein Verlag, 2017.

Geuter, Ulfried. "Die Zerstörung wissenschaftlicher Vernunft. Felix Krueger und die Leipziger Schule der Ganzheitspsychologie." *Psychologie heute* 80, April (1980): 35–43.

–. *Die Professionalisierung der deutschen Psychologie im Nationalsozialismus.* Frankfurt am Main: Suhrkamp, 1984.

Gigerenzer, Gerd. "Das Portrait des Schülers im Übertrittgutachten." *Zeitschrift für Sozialpsychologie* 18, no. 3 (1987): 191–208.

Götz, Margarete, and Uwe Sandfuchs. "Geschichte der Grundschule." In *Handbuch Grundschulpädagogik und Grundschuldidaktik.* Edited by Wolfgang Einsiedler, 13–30. Bad Heilbrunn: Klinkhardt, 2011.

Gresser-Spitzmüller, Ruth. *Lehrerurteil und Bildungschancen: Eine Untersuchung über den Einfluss des Grundschullehrers auf die Wahl weiterführender Schulen.* Weinheim: Beltz, 1973.

Grimm, Jacob, and Wilhelm Grimm. *Deutsches Wörterbuch. Volume 4.* Leipzig, S. Hirzel: 1935.

Hagel, Hans J. "Der prognostische Wert unserer heutigen Eignungsprüfungen und die Förderstufe des Rahmenplanes." PhD diss., Universität Münster, 1964.

Helbig, Marcel, and Rita Nikolai. *Die Unvergleichbaren. Der Wandel der Schulsysteme in den deutschen Bundesländern seit 1949.* Bad Heilbrunn: Klinkhardt, 2015.

Henschel, Paul. "Ein Schülerbild." *Aus dem Pädagogischen Universitätsseminar Jena* 2 (1890): 143–56.

Herbart, Johann F. *Umriss pädagogischer Vorlesungen.* Göttingen: Dieterich, 1841.

Hillmann, Karl-Heinz. *Wertwandel: Zur Frage soziokultureller Voraussetzungen alternativer Lebensformen.* Darmstadt: Wiss. Buchges, 1989.

Hofsäss, Thomas. *Die Überweisung von Schülern auf die Hilfsschule und die Schule für Lernbehinderte: Eine historisch-vergleichende Untersuchung.* Berlin: Spiess, 1993.

Hylla, Erich. *Der Übergang von der Grundschule zu weiterführenden Schulen: Bestimmungen, Erfahrungen, Vorschläge.* Leipzig: Klinkhardt, 1925.

Ingenkamp, Karlheinz. *Untersuchungen zur Übergangsauslese.* Weinheim: Beltz, 1968.

–. "Die Testaversion der deutschen Intellektuellen." In *Diagnostik in der Schule: Beiträge zu Schlüsselfragen der Schülerbeurteilung.* Edited by Karlheinz Ingenkamp, 153–79. Weinheim: Beltz, 1989.

–. *Pädagogische Diagnostik in Deutschland, 1885–1932. Geschichte der pädagogischen Diagnostik. Vol. I.* Weinheim: Dt. Studienverl, 1990.

Jacobi, Juliane. "Der Blick auf das Kind. Zur Entstehung der Pädagogik in den Schulen des Halleschen Waisenhauses." In *Das Kind in Pietismus und Aufklärung. Beiträge des internationalen Symposions vom 12.–15. November 1997 in den Franckeschen Stiftungen zu Halle.* Edited by Josef N. Neumann, 47–60. Tübingen: Verl. der Franckeschen Stiftungen Halle im Max-Niemeyer-Verl., 2000.

Kamm, Helmut. "Beurteilungskategorien und Perspektiven des Lehrers in Schülercharakteristiken." PhD diss. Eberhard-Karls-Universität zu Tübingen, 1972.

Kienzle, Richard. *Schülerbeobachtung und Schülerbeurteilung: Eine praktische Anleitung für Lehrer und Erzieher.* Eßlingen: Burg-Bücherei, 1951.

Krüger, Hans. "Wilhelm von Humboldts Charakterschilderungen im Rahmen seiner Persönlichkeitsforschung." *Zeitschrift für angewandte Psychologie und Charakterkunde* 66, 1, 2 (1943): 42–103.

Latscha, Fritz. "Der Einfluss des Primarlehrers." In *Die Ungleichheit der Bildungschancen: Soziale Schranken im Zugang zur höheren Schule.* Edited by Franz Hess, Fritz Latscha and Willi Schneider, 185–258. Olten: Walter-Verlag, 1966.

Laux, Hermann. *Pädagogische Diagnostik im Nationalsozialismus, 1933–1945.* Geschichte der pädagogischen Diagnostik. Volume 2. Weinheim: Dt. Studienverl, 1990.

Lübke, Silvia-Iris. *Schule ohne Noten: Lernberichte in der Praxis der Laborschule.* Opladen: Leske + Budrich, 1996.

Mattes, Peter. "Zur Kontinuität in der deutschen Psychologie über die Zeit des Nationalsozialismus hinaus." *Psychologie und Geschichte* 1, no. 3 (1989): 1–10.

McElvany, Nele. "Die Übergangsempfehlung von der Grundschule auf die weiterführende Schule im Erleben der Lehrkräfte." In *Der Übergang von der Grundschule in die weiterführende Schule. Leistungsgerechtigkeit und regionale, soziale und ethnisch-kulturelle Disparitäten. Zusammenfassung der zentralen Befunde.* Edited by Jürgen Baumert et al., 295–311. Berlin: Max-Planck-Institut für Bildungsforschung, 2010.

Muchow, Martha. "Notwendigkeit und Möglichkeit der Heranziehung des Lehrerurteils bei der Begabtenauslese." *Zeitschrift für Pädagogische Psychologie und Experimentelle Pädagogik* 20, no. 5 (1919): 302–8.

"Neuregelung der Schülerauslese an höheren Schulen." *Die Mittelschule* 49, no. 12 (1935).

Pfeifer, Wolfgang. *Etymologisches Wörterbuch des Deutschen.* Berlin: Akademie-Verlag, 1989.

Pohlmann, Sanna. *Der Übergang am Ende der Grundschulzeit: Zur Formation der Übergangsempfehlung aus der Sicht der Lehrkräfte.* Münster: Waxmann, 2009.

Rajičić, Dušan. *Berücksichtigung der Individualität in der Massenerziehung: Geschichte und Darstellung.* Belgrad: Neue Handelsdruckerei, 1899.

Reble, Albert. *Geschichte der Pädagogik.* Stuttgart: Klett, 1992.

Reh, Sabine, Kathrin Berdelmann, and Joachim Scholz. "Der Ehrbetrieb und unterrichtliche Honorierungspraktiken im Schulwesen um 1800. Die Entstehung des Leistungs-Dispositivs." In *Leistung.* Edited by Alfred Schäfer and Christiane Thompson, 37–60. Paderborn: Schöningh, 2015.

Richert, Peggy. *Elternentscheidung versus Lehrerdiagnose: Der Übergang von der Grundschule zur Sekundarschule.* Bad Heilbrunn: Klinkhardt, 2012.

Ringer, Fritz K. *Felder des Wissens: Bildung, Wissenschaft und sozialer Aufstieg in Frankreich und Deutschland um 1900.* Weinheim: Beltz, 2003.

Rudloff, Wilfried. "Ungleiche Bildungschancen: Bildungsforschung, öffentlicher Diskurs und Bildungsreform in England und der Bundesrepublik in den Jahren des Bildungsbooms." In *Bildung und Differenz: Historische Analysen zu einem aktuellen Problem.* Edited by Carola Groppe, Gerhard Kluchert and Eva Matthes, 361–86. Wiesbaden: Springer, 2016.

Ruttmann, Wilhelm J. *Die Begutachtung des Schülers im Dienste der Auslese: Ergebnisse der Schülerkunde und Wegweisungen der Praxis.* Nürnberg: Korn, 1936.

Schulte Ladbeck, Wolfgang. *Grundschulgutachten und Schulerfolg im Gymnasium: Längsschnittstudie dreier Schülerjahrgänge vom Übertritt ins Gymnasium bis zum Abitur.* (PhD diss., Universität Münster, 1989).

Schultze, Walter. "Die Begabtenförderung in ihrer Abhängigkeit vom Schulaufbau: Eine internationale Umschau." *Paedagogica Europea* 3 (1967): 25–45.

Schultze, Walter, Werner Knoche, and Elisabeth Thomas. *Über den Voraussagewert der Auslesekriterien für den Schulerfolg am Gymnasium.* Frankfurt am Main: Max-Traeger-Stiftung, 1964.

Sekretariat der Ständigen Konferenz der Kultusminister der Länder in der Bundesrepublik Deutschland. "Übergang von der Grundschule in Schulen des Sekundarbereichs I und Förderung, Beobachtung und Orientierung in den Jahrgangsstufen 5 und 6 (sog. Orientierungsstufe): Informationsschrift des Sekretariats der Kultusministerkonferenz Stand: 18.10.2010." Accessed November 19, 2014. http://www.kmk.org/fileadmin/veroeffentli chungen_beschluesse/2010/2010_10_18-Uebergang-Grundschule-S_eI1-Orientierungsstufe.pdf.

Simoneit, Max. *Über Kindercharaktere: Bewertung und Schülerauslese.* Berlin: Bernard & Graefe, 1952.

Steinkamp, Günter. "Die Rolle des Volksschullehrers im schulischen Selektionsprozess: Ergebnisse einer empirisch-soziologischen Untersuchung." *Hamburger Jahrbuch für Wirtschafts- und Gesellschaftspolitik* 12 (1967): 302–24.

Stelmaszyk, Bernhard. "Rekonstruktionen von Bildungsgängen preußischer Gymnasiasten sowie der zugehörigen Lehrergutachten aus Reifeprüfungsverfahren der Jahre 1926–1946." Habilitation, Johannes Gutenberg-Universität Mainz, 2002.

Stern, William. *Die Intelligenz der Kinder und Jugendlichen und die Methoden ihrer Untersuchung.* Leipzig: Barth, 1920.

Tent, Lothar. *Die Auslese von Schülern für weiterführende Schulen: Möglichkeiten und Grenzen. Beiträge zur Theorie und Praxis der Leistungsbeurteilung in der Schule.* Göttingen: Hogrefe, 1969.

Terhart, Ewald. "Zensurengebung und innerschulisches Selektionsklima - die Rolle der Schulleitung." *Zeitschrift für Soziologie der Erziehung und Sozialisation* 19, no. 3 (1999): 277–92.

–. "Die Beurteilung von Schülern als Aufgabe des Lehrers: Forschungslinien und Forschungsergebnisse." In *Handbuch der Forschung zum Lehrerberuf.* Edited by Ewald Terhart, Hedda Bennewitz and Martin Rothland, 699–717. Münster: Waxmann, 2011.

Titze, Hartmut, and Corinna M. Dartenne. "Lernfähigkeit und Geschlecht." In 'Bildung' *jenseits pädagogischer Theoriebildung? Fragen zu Sinn, Zweck und Funktion der allgemeinen Pädagogik; Festschrift für Reinhard Uhle zum 65. Geburtstag.* Edited by Detlef Gaus and Elmar Drieschner. 1. Aufl, 381–400. Wiesbaden: VS Verl. für Sozialwiss, 2010.

Tobias, Alfred. "Berücksichtigt bei der Schülerauslese die Eigenart der nordischen Rasse!" *Reichszeitung der deutschen Erzieher. Nationalsozialistische Lehrerzeitung* 2, no. 3 (1934): 12–13.

Ullrich, Heiner. "Exzellenz und Elitenbildung in Gymnasien. Traditionen und Innovationen. Edited by Heinz-Hermann Krüger and Werner Helsper, 181–201. Zeitschrift für Erziehungswissenschaft. Wiesbaden: Springer VS, 2014.

Undeutsch, Udo. "Zum Problem der begabungsgerechten Auslese beim Eintritt in die Höhere Schule während der Schulzeit." In *Begabung und Lernen: Ergebnisse und Folgerungen neuer Forschungen.* Edited by Heinrich Roth and Hans Aebli, 377–405. Stuttgart: Klett, 1971.

Urabe, Masashi. *Funktion und Geschichte des deutschen Schulzeugnisses.* Bad Heilbrunn: Klinkhardt, 2009.

Volkers, Achim. *Wissen und Bildung bei Foucault: Aufklärung zwischen Wissenschaft und ethisch-ästhetischen Bildungsprozessen.* Wiesbaden: VS Verlag, 2008.

Waldow, Florian. "Die internationale Konjunktur standardisierter Messungen von Schülerleistung in der ersten Hälfte des 20. Jahrhunderts und ihr Niederschlag in Deutschland und Schweden." In *'Der vermessene Mensch': Ein kritischer Blick auf Messbarkeit, Normierung und Standardisierung.* Edited by Martin Dust and Johanna Mierendorff, 75–86. Jahrbuch für Pädagogik 2010. Frankfurt am Main: Peter Lang, 2010.

Weigand, Gabriele. "Geschichte und Herleitung eines pädagogischen Begabungsbegriffs." In *Werte schulischer Begabtenförderung. Begabungsbegriff und Werteorientierung.* Edited by Armin Hackl, Olaf Steenbuck and Gabriele Weigand, 48–54. Frankfurt am Main: Karg-Stiftung, 2011.

Wiedemann, Franz. *Der Lehrer der Kleinen: Ein praktischer Rathgeber für junge Elementarlehrer; überhaupt aber ein Buch für alle, welche sich für die Erziehung der Kleinen interessieren.* Leipzig: Oehmigke, 1880.

Wörlein, Johann W. *Bibliologisches Lehrbuch der deutschen Volks-Pädagogik*. Sulzbach: Seidel, 1830.

Yates, Alfred, and D. A. Pidgeon. *Admission to Grammar Schools: Third Interim
   Report on the Allocation of Primary School Leavers to Courses of Secondary
   Education*. London, UK: Newnes, 1957.

Zietz, Karl. "Das Gutachten für die Schülerauslese. (Vorschläge zur Abfassung der
   Schülercharakteristik)." *Die deutsche Schule* 41, no. 2 (1937): 69–79.

Assessment and Psychologisation

Philippe Bongrand[2]

From the Promotion to the Neutralisation of Emotions in Student Assessment: Instituting the *Fiche Scolaire* for Vocational Guidance in France, 1918–1922[1]

Today, the French assessment culture in schools, and in particular in secondary schools, has three dominant characteristics. First, the primary instruments of formal evaluation are grades.[3] Second, the main criterion for grading students is their performance in various disciplines, especially in certain 'fundamental' disciplines (the humanities until the 1960s, mathematics ever since). Finally, the main function of grading is to rank students relative to one another: students are evaluated on their performance in comparison to their peers rather than on the skills they have mastered.[4]

These dominant traits cannot be explained by any consensus. The low reliability of the grading system has been established and widely discussed at least since the creation of docimology, the science of tests and exams, in the 1920s.[5] The importance given to certain disciplines has been denounced as an instrument for imposing one culture over others by the advocates of "comprehensive education," already identifiable by the mid-19th century,[6] for example, or, since the 1960s, by

---

1 Translation: Sarah Novak.

2 The author warmly thanks Ute Frevert, Margrit Pernau and the members of the Centre for the History of Emotions at the Max Planck Institute for Human Development, Berlin, where this research found its starting point. He also thanks Marcelo Caruso and Cristina Alarcón for their challenging support.

3 Pierre Merle, "L'école française et l'invention de la note. Un éclairage historique sur les polémiques contemporaines," *Revue française de pédagogie* 193 (2015).

4 Pascal Bressoux and Pascal Pansu, *Quand les enseignants jugent leurs élèves* (Paris: PUF, 2003); Joanie Cayouette-Remblière, *L'école qui classe* (Paris: Puf, 2016).

5 Jérôme Martin, "Aux origines de la 'science des examens', 1920–1940," *Histoire de l'éducation* 94 (2002).

6 Frédéric Mole, *L'école laïque pour une République sociale. Controverses pédagogiques et politiques,1900–1914* (Rennes: PUR, 2010).

sociologists who have it as the cornerstone of how schools legitimise inequality.[7] The logic behind ranking students has never been endorsed as an explicit single objective; the avowed aim of the French republican school system is, on the contrary, national unification.[8] This dominant culture is sometimes denounced as the mechanism of an educational system that teaches docility rather than emancipating its pupils, skews their (dis)tastes for certain subjects and turns tests into a vector for experiencing injustice or anxiety.[9] This criticism is widespread and hardly new but has had little influence on this or on other pillars of educational culture.[10]

To understand the dominance of this quantified, subject-matter based, normative assessment culture, one research strategy consists in studying the limited scope of attempts to evaluate students differently, in other words to focus on their unfulfilled possibilities.[11] In this perspective, the present chapter will focus on the promotion of tools that might enhance the affective aspects of student assessment. This goal is not only pursued by "alternative" schools and "new" pedagogies, which have often emphasised assessment without grading, freedom from official curricula, respect for the individual or the quest for "well-being."[12] Alternative assessment tools, which valorise the affective aspect, can also be promoted by those most directly responsible for developing school policies, which are particularly centralised in France. This was true of the multiple attempts made to adopt a *dossier scolaire* in France in the 20th century.

A *dossier scolaire* is a type of school record that follows a pupil throughout his or her studies and contains information from various actors (teachers, doctors, psychologists, parents…) that might concern his or her mastery of disciplines but also his or her family, health, physiology or psychology. Through the diverse kinds of information, it gathers, this school record questions categories of student

---

7   Pierre Bourdieu and Jean-Claude Passeron, *The Inheritors. French Students and their relation to culture*, trans. Richard Nice (Chicago, IL: University of Chicago Press, 1979 [1964]).

8   Eugen Weber, *Peasants into Frenchmen. The modernisation of rural France, 1870–1914* (Stanford, CA: Stanford University Press, 1976).

9   Fabrizio Butera, Céline Buchs and Céline Darnon, ed. *L'évaluation, une menace?* (Paris: PUF, 2011).

10 David Tyack and Larry Cuban, *Tinkering Towards Utopia: A Century of Public School Reform* (Cambridge, MA: Harvard University Press, 1995).

11 Quentin Deluermoz and Pierre Singaravélou, *Pour une histoire des possibles. Analyses contrefactuelles et futurs non advenus* (Paris: Seuil, 2016).

12 Marie-Laure Viaud, *Des collèges et des lycées différents* (Paris: PUF/Le Monde, 2005); Laurent Gutierrez, Laurent Besse and Antoine Prost, ed. *Réformer l'école. L'apport de l'Éducation nouvelle, 1930–1970* (Grenoble: Presses Universitaires de Grenoble, 2012).

assessment that are otherwise mainly quantitative, normative and based on subject mastery. 'Psychological' categories in school record forms can reveal the role of the affective aspect. For this reason, the school record constitutes a possible terrain for the history of emotions.[13]

In this perspective, I would like to look into the conception, development and implementation of school report files in order to observe the status that they give to students' feelings and, at the same time, to examine their importance in relation to the dominant culture of student assessment. This chapter focuses more specifically on the adoption, in 1922, of a national model for the *fiche scolaire* (report card) given to teachers in order to contribute to the vocational guidance of their pupils. This new report card was an instrument of change: it asked teachers to fill in extra-curricular rubrics, going beyond the habitual grade record (sometimes called the *livret scolaire*), and it did not aim at classifying students in relation to a given academic norm (in order to pass on to the next grade level or to provide certification) but instead in relation to differentiated futures. In the 1920s and 30s, movements in favour of prolonging and unifying education would transform this vocational guidance report card into a component of the *dossier scolaire* (school record). The original developer of this report form was asked in 1937 to create the first model of a student record that would be adopted on a national scale, and whose relationship can be seen with the school records instituted after the Liberation of France and used during the following decades. The episode examined here thus offers a possible starting point for the history of the school record in France, which remains incomplete and little studied to this day.

In the first part of this chapter, I will show how the different projects for developing a school record form around the 1920s give new emphasis to children's emotions among the preoccupations of educators. Using different approaches and terminologies, they consider the affective aspect as a source of meaningful data, as a goal to reach or as a tool to mobilise. The second part of this chapter will show that, while the academic institution encouraged teachers to use this new report card to assess pupils, the version that was adopted and the initial elements of its implementation reveal its meagre influence, at least in the short term, on the culture of student assessment.

---

13 The term "emotions" is here used somewhat loosely in order to avoid imposing anachronistic meanings, while at the same time remaining sensitive to the terminology in use during the period in question. See *Ute Frevert, Emotions in History. Lost and found* (Budapest: Central European University Press, 2011).

Evaluating Students' Emotions to Aid in their Vocational Guidance

The *dossier scolaire* came to exist when the public education administration imported into the school system the objectives and instruments belonging to vocational guidance. This type of counselling, which had up to that point been carried out mainly by people involved in labour policy and in the labour market, aimed at guiding students to apply for jobs that matched their tastes and aptitudes after they finished their studies.[14]

The promoters of a public vocational guidance service saw it as a way of contributing to the emergence of the affective state that is happiness.[15] This argument is found in the writings of the two most important authors of this movement. For Fernand Mauvezin, an engineer who directed the service of vocational guidance of the Chamber of Trades of the Gironde and South-West regions, "there is no doubt that the child will gladly seize upon the opportunity to learn a trade if it has been proven to him that this is the field that offers him the highest chance of success. Because he likes his trade, he will want to learn it in depth […]."[16] Whereas those who take the wrong path will become "failures," "malcontents," "put off by everything," and "must suffer because of this."[17]

According to Julien Fontègne, a teacher who took part in the creation of the office of vocational guidance at the Institut Jean-Jacques Rousseau in Geneva in 1918,[18] then organised a similar office in Strasburg starting in February 1921, "guiding the child towards a professional that suits his tastes [is] the only means

---

14 See André Caroff, *L'organisation de l'orientation en France. Évolution des origines à nos jours* (Paris: EAP, 1987); Jérôme Martin, "Le mouvement d'orientation professionnelle en France. Entre l'école et le marché du travail, 1900–1940. Aux origines de la profession de conseiller d'orientation" (PhD Diss., University of Paris-Sorbonne, 2011).

15 See Rémi Pawin, *Histoire du bonheur en France depuis 1945* (Paris: Robert Laffont, 2013).

16 Fernand Mauvezin, *Rose des métiers. Traité d'orientation professionnelle. Qualités et aptitudes nécessaires à l'exercice de 250 métiers différents et défauts rédhibitoires* (Paris: Éditions littéraires et politiques, 1922), 60.

17 Ibid, 15, 64, 75.

18 Astrid Thomann, Bernard Schneuwly and Valérie Lussi, "L'orientation professionnelle et les sciences de l'éducation: deux voies contrastées," in *Émergence des sciences de l'éducation en Suisse à la croisée de traditions académiques contrastées. Fin du 19ᵉ – première moitié du 20e siècle*, ed. Rita Hofstetter and Bernard Schneuwly (Berne: Peter Lang, 2007).

to lead him to happiness. [...]. And this happiness and individual well-being, this superior morality of the individual, cannot help but exert a highly positive influence on the *community*."[19] On the other hand, bad career guidance is a "moral influenza virus" that provokes "the hatred of failures, social malcontents for their community;" "leaves [them] all the more abandoned to individual passions or hereditary inclinations."[20]

F. Mauvezin's and J. Fontègne's writings, which were broadly disseminated and very influential, allow us to study in detail — beyond a mere slogan, however foundational and long-lasting — how vocational guidance, in particular with the help of a student record file, might have ended up with the production of happiness as its goal.

The conception and promotion of evaluation forms to be used by teachers

Encouraging teachers to handle the elements of a school record is one of the major points of both Fontègne's and Mauvezin's proposals. It can be found in the various publications that they addressed to children, teachers, employers or administrators.[21] These brochures indicate, first, the type of information that must be collected and the resources (tests, questionnaires) that can be used for the 'examination' of the child. They also contain 'professional monographs' that explain the qualities necessary for carrying out different types of tasks. The use of common descriptive categories thus makes it possible to identify which type would correspond to a given child. According to the writings of Fernand Mauvezin, in Bordeaux in 1918 at the latest,[22] this system of correspondences took on the form of a compass rose, under the title *Rose des métiers* (Rose of Trades). This tool intended for parents and "vocational counsellors" was already well known when it was published as a book in 1922.[23] Julien Fontègne published articles in various

---

19 Julien Fontègne, *L'orientation professionnelle et la détermination des aptitudes* (Neuchatel/Paris: Delachaux et Niestlé, 1921), 12.

20 Ibid.

21 See especially Fernand Mauvezin, *Avant de choisir son métier ou sa profession, conseils aux enfants (garçons et filles), aux parents, aux éducateurs* (Paris: Éditions littéraires et politiques, 1921); Julien Fontègne, *Avant d'entrer en apprentissage. Nouveaux entretiens sur l'orientation professionnelle* (Paris: Eyrolles, 1924).

22 This date varies according to different authors. This is the one given by Mauvezin in his book in 1922.

23 Some elements were published in the first issue of the journal *L'orientation professionnelle*: "Une école de vocation," *L'orientation professionnelle* 1 (1919): 29–31.

journals of psychology, pedagogy and vocational guidance, and then a book in which he developed these articles further.[24] These publications encouraged schools to keep a file of information on each pupil and to have teachers contribute to it. Let us examine how these two authors conceived of this record.

Evoking practices already in use in Bordeaux and Strasburg, F. Mauvezin suggests that, for every student, the teacher or principal should fill out a *fiche scolaire* made up of a 'physiological report for vocational guidance' and a 'pedagogical report for vocational guidance'. Far more than a simple grade record, this *fiche scolaire* (which might today be called a "school record") is quite a long document:

> "In it one can find everything that it is useful to know about each pupil: surname, given name, date and place of birth, school background, rankings, absences, successes, economic situation of the family: parents' professions, number of siblings, orphans, various gratuities, school mutual fund; vision, hearing, general health, accidents, operations, infirmities, vaccinations; notes regarding the pupil's aptitudes, morality and discipline; the wishes and observations of families; the teacher's personal observations. In other terms, the experience of each pupil is gathered before teacher's eyes on a small chart. At the end of each school year or when the student leaves, the teacher, with total sincerity and independence, adds notes from his personal experience. And this goes on until the end of each pupil's schooling."[25]

Filling out this report card was thus a step away from the assessment culture centred on academic testing, which, as F. Mauvezin regretfully writes, assimilates passing tests to intelligence, whereas "other qualities, very seldom mentioned, have as powerful an effect on a child's success as intelligence. By these I mean reflection, perseverance, strength of will."[26] To convince teachers to expand their professional viewpoint, F. Mauvezin argues that these reports can nourish their pedagogical thinking and allow them to examine such questions as these, for example: "Are very nervous children, or very apathetic children, moving toward a better balance over the course of their schooling?"[27] "Attention, intelligence, sensitivity, willpower, morality, taste, character — have these improved during the pupil's schooling?"[28] He speaks of reforming the objectives of school (vocational guidance) in association with the use of new instruments (the report card or "*fiche scolaire*") and of new assessment criteria (which, as we shall see *infra*, reconsider the role of emotions).

---

24 Julien Fontègne, *L'orientation professionnelle*.
25 Mauvezin, *Rose*, 18.
26 Mauvezin, *Rose*, 61.
27 Mauvezin, *Rose*, 19–20.
28 Ibid.

This can be found in the method of vocational guidance that J. Fontègne tested in Geneva. A vocational counselling session would be based on a file (individual report) containing eleven documents or 'folios' full of information about the child, provided either before the consultation by various adults (parents, doctor, teacher) or during it by the vocational counsellor himself as he interviewed the child (Fontègne favoured this over the questionnaire that Mauzevin had the child fill out) or administered tests as part of a 'psychological examination.' The child's teacher filled out four 'folios' concerning his grades in each subject, his physical and intellectual activity and his moral behaviour. In 1921, J. Fontègne helped create the office of vocational guidance of the of Chamber of Trades in Strasburg,[29] and one of its missions would be to distribute vocational guidance forms to schools.[30] Fontègne held meetings with groups of teachers during which he asked them to carry out a "meticulous study of the child in his games, in the street, in class, alone, among his peers, in order to give the Office of Vocational Guidance as much useful information as possible regarding his physical and intellectual activity; his moral and social behaviour and his diverse aptitudes."[31]

As an annex to his 1921 book, J. Fontègne provided a template for the booklet with eleven folios used in Geneva and, perhaps aware of the ambitiousness of the longer version, also provided a template of the smaller, simpler report card that was used in the vocational guidance office that he ran in Strasburg.

These publications, which became inevitable references for all other works on vocational guidance, contained templates that were ready for immediate use by their readers, especially by guidance counsellors. F. Mauvezin and J. Fontègne disseminated assessment forms throughout the regions where they worked, and provided models for similar forms in order to encourage their use as a national policy. Fontègne emphasises the reformative potential of his book: "I am not unaware that this 'individual report,' as I have envisaged it, will not become standard in our schools right away. I have nonetheless chosen to provide it here,

---

29 Reports and other preparatory documents for the opening of this office may be found at the French National Archives F17 14 404.

30 Hubert Ley and Julien Fontègne, *La chambre de métiers d'Alsace et de Lorraine. Son organisation administrative, sa mission et les résultats de son activité* (Paris: Association française pour la lutte contre le chômage, 1921), 10. Julien Fontègne, "L'office régional d'orientation professionnelle de Strasbourg," *Manuel général de l'instruction primaire* 26 (1921): 336–37.

31 "L'école et l'orientation professionnelle", *Gazette des métiers d'Alsace-Lorraine*, 25 (1921): 238.

for I am convinced that there are educational centres that will be interested in it and will adopt it as soon as they truly begin to take interest in the question of vocational guidance."[32] In each of these models for a report form, interpreted from the perspective of their authors, we can see the degree to which affective elements are taken into consideration as part of student assessment. It is at this point that the report card's power to affect the dominant assessment culture came into play.

Urging teachers to evaluate children's preferences

Compared to the usual assessment criteria (aptitudes, academic performance, etc.), one new characteristic of these reports is that they focus on children's feelings, specifically on their tastes — which would prove to be only one among a number of occurrences of the affective aspect. Identifying and materializing these tastes was of central importance in the forms filled out by counsellors. Mauvezin produced long questionnaires to be completed by children (sometimes with the help of teachers), inviting them to write down their likes and dislikes, because becoming aware of their tastes was supposed to help them turn towards a field that they enjoyed, to end up doing a job that they liked, and thus to lead a happy life. This wish to objectify tastes can also be seen in forms designed specifically for teachers to fill out, thus broadening the field of formal assessment. In the *fiche pédagogique* section in Mauvezin's record file, the teacher must indicate the student's "particular likes" and "particular dislikes."[33] On Fontègne's form, the teacher mentions whether the student prefers rest or action, "likes to read," and what his "dominant tastes" are.[34]

Teachers are not merely asked to identify and describe pupils' tastes. To keep students from aiming for careers not suited to their aptitudes, it is also necessary to modify their preferences and orient their affects. The vocational counsellor "will sometimes have to deflate excessive enthusiasms" during interviews.[35] To discourage a child from aiming for a career that is too high in the social hierarchy, he can use not only the maxims of conservative morality but also warnings of the misery of discovering that one is not cut out for the career he has worked for, or the shame of one who, having reached a higher social status through work, has

---

32 Fontègne, *L'Orientation*, 236.
33 Mauvezin, *Rose*, 28.
34 Fontègne, *L'Orientation*, 234.
35 Mauvezin, *Rose*, 33.

to 'blush' over his family background. Mauvezin argues in favour of counselling students when they are young and their tastes are still malleable. Work must be carried out on the child's emotions, and for this task Mauvezin recommends that teachers rely upon emulation:

> "Being inferior to one's age in knowledge, intellectual and even physical aptitudes, is always a painful thing to realise, and is sometimes humiliating; it inspires effort when all other pedagogical methods have resulted in inaction. Being superior to other students of one's own age is a satisfaction that maintains the zeal of the best students. Average students make an effort at least to maintain their rank, which the inferior students would like to snatch from them and surpass. As soon as he starts school, the child gets used to noticing superiority without being jealous. Superiority is, in his eyes, legitimate, whether it be a gift of nature or gained through an honourable effort of will. This principle of emulation is easy to use and is always effective. Appropriate commentaries must accompany this when it seems too harsh for children of good will but ill-favoured by nature."[36]

While J. Fontègne also encourages teachers to carry out an emotional labour, his goal is to modify students' attitudes towards manual labour. In Strasburg, the vocational bureau gathered teachers annually not only to give them individual school report forms (*fiche individuelle scolaire*) but also to encourage them to "exalt the value of work at all times."[37] Deeply inspired by Kerschensteiner,[38] J. Fontègne considers that in order to "make [children] enjoy work," teachers should find examples from the world of work to fit into their curricula, offer outings to factories, workshops and museums, use films for educational purposes, reassert the value of instructive manual labour, all this in order to "introduce a bit of practicality into teaching" and to place the child in a "professional atmosphere."[39] In order to create a true learning environment and help the child develop his own "professional mentality," Fontègne recommends emotional pedagogy.[40] While this pedagogical

---

36 Mauvezin, *Rose*, 22.

37 Fontègne, "L'office."

38 André Caroff, *Julien Fontègne. Un pionnier de l'orientation professionnelle* (Paris: INETOP, n.d.), 12–17.

39 Fontègne, *L'Orientation*, 51.

40 Later, in 1928, as the preface to a work in which this pedagogy is developed, J. Fontègne would include composition prompts, dictations, recitations, songs, maxims and ideas for essays, drawings or arithmetic problems exalting the values of work and of choosing a profession. These subjects illustrate emotional pedagogy: "French composition subject: 'People often speak of the joy procured by working. They also sing of the pleasantness of doing nothing. Have you experienced one or the other, and in which circumstances? Which did you prefer? Why?" "Demonstrate that work is a serious affair but not a sad one." "'Work, put yourself to the trouble', said La Fontaine. Why

work of guiding 'tastes' is not explicitly part of the school record file, the file follows up on this work and benefits from it. Though they are opposed on other political or methodological points, Mauvezin, like Fontègne, thus shows how children's preferences must be modelled in order to be simultaneously experienced as personal and, in substance, specified as reasonable. The two have an analogous viewpoint on this, and argue not only for guiding students according to affect but, indissociably, guiding them using affect or even guiding their affects.

Differing roles and definitions for affective phenomena

From a semantic point of view, it should be noted that the term 'emotions' does not appear on most of Mauzevin's or Fontègne's forms, whereas affective phenomena may be found under a number of headings. 'Tastes,' evoked previously, is only one meaning of the term.

A second meaning, biological in this case, for affective elements is found in Mauzevin's 'physiological report card.' The teacher, if possible with the help of a doctor, fills in information in two affective categories: "temperament" (which, in the tradition of the Hippocratic humours, refer to being "sanguine, nervous, bilious, lymphatic, strong or weak") and "character" (which, following psychological discussions from the end of the previous century, are divided into "sensitive, intellectual, strong-willed, indifferent, balanced").[41] These innate properties reduce the space of the child's possible preferences:

> "The apprentice who is indifferent or nonchalant will be forced to acknowledge that he has perhaps made a mistake, for every person beginning his trade should consider it the most beautiful and is interested in it with all his heart. He should thus seek another line of work, unless his apathy comes from inveterate laziness, in which case there is no remedy."[42]

Similarly, Fontègne indicates that, if they are "predisposed to nervousness (trembling — overexertion during the high season)," young women should not become

---

must we work, and is work always 'trouble'?" Teachers can thus appeal to their students' emotions in order to "teach them to love and honour all workers"; they must "call on the noblest sentiments that are latent within most students". Henry Lefebvre and Marcel Henry, *La préorientation professionnelle à l'école primaire* (Paris: Librairie de l'Enseignement technique, 1928).

41 Mauzevin, *Rose*, 29.

42 Mauzevin, *Rose*, 93.

telephone operators. In the file that he proposes, the "nervous" type appears under the physiological heading.[43]

Finally, a third meaning given to affective phenomena can be found in 'moral' qualities. Mauvezin and Fontègne both consider that career guidance must be based in large part on students' 'aptitudes,' which they divide into physical, intellectual and moral categories. If we look closely, the moral aptitudes attributed to children or demanded by certain professions can be understood in current terms as emotional competencies. The person who wishes to become a telephone operator must have "the ability to adapt, calmness, awareness, an even temper, a sense of teamwork [...];"[44] a milliner must have "good manners, curtesy, patience, affability."[45] In J. Fontègne's model, the sheet to be filled out by the teacher about the student's moral aptitudes focuses mainly on affective elements:

"Folio n° 7. Indications about the child's moral behaviour
1) How would you describe his nature? (cold, warm, passionate, easily excited, indifferent)
2) Does he show an aptitude to repress the expression of his emotions? (to dissimulate fear, worry, surprise, pain)
3) Violent or gentle character? (irritable, choleric, phlegmatic)
4) Does he seek out sensations, risk, danger?
5) What are his dominant tastes, his particular interests?
6) Is he conscientious? Does he have a sense of duty? Of responsibility?
[...]
11) Is he sincere? (lying, bragging)
12) Does he easily bend to discipline?
13) Is he shy? Arrogant?
14) How does he behave in regards to punishments? Rewards?
15) Does he demonstrate a special strength (or weakness) of will? Does he control himself easily?"[46]

Characterizing the status of emotions in these files is all the more complicated because it is not only the meaning given to emotions that differ but also their bearing on the student's career guidance. Tastes, which, as we have seen, are supposed to be guided by educators, are secondary in the choice of orientation. For F. Mauvezin, they are less significant than other criteria, the most important of

---

43 Julien Fontègne, "Le cabinet d'orientation professionnelle de l'Institut Jean-Jacques Rousseau, à Genève." *L'orientation professionnelle* 8 (1920): 35–44.
44 See *L'Orientation professionnelle* 8 (1920): 43.
45 See *L'Orientation professionnelle* 30 (1922): 24.
46 Fontègne, *L'Orientation*, 234.

which are the subject's aptitudes and his family background. He advises against letting career guidance be too strongly influenced by the desires of children:

> "The vast majority of parents do not dare broach the subject of their children's vocational guidance for they feel that the question is very serious and delicate, but instead, without emotion, let the matter be decided for them by a 13-year-old kid. If we listened to the desires of rural children, we would soon have in France hundreds of thousands of workers more or less vaguely qualified as mechanics, knowing nothing about agriculture, whereas we have a great need of agricultural workers who are knowledgeable about their field and who perhaps could make use of a few notions of mechanics."[47]

Fontègne also distances himself from the subjective expression of the young person, inevitably "mentally anarchical," who must "make choices at an unfortunately troubling and confusing period of his life."[48] This secondary status given to the preferences of the subject appears in the advice that, during the orientation meeting itself, "one should, as much as possible, avoid thwarting a *reasonable* wish on the part of the child."[49] Tastes are an insufficient but necessary condition. Fontègne congratulates himself on having managed to "guide young people away from careers in which they would certainly not have succeeded due to a lack of inclination, for instance."[50]

Emotions, in their moral or physiological sense, are given the characteristic status of "aptitudes" in Fontègne's writing during this period of the vocational guidance movement; this is to say that they are innate, often hereditary, not very trainable, and are thus a source of indications or counter-indications.[51] An example of a counter-indication related to emotive qualities appears when J. Fontègne acknowledges the usefulness of graphology:

> "Young men, even brilliant ones, who are too nervous (choppy handwriting even in moments of rest) or too impressionable (handwriting that is constantly uneven) or too reckless (disorganised handwriting, without downstrokes and upstrokes, with neglected punctuation and accents) must, in general, be discouraged from careers that require a difficult entrance examination demanding presence of mind; nor should they enter into

---

47 Mauvezin, *Rose*, 59, 15.
48 Fontègne, *L'Orientation*, 106, 10.
49 Julien Fontègne, "L'école primaire et l'orientation professionnelle," *Manuel général de l'enseignement primaire* 44 (1923): 840.
50 Fontègne, *L'Orientation*, 62.
51 Catherine Dorison, "Orienter selon les aptitudes. Enjeux institutionnels et pédagogiques, 1936–1959," in *En attendant la réforme. Disciplines scolaires et politiques éducatives sous la IVe République*, ed. Renaud D'Enfert and Pierre Kahn (Grenoble, Presses universitaires de Grenoble, 2010).

professions that, at some time, may require a great deal of attention or composure (those in which one's life may be at risk, sailor, explorer, mechanic, driver, roofer, etc.). For them, agricultural professions, which calm and relax the nerves and maintain health, seem the mostly highly recommendable [...]."[52]

These aptitudes are less discriminating factors for Mauvezin: while they are found in the report file, moral aptitudes are not found in the professional monographs.

The Vocational Guidance File is Appropriated and Redefined by the School System

Around 1920, the national vocational guidance policy began to follow the practices extolled by Fontègne and Mauvezin. The new policy required teachers to fill in forms that, according to their overt objective (vocational guidance) and their topic headings (which could include affective elements), seem to promote a new kind of assessment. However, despite this unprecedented call to fill in these forms, the composition and the implementation of the forms themselves reveal certain mechanisms that, in the short run, limited their influence on the assessment culture.

An unprecedented national campaign for a report card model with few innovations, 1921–1922

Within the ministry of Public Instruction, the general inspector Maurice Roger pushed to rehabilitate the role of school in career guidance, which had up to that point been managed by the Labour Ministry and by trade groups. When, starting in 1917, the annual report on the complementary work of public schools ("Oeuvres complémentaires de l'école," encompassing such things as continuation classes for adults and other community services) was assigned to him,[53] M. Roger took the initiative of highlighting vocational guidance in this report and of listing teacher participation in filling out career guidance forms among practices that he wished to disseminate. Already in the 1917–1918 report, he praises a school in Paris where teachers "write a text about each pupil mentioning his qualities and his degree of manual skill. These notes are then compared and can provide precise

---

52 Fontègne, *L'Orientation*, 73.
53 This annual report addressed to the National Assembly was published in the *Journal officiel*. The reports for the years 1916–1928 can be found in a document kept at the Bibliothèque nationale de France, Nr. FOL–R–646.

information."[54] The following years' reports mention similar student records used in other cities: Libourne (1919–1920), Nantes and Paris (1920–1921), Marseille, Alençon and Châlons (1921–1922). One report (1918–1919) expresses regret that some schools inform students about different trades (through films, visits or workshops) without making a connection with information about the students themselves — information that could specifically be found in student records. In most of these reports, the writings of J. Fontègne and F. Mauvezin are cited as essential references.

In February 1921, a national commission was set up as part of the Under-Secretariat of the State for Technical Instruction in order to coordinate the ministry's initiatives in the area of vocational guidance.[55] This commission was made up of eight representatives, four each from the Labour and Public Instruction Ministries respectively, with Maurice Roger and Julien Fontègne among them. In its first doctrinal text, from May 1921, the commission once again brought up the argument that vocational guidance should aim at "the highest possible satisfaction and well-being," "inner contentment," "the happiness of the individual and, by the same token, that of society."[56] Vocational guidance was to be handled by specialised 'offices' with the help of teachers, who had representatives in the oversight council and were required to fill out the forms. These 'individual school reports,' the printing cost of which was included in the budget, contained information about grades, moral aptitudes and, if the student had received any technical training, his manual skills. This text written by the Under-Secretary of the State thus considers schoolteachers to be competent to evaluate the emotions, understood in the sense of moral competencies. Furthermore, the forms were only supposed to be filled out after the students were exposed to "judicious propaganda, free of any charlatanism" intended to guide their aspirations towards fields with good job prospects.[57] This recommendation presupposes intervening upon students' emotions, here understood in the sense of tastes or preferences. From the perspective of teachers, urged to "apply all their knowledge and all their

---

54 Maurice Roger, "Rapport sur les œuvres complémentaires de l'école publique en 1917–1918" *Journal officiel de la République française* (1918): 239–240.

55 Caroff, *L'organisation*, 61–62.

56 "Projet de modèle-type d'Office d'Orientation professionnelle," Archives nationales, F17 14404. This document was disseminated by a circulary (May 14, 1921) and by the journals *Formation professionnelle* (June 1921) and *L'orientation professionnelle* (September 1921).

57 Ibid.

hearts to the careful observation of the child," the dominant assessment culture appeared to be at stake.[58]

On a national level, the administration reinforced its request by providing a ready-to-use assessment tool as well. A memorandum from January 20, 1922, requests from the national commission "a pedagogical and physiological report card [...] to serve as a model and be communicated to all schools in order to be put to use everywhere."[59] On July 10, 1922, the national commission adopted two forms, one medical and the other academic, that were sent "not as models but rather as examples" to vocational guidance centres.[60] In substance, these report card forms are direct descendants of the form created by J. Fontègne for the vocational guidance office in Strasburg. Below are the contents of one of these two forms intended for use in schools, to be filled out by students and teachers.

Model School Report Card

I. Information to be provided by the student

1° Name of school. Grade.
2° Last name and given name(s) of the graduating student
3° Date and place of birth
4° Address
5° Name and profession of parents
6° Number and ages of siblings
7° Profession desired by the student
8° Reasons for this choice of profession
9° In the event the student cannot enter into this profession, what other profession(s) would he consider?
10° Would he agree to go into an apprenticeship outside of...
11° Can his parents' house and feed him?
12° Can his parents pay the apprenticeship fees?
13° Do the student or his parents have any other plans for him?
14° If they do, where and starting on what date?

---

58 Ibid.
59 Caroff, *L'organisation*, 62.
60 "L'orientation professionnelle et le Sous-secrétariat d'État à l'Enseignement technique," *L'Orientation professionnelle* 41 (1922): 18–22.

II. Information to be provided by the teacher

1° Behaviour. Effort. General results. Did he receive his primary education diploma?

2° How well does the student express himself? Orally? In writing?

3° Yearly grade point average (out of 10) in spelling. In written arithmetic. In mental arithmetic.

4° What type of drawing does he prefer to do? How successful is he?

5° Have you noticed any special talents in this student?

6° Does he demonstrate any strong aptitudes?

7° Does he work fast or slowly?

8° Complementary observations: attention, memory, judgment, orderliness and cleanliness, character.

9° Grades in gymnastics.

III. Information to be provided by the manual work instructor

1° Type of work carried out

2° Results obtained

3° Would you advise this student to go into his desired field? If not, which field would you suggest?[61]

Compared to the model developed at Institut Jean-Jacques Rousseau and reproduced above, this report form seems rudimentary. The usual categories of academic assessment ("behaviour and effort," grades in each subject) are preeminent, while there is no 'psychological' form to fill out. The evaluation of emotions is here reduced to noting a student's taste for drawing, 'observing' a possible moral propensity for order and cleanliness and, finally, evaluating his character. This watering-down is all the more surprising because the national commission simultaneously adopted a model of a professional monograph in which emotions play an important role (with questions such as: "Can this trade be recommended to persons with unhealthy tendencies towards impatience? Melancholia? Worry? Lack of self-confidence? Nervous troubles?"),[62] thus calling for an affect-oriented examination of the child.

This contribution to establishing the school record file thus seems to show that there was the potential, though it would remain unrealised, for the value of emotions to be reasserted in teachers' assessments of pupils. Without any archives

---

61 Ibid.
62 Ibid.

from the commission's debates, I will try to identify elements of an explanation for this within the context of the development of the report card and later of its implementation.

A result of the perceived fragility of psychology?

The discreet role played by emotions in this form may arise from the impossibility of delineating a clear and acceptable repartition of all the assessment objects, instruments and skills between teachers and psychologists.[63] This hypothesis — which may appear overly retrospective when we consider the major role that psychology would later play — emerges from a comparison between the various publications of M. Roger. These publications, which reveal selected hints of the shifting ideas and practices of vocational guidance, show that expectations of psychology were quite unstable between 1917 and 1924. Initially, in 1917, M. Roger placed teachers at the centre of the guidance process:

> "What are the child's aptitudes? Who reveals them to parents, if they are unaware of them, who confirms or clarifies the suspicions that they may have? Teachers. No one is in a better position for informing parents of the degree and quality of [the child's] intelligence or attentiveness."[64]

Then, during the years 1918–1919, M. Roger shifted to the position that certain aptitudes are inaccessible to teachers and must be subjected to psychological testing — which, he regrets, is little used ("Binet-Simon tests are widely used, but not in France").[65] He clearly endorses Fontègne's positions: he quotes his conferences and publications (including the work that came out in 1921, a book which reproduces the Geneva school report form), the methods that he proposes (favouring interviews and tests, unlike Mauvezin), his examples from the German sphere (which Roger adds to examples that were initially exclusively Anglo-American) and his arguments in favour of creating a specialised office in charge of centralizing data for vocational guidance. M. Roger even presents the "rigorous method" of the Geneva office as an "indispensable model" in which the teacher, if he indicates in a report devoted to the student "all that he knows about his intelligence and his

---

63 This hypothesis recalls professional group dynamics as highlighted by Andrew Abbott, *The System of Professions. An Essay on the Division of Expert Labour* (Chicago, IL: University of Chicago Press, 1988).

64 Maurice Roger, "L'orientation professionnelle et l'école," *Manuel général de l'instruction primaire* 2 (1917): 13.

65 Maurice Roger, "Rapport sur les œuvres complémentaires de l'école publique en 1918–1919," *Journal officiel de la République française* (1920): 341.

manual abilities" and his aptitudes, takes part in the work of a counsellor.[66] Roger
expresses his confidence in "experimental psychology [which] makes it possible
to measure faculties with sufficient rigor, [… and] at the very least provides some
clues and contributes to determining aptitudes."[67] Finally, during a third period,
in writings from the years 1920–1921, M. Roger adopts an intermediary position.
Seeking support in the work of Théodore Simon,[68] who along with Binet invented
the first metric scale of intelligence, he insists on the inability of the fledgling
field of psychology to provide the tests and information needed to understand
the tastes and character of a child. Failing this, "the experience of schoolteachers,
acquired through practice and proven by results, provides indications that can
be trusted."[69] Thus, in late 1921, M. Roger placed intellectual and moral aptitudes
within the realm of competency of teachers, and saw the intervention of psychologists as pertinent only on rare occasions, regarding the 'very special qualities'
required by certain professions — such as aviation.

Reservations regarding psychology can thus be detected during the 1921–1922
school year, while the national commission was at work. When he gave his political support to the career guidance movement, Édouard Herriot, president of the
Radical Socialist party, turned this reserved attitude into a characteristic of the
French approach to vocational guidance:

> "as in everything, excesses must be avoided; the Office must be scientific without ped-
> antry and must not, as the German method sometimes does, overuse weights, measures,
> indexes of nervousness."[70]

These reservations resonate with the notable absence of any consensus among
guidance experts. The authors of school report forms present affective aspects, be
they tastes, moral aptitudes, temperament or character, as riddles to solve much
more than as objects of expert assessment. F. Mauvezin, not especially concerned
with being scientific, writes against psychological testing: "willpower, intelligence,
sensitivity, character, temperament, likes, dislikes, must be sought out by other

---

66 Maurice Roger, "Le choix du métier," *Manuel général de l'instruction primaire* 21 (1920):
    277.

67 Roger, Rapport, 1920: 341.

68 Théodore Simon, "La connaissance de l'enfant et l'orientation professionnelle,"
    L'orientation professionnelle 20 (1921).

69 Maurice Roger, "Rapport sur les œuvres complémentaires de l'école publique en
    1920–1921," *Journal officiel de la République française* (1922) : 196–97.

70 Édouard Herriot, "L'apprentissage," *Manuel général de l'instruction primaire* 9 (1921),
    111–113.

means [than measurements]."[71] Mauzevin, following the approach of F. Parsons,[72] proposes a self-administered questionnaire for the child to fill out. J. Fontègne rejects this questionnaire but, while he shares with contemporary psychology a concern for not reducing personality to intelligence[73] and a certain posture of humility,[74] offers no scientific alternative:

> "We all know that moral values play a very important role in the professional life of an individual. Why do psycho-professional questionnaires […], laboratory experiences, surveys, grant such little space to this factor? It is because psycho-moral research is extremely difficult: the child does not 'expose' himself morally as he does physically; often, in fact, he is ashamed to let himself be known as he truly is and many a child who would not hesitate to his reveal visual deficiency or memory problems would be extremely embarrassed to admit to the anxiety he feels about making decisions […]. Psychologists attempt to discover moral aptitudes through experimentation: there have been numerous experiments involving recollection, the association of ideas, suggestion, simulation, the electro-dermic reflex, etc., but nothing so far makes it possible to determine exactly what a vocational guidance service could borrow from these studies. Most of the time, therefore, we must rely on the observations about the child that his parents and teachers agree to share with us."[75]

In the absence of an agreement on the value of psychological testing and student questionnaires, asking teachers to evaluate emotions appeared as a last resort. The commission members then had to formulate a request in such a way as to make it acceptable to teachers. Giving teachers an assessment form with numerous and original headings, such as the Geneva report form, would not only have increased their workload but would also have harshly emphasised the lack of any legitimate instruments for carrying out these tasks. Conversely, removing all original emotional categories from the form, while waiting for counsellors equipped with testing material to be trained and hired, would have delayed and hindered the cause of vocational guidance. We may hazard the hypothesis that, in this context, disseminating an acceptable version of the report card form was

---

71 Mauvezin, *Rose*, 33.

72 Frank Parsons, *Choosing a vocation* (Boston, MA: Houghton Mifflin, 1909).

73 John Carson, *The Measure of Merit. Talents, Intelligence, and Inequality in the French and American Republics, 1750–1940*, (Princeton, NJ: Princeton University Press, 2006), 240–42.

74 A similar disparity may be seen between the existence of sophisticated intelligence tests and the perceived difficulty of evaluating character in Great Britain in the mid-1920s; See Pamela Dale, "A new approach to vocational guidance for school-leavers in the 1920s? Exploring key themes from an influential 1926 report," *History of Education* 41, no 5 (2012): 607, 610, doi : 10.1080/0046760X.2012.665948.

75 Fontègne, *L'orientation*, 75.

accomplished by mobilising a number of standard, traditional assessment categories (not supplementary ones) and, furthermore, by limiting the scope of the more groundbreaking categories of student 'observation.' Disqualifying any recourse to psychology would have also disqualified the evaluation of emotions as extracurricular categories.

From opposition against report cards to their neutralisation

In addition to disagreement regarding the categories to be included on the form, two series of objections seem to have undermined — at least temporarily — the influence of the new school report card on the dominant assessment culture. An initial wave of opposition came from parents. Their attitude, mentioned discreetly in a footnote in Roger's report for 1921–1922, became a major focus in the report for the following school year — during which the report card was put into circulation. The report expresses misgivings regarding families who are "rather hostile and [who] only grudgingly provide indispensable information," or families who are "indifferent."[76] The argument that these report cards were excessively objectifying was relayed by the press at the start of the 1922 school year, when a "long controversy"[77] began after a teacher decried that "individual student records are getting longer: the teacher, doctor and tradesman all add their observations to the file and the child is catalogued, measured and enlisted, and his future is determined."[78] We may hypothesise that these criticisms, in addition to explaining the diminished use of these report cards, were already known or anticipated while the commission was developing the model for the report card and that they led to the reduction of the most explicitly psychological categories, and in particular the emotional ones. A second series of oppositions to the new report card system came from teachers pleading lack of time, or lack of competence, or disagreement with the principle of orientation. At the Congress of the French Federation of School Principals, in 1923, the recorder, Labrunie, presented these arguments and concluded that the report card was useless and dangerous.[79]

---

76 Maurice Roger, "Rapport sur les œuvres complémentaires de l'école publique en 1921–1922." *Journal officiel de la République française* (1923): 427–428.

77 Jeanne Clément, *Le mouvement d'orientation professionnelle* (Aix-en-Provence: Paul Roubaud, 1924).

78 See "L'orientation professionnelle et la 'papillonne' de Fourier," *L'Orientation professionnelle* 40 (1922) : 22–23.

79 Caroff, *L'organisation*, 89–90.

It is especially enlightening to observe how the report card was defended in the face of this opposition. First, to convince families, the argument was given that report cards were filled out by teachers, who traditionally benefited from parents' trust. Second, to convince teachers that they were indeed competent to fill out these forms, it was argued that the new report card only recapitulated the usual assessment criteria. In a short article, J. Fontègne retorts, for example, that a gymnastics class is sufficient to characterise a pupil's level of "composure," and enumerates the categories in the report card to illustrate their lack of originality — though he significantly omits to mention the categories related to "character."[80] A third tactic presented the school report in a way that was completely unconnected with vocational guidance, thus avoiding the issue of opposition to the principle of guiding students. F. Duffieux, a school principal who worked in Bordeaux with F. Mauvezin, extolled the virtues of the report card as a tool for improving teaching and suggested filling it in not with psychological categories but rather with the usual classifications of academic assessment.[81] These three ways of defending the report card converged to neutralise, and decisively so, any reformative impact that this new assessment tool might have had. This was all the truer because these rhetorical arguments were accompanied by practical suggestions, encouraging teachers to apply their own habits of assessment to the report card. When J. Fontègne associated a school subject (gymnastics) with the aptitude (composure) of the child, he made a decisive connection that would work to safeguard school culture. This connection, which could later be seen as central in the history of the school record file,[82] was brought up in 1922 in response to the obstacles against adding extra-curricular categories to teachers' assessment work. The innovative characteristics and the impact of the *fiche scolaire*, a modest but key element of the advent of the modern school record, were thus held in check. It remains to be seen whether this hypothesis is confirmed by the implementation of report cards in local career orientation offices. In Nantes, the activity report for 1921–1923 suggests that the apparent success of the report card, used for nearly every school pupil in the city, was achieved by limiting the originality of its categories of assessment.[83]

---

80 Fontègne, "L'école".

81 F. Duffieux, "Le classement des élèves pour l'orientation professionnelle," *L'école et la vie* 5 (1922), 59–60.

82 See for example Jean-Yves Seguy, "Aptitudes, disciplines scolaires et orientation, entre approches pédagogique et psychologique", in *Problèmes de l'école démocratique, 18ᵉ–20ᵉ siècle*, ed. Bruno Garnier (Paris: CNRS éditions, 2013).

83 Ville de Nantes, *Le placement public et l'orientation professionnelle à Nantes et dans la région* (Nantes: Imprimerie du Commerce, 1921), 33–34.

Conclusion

In France, scholastic assessment culture is notoriously centred on subject-matter tests and intellectual aptitudes. Consequently, pupils' tastes, ambitions or personalities appear to be of secondary interest in the way their instructors establish judgments of them. The origins of this situation can be understood through the failure of the *dossier scolaire*, a long-term school record conceived as an alternative or complementary means of evaluation to grades and examinations. This document contains student assessments based on both academic and psychological criteria. This chapter more specifically examined the case of the *fiche scolaire*, a student report card that teachers were asked to fill out starting in the early 1920s for use in career guidance. Situating this report card in relation to other models that were in use at the time showed the status that it reserved for students' feelings, and the mechanisms that prevented it from drastically challenging the dominant assessment culture.

The conception of a national model for a report card or *fiche scolaire* was a turning point in the history of the advent of the modern school record file. It involved various changes: the objectives of vocational guidance were appropriated by the education system; psychological categories came to affect the work of teachers; the modification of school practices led families to question their legitimacy.

At the specific moment of the years surrounding 1920, the introduction of the school record was part of a merger between the school system and the vocational guidance movement. This convergence had clear pedagogical effects: teachers were given a newly important role in providing professional guidance and information (through talks, field trips etc.). However, there seems to be scant institutional interest accorded to emotions. Discourses inspired by the development of psychology and/or by vocational guidance, embodied by Mauvezin and Fontègne, certainly suggest that schools should take an interest in pupils' likes and dislikes and in their moral aptitudes. But different mechanisms — the absence of any alternative assessment technology for providing expert assessment, the constraints of legitimizing the orientation process in the eyes of students' families — made it necessary to meet the new objective of orientation using the traditional methods of school assessment, even if this required teachers or other specialists to reinterpret or reformulate them. They can thus be seen as mechanisms of neutralisation.

1918–1922 was nonetheless not an isolated episode, although the scope of the present study has been limited to its short-term effects. In the longer term, it can be seen as a turning point. The principle of the report card was adopted and began to be used on a national scale. Later in the decade, the focus shifted instead onto the mechanisms that would neutralise the new developments. Over the course of the 1920s, scientists worked to develop more rigorous observation forms, advocates of educational system reform reinterpreted the report card as an instrument of internal orientation within the school institution, and pedagogues would see in it an instrument of modernised education.

The elements that have been described here all came together to bring about a form of 'governmentality.' Reformers worked to perfect material technology, supported by specialised knowledge, in order to govern people by promising them individual and collective happiness, and by urging them to develop self-knowledge and follow their interests in order to reach this happiness. These technologies objectified people's individuality and inserted them into collective nomenclatures. They worked to define the personality of the student and at the same time to make the student aware that he was a person. In this context, the school record was able to place the psychological concepts of moral aptitudes, character and emotions in a performative situation. But the origins and development of these record forms show how much they filtered and recomposed these categories of apprehending individuality, so that we may say that they favoured not so much psychologizing mores as scholasticizing them.

To find out if and how these categories effectively modify the experience of the self, it would be necessary to study the emotional experience of students — as the history of emotions invites us to do.[84] While it has been shown here that the professional culture of teachers tended to reduce emotions to kinds of subject mastery, this approach, which appears unemotional, could in fact have very real effects on students' emotions. Behind the controversies surrounding the best way to assess students, there is a consensus that they must be assessed, categorised, graded, commented upon… which promotes the experience of being graded and ranked, an experience that, as we know, cannot help but provoke an emotional response.

Literature

Abbott, Andrew. *The System of Professions. An Essay on the Division of Expert Labour.* Chicago, IL: University of Chicago Press, 1988.

Bourdieu, Pierre, and Jean-Claude Passeron. *The Inheritors. French Students and their relation to culture,* translated by Richard Nice. Chicago, IL: University of Chicago Press, 1979 [1964].

---

84 See Noah Sobe, "Researching emotion and affect in the history of education," *History of Education* 41, no. 5 (2012): 689–95, doi: 10.1080/0046760X.2012.696150.

Bressoux, Pascal, and Pascal Pansu. *Quand les enseignants jugent leurs élèves.* Paris: PUF, 2003.

Butera, Fabrizio, Céline Buchs, and Céline Darnon, ed. *L'évaluation, une menace?* Paris: PUF, 2011.

Caroff, André. *L'organisation de l'orientation en France. Évolution des origines à nos jours.* Paris: EAP, 1987.

–. *Julien Fontègne. Un pionnier de l'orientation professionnelle.* Paris: INETOP, n.d., No. MO 8047, n.p.

Carson, John. *The Measure of Merit. Talents, Intelligence, and Inequality in the French and American Republics, 1750–1940.* Princeton, NJ: Princeton University Press, 2006.

Cayouette-Remblière, Joanie. *L'école qui classe.* Paris: PUF, 2016.

Clément, Jeanne. *Le mouvement d'orientation professionnelle.* Aix-en-Provence: Paul Roubaud, 1924.

Dale, Pamela. "A new approach to vocational guidance for school-leavers in the 1920s? Exploring key themes from an influential 1926 report." *History of Education* 41, no. 5 (2012): 505–615. doi: 10.1080/0046760X.2012.665948.

Deluermoz, Quentin and Pierre Singaravélou. *Pour une histoire des possibles. Analyses contrefactuelles et futurs non advenus.* Paris: Seuil, 2016.

Dorison, Catherine. "Orienter selon les aptitudes. Enjeux institutionnels et pédagogiques, 1936–1959." In *En attendant la réforme. Disciplines scolaires et politiques éducatives sous la IVᵉ République,* edited by Renaud D'Enfert and Pierre Kahn, 37–50. Grenoble: Presses universitaires de Grenoble, 2010.

Duffieux, F. "Le classement des élèves pour l'orientation professionnelle." *L'école et la vie* 5 (1922): 59–60.

Fontègne, Julien. "Le cabinet d'orientation professionnelle de l'Institut Jean-Jacques Rousseau, à Genève." *L'orientation professionnelle* 8 (1920): 35–44.

–. *L'orientation professionnelle et la détermination des aptitudes.* Neuchatel/Paris: Delachaux et Niestlé, 1921.

–. "L'office régional d'orientation professionnelle de Strasbourg." *Manuel général de l'instruction primaire* 26 (1921): 336–37.

–. "L'école primaire et l'orientation professionnelle." *Manuel général de l'enseignement primaire* 44 (1923): 840.

–. *Avant d'entrer en apprentissage. Nouveaux entretiens sur l'orientation professionnelle.* Paris: Eyrolles, 1924.

Frevert, Ute. *Emotions in History. Lost and found.* Budapest: Central European University Press, 2011.

Gutierrez, Laurent, Laurent Besse and Antoine Prost, ed. *Réformer l'école. L'apport de l'Éducation nouvelle, 1930–1970.* Grenoble: Presses Universitaires de Grenoble, 2012.

Herriot, Édouard. "L'apprentissage." *Manuel général de l'instruction primaire* 9 (1921): 111–113.

Lefebvre Henry, and Marcel Henry. *La préorientation professionnelle à l'école primaire.* Paris: Libraire de l'Enseignement technique, 1928.

Ley, Hubert, and Julien Fontègne. *La chambre de métiers d'Alsace et de Lorraine. Son organisation administrative, sa mission et les résultats de son activité.* Paris: Association française pour la lutte contre le chômage, 1921.

Martin, Jérôme. "Aux origines de la "science des examens", 1920–1940." *Histoire de l'éducation* 94 (2002): 177–199.

–. "Le mouvement d'orientation professionnelle en France. Entre l'école et le marché du travail, 1900–1940. Aux origines de la profession de conseiller d'orientation." PhD Diss., University of Paris-Sorbonne, 2011.

Mauvezin, Fernand. *Avant de choisir son métier ou sa profession, conseils aux enfants (garçons et filles), aux parents, aux éducateurs.* Paris: Éditions littéraires et politiques, 1921.

–. *Rose des métiers. Traité d'orientation professionnelle. Qualités et aptitudes nécessaires à l'exercice de 250 métiers différents et défauts rédhibitoires.* Paris: Éditions littéraires et politiques, 1922.

Merle, Pierre. "L'école française et l'invention de la note. Un éclairage historique sur les polémiques contemporaines." *Revue française de pédagogie* 193 (2015): 77–88.

Mole, Frédéric. *L'école laïque pour une République sociale. Controverses pédagogiques et politiques, 1900–1914.* Rennes: PUR, 2010.

Parsons, Frank. *Choosing a Vocation.* Boston, MA: Houghton Mifflin, 1909.

Pawin, Rémi. *Histoire du bonheur en France depuis 1945.* Paris: Robert Laffont, 2013.

Roger, Maurice. "L'orientation professionnelle et l'école." *Manuel général de l'instruction primaire,* 2 (1917): 13.

–. "Rapport sur les œuvres complémentaires de l'école publique en 1917–1918." *Journal officiel de la République française* (1918): 231–46.

–. "Rapport sur les œuvres complémentaires de l'école publique en 1918–1919." *Journal officiel de la République française* (1920): 331–52.

–. "Rapport sur les œuvres complémentaires de l'école publique en 1921–1922." *Journal officiel de la République française* (1923): 413–37.

–. "Le choix du métier." *Manuel général de l'instruction primaire,* 21 (1920): 277.

–. "Rapport sur les œuvres complémentaires de l'école publique en 1920–1921." *Journal officiel de la République française* (1922): 181–206.

Seguy, Jean-Yves. "Aptitudes, disciplines scolaires et orientation, entre approches pédagogique et psychologique." In *Problèmes de l'école démocratique, 18ᵉ–20ᵉ siècle*, edited by Bruno Garnier, 153–74. Paris: CNRS éditions, 2013.

Simon, Théodore. "La connaissance de l'enfant et l'orientation professionnelle." *L'orientation professionnelle* 20 (1921): 1–10.

Sobe, Noah. "Researching emotion and affect in the history of education." *History of Education* 41, no. 5 (2012): 689–95. doi: 10.1080/0046760X.2012.696150.

Thomann, Astrid, Bernard Schneuwly, and Valérie Lussi. "L'orientation profession-nelle et les sciences de l'éducation: deux voies contrastées." In *Émergence des sciences de l'éducation en Suisse à la croisée de traditions académiques contras-tées. Fin du 19ᵉ – première moitié du 20ᵉ siècle*, edited by Rita Hofstetter and Bernard Schneuwly, 291–320. Berne: Peter Lang, 2007.

Tyack, David, and Larry Cuban. *Tinkering Towards Utopia: A Century of Public School Reform*. Cambridge, MA: Harvard University Press, 1995.

Ville de Nantes. *Le placement public et l'orientation professionnelle à Nantes et dans la région*. Nantes: Imprimerie du Commerce, 1921.

Viaud, Marie-Laure. *Des collèges et des lycées différents*. Paris: PUF/Le Monde, 2005.

Weber, Eugen. *Peasants into Frenchmen. The modernisation of rural France, 1870–1914*. Stanford, CA: Stanford University Press, 1976.

Tanaka Koji

Retrospective and Prospective on the Educational Assessment in Post-war Japan

In educational methods research, it has only been in recent years that the theories and practices of 'educational assessment' have secured a clear position academically. In fact, two publications edited by National Association for the Study of Educational Methods — "Re-questioning the Post-war Educational Method Research: "The Results and Challenges of the National Association for the Study of Educational Methods in 30 Years" (1995)[1] and "50 Years after the War: Re-questioning Schools Now" (1996)[2] — contain no sections titled 'Educational Assessment'. Educational assessment finally received clear treatment in Lesson "Study of Japan, Volume II", edited by the same association.[3] In post-war education, there were circumstances specific to Japan and one main reason for the delay was likely due to its long orientation as a target or being a part of educational psychology. Thus, when reviewing the history of research on 'educational assessment' at the official level of academic societies — even when looking exclusively at post-war history — determining its precise chronology is one challenge going into the future.[4]

In this chapter, after stating that this is merely a hypothetical chronology, and noting the large impact the national curriculum has on the theoretical and

1   Nippon Kyoikuhouhougakkukai, "Sengo KyouikuhouhouKenkyu wo toinasu: Nippon Kyoikuhouhou gakkukai30 nen no seka to kadai", *Kyoikuhouhou* 24 (1995).
2   Nippon Kyoikuhouhougakkukai, "Sengo50nen ima gakko wo toinasu," *Kyoikuhouhou* 25 (1996).
3   Kanae Nishioka, (educationist), "Chapter 5: Educational Assessment and Lesson Study, Kyouikuhyouka to Juggyoukenkyu" in *Nippon no Jugyoukenkyu, Vol. II*, ed. Nippon Kyoikuhouhougakkukai (Tokyo: Gakubunsha, 2009).
4   For references related to educational assessment issued from 1945 to 1994, see Tanaka 1996 in the bibliography. For foundation work related to post-war educational assessment research history, see Koji Tanaka, *Jinbutu de tuzuru Sengokyoukuhyouka no Rekishi* (Shiga: Sangaku Publishing, 2009), 1–9; Koji Tanaka, "Kyouikumokuhyo Hyoukakenkyu no 20nen," in *Deciphering the Age of Assessment: Challenges and Outlook of Educational Goals/Educational Research, Vol. I, Vol. II*. Tokyo: (Nippon-Hyojun, 2010a), 10–21.

practical aspects of educational activities in Japan, I hypothesize the history of the post-war cumulative guidance record (*Shidoyoroku*),[5] as follows.

Division 1: Cumulative Guidance Record 1948 Version
– Reflecting on the 'Register' and Placing Importance on 'Guidance Function'

Division 2: Cumulative Guidance Record 1955
Cumulative Guidance Record 1961
Cumulative Guidance Record 1971
Strengthening of 'Relative Assessment' and Intensification of Contradictions

Division 3: Guidance Record 1980 and Cumulative Guidance Record 1991 – Appearance of the 'Viewpoint-based Academic Status' Column as a 'Solution' for Contradictions

Division 4: Cumulative Guidance Record 2001 and Cumulative Guidance Record 2010
– Full Adoption of 'Objective-referenced Assessment' and Combination of 'Objective-referenced Assessment' and 'Intra-individual Assessment'

Keeping this post-war history of the cumulative guidance record in mind, I developed the following structure by focusing on each revision period and its theoretical development.

History of Educational Assessment Research

Establishing the Concept of "Evaluation" in the Early Post-war Stages

As is commonly known, Japan in the post war period had been overwhelmingly influenced by the USA. The term 'educational assessment' comes from the translation of "evaluation," which was introduced from USA after World War II. "The

---

5   The cumulative guidance record is an official document whose contents are regulated by the MECSST (Ministry of Education, Culture, Sports, Science and Technology) and each regional board of education. It is a public (then not open because private information) certificate (with grades) given to each pupil and, has become the basis for 'school records' and the 'report card.' It consists of the evaluation of the academic achievements and behaviour of the students, and notes written by the teacher. For detailed analysis and examination of the record history, see Koji Tanaka, "History and Future of Cumulative Guidance Records," in *Points of Revision of the New Cumulative Guidance Record for Elementary Schools*, ed. Koji Tanaka (Tokyo:Nippon-Hyojun, 2010b), 130–150.

Research Meeting Records for Teacher Training (2)"[6] was recently reprinted. It records research meetings comprising the prehistory of the IFEL (Institute for Educational Leadership), which had been incorporated at the beginning stages of the post-war period. It introduces the new concept of 'evaluation,' which was later translated into Japanese as 'educational assessment.' It also considers the "Eight Year Study" by R. W. Tyler, an advocate for evaluation. Some enthusiasm for the educational reforms of the time can be observed here.

Unfortunately, this description has disappeared from the current course of study. However, in "Chapter 5: Examination of Academic Results" in the first "Course of Study (General Draft 1947)," and in the "Course of Study General Draft" of 1951, the sections on "educational assessment" were clearly positioned as "IV: Assessment of Curriculum" and "V: Assessment of Study Guidance Method and Academic Achievements."

The "Course of Study General Draft" of 1951 states, "Assessment of the curriculum and improvement of the curriculum is one continuous work, and each concept cannot be thought of separately from the other. In this sense, the assessment of the curriculum, along with its planning and development, is necessary work for effectively advancing the studies of children/students." Moreover, it clarifies, "In this sense, regarding the activities implemented by oneself, one must constantly examine and make the assessment at all junctures, and the responsibility to improve the process of assessment lies particularly with each individual teacher." The descriptions clearly reflect the fact that the course of study during the early post-war stages was considered a 'draft.'

Reflecting on the pre-World War II "School Register" (originally called the "school register" and renamed the "cumulative guidance record" in 1949), the "About the School Register of Elementary Schools" (November 12, 1948) — a notification signed by the Ministry of Education's superintendent of education — makes the following three points: "1. Record the course of development of each child comprehensively and continuously, and this record will become the original record that will be needed for guidance. 2. Looking at it from the new mentality of education, the particularly important records are selected. 3. It is made so that the development of a child can be recorded as objectively and simply as possible." Clearly, the "guidance function" was perceived as particularly important in point number 1. As a result of these policies, the development of enriched practices

---

6   Sponsor Ministry of Education (*Monbusho*), Imperial University Tokyo (*Tokyo Tekoku Digaku*), 1947.

related to 'educational assessment' in the early post-war stages has been retrieved and re-examined in recent research.[7]

The "Principles of Primary Education" (1951) is a typical case showing the Ministry of Education's understanding of 'educational assessment'. Here, "evaluation" is explained clearly through the following five points: "(i) Evaluation considers the entire lifestyle of the student, and promotes his or her development; (ii) Evaluation not only considers the results of education but places importance on the process; (iii) Evaluation is not only conducted by the teacher—student self-evaluation must also be considered an important aspect; (iv) Evaluation and its results are also conducted for the selection of more appropriate teaching materials and for the improvement of teaching methods; (v) Evaluation is necessary for effective learning activities."[8] This shows that 'educational evaluation' is the evaluation of one's educational activities, aimed at improving teacher guidance and children's academic activities (including self-evaluation).

The concept of 'evaluation' was introduced by Tyler[9] in the 1930s as a negative reaction to the concept of 'measurement' popularised by the educational measurement movement of the 1920s. Regarding 'educational evaluation', Tyler believed educational objectives were the fundamental, valid standards. He criticised the educational measurement movement for using statistical measuring methods that merely focused on 'trusting' measurements. Among Japanese educational psychologists of the time, Masaki Masashi (1905–1959) deeply understood the significance of Tyler's 'educational evaluation'. Considering measurement and evaluation processes based on the "Structure of the Reality of Education and Road of Historical Development,"[10] Masaki criticises the trend of "treating the technology during its peripheral discussion stage."[11] Furthermore, he warns that if "educational values/goals" are not questioned, the managerial and measurement-oriented nature of evaluation will become dehumanised. For example, "measurement standards" refer to "statistical averages" inductively and in terms of experience, but "evaluation

---

7   See Hayashi Msami, "Chibaken Hojopuran niokeru Nouryokuhyouka no hensen ni kansuru kenkyu," *Karikuramukenkyu* 6 (1997), 14–24; Seisuke Sakai, "Shokishyakaika "Tawaramotopuran" niokeru gakushuhyouka no tokuchitu," *Kyouikuhohoukenkyu* 34 (2009), 49–60.

8   Monbusho, *Shotookyouikugenri* (Tokyo: Toyokan Publishing, 1951), 217–19.

9   R. W. Tyler, *Constructing Achievement Tests* (Ohio: Ohio State University, 1934), 35–42.

10 Masaki Masashi (psychologist), "Kachi to Hyouka," in *Kouza:Kyouiku*. Vol. III. (Tokyo: Iwanami Shoten, 1952), 246.

11 Ibid., 244.

standards" refer to the "historical and social standard of the local society."[12] Masaki describes the significance of 'educational evaluation' in education as follows:

"Evaluation within the education process today is becoming more important. This does not mean that the issue of evaluation is being newly added to the education process, and that the interest for evaluation is growing. If anything, evaluation is a part that is integrated with the education process, and people are now aware of something that was unattended in terms of past conventional issues and methods. It means that the issues of evaluation have been segmented as part of a self-development of educational activities, and it is now being emphasised."[13]

Thus, Masaki identified important methodological points for realizing the philosophy/aim of 'educational evaluation' during the early post-war stages. However, although these ideas did not necessarily become part of the mainstream at the time, they were inherited later by Aritsune Tsuzuki.

Multilayered Structure of Post-war Educational Assessment

Tyler aimed to expand educational objectives through 'educational assessment' (i.e., setting goals that included high cognitive function and emotional aspects). However, discussions regarding the methods for assessing the results of such expanded educational objectives and standards remained insufficient. As a result, the 'measurement' concept, which emphasised reliability and objectivity, was maintained.[14]

Moreover, with Japan becoming a 'credentialist' society, there was a strong demand for a 'certification function' in the cumulative guidance record that would become the basis for school records with a 'high stakes' personality. Furthermore, a 'five-level relative assessment' was adopted as an overall rating in the revised cumulative guidance record of 1955 (the first post-war 'relative assessment' adopted for the cumulative guidance record was an analysis rating). In other words, 'relative assessment' was emphasised over 'educational assessment.' After this point, Japanese educational assessment research focused on criticizing 'relative assessment' and finding ways to overcome it.

Though 'relative assessment' became predominant, the structure of the cumulative guidance record at the time was not so one-sided. Hashimoto Shigeharu (1908–1992), a leader in post-war educational assessment research, considered the strengths and weaknesses of educational assessment views, examining the

---

12 Masashi Masaki, *Kyoiku no shinri* (Tokyo: Haneda Shoten, 1948), 352.
13 Masaki, "Kachi to Hyouka," 245.
14 See Appendix.

trend of tilting toward "absolute assessment (in this case, an 'objective-referenced assessment')."[15] Because of its great impact, I call this the 'Hashimoto Paradigm.'

According to the Hashimoto Paradigm, 'relative assessment' has many weak points when examined from the perspective of 'education.' This is where the focus turns to 'absolute assessment.' While it might look good from the perspective of 'education,' it is subjective and lacks reliability when considered in terms of 'educational measurement.' Therefore, against the cumulative guidance record, which has the function of external certification, 'absolute assessment' is unsuitable. For this purpose, 'relative assessment,' which has both 'objectivity' and 'reliability,' is effective. However, according to Hashimoto, because of its 'educational' weak points, 'intra-individual assessment' becomes necessary. As a background to this way of thinking, the revised cumulative guidance record of 1961 explains that relative assessment is applied in the 'rating' column, cross-cutting intra-individual assessment in the 'observation' column and vertical intra-individual assessment in the 'progress status' column. While this explanation does not clarify the position of absolute assessment, the 'standard one-by-one test' was adopted. With regard to the 'rating' column, it was positioned as 'absolute assessment added to relative assessment' (this 'added' 'absolute assessment' was actually 'intra-individual assessment'). Thus, the educational assessment structure in place for over half a century after the war was a multilayered structure based on 'relative assessment.'

Here, I would like to focus on fact that the role of 'intra-individual assessment' was attracting attention. When talking about post-war educational assessment theories, it is important to remember that 'intra-individual assessment,' along with 'relative assessment,' was adopted in the first post-war cumulative guidance records. 'Intra-individual assessment' adjusted to the child's perspective and tried to comprehensively assess the child's progress. It came about after reflecting on the pre-war 'examinations' that placed absolute trust in teachers.

However, the relationship between 'relative assessment' and 'intra-individual assessment' comprised a 'structure of hot and cold' (in context of sociology) in the field of education. Regarding these contrary notions discussed in the March 1961 issue of "Modern Educational Science" (Toyama Hiraku "Combining Education and Science" and Toui Yoshio's "Combining Education and Life"), I have proposed "combining attainment assessment and intra-individual assessment."[16] Hiraku Toyama (1909–1979) and Sakuji Kuwahara criticised 'relative assessment.' Toyama notes that to raise one's grades, someone must fall; therefore, relative

---

15 Hashimoto Shigeharu (psychologist), "Soutaihyouka to Zettaihyouka," *Kyoikushinri*, May Issue (1961), 356–362.

16 Tanaka Koji (educationist), *Gakuryoku Hyoukaron Nyumon* (Tokyo. Hosei Press, 1996).

assessment creates unnatural exclusive competition and creates the mentality, "The misfortune of others is my happiness."[17] He further notes, "The goal of education originally is for all children to get 5s, and the efforts of the teachers should also be aimed towards this goal. However, the five-level assessment squarely contradicts this idea."[18] Moreover, Kuwahara suggests that the work of education is to break down the regular distribution curve that is the trend of the majority in its natural state and recreate it as an "educational curve": "As a result of education, if you were to still indicate the standard curve, rather than being happy that the test was appropriate, one should look at it as a situation that requires reflection to see if the education itself was appropriate."[19] Such criticism of 'relative assessment' was rooted in a hope for the academic security of all children, and it later led to the introduction of 'attainment assessment.'

In the same issue, however, people like Yoshio Toui (1912–1991) and Mitsuo Sakamoto promote 'intra-individual assessment' as a method for describing the mental growth and development of children. They believed there was a non-educational aspect of relative assessment in its abstract scoring. Toui states: "There should be an improvement in the quality from '3' of the first semester to '3' in the second semester. It is more unreasonable to ask to look for the difference in the same '3.'"[20] Furthermore, "whether it is relative assessment or absolute assessment, I would like to oppose the idea of showing grades through numbers."[21] Incidentally, Kihaku Saito (1911–1981), an advocate for Taisho free education, had already pointed out before the war that an individual's vertical progress should be focused on instead of the horizontal relationship of the entire class.

Criticism of "Relative Assessment" and the Appearance of "Attainment Assessment" and its Challenges

The 'report card incident'[22] of February 1969 displayed absurdity on a national level. Afterward, report card reforms took place in elementary schools nationwide.

---

17 Toyama Hiraku (a researcher of mathematical domain), *Gendaikyouikukagaku*, March Issue (1961), 4.

18 Ibid.

19 Kuwahara, *Gendaikyouikukagaku* March Issue (1961), 33.

20 Toui Yoshio (a teacher of primary school), *Modern Educational Science* March Issue (1961), 10.

21 Ibid.

22 The 'report card incident' was that one father with fifth grade son criticised irrationality the of "relative Assessment" through TV (wide show program) in February 1969. See Tanaka Koji, *Educational Assessment* (Iwanami Shoten, 2008), 177.

It also affected the revision of cumulative guidance records in 1971, adding a note saying, 'do not assign grades in five levels in a machine-like manner.' This precipitated the decline of 'relative assessment.' At this time, Nakauchi Toshio established the "attainment assessment" theory with the scheme of "progressive objectives = relative assessment, attainment goal = attainment assessment."[23] Nakauchi was probably the first education scholar in Japan to systematically raise the issue of the significance and role of 'today' in educational assessment. "Theory of Academic Ability and Assessment" (1971) is his monumental publication. Actually, the term 'attainment assessment' first appeared in the 'long records' (Mission Report) of the Kyoto Prefectural Board of Education's "To Advance the Improvement of Attainment Assessment: Reference for Research Discussion."[24] The following is an excerpt from this text:

> "The basics of attainment assessment are the assessment in educational guidance where the goal is to have the academic abilities of each child reach the objectives in each of the grades and subjects. Therefore, for the development of all children in the future, it is something that is necessary, and it must be something that serves the purpose of educational guidance overall in organizing sufficient education."[25]

As theories of various researchers that directly and indirectly contributed to the establishment of 'attainment assessment,'[26] those of Tsuzuki Aritsune, Kajita Eichi, Murakoshi Kunio educational psychologist, and Bloom are introduced. Hiroo Inaba was a theoretical pillar of attainment assessment theory. Needless to say, Nakauchi Toshio, who emerged from the right to learn security theories, was one of the main triggers. At the same time, there is a need to clarify the differences among theorists who claimed 'attainment assessment.'

Tsuzuki, who was a student of Masaki Masashi, criticised the 'age-related (attendance/registration-governed) principle' of the past, claiming the "grade-related (achievement/goal-governed) principle," and regulates 'educational assessment' as follows: "Assessment is part of the activities of pursuing a goal in units of pursuing a goal–assessment–adjustment. Educational assessment is the act of checking the relationship between the results of the pursuit and goals in order to make

23 Nakauchi Toshio (educationist), "Kyouikumokuhyou · hyoukaron no kadai," *Kyoiku,* July Issue (1977), 36–41.
24 Kyoto Prefectural Board of Education, (Mission Report) "To Advance the Improvement of Attainment Assessment: Reference for Research Discussion," February (1975), 5.
25 Ibid.
26 Sasaki Motoki (an admistrator in Kyoto Prefecture), *Toutatudohyoukasonokangaekata to susumekata* (Meijitosho Shuppan, 1979).

adjustments, and providing feedback information."[27] This is a clear regulation, and by matching it with the 'grade-related principle,' Tsuzuki connected academic ability security theories with 'attainment assessment.' However, comparing it to the aforementioned "Principles of Primary Education" (1951), the evaluation of (ii) in particular emphasises the process, not just the results, of education. The evaluation of (iii) stresses not only the evaluation of teachers but also the self-evaluation of children. Since this perspective rejected, Tsuzuki's regulations create a machine-like and systematic impression. Here, we see traces of the behaviourist learning theories that were about to be introduced at the time. This attracted criticism in later years.

Let us summarize the criticisms of 'five-level relative assessment' that have accumulated over time by 'attainment assessment.' First, it is a non-educational assessment theory that assumes there are students who cannot keep up. For example, in a class of 40 students, a grade of 5 will be given to two to three students. However, a grade of 1 will also have to be given to two to three students. An underlying strain of Social Darwinism ('survival of the fittest') supported the educational measurement activities of the 1920s, which assumed that some students would excel, and others would fall behind, no matter how you guided them. This is where heartful teachers, such as Yoshio Toui, were troubled when filling out report cards using the five-level relative assessment. They were torn when they had to unreasonably allocate 2s and 1s, even though everyone in the class gave their utmost effort as a result of the teacher's guidance.

Yoshio Toui said, "Every time the semester comes to an end, there is a deep sigh. The pen in my hand is slow and it does not move forward. Then I close my eyes and fill out '2.' Then there is a sign again. [...] The grade I have to fill out in the report card is a '2' even though the student gave that much effort. [...] I would praise student T who was a slow learner and tell him he finally has the ability to express himself. But I have to give him a '1' on the report card. After graduation when the report cards are finished being passed out, I always feel stiffness in my cheek."[28] Then, Toui embarked on report card reform during his years as a principal of Yoka Elementary School.[29]

The second problem with 'relative assessment' is that by making exclusive competition the norm, it creates the perception that learning is a win/lose situation. When grade allocation rates are determined beforehand, someone has to fail for

---

27 Tsuzuki Aritsune (psychologist), *Kyouikuhyouka* (Tokyo: Dai-ichi Hoki, 1969), 27.
28 Toui, Yoshio *Yoshio Toui Collection*, Vol. IV (Tokyo: Meijitosho Shuppan, 1972), 7.
29 Toui Yoshio, *Tuchinbo no kaizo* (Tokyo: Meijitosho Shuppan, 1967).

another to receive a higher grade. Thus, relative assessment creates unnatural and exclusive competition, forming an idea that one person's happiness depends on another's unhappiness.[30] Needless to say, competition in general (e.g., the competition of emulation for everyone to receive 5s) is not being rejected; rather, exclusive competition is the problem.

The third problem is that 'relative assessment' does not reflect actual academic achievement. Even if a student receives a 5 in a five-level assessment, it only means the student's position is high relative to the group; it does not prove that his or her academic achievements reflect his or her educational objectives. Rather, it strengthens the perception of learning as a win-lose situation, and the question of what was learned is diluted. This is one of most significant issues regarding the academic abilities for entrance examination.

The fourth problem is that 'relative assessment' estimates the academic activities of children, and insofar as it creates hierarchy in the group, the only issues are effort (or lack of) and ability (or lack of). Therefore, it does not contain the following aspect: "assessment results are a reflection of the educational activities, and the teacher examines the education amount and its surrounding environment based on these reflections, and offers training."[22] This dominant academic perspective that 'studying is a win-lose situation' promotes a hollowing of the educational activities that form one's academic abilities.

The claim of 'attainment assessment,' which is an 'objective-referenced assessment' that criticises 'relative assessment,' as shown above, is articulated as follows. Above all, 'objective-referenced assessment' rehabilitated the original role of educational assessment. As mentioned above, the role of 'educational assessment' is to secure the academic abilities of all children, examine the guidance of teachers, and give students an outlook on their educational activities. Needless to say, with 'relative assessment,' the abilities and efforts of children may be questioned, but there is no opportunity to re-question the nature of education in practice. 'Objective-referenced assessment,' on the other hand, captures the degree to which children achieve objectives, and if guidance is insufficient, the teacher's activities can be modified, or support can be provided regarding the students' educational activities.

Furthermore, 'attainment assessment' originally served to rehabilitate the role of educational assessment, and the 'differentiation of the assessment function' was raised. 'Attainment assessment,' which attempts to secure academic abilities, tried to finely capture the reality of children's academic makeup through three assessments: 'diagnostic assessment,' which attempts to understand children's academic

---

30 Toyama, *Gendaikyouikukagaku*, March Issue (1961), 4.

makeup before they enter class; 'formative assessment', which adjusts the content and methods of guidance depending on the various reactions of children during class; and 'summative assessment', which captures how much of the goal has been achieved. In particular, "formative assessment" gained approval as an assessment model that could be utilised in guidance. Regarding the differentiation of these assessment functions, Bloom had influence at the time.[31] In addition, "Taxonomy of Educational Objectives," which inherits Tyler's ideas, stratifies the content of educational objectives and abilities simultaneously, and it had a global impact, not just in the USA.[32]

Now, I would like to discuss a case that occurred in the mid-1970s, at a time when 'relative assessment' was actualised and 'attainment assessment', as an 'objective-referenced assessment', was about to emerge. It is a case that cannot be ignored in terms of the educational assessment research that would come later. This disputed point continues even now.

During this period, the Ministry of Education and the Centre for Educational Research Innovation (CERI) of the Organisation for Economic Cooperation Development (OECD) co-held the "International Seminar Related to Curriculum Development" (held in Tokyo in 1974). During this seminar, J. M. Atkin proposed a curriculum, classwork, and two prototypical models: a 'Technological Approach' and a 'Rashomon Approach' related to assessment. The 'Technological Approach', which can be precisely compared to 'technology', displays the plans of the teacher and 'action objectives' based on the rational organisation of classes in line with an array of teaching materials. Furthermore, the assessment theory implemented here is 'objective-referenced assessment'. Meanwhile, in the 'Rashomon Approach', creative classes that emphasise improvisation are conducted with the goal of developing academic activities that are active and versatile. The assessment theory implemented here is an "assessment that does not get caught up in the objectives."[33] The academic values created by the meeting of children, teachers, and teaching materials are interpreted from perspectives. The name comes from the Kurosawa film *Rashomon* (1950), based on the story "In the Woods" (1921) by Akutagawa Ryunosuke.

---

31 See Bloom, Benjmain, *Educational Assessment Method Handbook*, trans. Kajita Eiichi. (Tokyo: Dai-Ichi Hoki, 1973) and Bloom, Benjamin, *The Right Academic Ability for All Children*, ed., trans. Inaba Hiroo Onishi Masaya (Tokyo: Meijitosho Shuppan, 1986).

32 See Ishii Terumasa (educationist), Gendai America no Gakuryokukeiseironno tenkai (Tokyo: Toshindo, 2010).

33 See Hirano Tomohisa (educationist), "Mokuhyouni torawarenai hyoukanituitenoichi-kousatu," *Nippon Kyoikuhouhougakkukai* 32 (1981), 29–36.

Comparing these two ways of thinking is an attempt to relativize the 'Technological Approach' and 'objective-referenced assessment.'[34] Furthermore, it can be said that at its core, there is a clear criticizing consciousness against the 'Technological Approach' and 'objective-referenced assessment.' Here, I will summarize the theoretical criticisms of 'attainment assessment' as 'objective-referenced assessment.' As mentioned earlier, Tsuzuki's assessment standards affected by behaviourist learning theory, and they give a rather systematic impression.

'Attainment assessment,' which was the typical form of 'objectives-referenced assessment,' has been criticised as merely checking whether students achieve the objectives that teachers conceive. It was said to "crush objective" and promote 'cramming knowledge.' To clarify, these problems did not arise in all classrooms where "attainment assessment" was practiced. Furthermore, countless efforts have been made to overcome these problems. In USA (the 'Behavioural objectives movement') under the students of Bloom, the differences between mastery learning and program learning have been pursued.[35]

Now, I will summarize the criticisms of 'objective-referenced assessment' through four points. This allows for a bonding with 'intra-individual assessment' as a challenge to 'objective-referenced assessment,' showing why the bond with the academic values of constructivism was demanded.

First, regarding 'objective-referenced assessment,' since the 'objectives' becomes the basis for teachers, there is the risk of overlooking the activities of children who stray from the path. To prevent this, 'engagement' by children, guardians, and citizens of the region had to be guaranteed. It was suggested that through this, it was possible to grasp educational activities on a multilateral and multilayered level. This was criticised by Scriven with his idea of "goal free" assessment.[36]

E. W. Eisner, who was involved in art education, was critical of 'objective-referenced assessment' from the early stages. His opinions became the foundation for the 'Rashomon Approach.'[37] Eisner's criticism can be summarised as follows: "The dynamic and complex process of education creates too many results;

---

34 See Tanaka Koji, "Kyouikumokuhyo to Karikuramkousei no kadai—Buruumu to Aisunaa no shosetu wo chushinnishite," *Kyoutodaigaku Kyouikugakubukiyou* 28 (1982), 101–13.

35 See Tanaka Koji, "OBE no genjyo to kadai," in *Kyoikuhouhougaku no saikouchiku*, ed. Hiroob Inaba (Tokyo: Ayumi Publishing, 1995).

36 See Nezu Tomomi, *Karikuramhyouka no Houhou* (Tokyo: Taga Shuppan, 2006).

37 See Elliot W. Eisner, *The Art of Educational Evaluation* (Brighton: The Falmer Press, 1985) and Nami Katsura, "Waakushopu Jugyoumoderuniyoru Hyougen no Jugyoukousei," *Nippon Kyoikuhouhougakkukai* 35 (2009), 59–70.

therefore, it is not possible to specify using behavioural and content terms."[38] Moreover, "curriculum theories which are regarded as the standard for measuring educational achievements of educational goals overlook various aspects of achievement that are unmeasurable."[39] In other words, 'objective-referenced assessment' considers education a factory assembly process. In making assessments, applying standards and making judgments should be differentiated.

Second, 'objective-referenced assessment' is an 'external assessment' for children. As such, I think an 'internal assessment' conducted by children themselves is not correctly positioned. Relying on others' assessments to value their own actions thus creates a state of constantly 'waiting for instruction' or 'waiting for assessment.' Criticisms of 'objective-referenced assessment' have noted the challenge of determining how to vitalize self-assessment among children.

Third, 'objective-referenced assessment' focuses too much on the results of children's studies and overlooks the challenge of understanding the 'process' behind those achievements and results. If the 'knowledge' the teacher has is far from the body of knowledge the children have, there will be 'conflict' and 'contradiction.' Cherishing such 'conflict' and 'contradiction' assures the dynamism of the class. Criticism has highlighted the question of the methodology for assessing this 'process.'

Lastly, with 'objective-referenced assessment,' to value objectivity, objective tests are often implemented. Of course, the objective test is not identical everywhere, but the range of measurement is naturally limited. In other words, people focus on the quantity aspect of assessment, while quality-based assessment targeting advanced academic abilities — and, for example, awareness of the mood that permeates the classroom — remains weak. Here, criticism has said that assessment tasks should be made more real, and there should be ways for children to express the academic abilities they have acquired. In summary, it tried to set goals for 'high quality' and demanded the security of subjective 'engagement' from the people associated with assessment (=stakeholder).

---

38 Eisner, *The Art*, 254.
39 Eisner, *The Art*, 257.

Challenges and Outlook of Educational Assessment Research

PISA (Program for International Student Assessment) and 'Authentic Assessment'

Educational reform, including educational assessment offered by PISA and implemented by the OECD, is coming to symbolize the globalisation of education.[40] In Japan, cultivating PISA-type academic abilities (= utilizing power), and discussions on revising the course of study are about to begin.[41] Furthermore, there is focus on the educational reforms in China and Korea, which maintain high PISA scores.[42] On behalf of 'domain-referenced assessment,' which is an old 'objective-referenced assessment,' the recommendation of 'standard-referenced assessment,'[43] which aims for high-quality academic abilities and the standards of all countries (especially Australia's efforts) are introduced. Thus, issues are arising regarding PISA-type academic abilities versus liberal-type academic abilities[44] along with the security of 'engagement' raised by 'authentic assessment' theories.

Since PISA is precisely oriented toward educational examination/educational assessment, 'authentic assessment' theories are attracting attention. Just before interest in such theories arose, there was a focus on 'portfolio assessment' in Japan. It concerns comprehensive learning, and as a method suited for educational assessment, it was actively examined after 1999.[45] Furthermore, Tetsuo Hori

---

40 See Sato, Manabu (educationist) ed. *Yurerusekai no Gakuryoku map* (Tokyo: Akashi Shoten, 2009).

41 See Katsuno Yorihiko, *Shakai no henkani taiousuru shishituyanouryoku wo ikuseisuru kyouikukateihensei no kihongenri* (Tokyo: National Institute for Educational Policy Research, 2013).

42 See Xiang Chun (educationist), *Gendai Chugoku niokeru Hyoukakaikaku* (Tokyo: Nippon-Hyojun, 2013); Kyoto University, Graduate School of Education, Centre of Collaboration in Innovation and Educational Practice, "Ajiani okeru PISA mondai," *Activity Report* (2007–2011) 2012, 371–440.

43 Suzuki Hideyuki (a teacher of secondary school *Sutandaadojunkyohyouka* (Tokyo: Toshobunka, 2013).

44 Against the literacy theories of PISA, critical discussions have been held in Germany, where there are traditions of *Bildung*, and in France, where there are traditions of *Esprit*. See Hisada Toshihiko, ed., *PISA go no kyouiku wo doutoraeruka — Doitu wo tooshitemiru* (Tokyo: Yachiyo Shuppan, 2013); Hosoo Moeko, "Huransu no Chutou-kyouiku niokeru kisogakuryokuronsou — chishi ka konpitenshi ka", in *Kinkidaigaku Ronbunshu* 26, no. 1 (2014), 17–46.

45 Nishioka Kanae, *Kyouka to Sougo ni ikasu Pootohoriohyoukahou* (Tokyo: Toshobunka, 2003).

developed the 'One Page Portfolio' as a method to easily use 'portfolio assessment' onsite.[46]

Given the growing interest in 'authentic assessment' theories, which are at the core of 'portfolio assessment' and 'performance assessment' approaches partially adopted by PISA, original texts are being translated.[47] I have identified the two principles of 'quality' and 'engagement' security as the main features of 'authentic assessment.'[48] Regarding "authenticity," I discussed the issue as follows: "The author focused on the two ambivalent meanings of 'intimacy' and 'difficulty' which are included in the meaning of 'authenticity.'"[49] Regarding this point, Fred Newmann introduced the concept of "authenticity" in education and used the terms "intimacy or relevance" and "difficulty or rigor" before defining "authenticity."[50] The former focusing on the empirical child was previously too strong for people, and in the work that comes with cultural and intellectual professions in the real world, the latter is the essential aspect.[51] Pursuing this concept of 'authenticity' is a challenge we face going into the future. Furthermore, 'performance assessment' is recommended in the 2010 revision of the cumulative guidance record. Creating a "rubric" is becoming a challenge in securing the "reliability" of the assessment.[52]

New Trends in Assessment Research

When large-scale examinations and assessments such as PISA start to take over, educational assessment becomes somewhat systematic, and there is a fear of deviating from everyday educational practice. As Kage points out: "In order to enrich

---

46 Hori Tetsuo (educationist), *Ichimai Pootohoriohyoukahou* (Tokyo: Toyokan Publishing, 2013).

47 Grant Wiggins and Jay McTighe., *Understanding by Design*, trans. Nishioka, Kanae (Tokyo: Nipponhyoujun 2012); Diane Hart, *Authentic Assessment: A Handbook for Educators*, trans. Koji Tanaka (Kyoto: Minerva Shobo, 2012).

48 Tanaka Koji, *Kyouikuhyouka to Kyoikujiisen no kadai* (Shiga: Sangaku Publishing, 2013).

49 Tanaka Koji, *Educational Assessment* (Tokyo: Iwanami Shoten, 2008), 73–74.

50 Fujimoto Nami, "Nyuman no Shinnsei no gakuryoku gainen ni kansuruichikosatu," *Kyouikumokuhyo hyouka gakaikiyou* 23 (2013), 50–59.

51 Tanaka, *Kyouikuhyouka to Kyoikujiisen no kadai*, 22.

52 During the early post-war stages, Komiyama Eichi proposed the "rating-scale method," which is a primitive form of today's rubric. See Eichi Komiyama, "Hyouka no kyouikutekiigi", in *Kyouikudaigakukouza Vol. XXXII: Kyouikuhyouka*, ed. Research Laboratory of Tokyo University of Education (Tokyo: Kanekoshobo, 1950). See also Koji Tanaka, *Paahomansehyouka* (Tokyo: Gyosei, 2001), 37.

educational assessment as a practice, or in order to heighten the 'quality' of education, the teachers must first polish the 'eye' and train to learn how to 'listen.'"[53]

In recent 'educational method research,' especially among young researchers, there is a focus on assessment inherent in educational practice that can be called 'assessment for learning' or 'assessment as learning.' For example, Ninomiya discusses 'formative assessment' based on constructivism, which is being initiated in England.[54] Kitagawa examines essay assessment based on a naturalistic approach, which Cuba and Lincoln call the "four generation assessment."[55] Hirata applies dynamic assessment based on Vygotsky theory in a math class.[56] Moreover, I focused on the 'Educational Practice Record,' which is unique to the assessment culture of Japan, and examined the 'Practice Record' as an "educational assessment theory."[57] How to plan the combination of 'authentic assessment' theories and assessment theories that are embedded in practice is a challenge for the future.

With its systematic design, educational assessment strongly affects daily educational practice. In particular, the entrance examination system has a large influence in Japan. According to newspaper reports (Asahi Shimbun, 11/1/2013, 1/9/2015) the Central Council made plans to reform college entrance examinations following a meeting on rebuilding education.[58] According to the report, a 'college entrance academic ability test' is being planned. This is beyond the scope of the present essay, but these reforms will affect the entire educational design of Japan in the future. I will take up this topic another time.

---

53 Kage Masaharu (psychologist), *Kodomo no sugatanimanabu Kyoushi* (Tokyo: Kyoiku Shuppan, 2007), 101.

54 Ninomiya Shuichi, "Igirisu no ARG niyoru gakushyu no tameno hyouka"ron noichik-ousatu," *Nippon Kyoikuhouhougakkukai* 38 (2012), 97–107.

55 Kitagawa Takeshi, "Kontentu riterasi toshiteno kakuchikara no hyouka ni kansuru kenkyu" *Kyoikuhouhou* 32 (2006), 49–59.

56 Hirata Tomomi, "Hatatu no Saikinseturyoiki no hyouka nikansuru jiisentekikenkyu sansuujugyo niokeru Dainamiku Asesumento no kokorom," *Nippon Kyoikuhouhougak-kukai* 33 (2007), 13–24.

57 See Tanaka, *Kyouikuhyouka to Kyoikujiisen no kadai.* Chapter 7.

58 See Koji Tanaka, *Educational Assessment* (Tokyo: Iwanami Shoten, 2008a), Chapter 6 and Arai Katsuhiro and Hashimoto Akihiko, *Koukoo to Daigaku no Setuzoku — Nyushisenbatu kara Kyouikusetuzoku he* (Tokyo:Tamagawa University Press, 2005).

Literature

Amano, Masateru. Kyouikuhyokashikenkyu. Tokyo: Toshindo, 1993.

Arai, Katsuhiro and Akihiko Hashimoto. *Koukoo to Daigaku no Setuzoku – Nyushisenbatu kara Kyouikusetuzoku he.* Tokyo: Tamagawa University Press, 2005.

Bloom, Benjamin. *Educational Assessment Method Handbook.* Trans. Eichi Kajita. Tokyo: Dai-Ichi Hoki, 1973.

Bloom, Benjamin. *Learning Assessment Handbook.* Trans. Eichi Kajita. Tokyo: Dai-Ichi Hoki, 1974.

Bloom, Benjamin. *The Right Academic Ability for All Children.* Trans Hiroo Inaba and Masaya Onishi. Tokyo: Meijitosho Shuppan, 1986.

Eisner, E. W. *The Art of Educational Evaluation.* Brighton, UK: The Falmer Press, 1985.

Fujimoto, Nami. "Nyuman no Shinnsei no gakuryoku gainen ni kansuruichikosatu." *Kyouikumokuhyo hyouka gakaikiyou* 23 (2013): 50–59.

Hart, Diane. *Authentic Assessment: A Handbook for Educators.* Trans. Koji Tanaka. Kyoto: Minerva Shobo, 2012.

Hashimoto, Shigeharu. "Soutaihyouka to Zettaihyouka," *Kyoikushinri*, May Issue (1961): 356–62.

Hayashi, Msami. "Chibaken Hojopuran niokeru Nouryokuhyouka no hensen ni kansuru kenkyu." *Karikuramukenkyu* 6 (1997): 14–24.

Hirano, Tomohisa. "Mokuhyouni torawarenai hyoukanituitenoichikousatu." *Nippon Kyoikuhouhougakkukai* 32 (1981): 29–36.

Hirata, Tomomi. "Hatatu no Saikinseturyoiki no hyouka nikansuru jiisentekikenkyu sansuujugyo niokeru Dainamiku Asesumento no kokorom." *Nippon Kyoikuhouhougakkukai* 33 (2007): 13–24.

Hisada, Toshihiko, ed. *PISA go no kyouiku wo doutoraeruka — Doitu wo tooshitemiru.* Tokyo: Yachiyo Shuppan, 2013.

Hori, Tetsuo. *Ichimai Pootohoriohyoukahou.* Tokyo: Toyokan Publishing, 2013.

Hosoo, Moeko. "Huransu no Chutoukyouiku niokeru kisogakuryokuronsou — chishi ka konpitenshi ka." *Kinkidaigaku Ronbunshu* 26, no. 1 (2014): 17–46.

Ishii, Terumasa. *Gendai America no Gakuryokukeiseironno tenkai.* Tokyo: Toshindo, 2010.

Kage, Masaharu. *Kodomo no sugatanimanabu Kyoushi.* Tokyo: Kyoiku Shuppan, 2007.

Katsuno, Yorihiko, *Shakai no henkani taiousuru shishituyanouryoku wo ikuseisuru kyouikukateihensei no kihongenri.* Tokyo: National Institute for Educational Policy Research, 2013.

Nami, Katsura. "Waakushopu Jugyoumoderuniyoru Hyougen no Jugyoukousei," *Nippon Kyoikuhouhougakkukai* 35 (2009): 59–70.

Kitagawa, Takeshi. "Kontentu riterasi toshiteno kakuchikara no hyouka ni kansuru kenkyu," *Kyoikuhouhou* 32 (2006): 49–59.

Xiang, Chun. *Gendai Chugoku niokeru Hyoukakaikaku*. Tokyo: Nippon-Hyojun, 2013.

Komiyama, Eichi. "Hyouka no kyouikutekiigi." in *Kyouikudaigakukouza 32: Kyouikuhyouka*, edited by Research Laboratory of Tokyo University of Education, 79–88. Tokyo: Kanekoshobo, 1950.

Masaki, Masashi. *Kyoiku no shinri*. Tokyo: Haneda Shoten, 1948.

Masaki, Masashi. "Kachi to Hyouka." In *Kouza Kyouiku*. Vol. III. Tokyo: Iwanami Shoten, 1952.

Monbusho. *Shotookyouikugenri*. Tokyo: Toyokan Publishing, 1951).

Sadao, Nagashima. "Kyoikuhyouka," in *Shinkyouikujiten*. (Tokyo: Heibonsha, 1949): 27–28.

Nakauchi, Toshio. "Kyouikumokuhyou · hyoukaron no kadai," *Kyoiku*, July Issue (1977): 36–41.

Nezu Tomomi. *Karikuramhyouka no Houhou* (Tokyo: Taga Shuppan, 2006).

Ninomiya Shuichi. "Igirisu no ARG niyoru gakushyu no tameno hyouka"ron noichikousatu." *Nippon Kyoikuhouhougakkukai* 38 (2012): 97–107.

Kanae, Nishioka, "Kyouikuhyouka to Juggyoukenkyu." In *Nippon no Jugyoukenkyu, Volume II*, edited by Nippon Kyoikuhouhougakkukai. Tokyo: Gakubunsha, 2009.

Nishioka, Kanae. *Kyouka to Sougo ni ikasu Pootohoriohyoukahou*. Tokyo: Toshobunka, 2003.

Orata, Pedro T. "Evaluating Evaluation," *Journal of Educational Research* 33, no. 9 (1940): 641–61.

Seisuke, Sakai. "Shokishyakaika "Tawaramotopuran" niokeru gakushuhyouka no tokuchitu," *Kyouikuhohoukenkyu* 34 (2009): 49–60.

Sasaki, Motoki. *Toutatudohyoukasonokangaekata to susumekata*. Meijitosho Shuppan, 1979.

Sato, Manabu, ed. *Yurerusekai no Gakuryoku map*. Tokyo: Akashi Shoten, 2009.

Suzuki, Hideyuki. *Sutandaadojunkyohyouka*. Tokyo: Toshobunka, 2013.

Tanaka, Koji, "Kyouikumokuhyo to Karikuramkousei no kadai Buruumu to Aisunaa no shosetu wo chushinnishite," *Kyoutodaigaku Kyouikugakubukiyou* 28 (1982): 101–13.

–. "OBE no genjyo to kadai", in *Kyoikuhouhougaku no saikouchiku,* edited by Hiroob Inaba, 238–58. Tokyo: Ayumi Publishing, 1995.

–. *Paahomansehyouka.* Tokyo: Gyosei, 2001.

–. *Jinbutu de tuzuru Sengokyoukuhyouka no Rekishi.* Shiga: Sangaku Publishing, 2009.

–. *Educational Assessment.* Tokyo: Iwanami Shoten, 2008.

–. "Kyouikumokuhyo Hyoukakenkyu no 20nen," in *Deciphering the Age of Assessment: Challenges and Outlook of Educational Goals/Educational Research,* Vol. I, Vol. II. Tokyo: (Nippon-Hyojun, 2010a), 10–21.

–. *Kyouikuhyouka to Kyoikujiisen no kadai.* Shiga: Sangaku Publishing, 2013.

–. "History and Future of Cumulative Guidance Records." In *Points of Revision of the New Cumulative Guidance Record for Elementary Schools,* edited by Koji Tanaka, (2010b):130–150. Tokyo: Nippon-Hyojun.

Toui, Yoshio. *Yoshio Toui Collection, Vol. IV.* Tokyo: Meijitosho Shuppan, 1972.

Toui, Yoshio. *Tuchinbo no kaizo.* Tokyo: Meijitosho Shuppan, 1967.

Toyama, Hiraku. *Gendaikyouikukagaku,* March Issue (1961): 4.

Tsuzuki, Aritsune. *Kyouikuhyouka.* Tokyo: Dai-ichi Hoki, 1969.

Tyler, Ralph W. Constructing Achievement Tests. Columbus, OH: Ohio State University, 1934.

–. "General Statement on Evaluation," *Journal of Educational Research* 35, no. 7 (1942):492–501.

–. "General Statement on Evaluation," *Journal of Educational Research* 35, no. 7 (1942):492–501.

Wiggins, Grant and Jay McTighe. *Understanding by Design.* Trans. Nishioka Kanae. (Tokyo: Nippon-Hyojun, 2012.

Woody, Clifford, "Nature of Evaluation," *Journal of Educational Research* 35, no. 7 (1942): 481–91.

Appendix: Educational Assessment Controversy

It is important to recall the 'educational assessment controversy', a dispute that took place during the 1940s in the "Journal of Educational Research" between the 'measurement group'[59] and the 'evaluation group'.[60] Criticism of the 'evaluation group' by the 'measurement group' was organised as follows by Nagashima:

"1. These tools of evaluation are the primary tools, and in the same way as measurement tools, it is a paper test, and one cannot escape the common limitations found in these tools.

2. Measurement tools have been criticised in the sense that they lack validity, but it cannot be said for certain that evaluation tools have sufficient validity in the growth/development processes of children.

3. Focusing on qualitative differences means that one side will tolerate subjectivity; the issue then becomes how to secure reliability.

4. For measurement, expressing quality with quantity has been attacked, but it must be said that this also applies to evaluation tools.

5. Educational measurement has been criticised for demanding fixed answers, but answers of free expression are not necessarily demanded for evaluation tools either.

6. It has been pointed out that evaluation tools also focus on the academic results rather than describing the academic process."[61]

We can see from this dispute that against the 'educational evaluation' theories of the time — which focused on quality — reliability, validity, and diversity were demanded in the assessment standard. It can be said that theories of 'authentic assessment' were among the answers for this issue.

---

59 Pedro T, Orata, "Evaluating Evaluation," *Journal of Educational Research* 33, no. 9 (1940): 641–61; Clifford Woody, "Nature of Evaluation," *Journal of Educational Research* 35, no. 7 (1942): 481–91.

60 Ralph W. Tyler, "General Statement on Evaluation," *Journal of Educational Research* 35, no. 7 (1942): 492–501.

61 Sadao Nagashima, "Kyoikuhyouka," in *Shinkyouikujiten* (Tokyo: Heibonsha, 1949), 27–28.

Actors of Assessment

Florian Waldow

Constellations of Actors and Fairness in Assessment in Germany, Sweden and England

Meritocracy, fairness and assessment

What should be considered "fair" in matters of pupil assessment is an explosive and contentious issue in many contexts and has been so for a long time.[1] The main reason why this question is so highly charged is the role educational assessment plays in the allocation of life chances. In all Western democratic societies, life chances are supposed to be distributed on the basis of individual merit, not ascriptive factors such as wealth, social or ethnic background, migration status etc. A social order in which life chances are distributed on the basis of merit is called a "meritocracy."[2]

However, 'merit' is a latent trait and therefore needs to be operationalized in order to be usable for the allocation of life chances. This is where education comes into play, as educational certificates are the "basic currency"[3] in which merit is expressed and which can be converted into life chances. It is important to note that it is not education 'as such,' i.e. the fact of being educated or possessing certain competencies that constitutes the currency that can be converted into life chances; in order to be convertible into life chances, competences, skills and knowledge need to be codified in the form of certificates,[4] e.g. a school leaving certificate like the German *Abitur*.

---

1   See Karlheinz Ingenkamp, ed. *Die Fragwürdigkeit der Zensurengebung: Texte und Untersuchungsberichte* (Weinheim: Beltz, 1989).

2   The term "meritocracy" was originally coined in 1958 by the British educational sociologist Michael Young to denote a dystopian future in which allocation of life chances by merit reigns supreme, leading to a society that is deeply divided along the lines of intelligence; see Michael Young, *The Rise of the Meritocracy, 1870–2033: An Essay on Education and Equality* (London, UK: Thames & Hudson, 1958). Today, however, the term "meritocracy" is usually used in an affirmative sense.

3   Morton Deutsch, "Education and Distributive Justice – Some Reflections on Grading Systems," *American Psychologist* 34, no. 5 (1979): 393.

4   Heike Solga, "Meritokratie – die moderne Legitimation ungleicher Bildungschancen," in *Institutionalisierte Ungleichheiten: Wie das Bildungswesen Chancen blockiert*, ed. Peter A. Berger and Heike Kahlert (Weinheim: Juventa, 2005), 28.

Educational certificates are usually based on summative assessment of some sort; in this way, pupil assessment becomes the key operation of the allocation of life chances in meritocratic societies, and the actors controlling and conducting assessment assume the role of gatekeepers. For this gatekeeping process to possess legitimacy, the assessment connected to it needs to be perceived as fair.[5] However, what is considered fair in determining merit — a question that is bound up with a range of other questions such as who is supposed to determine merit — is far from self-evident and universal. Rather, the concept of fairness is highly context- and actor-specific.

The present chapter aims to uncover some of these differing conceptions of fairness that are embedded in the institutional "blueprints"[6] of the assessment systems of Germany, Sweden and England. It will present an institutional analysis focussing on the conceptions of fairness that are embedded in constellations of actors involved in pupil assessment. The chapter focuses on summative assessment, as this is the type of assessment that is most relevant for the allocation of life chances.

The chapter focuses on the role of actors assessing pupils, such as teachers or exam boards. However, it would be a misconception to assume that pupils have a completely passive role in the process of assessment, selection and allocation of life chances. Pupil assessment does not just produce knowledge on the basis of which pupils can be "processed" by others, but also knowledge on the basis of which pupils perform acts of self-selection, adjusting their plans to what seems attainable.[7]

Despite the fact that "meritocracy" is a very powerful normative ideal, it has been demonstrated again and again that in practice, criteria such as social or ethnic background and wealth continue to be key for succeeding in the education system and thereby in extension for the allocation of life chances in societies

---

5   Olaf Struck, "Gatekeeping zwischen Individuum, Organisation und Institution: Zur Bedeutung und Analyse von Gatekeeping am Beispiel von Übergängen im Lebensverlauf," in *Institutionen und Lebensläufe im Wandel: Institutionelle Regulierungen von Lebensläufen*, ed. Lutz Leisering, Rainer Müller, and Karl F. Schumann (Weinheim: Juventa, 2001), 45.

6   Stefan Liebig, "Soziale Gerechtigkeit – Modelle und Befunde der soziologischen Gerechtigkeitsforschung," in *Fachgespräch Gerechtigkeit*, ed. Otfried Höffe, Stefan Liebig, and Bernd von Maydell (Berlin: Berlin-Brandenburgische Akademie der Wissenschaften, 2006), 23–24.

7   Monika Falkenberg and Herbert Kalthoff, "Das Feld der Bildung: Schulische Institutionen, Schulbevölkerung und gesellschaftliche Integration," in *Lehr(er)buch Soziologie: Für die pädagogischen und soziologischen Studiengänge*, ed. Herbert Willems (Wiesbaden: VS Verlag für Sozialwissenschaften, 2008).

following the "meritocratic" ideal.[8] Therefore, characterising a society as "meritocratic" refers to its "normative self-definition"[9] rather than its actual mode of functioning. Thus, even in societies that define themselves as meritocratic, families can still pass on social advantages from one generation to the next. However, it is a sign for the power of the meritocratic ideal that families can increasingly no longer pass on privilege *directly* to their offspring, but have to take the "detour" through the education system, converting ascriptive traits into legitimate advantages in the shape of educational certificates.[10]

An institutional analysis of the constellations of actors involved in pupil assessment such as the one attempted here reveals a great deal about underlying conceptions of justice. Which actors get to perform the allocation of a social good in which ways and what is supposed to safeguard this allocation are aspects of the allocation process that are important parts of conceptions of fairness concerning the allocation process.[11] The basic ground rules of pupil assessment — including the constellations of actors stipulated by the rules and regulations — may not completely determine actors' conceptions of fairness, but they do provide a certain framework actors' conceptions have to relate to.

All education systems that follow the meritocratic ideal have to ensure that allocation-relevant assessment is conducted on a more or less comparable basis for all pupils. This is an important aspect of the demand for "equality of opportunity" that is usually connected to the meritocratic ideal.[12] However, comparability can be achieved in different ways, involving different actors in different roles:

---

8   See Rolf Becker and Alexander Schulze, "Kontextuelle Perspektiven ungleicher Bildungschancen – eine Einführung," in *Bildungskontexte*, ed. Rolf Becker and Alexander Schulze (Wiesbaden: Springer, 2013).

9   Solga, "Meritokratie," 23.

10 See David P. Baker and Gerald K. LeTendre, *National Differences, Global Similarities: World Culture and the Future of Schooling* (Stanford, Calif.: Stanford University Press, 2005), chapter 3.

11 See Gerald S. Leventhal, "What Should Be Done with Equity Theory? New Approaches to the Study of Fairness in Social Relationships," in *Social exchange: Advances in theory and research*, ed. Kenneth J. Gergen, Martin S. Greenberg, and Richard H. Willis (New York: Plenum Press, 1980); Gerald S. Leventhal, Jurgis Karuza jr. and William Rick Fry, "Beyond Fairness: A Theory of Allocation Preferences," in *Justice and social interaction: Experimental and theoretical contributions from psychological research*, ed. Gerold Mikula (Bern: Hans Huber, 1980).

12 On the ambivalent meanings of "equality of opportunity" see Johannes Giesinger, "Was heißt Bildungsgerechtigkeit?," *Zeitschrift für Pädagogik* 53, no. 3 (2007).

"At one extreme this has taken the form of highly formalized "standardized tests" which are entered under standard conditions and marked in a common way and where considerable efforts are devoted to the attempt to maintain "standards" across time and space. At the other extreme there has been a reliance on "professional judgement" to try to ensure an acceptable level of comparability."[13]

Most education systems can be located somewhere between these two extremes. Germany is quite close to the 'professional judgement'-pole, while England is quite close to the 'standardized tests/examinations' -pole, with Sweden somewhere in between. Due to these different ways of pursuing 'equality of opportunity,' a central tenet of 'meritocracy' in all three education systems analysed here, these three countries' systems of pupil assessment make for an interesting comparison with the aim of, in Charles Tilly's terminology, "variation finding."[14]

A final note on the choice of units of comparison concerns the German case. In Germany, individual federal states are responsible for educational matters. However, the chapter will not discuss the differences between different federal states in Germany, which in some areas can be quite significant.[15] However, as the basic constellations of actors involved in pupil assessment are similar in all federal states, especially if compared to Sweden and England, these differences will be largely ignored for the purposes of this chapter.

The following section will provide a short overview over actor constellations in assessment in the three countries studied. Already in this section, some tentative interpretations of which conceptions of fairness are embedded in actor constellations will be made. The section that follows will discuss some selected aspects in a comparative and more systematic way. The conclusion will summarise the

13 Harvey Goldstein and Toby Lewis, "The Scope of Assessment," in *Assessment: Problems, developments, and statistical issues: A volume of expert contributions*, ed. Harvey Goldstein and Toby Lewis (Chichester: Wiley, 1996), 2.

14 Charles Tilly, *Big Structures, Large Processes, Huge Comparisons* (New York: Russell Sage Foundation, 1984), 82. The choice of these three countries as units of comparison can also be justified from the perspective of "educational regimes". Political scientists have identified different educational regimes analogous to welfare regimes, and each of the countries analysed here can be assigned to different regime types. See Anne West and Rita Nikolai, "Welfare Regimes and Education Regimes: Equality of Opportunity and Expenditure in the EU (and US)," *Journal of Social Policy* 42, no. 3 (2013), doi: 10.1017/S0047279412001043.

15 For an overview, see Marcel Helbig and Rita Nikolai, *Die Unvergleichbaren: Der Wandel der Schulsysteme in den deutschen Bundesländern seit 1949* (Bad Heilbrunn: Klinkhardt, 2015).

results and discuss their limitations and possible extensions. It will end with some general considerations on the character of meritocracy/meritocracies.

Actor constellations in pupil assessment in Germany, Sweden and England

Germany

Traditionally, a centralised educational administration (centralised on the level of individual federal states, not on the level of the nation state as a whole), detailed curricula and a more or less centralised and centrally controlled system of teacher education and teacher certification were seen as a sufficient safeguard to ensure that pupil assessment, especially grading, would be carried out in a comparable way across the country or at least the federal state. Over a period of time stretching at least from the 1930s to the present, there was recurrent criticism of the "questionability of grading,"[16] drawing attention to the fact that different teachers grade the same piece of work differently and even the same teacher will grade the same piece of work differently at different times. However, this did not lead to any thorough revisions of the assessment system or to the adoption of a psychometric test culture as in the United States or Sweden.[17] Generally, the development of assessment systems in Germany over the course of the 20th century is characterised by slow and incremental change at best. In the course of the last 15 years, developments seem to have accelerated somewhat, but some basic traits of German assessment culture still persist, such as the comparatively high degree of autonomy of individual teachers when it comes to assessment.

The existing official rules on pupil assessment tend to be quite unspecific when it comes to the act of assessment itself. They mainly regulate "technical" details such as the number of examination papers to be sat and the possibilities of the school head to intervene into individual teachers' assessment. Even fundamental questions such as whether assessment should be norm-, criterion- or individually-referenced tend not to be stipulated unambiguously by official regulations.[18] According to Falko Rheinberg, many regulations implicitly assume that assessment

---

16 This was the title of a very successful book edited by Karl-Heinz Ingenkamp (*Die Fragwürdigkeit der Zensurengebung*).

17 See Florian Waldow, "Die internationale Konjunktur standardisierter Messungen von Schülerleistung in der ersten Hälfte des 20. Jahrhunderts und ihr Niederschlag in Deutschland und Schweden," *Jahrbuch für Pädagogik* 21 (2010).

18 Ingo Richter, *Recht im Bildungssystem: Eine Einführung*, Grundriss der Pädagogik/ Erziehungswissenschaft 23 (Stuttgart: Kohlhammer, 2006), 98.

is to be carried out criterion-referenced.[19] However, the assessment criteria tend to be defined very vaguely at best. There is no connection between the goals defined in the curricula and grade criteria. Grades are defined in a very vague way, based on an agreement reached between the different federal states 50 years ago (*Hamburger Abkommen*).[20]

Thus, the official regulations leave a wide scope to teachers, and individual teachers' autonomy is quite high in Germany when it comes to assessment. A key concept in this respect is individual teachers' 'pedagogical responsibility' (*pädagogische Verantwortung*) and, complementarily, 'pedagogical freedom' (*pädagogische Freiheit*). Teachers' pedagogical freedom is stipulated in all federal states' education laws. It denotes the teacher's scope of autonomously handling instruction and education in a wider sense, including assessment.[21] Individual teachers' 'pedagogical freedom' is not boundless, but limited by the rules and regulations on the one hand and by the heads of individual subjects (*Fachbetreuer*), school heads and school administration on the other. Federal states and school types differ in how much influence they allow subject heads and school heads. However, how far school heads may intervene in assessment and where the boundaries of individual teachers' 'pedagogical freedom' are to a certain extent is open to interpretation and sometimes becomes the subject of court cases.

In 1999, Ewald Terhart characterised pupil assessment in Germany as being grounded in a non-explicit practice that is passed on from one generation of teachers to the next:

> "The actual practice [of pupil assessment] and its accompanying mental processes are primarily supported by a tradition that is practice-based and only partly made explicit. It is a part of professional culture and is specific to different school types and individual schools. Novices to the profession (who have been to school for at least 13 years and gone through teacher education for [...] 6–8 years, a time during which they were permanently graded themselves; therefore, they are not really novices to the system!) are [...]

19 Falko Rheinberg, "Bezugsnormen und schulische Leistungsbeurteilung," in *Leistungsmessungen in Schulen*, ed. Franz E. Weinert (Weinheim: Beltz, 2002), 66.
20 The agreement was modified in 1971. See Kultusministerkonferenz, "Abkommen zwischen den Ländern der Bundesrepublik zur Vereinheitlichung auf dem Gebiete des Schulwesens (Vom 28.10.1964 in der Fassung vom 14.10.1971)," accessed September 3, 2015, http://www.kmk.org/fileadmin/veroeffentlichungen_beschluesse/1964/1964_10_28_Hamburger_Abkommen.pdf.
21 Richter, *Recht im Bildungssystem*, 121; Hermann Avenarius, "Welche Rechte und Pflichten haben Lehrkräfte, Schulleitungen und Schulaufsicht bei der Qualitätsentwicklung der Schulen und bei der Sicherung gleicher Lebenschancen?," *DIPF informiert*, no. 4 (2003): 13.

gradually socialised into the general principles of this tradition. Living the tradition on a daily basis leads to the preservation, but also to the gradual development of a practice that is described and experienced as being based on a "broad consensus", a consensus, however, that has never actually been critically examined and has never been explicitly [...] agreed on."[22]

Terhart published the text from which the above quote is taken in 1999. Since then, there have been significant changes in the German system of education. E.g., almost all German federal states introduced centralised final examinations.[23] However, the degree of centralisation and standardisation of these examinations is very moderate when compared to other centralised examination systems such as the English system.[24] Local components of these examinations still play an important role, e.g. in the Abitur-exams, the examination at the end of the academic-track upper secondary school regulating university admissions. Despite the fact that these examinations are now called "centralised" *(Zentralabitur)* in all but one federal states, the centralised component of the final Abitur-grade does not exceed 23 per cent in any federal state, the rest is determined locally.[25]

Another reform that has taken place since the publication of Terhart's text is the introduction of educational standards.[26] In the wake of standards-based reform, a variety of testing instruments were introduced that make comparisons of assessment beyond the individual school class possible (i.e. comparing the whole school, schools within a federal state or even federal states).[27] However, the introduction of these instruments was usually not justified by their possible

---

22 Ewald Terhart, "Zensurengebung und innerschulisches Selektionsklima – die Rolle der Schulleitung," *Zeitschrift für Soziologie der Erziehung und Sozialisation* 19, no. 3 (1999): 281.

23 See Svenja Mareike Kühn, *Steuerung und Innovation durch Abschlussprüfungen?* (Wiesbaden: VS Verlag für Sozialwissenschaften, 2010).

24 Esther D. Klein et al., "Wie zentral sind zentrale Prüfungen? Abschlussprüfungen am Ende der Sekundarstufe II im nationalen und internationalen Vergleich," *Zeitschrift für Pädagogik* 55, no. 4 (2009): 618.

25 Ibid., 607.

26 Olaf Köller, "Bildungsstandards," in *Handbuch Bildungsforschung*, ed. Rudolf Tippelt and Bernhard Schmidt (Wiesbaden: VS Verlag für Sozialwissenschaften, 2009).

27 Isabell van Ackeren and Gabriele Bellenberg, "Parallelarbeiten, Vergleichsarbeiten und Zentrale Abschlussprüfungen: Bestandsaufnahme und Perspektiven," *Jahrbuch der Schulentwicklung*, no. 13 (2004); Dirk Richter et al., "Überzeugungen von Lehrkräften zu den Funktionen von Vergleichsarbeiten. Zusammenhänge zu Veränderungen im Unterricht und den Kompetenzen von Schülerinnen und Schülern," *Zeitschrift für Pädagogik* 60, no. 2 (2014).

contribution to standardising the levels of educational assessment and thereby the fairness of assessment. In 2006, the Standing Conference of the Ministers of Education and Cultural Affairs of the federal states passed a "Comprehensive strategy on educational monitoring." This document sees the main goals of the new testing instruments on the one hand in the area of system monitoring, on the other in the field of school development. Improving fairness in assessment does not play a role.[28] Empirical results vary as to how intensively teachers use the new tests in their assessment; however, the degree often seems to be quite limited.[29] So, despite the changes in recent years in the wake of standards-based reform, fairness in assessment is still largely based on the non-standardized and 'holistic' professional judgement of teachers assessing pupils they have taught and know personally.

However, it is not certain that the situation will remain so. E.g., the Standing Conference of Education Ministers of the German federal states is working on a joint pool of examination questions for the *Abitur*-examination, thereby increasing standardisation. This and other developments may herald a slow departure from the German system as we know it. While institutional structures that are as ingrained as assessment systems may change quite slowly as a rule, they are not completely immutable.

Sweden

The Swedish system lacks final examinations like the British or German systems. Instead, for the purposes of the allocation of life chances, the grades received in

---

28 See Kultusministerkonferenz, "Überblick: Gesamtstrategie zum Bildungsmonitoring," Kultusministerkonferenz, accessed September 3, 2015, http://www.kmk.org/bildung-schule/qualitaetssicherung-in-schulen/bildungsmonitoring/ueberblick-gesamtstrat egie-zum-bildungsmonitoring. html. A revised version was passed in 2015, still with no mention of fairness in assessment; see Kultusministerkonferenz, "Gesamtstrategie der Kultusministerkonferenz zum Bildungsmonitoring: Beschluss der 350. Kultusmi-nisterkonferenz vom 11.06.2015," (Berlin: Kultusministerkonferenz, 2015). However, the potential of these instruments for a standardisation of assessment has not passed unnoticed among researchers in the field; see van Ackeren and Bellenberg, "Paralle-larbeiten, Vergleichsarbeiten und Zentrale Abschlussprüfungen," 125.

29 Results vary mainly between different federal states and different subjects. See Uwe Maier, *Wie gehen Lehrerinnen und Lehrer mit Vergleichsarbeiten um? Eine Studie zu testbasierten Schulreformen in Baden-Württemberg und Thüringen* (Baltmannsweiler: Schneider Verlag Hohengehren, 2009); Richter et al., "Überzeugungen von Lehrkräften zu den Funktionen von Vergleichsarbeiten."

the last year of lower secondary schooling (year 9 of *grundskola*) and the grades received in upper secondary schooling (year 10–12, *gymnasieskola*) are particularly used for allocation purposes, the former regulating access to the different national programmes of upper secondary schooling and individual schools[30] and the latter for access to higher education. These grades are set by the teachers.

However, while teachers are ultimately responsible for pupil assessment, in contrast to Germany there is a system of centralised national tests with the primary goal of standardising assessment nationwide. This system was already set up in the 1940s in the primary and lower secondary sector and in the 1960s in the upper secondary sector. Tests were first introduced for the main subjects Swedish and mathematics. The explicit aim of the tests was to standardise teachers' assessment across the whole country.[31] According to Christian Lundahl, the debate around the introduction and use of standardized tests in school from the perspective of a sociology of professions can be seen as a struggle between teachers and psychologists on who was to "own" assessment; on the one side the teachers with their traditional, 'holistic' methods of assessment and their personal knowledge of pupils, on the other psychologists with their scientific psychometric methods. Even though teachers remained ultimately responsible for assessment and even though the national tests were supposed to *support* teachers' assessment, not replace it, Lundahl claims (plausibly) that the psychologists won this struggle.[32] The psychologists' 'clinical gaze' to a certain degree has replaced the teachers' perspective. Lundahl sees this loss of autonomy in the field of assessment as a partial deprofessionalisation of the teaching profession. From the beginning, researchers were involved in the development of the tests. Today, they are developed by university institutes on behalf of the National Agency of Education.

Until the early 1990s, Sweden had a norm-referenced system of assessment with the whole age group in the entire country as reference group.[33] This means

---

30   The upper secondary school *(gymnasieskola)* in Sweden is tracked into 18 national programmes (with local variants), some with a main focus on preparing for university studies, some with a focus on preparing for working life.

31   Christian Lundahl, *Varför nationella prov? Framväxt, dilemman, möjligheter* (Stockholm: Skolverket, 2009).

32   Christian Lundahl, *Viljan att veta vad andra vet: Kunskapsbedömning i tidigmodern, modern och senmodern skola*, Arbetsliv i omvandling 2006:8 (Stockholm: Arbetslivsinstitutet, 2006), 262.

33   Håkan Andersson, *Relativa betyg: Några empiriska studier och en teoretisk genomgång i ett historiskt perspektiv*, Akademiska avhandlingar vid Pedagogiska institutionen, Umeå universitet, 29 (Umeå: Universität, 1991).

that the entire age group was to be placed in a normal distribution according to its performance. Which percentage of pupils could reach which grade was determined from the outset. Grades were calibrated with the help of the national tests. While the tests themselves did not function as exams and did not enter into the calculation of individual grades, the average grade of an individual class was not allowed to differ to widely from the average result of the tests in that class.

In the early 1990s, the Swedish school system underwent a thoroughgoing reform. Traditional curricula were replaced by educational standards and the norm-referenced system of assessment was replaced by a criterion-referenced system. Competence levels were defined and coupled to certain grades. Now, grades were no longer supposed to reflect the relative position of pupils within their age group, but supposed to reflect whether pupils had reached a certain competence level, irrespective of how many other pupils reached the same level.

The grading system was again thoroughly revised in 2011. Criterion-referencing remained in place, but the radical competence orientation of the former system was rolled back to a certain extent, with more content being stipulated in the curricula again. The curriculum documents contain detailed grade criteria, with a clear link between competencies and grades. In contrast to Germany there are no detailed regulations on technical details such as what relative weight written work should have in assessment in relation to oral contributions etc.

With the criterion-referenced system introduced in the early 1990s, the systemic necessity of having national tests to calibrate grades came to an end, as grades are now determined by criteria irrespective of how many pupils are awarded the grade. However, tests were not abolished. On the contrary, the number of tests and the number of subjects in which there are tests were even increased. Safeguarding comparable standards of assessment throughout the country is still seen as the most important function of the national tests, even though now school development and system monitoring have been added as additional functions.[34] The National Agency of Education and large parts of the media continue to see the system of national tests as an important safeguard of fairness in assessment in Sweden. Evidence that the grades awarded by teachers diverge too far from test results are still seen as a threat to fairness.[35]

---

34 Lundahl, *Varför nationella prov?*, 121; Skolverket, "Nationella prov," Skolverket, accessed August 3, 2015, http://www.skolverket.se/bedomning/nationella-prov.

35 Skolverket, *Provbetyg-slutbetyg-likvärdig bedömning? En statistisk analys av sambandet mellan nationella prov och slutbetyg i grundskolans årskurs 9, 1998–2006*, Skolverkets rapport 300 (Stockholm: Skolverket, 2007).

The tests are supposed to put pupil assessment on a rational, scientifically based footing. The intention and symbolic function of the tests is to safeguard that the same grade will represent the same level of knowledge and skills in different schools and different classrooms. In practice, this is only fulfilled to a certain degree. Preparation for tests differs strongly between schools. Also, the test formats used give pupils of certain upper secondary tracks an advantage over others.[36]

The National Agency of Education does not just become involved in teachers' assessment through administering the national tests. In addition to the national tests, the Agency produces a wealth of additional materials to aid teachers in their assessment, such as assessment matrices, detailed guidelines and diagnostic material of different types.[37]

So, while the final responsibility for pupil assessment in Sweden lies in the hands of the teachers, the National Agency of Education is there as a kind of 'third actor', providing assessment support or, put negatively, constraining teachers' freedom of assessment.

England

In England, educational certificates relevant for selection purposes such as access to higher education are not awarded directly by schools, but by external awarding bodies known as examination boards. Assessment that is selection relevant is thus mostly in the hands or at least tightly controlled by a body that is not directly connected to the school.

England has a long tradition of external exams, ultimately going back to the first university admissions exams in the first half of the 19th century and the civil service selection exams introduced in the mid-19th century.[38] Academic school leaving examinations not tied to university admission were only available from 1911.[39] In the English tradition, educational certificates relevant for selection purposes such as access to higher education are not awarded by the schools, but

36 Helena Korp, *Lika chanser i gymnasiet? En studie om betyg, nationella prov och social reproduktion* (Malmö: Holmbergs, 2006).
37 See e.g. Skolverket, "Bedömningsportalen," accessed August 3, 2015, https://bp.skolverket.se/.
38 Patricia Broadfoot et al., "What Professional Responsibility Means to Teachers: National Contexts and Classroom Constants," *British Journal of Sociology of Education* 9, no. 3 (1988), 266.
39 Jo-Anne Baird, "Country-Case Study: England," in *Secondary school external examination systems: Reliability, robustness and resilience*, ed. Barend Vlaardingerbroek and Neil Taylor (Amherst, NY: Cambria, 2009).

by external awarding bodies known as examination boards. Exams are devised, administered and graded by these boards. Currently, there are five competing examination boards offering the GCSEs (General Certificate of Secondary Education) and A-levels (General Certificate of Education Advanced Level), the two most important examinations at the end of lower secondary and upper secondary schooling, respectively. There is a wealth of other bodies offering a large number of other qualifications.[40] Schools buy the examinations from the examination boards; they can buy examinations in different subjects from different boards. Pupils are quite free in choosing in which subjects they want to take exams. Certain parts of the examinations can be carried out and supervised locally (formerly called "coursework," today "controlled assessment"), but the "controlled assessment"-parts of examinations, too, are monitored closely by examination boards.[41] Recently, controlled assessment has been rolled back in most subjects.[42]

For a long time, grading of external examinations was purely norm-referenced. In the 1980s, grade criteria for some grades were introduced; these however are formulated in quite a vague way, and the translation of rough marks into grades is still conducted primarily on the basis of the professional judgment of the awarders at the examination boards, many of whom also work as teachers or are former teachers. Thus, in grading exams, a mixture of norm- and criterion-referencing is used.[43] However, professional judgements made by awarders are strongly guided by statistics based on results of previous years. Actors involved in examining and awarding in exam boards are tightly controlled by numerous regulations, and their activities are tightly monitored by a regulating authority, the Office of Qualifications and Examinations Regulation (Ofqual).

The system of external exams means that the constellation of actors involved differs significantly from that to be found in Germany and Sweden. In Germany

---

40 Accredited Qualifications, "Accredited Qualifications," accessed October 19, 2015, http://www.accreditedqualifications.org.uk/qualification-types-in-the-uk.html.

41 Tina Isaacs, "Educational Assessment in England," *Assessment in Education: Principles, Policy & Practice* 17, no. 3 (2010).

42 It should be mentioned that the teachers' role in non-examination types of assessment has also been rolled back since the 1990s, reflecting, according to Black & Dylan, a deep distrust of the teaching profession. See Paul Black and Dylan Wiliam, "Lessons from around the World: How Policies, Politics and Cultures Constrain and Afford Assessment Practices," *Curriculum Journal* 16, no. 2 (2005): 259, doi: 10.1080/09585170500136218.

43 Colin Robinson, "Awarding Examination Grades: Current Processes and Their Evolution," in *Techniques for monitoring the comparability of examination standards*, ed. Paul Newton et al. (London, UK: Qualifications and Curriculum Authority, 2007).

and Sweden, teachers combine the roles of instructor and judge (in the sense of judging what pupils have learnt). In England, teachers do not judge pupils themselves (at least in examinations), but try to *coach* them to score as highly as possible in the external examinations.[44] In direct contrast to the German and the Swedish case, the examiners are not supposed to know the pupils they are assessing personally and are not allowed any personal interest in the schools from which the pupils they assess come.

Within the English examination system, the fact that examinations are conducted by an agency external to schools in which pupils have been taught is considered a central safeguard for exams to be regarded as fair. Even crises such as the one erupting around the A-levels in 2002, when allegations were made that the examination process had been tampered with in order to counteract grade inflation,[45] were not able to shatter confidence in the system of external examinations as such: "Regardless of the demonstrable inherent unreliability of all forms of assessment, public confidence in the reliability of externally provided assessment remained high, as did the belief that assessments carried out by teachers could not be relied on."[46]

The fact that competing examination boards exist in England creates special problems of comparability, which was noted already in the beginning of the 20th century.[47] The debate whether the different examination boards apply the same standards in their examinations is never ending, occasionally leading to the demand that the different examination boards be merged.[48] There are even discussion groups on the Internet about differences in examination standards in the different examination boards, such as this one: "Edexcel vs Cambridge (OCR/CIE), which one is tougher?"[49] Also, there have been several inquiries into examination standards over the years.[50] Questions of inter-subject comparability

---

44 Bernd Zymek, "Auslese und Selbsteliminierung. Die Gymnasien zwischen elitärem Selbstanspruch und Multifunktionalität, 1945–1970," *Zeitschrift für Pädagogik* 61, no. 1 (2015).

45 Isabel Nisbet and Alan Greig, "Educational qualifications regulation," in *Centre for the study of Regulated Industries (CRI) regulatory review 2006/2007*, ed. P. Vass (Bath, UK: CRI, 2007).

46 Katherine Tattersall, "A brief history of policies, practices and issues relating to comparability," in *Techniques for monitoring the comparability of examination standards*, ed. Paul Newton, et al. (London, UK: Qualifications and Curriculum Authority, 2007), 81.

47 Nisbet and Greig, "Educational Qualifications Regulation."

48 William Stewart, "Poll Backs Merger to Create Single Exam Board," *TES*, May 14, 2010.

49 The Student Room, "Edexcel vs Cambridge (OCR/CIE), which one is tougher?," accessed September 3, 2015, http://www.thestudentroom.co.uk/showthread.php?t=547887.

50 Tattersall, "A Brief History of Policies, Practices and Issues Relating to Comparability."

have also played a major role,[51] acerbated by the fact that pupils select a limited number of subjects for A-levels.

The high reliance on and trust in external examinations is perhaps partly due to the high degree of decentralisation and fragmentation that has been typical for the English education system for a long time. The English education system, including the teaching profession, traditionally was much less unified than the German and Swedish education systems, and external exams were almost the only means of controlling and evaluating outcomes.

Different constellations of actors, different conceptions of fairness

Teacher: examiner or coach?

In the context of the topic of this chapter, a central question is who "owns" assessment, i.e. who is responsible for assessment: schools and teachers themselves, or an external body such as an examination board or educational ministry?[52] If the latter is the case — as in the English system —, the school becomes the pupil's "ally" vis-à-vis the examining body. If the former is the case — as in Germany and Sweden —, the school is itself the examining body. This has consequences e.g. for the pupils' tendency to appeal against grades. In the German case, the appeal is directed against the school, meaning that schools will try and keep appeals at a minimum. In contrast, in the English case, it is not uncommon for schools to *encourage* pupils to appeal against examination boards' assessments.[53]

Actor constellations in assessment interact strongly with conceptions of the teachers' role and conceptions of teacher professionalism.[54] The rules governing teacher professionalism (including rules that are not laid down in the form of

---

51 Paul E. Newton, "Making Sense of Decades of Debate on Inter-Subject Comparability in England," *Assessment in Education: Principles, Policy & Practice* 19, no. 2 (2012), doi: 10.1080/0969594X.2011.563357.

52 See Helmut Fend, *Schule gestalten: Systemsteuerung, Schulentwicklung und Unterrichtsqualität* (Wiesbaden: VS Verlag für Sozialwissenschaften, 2008), 356.

53 In the Swedish case, appealing formally against grades is not possible. See Florian Waldow, "Conceptions of Justice in the Examination Systems of England, Germany and Sweden: A Look at Safeguards of Fair Procedure and Possibilities of Appeal," *Comparative Education Review* 58, no. 2 (2014), doi: 10.1086/674781.

54 See Ewald Terhart, "Lehrerberuf und Professionalität: Wandel der Begrifflichkeit – Neue Herausforderungen," in *Pädagogische Professionalität*, ed. Werner Helsper and Rudolf Tippelt, *Zeitschrift für Pädagogik Beiheft 57* (Weinheim: Beltz, 2011).

formalised regulations and that teachers may not even be explicitly aware of) are a key element of the institutional logics of any education — and assessment — system. Key questions in this context are, as stated above, how autonomous teachers are when it comes to pupil assessment and which instruments there are to aid teachers in assessment (or, depending on the perspective, constrain their freedom of judgement).

Objective methods vs. holistic judgement on the basis of personal knowledge

Connected to the question who "owns" examinations is the question whether examiners should know the examinees personally or not. In Germany and Sweden, knowing the assessed pupil personally is seen as an advantage, or even a precondition, for assessing a pupil fairly. In the first Swedish curriculum for the comprehensive school from 1962, this was made explicit when it stated that teachers should take extra care when awarding the best and the worst grades in the half-term school report, because they have not had a chance to get to know the pupils sufficiently well then.[55] Thus, a "holistic" assessment of pupils on the basis of thorough personal knowledge is what the institutional blueprint of the system requires. This is even true for 'centralised' examinations in those German federal states where the teacher marks and grades the centralised examinations of his pupils. In contrast, in England, awarders must not have a 'personal interest' in the school or know the pupils assessed personally. In this system logics, *not* knowing the pupil personally is seen as a precondition for fair assessment. What counts as 'holistic' in the German and Swedish systems would count as an undesired halo effect in the English. There, the fact that assessment is external and anonymous is seen as a safeguard of fairness. So, what is seen as a *prerequisite* for fair assessment in Germany and Sweden is seen as an *obstacle* for fair assessment in England.

Specific assessment cultures have specific trouble spots

Specific assessment systems have specific trouble spots or institutional 'fault lines' whose location depends on the architecture of the system, especially constellations of actors. Discussions about fairness have a tendency to concentrate on these spots, and accusations of 'unfairness' often arise in connection to them.

---

55 Skolöverstyrelsen, *Läroplan för grundskolan*, Skolöverstyrelsens skriftserie, (Stockholm: Skolöverstyrelsen, 1962), 90.

Often, these trouble spots are located at places where questions of comparability (between examiners, between subjects, over time ...) are at stake.

E.g., the question of the comparability of the different German federal states' *Abitur*-grades has long been such a trouble spot due to the importance of the *Abitur* for admittance to higher education.[56] Due to the fact that England and Sweden are not federal countries, this issue has not played a role there. The question whether the different external exam boards operate according to comparable standards has been a contentious issue in England for a long time. This question has not arisen in Germany and Sweden, which do not possess exam boards. Special safeguards are often introduced to ensure that comparability is ensured at the trouble spots. E.g., in admittance to German higher education, the die *Zentralstelle für die Vergabe von Studienplätzen* (ZVS) has used different procedures to try and balance out differences between federal states in admitting students to university.[57] In England, the regulating body Ofqual is responsible for ensuring that exam boards apply comparable standards.

The fact that discussions about fairness often focus on these trouble spots sometimes deflects attention from other areas where problems of comparability are at least as grave as at the trouble spots. E.g., when the possibilities of choosing exam subjects were widened massively in Germany in the upper classes of upper secondary schooling in the so-called *Oberstufenreform*, massive problems concerning the comparability of *Abitur*-grades arose: Can a good grade in Maths be seen as equivalent to a good grade in Arts? These problems were not unknown to educational administrators at the time,[58] and pupils, too, tended to be aware of the fact that different combinations of subjects were regarded as 'softer' than others. Still, these problems of comparability did not lead to a massive scandalisation and the introduction of special safeguards.

Generally speaking, it is possible to say that if the same qualification (such as the *Abitur* or A-levels) is offered by different institutions (e.g. different federal states or different exam boards), this often leads to the perception that there is a

---

56 Arnold J. Heidenheimer, *Disparate Ladders: Why School and University Policies Differ in Germany, Japan, and Switzerland* (New Brunswick, N.J.: Transaction Publishers, 1997), 76, 121.

57 Sebastian Braun and Nadja Dwenger, "Success in the University Admission Process in Germany: Regional Provenance Matters," DIW, accessed January 15, 2016, http://www.diw.de/documents/publikationen/73/83278/dp789.pdf.

58 Abteilung Gymnasium Staatsinstitut für Schulpädagogik, *Handreichungen für die Leistungsmessung in der Kollegstufe* (München: Staatsinstitut für Schulpädagogik, 1974).

problem of comparability. These problems are treated (if not solved) by special bodies such as the ZVS and Ofqual.

Pupils' role in assessment

In all three countries, pupils are to be informed about the criteria according to which they are going to be assessed, but are not supposed to have an active part in the act of assessing themselves and their peers or the formulation of the criteria on the basis of which assessment is to be carried out. Before the most recent reform of the assessment system, Swedish pupils were supposed to have a say in how the (very general) goals stipulated in the curriculum documents were to be "translated" into concrete (and school-specific) goals and grade criteria. As concrete grade criteria are no longer supposed to be school-specific, this is no longer the case.

Thus, none of the three countries breaks the (unwritten) rule that (summative) pupil assessment as a rule should not be carried out by the pupil him- or herself or by his or her peers. This is less natural than it may seem at first glance, as it has been shown that in some situations a pupil's peers are in a particularly good position to assess a pupil's knowledge and skills.[59]

Related to the question in how far pupils are to have a say in the assessment process is the question whether it is possible to appeal against assessments once they have been made, a question that for reasons of space cannot be discussed here and that has been treated more fully elsewhere.[60]

The addressee(s) of fairness

Fairness in assessment concerns first and foremost those who are affected most strongly by assessment, i.e. the pupils that are assessed and, more indirectly, their parents. However, due to the importance of pupil assessment for the allocation of life chances in systems subscribing to the meritocratic myth, fairness in assessment is a concern that affects the society as a whole. If assessment systems are not perceived as fair, ultimately the legitimacy of the whole allocation of differential life chances and the justification of social inequality is at stake.

In this way, the 'addressees' of the attempts to make assessment systems (appear) fair go beyond the circle of those directly affected by assessment. There is

---

59 See Deutsch, "Education and Distributive Justice," 395.
60 See Waldow, "Conceptions of Justice in the Examination Systems of England, Germany and Sweden."

a strong symbolic component here that is bound up with wider concerns about the legitimacy of the order of society as a whole.

The degree to which the general public is seen as an addressee of fairness in assessment differs markedly in the three countries studied here. The English regulations stress again and again that the actors carrying out educational assessment need to make sure to keep public confidence in the system intact. This is not stressed to the same degree in the German and Swedish regulations. Especially in Germany, the addressees of fairness in assessment are mainly individual pupils and their parents.

One possible explanation for these differences (that, however, would need more empirical substantiation and therefore at this point in time has to be treated as a hypothesis) is the different degree to which the myth of "accountability" has permeated the various education systems.[61] England and Germany, respectively, mark the two extremes here among the countries studied in this chapter. The English education system relies very strongly on accountability as a steering mechanism. Schools' operations and output are supposed to be very transparent in the sense that a large amount of data, especially on performance, is produced. A school inspection regime exists that has very strong sanctions at its disposal.[62] One important, if not the most important, indicator on which schools are judged is pupil performance, leading to massive washback effects for schools. Germany, on the other hand, is still strongly characterised by the tradition of "process control",[63] with comparatively little control of 'product' (although this may be slowly changing) and weak accountability of schools for their output. School inspectors do not have access to powerful sanctions to punish 'underperforming' schools like their English colleagues do. Sweden occupies a middle ground between Germany and England, with stronger accountability and a more powerful school inspectorate than the German system, but less accountability and a weaker inspectorate than in England.

---

61 See Michael Power, *The Audit Society: Rituals of Verification* (Oxford: Oxford University Press, 1997).

62 Fanny Oehme, "Konzeptionen 'gerechter Schulinspektion' aus einer institutionen- und einstellungsanalytischen Perspektive: Ein Blick nach England," in *Zur Gerechtigkeit von Schule*, ed. Veronika Manitius, Björn Hermstein, and Nils Berkemeyer (Münster: Waxmann, 2015).

63 Stefan Thomas Hopmann, "On the Evaluation of Curriculum Reforms," *Journal of curriculum studies* 35, no. 4 (2003).

Conclusion: Fairness in assessment and pupil assessment cultures

Summary: Fairness and different constellations of actors in the three countries

This chapter has started from the premise that in the institutional 'blueprints' or 'logics' of assessment systems, certain conceptions of fairness are embedded. The chapter has focused on one aspect of these institutional logics, the conceptions of fairness embedded in the constellations of actors. It has become apparent that the teachers' role and conceptions of teacher professionalism are key issues in this context, as the rules governing teacher professionalism (including the unwritten ones) are a key element of the institutional logics of any educational system.[64]

In Germany, pupil assessment is still mostly grounded in a non-explicit professional practice teachers are socialised into during their training and through their school practice. Despite the introduction of centralised tests and exams, the individual teacher is still key actor when it comes to safeguarding the fairness of assessment.

In Sweden, pupil assessment appears — at least if we look at the intended 'institutional logics' of the system — as a practice whose basis is made more explicit. Compared to Germany, pupil assessment is to be grounded more in scientific rationality in the sense of psychological diagnostics (which, in turn, generates a number of different problems of its own). The national tests produced by the National Agency of Education are an important safeguard of fairness in assessment, possessing a strong symbolic function (see below). So, individual teachers play the key role for pupil assessment, but their activity is heavily framed by the tests and materials provided by National Agency of Education.

In England, the key actors for pupil assessment of the type this chapter is interested in are not internal to the school, but external: the examination boards. Rational, psychometric methods and statistical knowledge gained from previous examinations are important for awarding decisions. Teachers coach their pupils, but are not responsible for the examining.

---

64 Ian Grosvenor and Martin Lawn, "'This is Who We Are and This Is What We Do': Teacher Identity and Teacher Work in Mid-Twentieth Century English Educational Discourse," *Pedagogy, Culture & Society* 9, no. 3 (2001).

Wider constellations of actors

This chapter has discussed the main actors in the field of pupil assessment and their constellations in different education systems: teachers, pupils, bodies external to the school such as exam boards or national agencies of education, partly the general public. It should be noted that these groups of actors and their constellations are woven into larger constellations of actors, which also impact the institutional logics of assessment systems, but which could not be discussed in this chapter for reasons of space. Among the actors not discussed here are employers and educational institutions such as universities. Especially in a system in which *entrance* exams rather than *exit* exams play an important role, such as the English one, university admittance procedures have massive washback effects on pupil assessment.[65] Another group of actors that could only be touched upon is the parents.

Actors' perceptions vs. "institutional logics"

This chapter has analysed an aspect of the conceptions of fairness embedded in the institutional 'blueprints' or 'logics' of assessment cultures. These conceptions are not necessarily in accordance (or even in harmony) with the conceptions of justice held by different (groups of) actors.

This chapter was written in the context of an ongoing project studying not only the "institutional logics" of assessment systems, but also the conceptions of fairness held by crucial groups of actors, i.e. teachers, pupils and school inspectors.[66] Already at this point in time, it is possible to see that actors' conceptions and beliefs about fairness are *framed*, but not wholly *determined* by the conceptions embedded in regulatory systems. The conceptions of fairness embedded in the institutional logics including the constellations of actors are connected to the conceptions of fairness of actors, but often there is considerable tension between the two.[67]

---

65 Baird, "Country-case study: England."
66 The project has the title "Different worlds of meritocracy? Educational assessment and conceptions of justice in Germany, Sweden and England in the age of 'standards-based reform'", is financed by the German Research Foundation and is based at Humboldt University, Berlin. See https://www.erziehungswissenschaften.hu-berlin.de/en/vew-en/forschung/unterschiedliche-welten-der-meritokratie?set_language=en.
67 Kathleen Falkenberg, Bettina Vogt and Florian Waldow. "Ständig geprüft oder kontinuierlich unterstützt? Schulische Leistungsbeurteilung in Schweden zwischen formativem Anspruch und summativer Notwendigkeit." *Zeitschrift für Pädagogik* 63, no. 3: 317–33.

Assessment cultures as symbolic orders

According to Barbara Stollberg-Rilinger, any institutional order needs "symbolic-ritualistic embodiments" (*symbolisch-rituelle Verkörperungen*) and is based on shared myths.[68] Pupil assessment cultures are no exception; they, too, possess elements that function as symbolic safeguards of fair assessment and buttress the assessment system's legitimacy. Thus, pupil assessment cultures are partly symbolic orders, and this includes aspects of the constellations of actors involved in assessment. Elements of assessment cultures with high symbolic content are e.g. the national tests in Sweden or external examinations in England.

The "symbolic-ritualistic embodiments" of a meritocratic system of assessment do not necessarily have to be spectacular and conspicuous in any way, even though they can be. Under "normal" operational conditions, an assessment system is supposed to produce assessments with a minimum of friction and noise; most of the time, the question whether assessments are fair is not even asked.[69] This is the actual function of such an institutional and symbolic order: it stabilises expectations concerning behaviour and collective sense-making processes and in this way makes sure that not every operation of the system has to be checked for its legitimacy and fairness. In this way, the symbolic order ensures the (mostly) friction- and noiseless working of assessment systems by stabilising and making plausible existing institutions.

One meritocratic myth — different meritocracies

It has become clear that there are considerable differences between the conceptions of fairness embedded in pupil assessment systems. Despite attempts at reform, these differences are often quite stable over time and can only be understood against the backdrop of the history of the systems in question. Which forms of assessment are seen as legitimate depends strongly on the cultural context and cannot be reduced to the question of the diagnostic quality of pupil assessment from a psychometric perspective.[70] Assessment cultures develop in strongly

---

68 Barbara Stollberg-Rilinger, *Des Kaisers alte Kleider: Verfassungsgeschichte und Symbolsprache des Alten Reiches* (München: C. H. Beck, 2008), 9.

69 See Terhart, "Zensurengebung und innerschulisches Selektionsklima – die Rolle der Schulleitung," 290.

70 See Ewald Terhart, "Giving Marks: Constructing Differences: Explorations in the Micro-Politics of Selection in Schools," in *Gleichheit und Gerechtigkeit: Pädagogische Revisionen*, ed. Heiner Drerup and Werner Fölling (Dresden: TUDpress, 2006), 123.

path-dependent ways, and at the end of the day, every conception of fairness is a cultural and political construct, i.e. has — explicitly or implicitly — been *agreed* on by those concerned.[71]

For the legitimacy of the allocation of life chances in a given education system and the pupil assessment connected to it, the quality of assessment according to purely scientific criteria is of secondary importance. Crucial, on the other hand, is whether the system is *accepted* by those affected by it; and as we have seen, systems of assessment ultimately affect the whole population. What counts as fair can therefore not be determined independently of the specific conceptions of justice particular to a certain system or a certain group of actors.[72]

In sum, educational systems in Western democracies may share adherence to the common meritocratic myth, but their isomorphism probably ends at a fairly high level of abstraction. The shared myth does not lead to identical pupil assessment cultures. What 'meritocracy' is supposed to mean depends heavily on where you look and whom you ask.

Literature

Accredited Qualifications. "Accredited Qualifications." Accessed October 19, 2015. http://www.accreditedqualifications.org.uk/qualification-types-in-the-uk.html.

Andersson, Håkan. *Relativa betyg: Några empiriska studier och en teoretisk genomgång i ett historiskt perspektiv*, Akademiska avhandlingar vid Pedagogiska Institutionen, Umeå universitet, 29. Umeå: Universität, 1991.

Avenarius, Hermann. "Welche Rechte und Pflichten haben Lehrkräfte, Schulleitungen und Schulaufsicht bei der Qualitätsentwicklung der Schulen und bei der Sicherung gleicher Lebenschancen?" *DIPF informiert*, no. 4 (2003): 9–15.

Baird, Jo-Anne. "Country-Case Study: England." In *Secondary School External Examination Systems: Reliability, Robustness and Resilience*, edited by Barend Vlaardingerbroek and Neil Taylor, 29–54. Amherst, NY: Cambria, 2009.

Baker, David P., and Gerald K. LeTendre. *National Differences, Global Similarities: World Culture and the Future of Schooling*. Stanford, CA: Stanford University Press, 2005.

---

71 Bernd Wegener, "Auf dem Weg zur Interdisziplinarität in der sozialen Gerechtigkeitsforschung? Anmerkungen zu Scherer, Elster, Rawls und Walzer," *Berliner Journal für Soziologie* 5 (1995).

72 See Black and Wiliam, "Lessons from around the World."

Becker, Rolf, and Alexander Schulze. "Kontextuelle Perspektiven ungleicher Bildungschancen – Eine Einführung." In Bildungskontexte, edited by Rolf Becker and Alexander Schulze, 1–30. Wiesbaden: Springer, 2013.

Black, Paul, and Dylan Wiliam. "Lessons from around the World: How Policies, Politics and Cultures Constrain and Afford Assessment Practices." Curriculum Journal 16, no. 2 (2005): 249–61. doi: 10.1080/09585170500136218.

Braun, Sebastian, and Nadja Dwenger. "Success in the University Admission Process in Germany: Regional Provenance Matters." DIW. Accessed January 15, 2016. http://www.diw.de/documents/publikationen/73/83278/dp789.pdf.

Broadfoot, Patricia, Marilyn Osborn, M. Gilly, and A. Paillet. "What Professional Responsibility Means to Teachers: National Contexts and Classroom Constants." British Journal of Sociology of Education 9, no. 3 (1988): 265–87.

Deutsch, Morton. "Education and Distributive Justice – Some Reflections on Grading Systems." American Psychologist 34, no. 5 (1979): 391–401.

Falkenberg, Kathleen, Bettina Vogt, and Florian Waldow. "Ständig geprüft oder kontinuierlich unterstützt? Schulische Leistungsbeurteilung in Schweden zwischen formativem Anspruch und summativer Notwendigkeit." Zeitschrift für Pädagogik 63, no. 3: 317–33.

Falkenberg, Monika, and Herbert Kalthoff. "Das Feld der Bildung: Schulische Institutionen, Schulbevölkerung und gesellschaftliche Integration." In Lehr(er) Buch Soziologie: Für die pädagogischen und soziologischen Studiengänge, edited by Herbert Willems, 797–816. Wiesbaden: VS Verlag für Sozialwissenschaften, 2008.

Fend, Helmut. Schule gestalten: Systemsteuerung, Schulentwicklung und Unterrichtsqualität. Wiesbaden: VS Verlag für Sozialwissenschaften, 2008.

Giesinger, Johannes. "Was heißt Bildungsgerechtigkeit?" Zeitschrift für Pädagogik 53, no. 3 (2007): 362–81.

Goldstein, Harvey, and Toby Lewis. "The Scope of Assessment." In Assessment: Problems, Developments, and Statistical Issues: A Volume of Expert Contributions, edited by Harvey Goldstein and Toby Lewis, 1–7. Chichester: Wiley, 1996.

Grosvenor, Ian, and Martin Lawn. "'This Is Who We Are and This Is What We Do': Teacher Identity and Teacher Work in Mid-Twentieth Century English Educational Discourse." Pedagogy, Culture & Society 9, no. 3 (2001): 355–70.

Heidenheimer, Arnold J. Disparate Ladders: Why School and University Policies Differ in Germany, Japan, and Switzerland. New Brunswick, N.J.: Transaction Publishers, 1997.

Helbig, Marcel, and *Rita Nikolai. Die Unvergleichbaren: Der Wandel der Schulsysteme in den deutschen Bundesländern seit 1949.* Bad Heilbrunn: Klinkhardt, 2015.

Hopmann, Stefan Thomas. "On the Evaluation of Curriculum Reforms." *Journal of Curriculum Studies* 35, no. 4 (2003): 459–78.

Ingenkamp, Karlheinz, ed. *Die Fragwürdigkeit der Zensurengebung: Texte und Untersuchungsberichte.* Weinheim: Beltz, 1989.

Isaacs, Tina. "Educational Assessment in England." *Assessment in Education: Principles, Policy & Practice* 17, no. 3 (2010): 315–34.

Klein, Esther D., Svenja M. Kühn, Isabell van Ackeren, and Rainer Block. "Wie zentral sind zentrale Prüfungen? Abschlussprüfungen am Ende der Sekundarstufe II im nationalen und internationalen Vergleich." *Zeitschrift für Pädagogik* 55, no. 4 (2009): 596–621.

Köller, Olaf. "Bildungsstandards." In *Handbuch Bildungsforschung,* edited by Rudolf Tippelt and Bernhard Schmidt, 529–48. Wiesbaden: VS Verlag für Sozialwissenschaften, 2009.

Korp, Helena. Lika chanser i gymnasiet? En studie om betyg, nationella prov och social reproduktion. Malmö: Holmbergs, 2006.

Kühn, Svenja Mareike. Steuerung und Innovation durch Abschlussprüfungen? Wiesbaden: VS Verlag für Sozialwissenschaften, 2010.

Kultusministerkonferenz. "Abkommen zwischen den Ländern der Bundesrepublik zur Vereinheitlichung auf dem Gebiete des Schulwesens (vom 28.10.1964 in der Fassung vom 14.10.1971)." Accessed September 3, 2015. http://www.kmk.org/ fileadmin/veroeffentlichungen_beschluesse/1964/1964_10_28_Hamburger _Abkommen.pdf.

–. "Gesamtstrategie der Kultusministerkonferenz zum Bildungsmonitoring: Beschluss der 350. Kultusministerkonferenz vom 11.06.2015." Berlin: Kultusministerkonferenz, 2015.

–. "Überblick: Gesamtstrategie Zum Bildungsmonitoring." Accessed September 3, 2015. http://www.kmk.org/bildung-schule/qualitaetssicherung-in-schulen/bil dungsmonitoring/ueberblick-gesamtstrategie-zum-bildungsmonitoring.html.

Leventhal, Gerald S. "What Should Be Done with Equity Theory? New Approaches to the Study of Fairness in Social Relationships." In *Social Exchange: Advances in Theory and Research,* edited by Kenneth J. Gergen, Martin S. Greenberg and Richard H. Willis, 27–55. New York, NY: Plenum Press, 1980.

Leventhal, Gerald S., Jurgis Karuza jr., and William Rick Fry. "Beyond Fairness: A Theory of Allocation Preferences." In *Justice and Social Interaction: Experimental and Theoretical Contributions from Psychological Research,* edited by Gerold Mikula, 167–218. Bern: Hans Huber, 1980.

Liebig, Stefan. "Soziale Gerechtigkeit — Modelle und Befunde der soziologischen Gerechtigkeitsforschung." In *Fachgespräch Gerechtigkeit*, edited by Otfried Höffe, Stefan Liebig and Bernd von Maydell, 23–44. Berlin: Berlin-Brandenburgische Akademie der Wissenschaften, 2006.

Lundahl, Christian. Varför nationella prov? Framväxt, dilemman, möjligheter. Stockholm: Skolverket, 2009.

–. *Viljan att veta vad andra vet: Kunskapsbedömning i tidigmodern, modern och senmodern skola.* Arbetsliv i omvandling 2006:8. Stockholm: Arbetslivsinstitutet, 2006.

Maier, Uwe. Wie gehen Lehrerinnen und Lehrer mit Vergleichsarbeiten um? Eine Studie zu testbasierten Schulreformen in Baden-Württemberg und Thüringen. Baltmannsweiler: Schneider Verlag Hohengehren, 2009.

Newton, Paul E. "Making Sense of Decades of Debate on Inter-Subject Comparability in England," *Assessment in Education: Principles, Policy & Practice* 19, no. 2 (2012): 251–273. doi: 10.1080/0969594X.2011.563357.

Nisbet, Isabel, and Alan Greig. "Educational Qualifications Regulation." In *Centre for the Study of Regulated Industries (Cri) Regulatory Review 2006/2007*, edited by P. Vass, 49–69. Bath, UK: CRI, 2007.

Oehme, Fanny. "Konzeptionen 'gerechter Schulinspektion' aus einer institutionen- und einstellungsanalytischen Perspektive: Ein Blick nach England." In *Zur Gerechtigkeit Von Schule*, edited by Veronika Manitius, Björn Hermstein and Nils Berkemeyer, 291–315. Münster: Waxmann, 2015.

Power, Michael. The Audit Society: Rituals of Verification. Oxford, UK: Oxford University Press, 1997.

Rheinberg, Falko. "Bezugsnormen und schulische Leistungsbeurteilung." In *Leistungsmessungen in Schulen*, edited by Franz E. Weinert, 59–71. Weinheim: Beltz, 2002.

Richter, Dirk, Katrin Böhme, Michael Becker, Hans Anand Pant, and Petra Stanat. "Überzeugungen von Lehrkräften zu den Funktionen von Vergleichsarbeiten. Zusammenhänge zu Veränderungen im Unterricht und den Kompetenzen von Schülerinnen und Schülern." *Zeitschrift für Pädagogik* 60, no. 2 (2014): 225–44.

Richter, Ingo. Recht im Bildungssystem: Eine Einführung, Grundriss der Pädagogik/ Erziehungswissenschaft 23. Stuttgart: Kohlhammer, 2006.

Robinson, Colin. "Awarding Examination Grades: Current Processes and Their Evolution." In *Techniques for Monitoring the Comparability of Examination Standards*, edited by Paul Newton, Jo-Anne Baird, Harry Goldstein, Helen Patrick and Peter Tymms, 97–123. London, UK: Qualifications and Curriculum Authority, 2007.

Skolöverstyrelsen. Läroplan för grundskolan. Stockholm: Skolöverstyrelsen, 1962.

Skolverket. "Bedömningsportalen." Accessed August 3, 2015. https://bp. skolverket.se/.

–. "Nationella prov." Skolverket. Accessed August 8, 2015. http://www.skolverket. se/bedomning/nationella-prov.

–. *Provbetyg-slutbetyg-likvärdig bedömning? En statistisk analys av sambandet mellan nationella prov och slutbetyg i grundskolans årskurs 9, 1998–2006.* Skolverkets rapport 300. Stockholm: Skolverket, 2007.

Solga, Heike. "Meritokratie — Die moderne Legitimation ungleicher Bildungschancen." In *Institutionalisierte Ungleichheiten: Wie das Bildungswesen Chancen blockiert*, edited by Peter A. Berger and Heike Kahlert, 19–38. Weinheim: Juventa, 2005.

Staatsinstitut für Schulpädagogik, Abteilung Gymnasium. Handreichungen für die Leistungsmessung in der Kollegstufe. München: Staatsinstitut für Schulpädagogik, 1974.

Stewart, William. "Poll Backs Merger to Create Single Exam Board." *TES*, May 14, 2010.

Stollberg-Rilinger, Barbara. *Des Kaisers alte Kleider: Verfassungsgeschichte und Symbolsprache des Alten Reiches.* München: C. H. Beck, 2008.

Struck, Olaf. "Gatekeeping zwischen Individuum, Organisation und Institution: Zur Bedeutung und Analyse von Gatekeeping am Beispiel von Übergängen im Lebensverlauf." In *Institutionen und Lebensläufe im Wandel: Institutionelle Regulierungen von Lebensläufen*, edited by Lutz Leisering, Rainer Müller and Karl F. Schumann, 29–54. Weinheim: Juventa, 2001.

Tattersall, Katherine. "A Brief History of Policies, Practices and Issues Relating to Comparability." In *Techniques for Monitoring the Comparability of Examination Standards*, edited by Paul Newton, Jo-Anne Baird, Harry Goldstein, Helen Patrick and Peter Tymms, 42–96. London, UK: Qualifications and Curriculum Authority, 2007.

Terhart, Ewald. "Giving Marks: Constructing Differences: Explorations in the Micro-Politics of Selection in Schools." In *Gleichheit und Gerechtigkeit: Pädagogische Revisionen*, edited by Heiner Drerup and Werner Fölling, 114–25. Dresden: TUDpress, 2006.

–. "Lehrerberuf und Professionalität: Wandel der Begrifflichkeit – Neue Herausforderungen." In *Pädagogische Professionalität*, edited by Werner Helsper and Rudolf Tippelt, 20–24. Weinheim: Beltz, 2011.

–. "Zensurengebung und innerschulisches Selektionsklima – Die Rolle der Schulleitung." *Zeitschrift für Soziologie der Erziehung und Sozialisation* 19, no. 3 (1999): 277–92.

The Student Room. "Edexcel vs Cambridge (OCR/CIE), Which One Is Tougher?" Accessed September 3, 2015. http://www.thestudentroom.co.uk/showthread. php?t=547887.

Tilly, Charles. Big Structures, Large Processes, Huge Comparisons. New York: Russell Sage Foundation, 1984.

van Ackeren, Isabell, and *Gabriele Bellenberg.* "Parallelarbeiten, Vergleichsarbeiten und zentrale Abschlussprüfungen: Bestandsaufnahme und Perspektiven." *Jahrbuch der Schulentwicklung,* no. 13 (2004): 125–59.

Waldow, Florian. "Conceptions of Justice in the Examination Systems of England, Germany and Sweden: A Look at Safeguards of Fair Procedure and Possibilities of Appeal." *Comparative Education Review* 58, no. 2 (2014): 322–43. doi: 10.1086/674781.

–. "Die internationale Konjunktur standardisierter Messungen von Schülerleistung in der ersten Hälfte des 20. Jahrhunderts und ihr Niederschlag in Deutschland und Schweden." *Jahrbuch für Pädagogik* 21 (2010): 75–86.

Wegener, Bernd. "Auf dem Weg zur Interdisziplinarität in der sozialen Gerechtigkeitsforschung? Anmerkungen zu Scherer, Elster, Rawls und Walzer." *Berliner Journal für Soziologie* 5 (1995): 251–64.

West, Anne, and *Rita Nikolai.* "Welfare Regimes and Education Regimes: Equality of Opportunity and Expenditure in the EU (and US)." *Journal of Social Policy* 42, no. 3 (2013): 469–93. doi: 10.1017/S0047279412001043.

Young, Michael. The Rise of the Meritocracy, 1870–2033: An Essay on Education and Equality. London, UK: Thames & Hudson, 1958.

Zymek, Bernd. "Auslese und Selbsteliminierung. Die Gymnasien zwischen elitärem Selbstanspruch und Multifunktionalität, 1945–1970." *Zeitschrift für Pädagogik* 61, no. 1 (2015): 8–23.

Alicia Méndez

The Place of the Entrance Assessment in the Building of a Meritocratic Career Path in Argentina, 1863–2013

In the meetings and in the papers where Latin American scholars discuss the process of formation of educational elites, any attempt to classify and systematize the schools for the privileged runs up against 'the case' of a paradigmatic Argentinian institution: the *Colegio Nacional de Buenos Aires* (*CNBA*); *El Colegio* (the school).[1] The difficulty in including this institution in a series, either with other Latin American or other Argentinian 'cases', resides mainly in the singularity of its entrance system and its assessment culture.

El Colegio, as it is known among its students, was founded in the civic, religious and economic centre of Buenos Aires by Bartolomé Mitre, a politician, military, historian and translator that as president embodied *porteño*[2] interests and fostered a state project — that accounts for the existence of this school — to educate future 'government men'[3] and the nation itself: "A modern, Western, republican and democratic nation, with an advanced economy."[4] The creation of the *CNBA* was part of the decisive impulse for the development of a local secondary public education system given by the decree for the creation of national schools in several provincial capitals in 1863.[5] The first of these schools, founded that same year, was, effectively, the *CNBA*.

---

1   It is frequent to hear *CNBA* graduates from different periods in its history refer to their *Colegio* as 'the' *Colegio*; the one that has been for many years 'the centre of Argentinian culture', 'the school of the nation', 'the best and the worst', according to its alumni's accounts.

2   This term refers to the dwellers of the City of Buenos Aires and has been coined because of the city's proximity to the port, one of the main communication and exchange channels between Argentina and the World.

3   Juan Álvarez, *Las guerras civiles argentinas y el problema de Buenos Aires en la República* (Buenos Aires: La Facultad, 1936).

4   Tulio Halperin Donghi 'Interview' in Roy Hora and Javier Trímboli, *Pensar la Argentina: los historiadores hablan de historia y política* (Buenos Aires: El cielo por asalto, 1994), 54.

5   Inés Dussel, *Currículum, humanismo y democracia en la enseñanza media*, 1863–1920 (Buenos Aires: Eudeba, 1997).

The core ideology of the founders of the *CNBA* was not that of the *pampa*, but that of a European non-Hispanic cultural beacon: French culture. Its distinctive sign, a high valuation on merit, was the means to establish, at least on an aspirational level, an affiliation to French tradition, since merit and ability were enshrined in liberal tradition when inscribed in the Declaration of the Rights of Man. Throughout Argentine's turbulent history, the *CNBA* remained a reference for youth education: it trained a small number of noteworthy representatives of the public and private top administration, liberal professions, the sciences and the arts who contributed to maintain the school's prestige with their professional achievements. This saga began with the *Generation of 1880*, many of whose members constituted the first graduating class, "the vegetal layer of this country," those who "fill the parliament, the press, the forum, hold professorships, set ideas in motion," according to Paul Groussac.[6]

People who are not necessarily former students of the Bolívar street institution concur in a valuation of the school that situates it at the very heart of our national identity. This view is grounded in the testimonies of important figures in the political and cultural life of the last century. These people, among who there are teachers, authorities, parents of students, alumni, refer to it) in an 'egalitarian' society — in a mundane sense of the word. The student body between the end of the nineteenth century and the 1930s was socially quite heterogeneous. It comprised children from traditional and influential families but the majority of students were of immigrant origin. Progressively these families became middle-class and constituted the most important social group in the school alongside a few children either from very wealthy or very humble homes.

In this work we aim to show the entrance process to the *CNBA*, its changes throughout the institutional history of the school, and its elements in common with other elite schools and other national schools. We intend to consider whether it is possible to speak of an assessment culture in this school and to seek similar features in the wider Argentinian assessment culture.

This article arises from a research in which field observations were made and over fifty interviews were conducted with the aim of documenting the social

---

6   Paul Groussac goes on: "(the men who) set ideas and capitals in motion, who act today in the height of development; head, hart and arm of Argentinian people" (quoted in Martín García Mérou, *Recuerdos literarios* (Buenos Aires: Eudeba, 1973), 317). Groussac was a young French adventurer who arrived in Argentina with no other education than an incomplete course at a military academy and there became director of the National Library. He was able to characterize the Generation of 1880 from a perspective that combined personal acquaintance and evaluating distance in optimal proportions.

origin and sociability of *CNBA* alumni. It is also based on the analysis of autobiographies, a prosopographic study and the analysis of socio-demographic data that was borrowed from a study that includes *CNBA* student records spanning from 1897 to 1999. Furthermore, it is based on twelve samples (comprising 773 entering students chosen at random) from two non-consecutive years every twenty years. Their results are gathered in a book called: *El Colegio. La formación de una elite meritocrática en el Nacional Buenos Aires.*

Many different modalities of admission were implemented at the *CNBA* throughout its history. These changes reflected the weakness of Argentinian school autonomy from institutional discontinuities, political-ideological confrontations, and changes in educational doctrines. Firstly, we will situate the *CNBA* admission culture in the context of examination modalities, both in the Argentinian system of secondary education and in the different configurations that compose the elite-formation system in Buenos Aires city and in Buenos Aires province in particular. Then we will describe the *CNBA* entrance process in detail, examining its long-term effects, to delve, lastly, into the specifics of the assessment culture at the *CNBA*.

The *CNBA* entrance process

In an Argentinean context which favours the abolishment of entrance examinations for admission to secondary school, the *CNBA* uses a very strict supervised selection process; a transitional moment narrated by its actors (people between 80 and 13 years old) in terms of 'rigor and effort.' In this rigor and this effort lies the perception, shared by *CNBA* alumni at any moment in the history of the school, that they belong to an institution in which the leading moral principle is merit. In analytical terms, they constitute a meritocracy; an expression that has entered everyday language in the last four or five years.

In the training system for Argentine elites, the *CNBA* is part of one of the different institutional configurations serving different audiences. Until the mid-1980s, the education system could be understood as an integrated field, in which elite institutions constituted a series of segments. Since the so-called Crisis of 2001, any reference to it as a whole or to a central entity that coordinates its various actors and institutions seems to have vanished. Thus, Guillermina Tiramonti prefers to speak of "fragments" which, as we will see, use very different styles and criteria to evaluate and select their students.[7] There are schools that "educate

---

7   Guillermina Tiramonti, "De los segmentos a los fragmentos. La nueva configuración del sistema educativo." Accessed July 24, 2011. http://www.bnm.me.gov.ar/giga1/documentos/EL001242.pdf.

for competition," schools that "educate in and for the conservation of Christian values" and schools that educate for "intellectual distinction."[8] The first two ideal types include private schools and the last type includes only state-funded schools, the so-called university schools. Thus, it must be noted that in Argentina, contrary to other countries, the dividing line is not between private and state schools but between state and private schools for the poor, and those, state or private, that target the narrow strip of the most privileged social sectors.[9]

In schools that 'educate in and for the conservation of Christian values,' schools themselves foster ties between families and school through their admission procedures: priority is given not only to siblings of current students, but also to anyone with relatives who were former students of the institution. The student selection process takes a year. Candidates must first submit a form including information about their parents, the schools they attended, their surnames and their current job positions as well as a photo of the family and data regarding the children. At a second stage, adults are evaluated through a personal interview. Finally, children must take examinations in English, language and maths, as well as a psycho-educational test. It is only at the end of the year that families will receive a letter informing them whether their application was accepted or not. Justification of the final decision is never made public. Some institutions request the payment of an admissions fee when initiating primary school. This membership creates cohesion among the families 'that belong.'[10] The process is quite similar in 'schools that educate for competition', where the examination is not a critical instance and, in general, what decides admission is the interview, which evaluates mainly non-academic aspects.

In the entrance process to the *CNBA* the examination is definitely a critical instance and there is not an interview with the candidate's family. However, it has not always been like this; at some moments in the past, the student's family relations were very important and the instance of evaluation was not as demanding as it would be decades later; at other moments, the interview led the selection process; and, for a short period in the mid-1970s, there was no entrance examination at all.

---

8   Sandra Ziegler, "La escolarización de las elites: un acercamiento a la socialización de los jóvenes de sectores favorecidos en la Argentina actual", in *La Trama de la Desigualdad Educativa. Mutaciones Recientes de la Escuela Media,* ed. Guillermina Tiramonti (Buenos Aires: Manantiales, 2004), 73–77.

9   María Rosa Neufeld and Jens A. Thisted, "Investigadores implicados: la investigación educativa en espacios barriales de la ciudad de Buenos Aires" (Paper presented at the VI Reunión de Antropología del Mercosur. Montevideo, 2005).

10 Ziegler, "La escolarización de las elites," 46.

Since 1957 there has been a compulsory entrance procedure for all the applicants to the *CNBA*. All of them are awarded the same diploma upon leaving school and, despite being considered an 'elite school,' nobody is granted access to a higher position in professional life for being an 'ex-*CNBA*,' since there is no acknowledged formal system or institutional circuit set to this end; which does not mean they do not reach those positions for their intellectual ability, for being part of alumni informal networks, or for having learned how to do it from older former students with successful careers, among other possibilities.

When there was a discretionary regime to enter the *CNBA*, for example, between 1924 and 1941, this condition introduced a double status among students; those in the first class, the ones who "entered through the window," "the apple of the principal's eyes," were assigned the best teachers.[11] Both the teachers and the students considered themselves privileged to be part of this 'elite within the elite,' because it implied that they had family resources in the field of interpersonal relations. People who could spare their child or a family friend's child the experience of the examination were normally teachers at the *Colegio*, although it could also be the owner of the bookstore opposite the school or a messenger of the Pope who played the role. In spite of having enjoyed a prestigious position gained from their social origin during school socialisation, some of these former students felt embarrassed, during our research interview, to admit in front of a stranger that they had been spared the entrance examination. In fact, it was difficult to find someone among the people who graduated before 1957 who was willing to admit, either in public or in private, that they "wangled their way onto *el Colegio*."[12] This reluctance goes hand in hand with their concern for the point of view of the wider society regarding the legitimacy of individual effort as part of the assessment culture at the *CNBA*. This concern was very explicit in people who were presenting their school, the *CNBA*, to a 'non-ex-*CNBA*' like this researcher.

It was the military who seized power in 1955 that made the changes which led to the implementation of a compulsory entrance examination to the *CNBA*. It was a written examination, to be taken on two successive days: two examination papers of two hours each. The examination was divided into four parts: Mathematics, Geography, Language and History. Each student would prepare for it on his/her own. In the following thirty years, many changes were made to

---

11 Many of the interviews with graduate students conducted between 2004 and 2010 in Buenos Aires have similar accounts of this.

12 This was the way other interviewees referred to the fact of having been exempt from the exam. Sometimes they referred to it by saying that someone 'entered through the window.'

this admission process. For instance, towards the end of 1973, as a result of an agreement between the authorities, the students and some teachers, a draw was used as the only admission procedure. This was a short-lasting initiative that, in consonance with the atmosphere of the period, aimed to enable the admission of workers' children.[13]

In the *Colegio* from the mid-seventies, more precisely in the years spanning from the military coup in 1976 to the Malvinas Islands War, the intervening authorities appointed by the military government encouraged the admission of 'neighbourhood kids' to the detriment of that of children who came from traditional elite families. In order to narrow down the list of candidates they required an interview with the family. Apparently, they wanted to rule out students of humble origins and children of divorced parents or of parents with 'suspicious' occupations, linked in some way to a broad spectrum of the so called 'liberal ideas.' These included secularism, supporting the right to divorce, being on the moderate left in politics, all of which are usually associated, in Argentina, with university educated urban groups and people with some contact with higher education and the world of books. None of these characteristics is exclusive. Anyway, children of divorced, political and agnostic parents, who used to participate in the cultural world of the previous period and, in some cases, had to live in exile for a while during the dictatorship, were admitted in the *Colegio*. These families practiced for the entrance interview so that their behavior and body language would not give away their 'liberal' beliefs. The requirement of the interview has been abolished since the last democratic restoration (1983).

A *CNBA* graduate, who is a *Licenciada en Letras* (equivalent to a Master in Spanish and Literature) and holds a high position in the Argentinian offices of an important publishing house, remembers the crucial moment of the interview at the time when the criteria used by authorities in order to select their students did not have much to do with academic aspects.

"An amusing anecdote is that as part of the entrance process we had to have a meeting with the authorities and our parents — I think it was called a colloquy —, just for them to meet the family and evaluate us. My parents were divorced. It was common knowledge that children of divorced parents were unlikely to be admitted. So my parents, who hadn't talked to each other for years, had to get together to rehearse the *mise-en-scène*. It was funny, because, as they both had children of the same age with their new partners, we had to learn a false family structure. My father, who had been a very successful advertising executive as a young man, had by then given it all up to go on the stage. As we thought

---

13 Santiago Garaño and Werner Pertot, *La otra juvenilia. Militancia y represión en el Colegio Nacional de Buenos Aires, 1971-1986* (Buenos Aires: Biblos, 2002).

that acting would be considered a suspicious occupation, he pretended to be still directing Walter Thompson,[14] a post he had resigned ten years before. Actually, it was fun planning it all. Even then, at the moment of the meeting — which turned out perfectly well — it was *dantesque* being so terribly nervous — the whole entrance process is terrible pressure for a twelve-year-old child — and watching ourselves acting it all out."[15]

Since the restoration of democracy in 1983, the *Colegio* implemented a full-year preparatory course to be attended by students while they were completing their last year of primary school. In 1987 a new system was tried by which the examination was divided into several midterm examinations for each subject; since then, the course has been made compulsory. Apparently, this system aimed to offer equal opportunity to all candidates, regardless of social origin or financial situation. However, the majority of candidates still attend some institutes offering private preparation courses, and some of them even do it for two years, during their last two years of primary school. In some exceptional cases, candidates prepare on their own, or with their parents' or a tutor's help. These are usually outstanding students from outlying neighbourhoods whose primary school teachers have acted as informal recruiters.

For those who sat the single comprehensive examination given until 1987, the experience seems to have been, at least, unforgettable: students arrived at a place where everything was unfamiliar to them and, once seated, they had to wait until invigilators had counted all the candidates and handed out the examination papers. Since 1987 students are given several midterm examinations for each subject during the year (the number of which has varied with the years and according to each subject). Based on the resulting grade averages, the *Colegio* prepares what they call an *orden de mérito*.[16] Compared to the single comprehensive examination, this experience is more gradual and, certainly, easier to deal with: when they get to take their first examination, they find themselves surrounded by the familiar faces of their classmates at the *CNBA* compulsory course and, if they attend a private course — most of them do —, by those of their classmates at the institute. As the entrance year progresses, they familiarize themselves with the school premises and with the *Colegio* rules, which are very different from those of the wider society.

According to a teacher who worked in the *CNBA* entrance course, the influence of the private institutes is difficult to counteract. For example, the language

---

14 A prestigious advertising agency.
15 Interview in Buenos Aires, July 2016.
16 A list ranking the students according to their examination results from the highest to the lowest.

examination that has been given in the recent years at the *Colegio* consists of four parts: syntax analysis, a writing task — a story that includes a dialogue and finishes with a brief argumentation—, recognition of grammatical categories — in verbs and other parts of speech —, and reading comprehension. It is not, however, an examination that a student with good knowledge of primary school topics would be able to pass. The answer key was tabulated, and it was very difficult to write a 'correct' examination answer without having been trained on the best way to do this specific examination. In order to be successful, it was necessary to follow a particular strategy for text organisation, which is taught only at private institutes. "Each institute taught how to write with certain specific methods, which were quite detectable. One institute, for example, taught how to write stories beginning with minor sentences. What [the *CNBA*] teaches them is how to best meet the questions requirements, to speculate and, in short, to survive."[17]

Regardless of the preparation method employed, the examination remains a critical instance: around 45% of the applicants have been admitted in recent years.[18] A *CNBA* graduate, who is a Literature PhD and a professor at the *Universidad de Buenos Aires (UBA)*, remembers his experience of the examination when "you had to risk it all in two days", that is, before 1987:

> "You are surrounded by thirty guys you haven't met before, waiting for your examination. On a desk, a phrase was written: 'Belgrano[19] has been here.' It wasn't that you weren't aware that it hadn't been the founding father himself who had written the phrase; what was curious was that such a joke could be made. We had arrived at eight o'clock in the morning, each one of us with their number; you had to wait until everyone had entered and all of us had been counted which left you for one hour and a half in the company of thirty guys who were all frantic. After a while, you start a conversation with a fellow sufferer and, as usually happen with the people from the *Colegio*, then and always: you feel like shit, because you never have achieved what you were supposed to. They ask you, for instance, 'How many rivers run across [the province of] Santa Cruz?' And what would I know!"[20]

Measures taken by the *Colegio* to ensure transparency in the admission process are, and have always been, very strict. Since the compulsory entrance course was

---

17 Interview, Buenos Aires, August 2008.
18 Interview with the current Dean of the *CNBA*, Gustavo Zorzoli, conducted by researcher Mariana Mataluna. Unpublished, July 2015.
19 Manuel Belgrano (1770–1820). Hero of the *Revolución de Mayo*, member of the first national government and creator of the national flag. The joke alludes to the fact that the founding father was, in fact, a student of the *Real Colegio de San Carlos*, antecedent of the *CNBA* in one of its successive foundations.
20 Interview, Buenos Aires, February 2006.

implemented, teachers are prevented from having their own course students as examinees. This is certainly exceptional in a country with a generalised assessment system in which the person teaching a class is also the one assessing students' progress. Examinations arrive on the desks of the teachers in charge of grading them with no candidate identifying mark other than a code number. No interpretation of the examination paper or response to a query is allowed during the examination. Candidates cannot make questions. "It is thoroughly supervised", commented a teacher who has worked in the entrance examination:

> "Each individual examination is assessed by three different examiners — in fact, two of these instances are checks —; each instance performed by an examiner with an institutional hierarchy higher than that of the previous one. Grading is entirely done inside the school premises. No examiner is allowed to take examinations home, which makes it likely for them to spend whole weekends there, until late at night."[21]

The intended message seems to be: 'we want to choose, with the most transparency, the best candidates.' After the examination, when the moment comes to allocate the places available in first year, the first twenty-five students in the 'order of merit'[22] get to choose which school session to attend: they are 'the elite within the elite, the most brilliant,' as former students themselves put it. This is characteristic of the elitist mechanisms fostered by socialisation at the *CNBA*; a group that is already considered exclusive generates smaller groups within itself, even more selective than the first one. Student records show hundreds of requests asking to be changed to a different session class (in order to attend the morning session, the most sought-after), the vast majority of them rejected.

Entering

During his welcome speech to the freshman class of 2006, the then principal congratulated the students on having "successfully passed the entrance examination" and advised them that "nothing is achieved without effort," despite the "culture of excess and frivolous consumerism" prevailing in society.[23] "Belonging to this school entails a serious social responsibility — he said — because the whole community supports it and expects us to show results according to their

---

21 Interview, Buenos Aires, August 2008.

22 In the testimonies obtained from actors in interviews conducted between 2004 and 2010 there is a coincidence on this denomination.

23 These words were pronounced by the then principal, Horacio Sanguinetti, during his welcome speech to the freshman class of 2006, which this researcher attended as part of her field work.

sacrifice."[24] Hence, "the three-part motto, the golden rule: 'Do not waste time, do not damage the building, do not offend anyone.'"[25] Here is the core of the secular morality that establishes the relationship between the entrants and the *Colegio*.

One of the freshmen's mothers, who was sitting next to this writer in the auditorium, had on her face an expression of pride that soon turned into one of devastation. She knew of the strictness of the *Colegio*: her husband had been a student there during the military dictatorship (1976–1983) and his experience at school had been so traumatic that he still found it very difficult to attend the regular alumni reunions, whether they were organised by the *Colegio* or by the former students themselves. As she heard the principal's speech, she found out that her son would have to attend preparatory course classes twice a week, during after-school hours, at the school sports field in Puerto Madero, on the east of the city, and that he would not be able to continue doing what he enjoyed the most, playing basketball, because on some of the other weekdays he would have to go to school an hour earlier than the usual in order to attend some of his classes. The woman was beginning to realize that the young man's life would change, and indeed it did: towards the end of our investigation, which took six years, the boy, who was already in fourth year, appeared in the Sunday magazine of an important national newspaper as a young 'opera-lover,' a habitué.

Having gone through the socialisation process that the *CNBA* admission process really is entails many of the children differentiating from their neighbourhood friends or friends from primary school who have free time for leisure. This distancing is plain to see during the very morning of the examination, when parents are left outside the iron bars that protect the entrance to the *Colegio*. Many adults stay in front of the school doing their children's examinations — copies of which are provided by the school authorities — since the doors are closed as soon as the students have entered the building. Once the examination stage is over, differentiation continues. Those iron bars separating examinees from their parents on the very same day of the test mark a first difference, regarding their families. Then, the decimal fractions that separate those who succeeded at the examination with the required minimal mark from those who failed establish an essential division, even though everybody knows that passing the examination is a relative possibility which depends on a requirement that changes every year depending on the general results obtained. In fact, there is not a set minimal grade; there is a limited number of places offered, and the necessary condition to enter

---

24 Ibid.
25 Ibid.

the school does not depend on the specific grade obtained but on the fact that it is higher than the cut-off grade set for the year in question. These, however, will be lifelong differences with long-lasting effects on very diverse aspects of life. The entrance examination, therefore, constitutes a moment of passage between two different kinds of logic: the family/neighbourhood logic, in which meritocratic values are rarely used, and that of the *Colegio*.

The long-term effect of the entrance process experience at the *CNBA*

The admission process to the *CNBA* is one of those moments in social life in which individuals internalize new norms and obligations and, at the same time, build their identities and demarcate otherness in ways that often imply, both in the short and in the long-term, social difference. The most interesting effect of this experience is probably the fact that it has allowed access to quality education, in the different moments of the history of the *Colegio*, to young students of diverse social origins regardless of their financial situation or the school their parents and siblings have attended, and irrespective of who their friends were or the social sphere they moved in.

Graduate students' records show the presence of a small number of students from the outskirts of Buenos Aires (at least since the 1970s, there were approximately a 10% with this residential pattern, which, of course, does not say much for certain about their cultural level) among a vast majority of professional parents' children, who live in areas easily reached by public transport. During the interviews we learned of the 'unusual' ways in which those whose families had no previous information about the *CNBA* chose to attend this downtown school: some were encouraged by their primary school teachers because they had had a particularly good school performance; others were motivated by a cousin or a friend from downtown who told them about their experience at the School, or by anecdotes recalled by a distant relative who happened to be a *CNBA* alumnus. Others saw the School entrance marble staircase, 'unique in its kind in Latin America,' on television and, taken by it, insisted on attending that school; these were some of the ways, among many others. Although they comprise a low percentage, these 'peripheral' students are very important, because they can show other 'neighbourhood kids' unusual models of successful career paths: neighbours, siblings, cousins, or younger students of their public or private primary school. They are not relevant in quantitative terms, but they are central to the approach we adopted on collecting and examining these data: ethnography. This method allows the researcher to learn of informal ways of dealing with unwritten and explicit rules, and also to observe the way in which individuals administer their resources and try to compensate for or create those they lack of in order to be able to cope with both the admission process and the adjustment to their new school; this makes ethnography invaluable in the study of elites.

The ascending trajectories of some former students who have reached, unlike their parents, positions of leadership, of power or prestige either in the State or the private sector show a certain margin of indeterminacy in the dynamics of social reproduction in an institution where some persons strengthen their intellectual, professional or political networks as 'sons/daughters' or 'grandchildren' while other persons build them as 'schoolfellows' in the game of school social interaction. During socialisation, these children of different social origins who learned together how to 'survive' a 'fierce' entrance examination and a very strict school life acquire more than new networks and a way of coping with the rigors of academic life: they learn how to discuss national politics and how to manage student unions and school politics ('they learn the ropes' as a *CNBA* teacher has put it), to exercise leadership or watch somebody else doing it, to amaze other people, to make useful contacts for their future professional lives, among other resources that some authors consider to be part of a practical category called "talent."[26]

A scholarship program funded by the *UBA* was implemented in the *Colegio* following 1955 as a stimulus for students with financial difficulties and a good school performance.[27] Some of these students earned their secondary school diploma at the *CNBA*, went on to university and are professionals nowadays. But most of them gave up soon after entering the School; they were not able to adjust themselves to the closely intertwined school and social aspects of daily interaction with their classmates. They encountered the same difficulties as those good students of humble distant homes who would enter the *Colegio* twenty-five years

---

26 Phillip Brown, Hugh Lauder and Johnny Sung, "Higher Education, Corporate Talent and Stratification of Knowledge Work in the Global Labour Market," in *World Year Book of Education 2015. Elites, Privilege and Excellence: The National and Global Redefinition of Educational Advantage*, eds. Agnès van Zanten, Stephan Ball, and Brigitte Darchy-Koechlin (London, UK: Routledge, 2015), 217.

27 A *CNBA* graduate told me he had had the privilege of living "the golden age of the reform at university" following 1955, which is known for a series of measures taken with the aim of promoting teaching and research. For the *CNBA*, these reforms meant being able to offer grants, given by the UBA, for students with low family incomes and good primary school grade-point averages. This 'reformist' movement, composed of socialist, communist and radical students and professors (poorly represented at *El Colegio*) appeared in university politics as the political rival to a different ideological tradition: Humanism.

later: living so far from the *Manzana de las Luces*, where the school is located, and from the North highway corridor, where most of its students live, they found it very difficult to make friends, since they could not count on commuting as an opportunity for socializing. Not being able to buy the books or the kind of clothes the other children wore (which sometimes dissuaded them from going to their parties) was also a problem, as well as speaking with a different vocabulary or being louder; and the fact that they did not share the same leisure centres on weekends or the same holiday destinations did not increase opportunity for integration either. These differences, felt like flaws, were in the short term a decisive factor for some of these persons, and they show what 'merit' means in practical terms for those who lack the resources needed: a sort of Janus face that legitimises the privilege earned by those who would have achieved it anyway and explains the exclusion of those who "did not know how to adjust."[28] The differential between these two groups, a very small number of students, represents the most genuine version of meritocracy; few persons indeed, but essential to the point of view of our research: ethnography.

Final Remarks

The *CNBA* still exhibits marks not only on its desks but also in its institutional discourse of a prestigious past and a highly regarded tradition, rooted in the French Enlightenment, whose holders were some of its distinguished alumni, "the Young men of the Generation of 1880."[29] The most famous of them, Miguel Cané, wrote an autobiography, *Juvenilia*, which is mandatory reading material for freshmen, where he tells the story of his life as a boarding-school pupil at the school founded by Bartolomé Mitre. For persons like Cané, intellectual life and writing were synonymous with a refutation of utilitarianism, with an appreciation of "the bright and clear, the unusual and diverse" and a "clear, transparent, fluent, elegant style."[30] Matters of form and gracious manners, characteristic of a good taste that, in their terms, was synonymous with aristocracy, constituted a real concern to the young members of this literary coterie.

---

28 The phrase belongs to an interviewee who is a *CNBA* graduate and a *Licenciada* in Political Science. Paris, December 2004.

29 We are referring to authors like Miguel Cané and Martín García Mérou, *CNBA* graduates, as well as to Pedro Goyena, who was a teacher at the institution, Mariano de Vedia and Paul Groussac himself.

30 *García Mérou, Martín. Recuerdos literarios* (Buenos Aires: Eudeba, 1973), 317.

The *CNBA* has been described on several occasions as a sort of 'fortified town,' an institution with its own standards regarding assessment methods and expectation levels, and the style of their students and alumni. Some of the characteristic features of education at the *CNBA* are an extremely high level of expectations; the ability to maintain an assessment system that also functions as a socialisation process, with observable consequences in the constitution of a distinctive 'identity' for the group of alumni; an emphasis upon written culture, in a school where Latin is a compulsory subject. In a constantly changing assessment culture, these enduring elements functioned in the initial stages as a model for the rest of the national schools. These schools, most of them founded shortly after the *CNBA*, also selected their student body by virtue of an entrance examination, a practice which extended until the beginning of the 21ˢᵗ century. As Martín Legarralde states, these schools maintained the same educational project for thirty years, one based on the curriculum designed in 1865 by the French philosopher Amadeo Jacques, first director of studies at the *CNBA*.[31] However, each of them represent, in their respective foundations and refoundations, the different moments in national life at which they were created, as well as the political projects of the provincial or national ruling groups, often antagonistic, that shaped them. These groups were divided by issues regarding the organisation of the Nation, regional history, community values and scale, but nevertheless they were able to establish an assessment culture in which the written word, evaluated by virtue of a teacher's criterion (normally supervised), was central — at least until the end of the 20ᵗʰ century, when many of these national secondary schools either under university control or not adopted an open entrance system. An easy relationship with written language, brought to light by the ability to express ideas in a clear, concise and organised way, using an appropriate register and a variety of lexical items, was a central aspect to be observed. If this model influenced other institutions, it was national schools, at least until the beginning of the 21ˢᵗ century, when some of them still required an entrance examination. This emphasis on written language and its evaluation differentiates Argentinian assessment culture from other national assessment cultures, which prioritize standardized multiple-choice tests.

A well-known Argentinian sociologist has encapsulated in one phrase the way in which, in his view, an institution that has merit as a legitimate form of distinction coexists with the rest of society. He said that the *CNBA* is "an island of merit

---

31 *Legarralde, Martín R.* "La fundación de un modelo pedagógico: los colegios nacionales entre 1862–1887." *Propuesta educativa* 10, no. 21 (1999–2000): 38–43.

in a country where the winds blow another way."[32] It is true that in the wider society winds blow "another way," as they say, the way of "egalitarianism": If we map national schools or, more accurately, the ones formerly known as such today, both the ones in provincial capital cities and the ones in Buenos Aires city and province, it is clear that a culture of admission centred in a compulsory entrance examination gave way to one that established an open entrance system, based on an integrating entrance course or on a draw, among other admission modalities. In spite of its remaining 'aristocratic' features, it is difficult to consider the *CNBA* as an island. If it were an island, it would have probably sunk: there would not be, every year, a group of teenagers willing to make the effort required to enter an institution like the *CNBA*. It is a school that offers quality education and a sort of guarantee of dignity "that spares its possessor permanently from the obligation to undergo tests, from having to demonstrate their abilities"[33] but does not ensure its students access to the best positions later in their professional careers.

The observation of the rules that are the same for everyone, the cornerstone of the *CNBA* admission culture, is perceived as elitist in an immigration society like the Argentinian one. Exceptions, however, and particularly the 'wit' to break the rules without being punished, are object of praise. The Argentinian historian Roy Hora has written that since 1920 and 1930 "distinction has been regarded unfavourably by an anti-elite and anti-oligarchy discourse of immigrant origin."[34] But, curiously enough, since the 1920s and 1930s, this same society has valued progress through education very highly, which, on the one hand, questions whether autonomous assessment cultures that go against the grain could exist in this context, but, on the other hand, enables the possibility of finding elements of the tradition embodied in the *CNBA* in other educational institutions.

Literature

Álvarez, Juan. *Las guerras civiles argentinas y el problema de Buenos Aires en la República*. Buenos Aires: Librería y Editorial La Facultad, 1936.

Bourdieu, Pierre. *La Nobleza de Estado*. Buenos Aires: Siglo XXI Editores, 2013.

Brown, Phillip, Hugh Lauder, and Johnny Sung. *"Higher Education, Corporate Talent and Stratification of Knowledge Work in the Global Labour Market."* In World Year Book of Education 2015. Elites, Privilege and Excellence: The

---

32 Interview, Buenos Aires, September, 2009.
33 Pierre Bourdieu, *La Nobleza de Estado* (Buenos Aires: Siglo XXI Editores, 2013), 172.
34 Roy Hora, "La 'oligarquía' del 8-N, un enemigo a la medida K," in *La Nación*, November 11, 2012.

National and Global Redefinition of Educational Advantage, edited by Agnès van Zanten, Stephan Ball, and Brigitte Darchy-Koechlin, 217–230. London, UK: Routledge, 2015.

Dussel, Inés. *Currículum, humanismo y democracia en la enseñanza media, 1863–1920.* Buenos Aires: Eudeba, 1997.

Garaño, Santiago, and Werner Pertot. *La otra juvenilia. Militancia y represión en el Colegio Nacional de Buenos Aires, 1971–1986.* Buenos Aires: Biblos, 2002.

García Mérou, Martín. *Recuerdos literarios.* Buenos Aires: Eudeba, 1973.

Gessaghi, Victoria. La educación de la clase alta argentina, entre la herencia y el mérito, Buenos Aires: Siglo XXI, 2017.

Halperin Donghi, Tulio. *"Entrevista."* In Roy Hora y Javier Trímboli, *Pensar la Argentina,* 26–79. Buenos Aires: El Cielo por Asalto, 1994.

Hora, Roy. *"La 'oligarquía' del 8-N, un enemigo a la medida K."* In La Nación, November 11, 2012.

Hora, Roy, and Javier Trimboli. *Pensar la Argentina: los historiadores hablan de historia y política.* Buenos Aires: El cielo por asalto, 1994.

Legarralde, Martín R. *"La fundación de un modelo pedagógico: los colegios nacionales entre 1862–1887."* Propuesta educativa 10, no. 21 (1999–2000): 38–43.

Méndez, Alicia. El Colegio. *La Formación de una Elite Meritocrática en el Nacional Buenos Aires.* Buenos Aires: Sudamericana, 2013.

Neufeld, María Rosa, and Jens A. Thisted, *"Investigadores implicados: la investigación educativa en espacios barriales de la ciudad de Buenos Aires."* Paper presented at the VI Reunión de Antropología del Mercosur. Montevideo, 2005.

Tiramonti, Guillermina. *"De los segmentos a los fragmentos. La nueva configuración del sistema educativo."* Accessed July 24, 2011. http://www.bnm.me.gov.ar/giga1/documentos/EL001242.pdf.

Ziegler, Sandra. *"La escolarización de las elites: un acercamiento a la socialización de los jóvenes de sectores favorecidos en la Argentina actual."* In La Trama de la Desigualdad Educativa. Mutaciones Recientes de la Escuela Media, edited by Guillermina Tiramonti, 73–100. Buenos Aires: Manantiales, 2004.

Camilla Addey[1]

The Assessment Culture of International Organisations: "From Philosophical Doubt to Statistical Certainty"[2] through the Appearance and Growth of International Large-Scale Assessments

This chapter recounts how education indicators and proxies were displaced in the pursuit of educational quality and comparative assessment data on learning outcomes in the second half of the 20th century. When the first international assessment programmes started testing and comparing student learning outcomes and the skills of adults across countries, widespread philosophical debates questioning the validity of such practices were side-lined in favour of universal learning metrics and comparative data-based evidence for policy.

Administered by a small number of authoritative international organisations and steered by selected experts, the recent International Large-Scale Assessments (ILSAs) phenomenon was not only made possible by methodological and theoretical advancements in assessment and psychometrics.[3] The phenomenon of ILSAs, and in particular the policy impact of the OECD's Programme for International Student Assessment (PISA), could not have occurred without a significant assessment culture shift "from philosophical doubt to statistical certainty."[4] For clarity, in this chapter assessment culture refers to the emergence and acceptance of assumptions upon which ILSAs are developed and understood as valid, and how they are valued.

---

1   The author wrote this chapter during a Fritz Thyssen Foundation fellowship awarded to carry out an ILSA research project called PISA4D4Pol. The author would like to thank Néstor López, Bryan Maddox, Kerstin Martens, Oren Pizmony-Levy, and Stephen Heyneman for valuable feedback on this chapter.
2   This is a phrase from Miriam Henry et al., *The OECD, Globalisation and Education Policy* (London, UK: Pergamon, 2001), 90.
3   See William Thorn, "International Adult Literacy and Basic Skills Surveys in the OECD Region," *OECD Education Working Papers* 26 (2009), doi: 10.1787/221351213600.
4   Henry, *The OECD*, 90.

Although today's main players in ILSAs once questioned the validity of educational and skill performance comparisons, they now rate and rank educational performance and skills, framing comparisons as an essential policy tool. Following the historical development of the ILSA phenomenon, this chapter highlights the events and actors playing a significant role between the late 1950s and 2016 in changing the global assessment culture which allowed the phenomenon of International Large-Scale Assessments to take on a key role in education policy, practice and research. Drawing on empirical research by Martens,[5] Pizmony-Levy,[6] Addey[7] and the experience of Heyneman,[8] this chapter unfolds how the Organisation for Economic Cooperation and Development (OECD), the International Association for the Evaluation of Educational Achievement (IEA), and the UNESCO Institute for Statistics (UIS) dealt with conceptual challenges and pressures in measuring educational progress but then turned them into an opportunity to increase their influence, changing their own culture of assessment and the approach to assessment around the world. The chapter highlights the 1990s as a key decade and zooms in on it to dig deeper into how the assessment culture shift happened. Understanding the ILSA phenomenon as a global political project helps understand the political and pragmatic rationales driving the "comparative turn"[9] in assessment culture but also the growth of the phenomenon.

The chapter concludes with a reflection of the latest developments in ILSAs — which have included moving towards a universal PISA learning outcomes metric, measuring pre-primary skills on a single metric for all countries, and the need to change national cultures of assessment in order for ILSAs to have greater impact on policy and practice — but also geopolitical changes that underlie the

---

5   Kerstin Martens, "How to Become an Influential Actor — the 'Comparative Turn' in OECD Education Policy," in *New Arenas in Education Governance*, ed. Kerstin Martens et al. (New York: Palgrave Macmillan, 2007).

6   Oren Pizmony-Levy, "Power, Conflict, and Change in World Society: The Case of International Association for the Evaluation of Educational Achievement" (Lecture at Beijing Normal University, China, 2015).
    Oren Pizmony-Levy, "Testing for All: The Emergence and Development of International Assessments of Student Achievement, 1958–2012" (PhD diss., Indiana University, 2013).

7   Camilla Addey, "Why do Countries join International Literacy Assessments? An Actor-Network Theory Analysis with Cases Studies from Lao PDR and Mongolia" (PhD diss., University of East Anglia, 2014).

8   Stephen P. Heyneman, "The Struggle to Improve Education Statistics in UNESCO: 1980–2000" (Paper presented at the World Bank, May 21, 2012).

9   Martens, "How to Become an Influential Actor."

emergence of ILSAs. This history of how international assessment culture changed but also observing the latest ILSA developments, calls for an ethical reflection on the implications for educational policy and practice.

Measuring Learning Outcomes — a Genesis

Adult literacy and educational achievement have historically been measured without assessing what has been learnt or is known. In the last two centuries,[10] the skills of people 15-year olds and older were measured in a dichotomous manner (which assumes there is a cutting off point at which point one is either literate or not) by asking individuals[11] either 'Are you literate?' or 'Can you read and write?' and offering only yes/no as possible answers. Although literacy measured as a dichotomy has historical longitudinal value, it is a subjective measure based on individuals' understanding of literacy thresholds (not reported in the survey answers). The dichotomous measure based on the 'literate and illiterate' distinction increasingly acknowledged by multiple disciplines and institutions as oversimplified, unable to capture the pluralities of literacy practices, and poorly informative for policy and planning.[12] Although this book deals with student assessment, the history of assessment culture at international organisations grows out of national and international large-scale assessments of adult skills, making them a crucial part of this history.

In the case of educational progress at all levels of schooling, this was historically measured in terms of access and school completion. With increasing awareness that the universalisation of education was not leading to basic learning outcomes, global educational commitments (i.e. Jomtien education conference in 1990,[13] the Education for All goals in 2000, and the Sustainable Development Goals in 2015) and the global education community came to devalue such indicators and proxies considered unreliable and shifted their focus to educational quality. International

---

10   See Bryan Maddox, "Secular and Koranic Literacies in South Asia: From Colonisation to Contemporary Practice," *International Journal of Educational Development* 27 (2007).

11   Often a member or head of a household is asked to define the household occupants' literacy or illiteracy status.

12   See Bryan Maddox and Lucio Esposito, "Sufficiency Re-examined: A Capabilities Perspective on the Assessment of Functional Adult Literacy," *Journal of Development Studies* (2011).

13   It was agreed that education progress had to be measured in terms of what students learnt.

commitments, agreed frameworks for educational development[14] but more broadly a widely shared concern for quality education, called for new ways to measure educational progress. As we will see in the next part of this chapter, this shift alone does not explain the growth of international assessments.

In the second half of the 20th century, national assessments were conducted as a way to measure learning outcomes but also adult skills, especially in North America.[15] In 1975, the U.S. Office of Education carried out the Adult Performance Level Study (APL) to evaluate reading, writing, numeracy and problem-solving. This was followed in 1985 by the Young Adult Literacy Assessment[16] (YALS), and in 1992 by the National Adult Literacy Survey (NALS) and the Survey of Workplace Literacy. In 1989, the Canadian Survey of Literacy Skills Used in Daily Activities (LSUDA) was carried out based on the U.S. assessments but applied the methodology to a bilingual context. The LSUDA represented a significant step in the history of international assessments: it was carried out in English and French and "demonstrated that they were able to provide comparable information regarding the literacy skills of the English and French speaking populations in Canada."[17] In this OECD working paper, Thorn[18] states that the work of the US-based ETS[19] and Statistics Canada (the OECD's main partners in its first international assessment endeavours) set the example of what could be measured with the YALS and the NALS by combining "advances in psychometrics, reading theory and large-scale assessment with household survey methodologies"[20] and that with the LSUDA, they proved that large-scale assessments could produce comparable data across languages and cultures. In 1988 and 1991, ETS developed and administrated the International Assessment of Educational Progress, drawing on the National Assessment of Educational Progress (NAEP), and funded by U.S. National Center for

---

14 The latest international framework for action, the *Belem Framework for Action* (2010), specifically address the need to develop comparable indicators to measure literacy as a continuum.

15 As early as 1916, immigrants arriving in New York State were asked to carry out the *Literacy Test*, as a form of screening and rejection. For a detailed account of the first North American large-scale assessments, see Kirsch and Murray (1998).

16 This is the first large-scale education assessment to use a household survey methodology.

17 See Thorn, "International Adult Literacy," 5.

18 Ibid.

19 ETS (the name originates from its earlier name Educational Testing Service) is a non-profit, private consultant firm which is mainly contracted to develop test items for ILSAs.

20 Thorn, "International Adult Literacy," 5.

Education Statistics and US National Science Foundation (as we shall see, these are key players in the history of ILSAs). These early assessment endeavours are key to the IEA and OECD international large-scale assessments in the early 1990s;[21] but also to the way the global actors and assessment culture changed. In order to understand how this happened, I will recount how the three main organisations (IEA, OECD and UNESCO) administrating international assessments and publishing data on education around the world developed international assessments whilst changing their assessment culture.

To measure or not to measure: changing global education actors

Although the main international organisations developing and administrating international assessments have value-laden agendas, they present themselves and are perceived as impartial, legitimate authorities,[22] which gives them the power to establish and be depositories of norms, values and standards.[23] The ILSAs they develop are perceived in the same way, though the IEA, OECD and UNESCO reinforce this by presenting the data as being objective[24] evidence of what works. However, as argued by Barnett and Finnemore,[25] international organisations do not only gather, manipulate, analyse and interpret information, they invest the information with meaning and transform it into knowledge. As argued by Darville,[26] knowledge produced by ILSAs is closely aligned with economic and political

21 See Oren Pizmony-Levy and James Harvey et al., "On the Merits of, and Myths about, International Assessments," *Quality Assurance in Education* 22, no. 4 (2014); and Gary W. Phillips, "International Assessment of Educational Progress (IAEP)," in *Encyclopedia of Quality of Life and Well-Being Research*, ed. Alex C. Michalos (Netherlands: Springer, 2014).

22 Kerstin Martens and Dennis Niemann, "When do Numbers Count? The Differential Impact of the PISA Rating and Ranking in Education Policy in Germany and the US," *German Politics* 22, no. 3 (2013), doi: 10/1080/09644008.2013.794455.

23 See Kerstin Martens, "How to become an influential actor"; and Bob Deacon, *Global Social Policy and Governance* (London, UK: Sage, 2007).

24 Indeed, Mitchell L. Stevens and Wendy Nelson Espeland, "Commensuration," *Encyclopedia of Social Measurement* 1 (2005) argue that the authority of commensuration hinges on its objectivity claims. "*Commensuration*."

25 Michael N. Barnett and Martha Finnemore, *Rues for the World, International Organisations in Global Politics* (Cornell, NY: Cornell University Press, 2004).

26 Richard Darville, "Knowledges of Adult Literacy: Surveying for Competitiveness," *International Journal of Educational Development* 19 (1999).

mandates. It is also worth noting that the international organisations developing and administrating ILSAs rely heavily on private companies, making the data heavily invested of multiple agendas.

Although common knowledge, for clarity purposes it is worth mentioning in what way the actors mentioned in this chapter differ in terms of the categories they belong to as this impacts on how they work. The OECD and UNESCO (and its Institute for Statistics) are international intergovernmental organisations whose Member States finance and decide the organisations' activities, whilst the IEA is an international, non-profit, non-governmental research-oriented association. Statistics Canada and the U.S. NCES are national government agencies which rely on public resources to carry out activities which are deemed necessary for government purposes.

The order in which I discuss the three main international organisations[27] presented in this chapter, relates to the chronological order in which they engaged in ILSAs.

The International Association for the Evaluation of Educational Achievement (IEA) and ILSAs

The International Association for the Evaluation of Educational Achievement (IEA) is now widely recognised for its two international large-scale assessments: The Trends in International Mathematics and Science Study - TIMSS (implemented every four years amongst fourth and eighth grade students) and the Progress in International Reading Literacy Study — PIRLS (implemented every five years amongst fourth grade students) which are international curriculum-based tests for children in school. In 2016, PIRLS (at its fourth implementation) was implemented by 50 countries (or smaller national entities), whilst in 2015, TIMSS (at its sixth implementation) was implemented by 59 countries (or smaller national entities).

Emerging from a working group convened by the UNESCO Institute for Lifelong Learning (UIL), the IEA was established by a group of scholars in 1958. Pizmony-Levy argues that IEA was initially driven by intellectual curiosity and, as stated in its 1968 mission, it justified its international testing activities in terms of international-scale education research. Between 1958 and the late 1980s, IEA

---

27 It is beyond the scope of this chapter to discuss all actors involved, though there are many important contractors (i.e. ETS, Pearson, ACER) which have played an important role in ILSAs. However, they have acted as contracted private companies to the ILSA-administrating organisations.

was the only institution testing across countries. Before becoming widely known for TIMSS and PIRSLS, the Association went through important changes in its approach to comparatively measuring learning outcomes. Kamens[28] argues that in the early days of the IEA, "Torsten Husén and his colleagues viewed national education systems as distinctive, historic systems. In their view they were like apples and oranges: non-comparable. Thus the early math and science testing regimes were not conducted with the idea of locating 'best practice' models that produced high achievement. They were designed with more pragmatic policy considerations at the fore."[29] Postlethwaite[30] and Kamens[31] clarify that IEA did accept that comparisons could be made amongst educational systems, however they only compared macro educational factors, suggesting micro comparisons were "of little use."[32] Kamens states that "Husén and the IEA did not imagine that they could pick and choose 'best practices' at the meso and micro level to affect particular outcomes that policy makers wanted to alter."[33] A few decades later, IEA no longer saw national educational systems as unique national projects, but as part of a world project. In order to understand how this happened, this section draws entirely on outstanding research carried out by Oren Pizmony-Levy[34] which meticulously reconstructs how the Association changed between 1958 and 2012.

Taking a World Culture theoretical approach, Pizmony-Levy[35] studied the emergence and institutionalisation of the field of international assessments as a global educational script/blueprint — arguing that its acceptance is evident in the increasing number of countries participating in ILSAs. Pizmony-Levy's historical reconstruction of the IEA's approach to assessment shows how the explosion of the ILSA phenomenon was accompanied by "dramatic changes in the field" mainly concerning the actors, logics and rationales.[36] Drawing on interviews with

---

28 David H. Kamens, "Globalisation and the Emergence of an Audit Culture: PISA and the Search for "Best Practices" and Magic Bullets," in *PISA, Power, and Policy the emergence of global educational governance*, ed. Heinz-Dieter Meyer and Aaron Benavot (Didcot, UK: Symposium Books, 2013).

29 Kamens, "Globalisation and the Emergence of an Audit Culture", 120.

30 Neville Postlethwaite, "Torsten Husén (1916-)," *Prospects: The Quarterly Review of Comparative Education. UNESCO: International Bureau of Education* XXIII (2000).

31 Kamens, "Globalisation and the Emergence of an Audit Culture," 121.

32 Ibid.

33 Ibid.

34 Pizmony-Levy, "Power, Conflict, and Change"; Pizmony-Levy, "Testing for All"; Pizmony-Levy et al. "On the Merits."

35 Pizmony-Levy, "Testing for All."

36 Pizmony-Levy, "Testing for All," 2.

key informants, archival research, and participant observations of IEA meetings, Pizmony-Levy shows how IEA went from being "a field organised/oriented toward educational research to a field organised/oriented toward educational audit and accountability."[37] He argues this change is twofold: an ownership shift from research to government affiliates, and a purpose shift from research to policy.

The IEA is governed by a General Assembly (GA) which includes representatives from countries involved in its ILSAs. In the IEA early days, the majority of countries chose to be represented in the IEA GA by individuals who had an academic or research affiliation, given the Association's intellectual mission. Pizmony-Levy highlights how, as of the mid-1990s, IEA ownership transitioned from researchers to governments, with country representatives increasingly affiliated with government bodies: "In 1986, the proportion of representatives from governmental agencies was 43.3 per cent; this figure jumped to 59.6 per cent in 1998 and to 73.4 per cent in 2012. Representatives from academic and research institutes correspondingly declined from 56.7 to 40.4 per cent and then to 26.6 per cent."[38] This change can be understood through the changes engineered after the implementation of the IEA's Second International Mathematics Study.

From their first days, IEA conceptualised and tested a framework to carry out national large-scale assessments, which was used in the First International Mathematics Study (FIMS) in 1964, followed by the Second International Mathematics Study (SIMS) between 1980 and 1982, and the Trends in International Mathematics and Science Study (TIMSS) in 1995 (the first time). Although rather unknown in the ILSA world, SIMS is key to understanding the development of IEA but also the educational statistics crisis at UNESCO in the 1990s. As recounted by Stephen Heyneman, when the SIMS data was released (showing the U.S. as doing badly compared to its reference societies), "the American government was not only embarrassed, but angry."[39] The government argued that the tests and the sampling frame used by the IEA had not been: "cleared by any government agency," and Congress held the U.S. Office of Education accountable.[40] The U.S. National Centre for Education Statistics hired Jeanne Griffith to ensure a similar mistake would never be repeated. It was decided that in order for the U.S. to make its criticism and voice welcome, it would have to do it "under the cover of the National

---

37 Ibid.
38 Pizmony-Levy et al. "On the Merits," 321.
39 Heyneman, "The Struggle," 2.
40 Stephen Heyneman, personal communication.

Academy of Sciences, an organisation which has more international credibility than the federal ministries."[41]

In 1988, Griffith had the National Academy of Sciences' Board on International Comparative Statistics in Education (BICSE) financed by the U.S. Department of Education and the National Science Foundation. It is through the BICSE, perceived as politically neutral,[42] that the U.S. would engineer global changes. Not only did BICSE remove a professor from the IEA GA and replace him with a government official, but it established the reasons for ILSA participation, an ILSA participation code of ethics, guided the implementation of IEA's TIMSS, and justified the use of both curriculum-based (i.e. TIMSS) and skill-based assessments (i.e. PISA).[43] Heyneman, who was part of the BICSE in those years, stated:

> "(i) that outside of OECD international organisations had a wide variety of capacities to understand the need for and implementation of technical standards; and (ii) that many important trading partners of the United States, including Russia, China, India, Mexico, Brazil, Indonesia had no access to the professional standards in education statistics which had been established either through IEA or OECD. The problem was UNESCO."[44]

As we shall see in the section dedicated to UNESCO, this led to the UNESCO 1990s' education statistical crisis induced by the U.S.

Pizmony-Levy reports that in an IEA meeting in 1960, the Association's positions on country performance comparisons was made clear: "The question we wish to ask is not 'Are the children of country X better educated than those of country Y?'" To us this seemed a false question begging all the important issues we need to study.[45] Archival documents from 1960, reveal concern at IEA regarding the 'horse-race' reception of the comparative studies in countries and that a clear statement was made, stating it was neither advisable nor possible. It is therefore surprising to read that in 2016, the IEA states its comparative research and assessment projects aims are quite the opposite to its early day aims. In 2016 the IEA website states that the IEA aims to: 1) provide international benchmarks

---

41 Stephen Heyneman, personal communication.

42 Stephen P. Heyneman and Chad R. Lykins, "The Evolution of Comparative and International Education Statistics," in *Handbook of Research in Education Finance and Policy*, ed. Helen F. Ladd and Edward B. Fiske (London, UK: Routledge, 2008).

43 Heyneman, "The Struggle," 3.

44 The implication being that the educational statistics that the U.S. would have been interested in (on Russia, China, India, Mexico, Brazil and Indonesia) would have been available from UNESCO, which is was no longer a Member State of and therefore had no legal power over. See Heyneman, "The Struggle," 3.

45 Pizmony-Levy, "Testing for All," 10.

to assist policymakers in identifying the relative strengths and weaknesses of their education systems; 2) provide high-quality data to increase policymakers' understanding of key school- and non-school-based factors that influence teaching and learning; 3) provide high-quality data that will serve as a resource for identifying areas of concern and action, and for preparing and evaluating educational reforms; 4) develop and improve the capacity of education systems to engage in national strategies for educational monitoring and improvement; 5) contribute to the development of a worldwide community of researchers in educational evaluation.[46]

Pizmony-Levy's research also documented how the IEA's change of assessments was a response to U.S. pressure in 1990, which was keen to fund an institution which was not perceived as a U.S. agency, but which would collect international data including a specific group of reference societies the U.S. was keen to compare with. Pizmony-Levy's forthcoming monograph on the history of IEA, recounts how in a similar manner to the financial contribution used to pressure the OECD towards developing international comparative education indicators, the IEA was also re-directed in its assessment work with U.S. financial support. TIMSS was developed under the influence of the U.S. As we shall see in the analysis of the OECD's assessment culture shift, Martens'[47] empirical data identifies similar pressure from the U.S.

Clearly showing how in the early days of IEA, both staff and documents avoided ranking tables and a competitive analysis of the data (i.e. analysis were presented by country alphabetical order), Pizmony-Levy's research captures the culture assessment shift that occurred in the IEA. From assessment as an intellectual endeavour, the IEA shifted to a culture of assessment based on rankings, feeding into what Martens[48] has termed governance by comparison, and Lehmkuhl[49] has called governance by rating and ranking.

---

46   "IEA, Researching Education, Improving Learning," accessed May 5, 2016, http://www. iea.nl/?id=72.

47   Martens, "How to become an influential actor."

48   Ibid.

49   Dirk Lehmkuhl, "Governance by Rating and Ranking," *Paper presented at the Annual Meeting of the International Studies Association (ISA)* (Honolulu, 2005).

The Organisation for Economic Cooperation and Development (OECD) and ILSAs

The Organisation for Economic Cooperation and Development (OECD) is the administrator of the most influential ILSA — the PISA, but also an important advocate for international education indicators for policy. As opposed to UN-ESCO, the OECD's education work is not by mandate and is deeply rooted in the Organisation's economic mandate. Until 1975, education had an "inferred role" role in the OECD's mandate and activities,[50] and it was only given a more structural presence in the restructuring of the Organisation with the constitution of the Directorate for Social Affairs, Manpower, and Education, which in 1991 was once again restructured into the Directorate for Education, Employment, Labour and Social Affairs — giving education a more prominent role, but still closely linked to the Organisation's economic mandates. Since then education has become a fundamental dimension of the Organisation's economic mandate, making it increase its presence, work and budget in education in the mid-1990s. The success of the OECD's ILSAs influenced the establishment of its Department of Education in 2002.

Although the OECD's shift to education is rather recent, the Organisation has achieved outstanding prominence in the global educational arena. Global prestige is conferred to countries for simply joining the OECD ILSA rankings, whatever their results. Scholars would unanimously agree that through PISA, the OECD has become a powerful policy actor in education policy processes[51] — from policy priority setting, justifying reforms, informing reformulation, all

---

50 George S. Papadopoulos, *Education 1960–1990: The OECD Perspective* (Paris: OECD, 1994).

51 See Fazal Rizvi and Bob Lingard, *Globalizing Education Policy* (London, UK: Routledge, 2010); Heinz-Dieter Meyer and Aaron Benavot, eds., *PISA, Power, and Policy the Emergence of Global Educational Governance* (Didcot, UK: Symposium Books, 2013); Sam Sellar and Bob Lingard, "PISA and the Expanding Role of the OECD in Global Education Governance," in *PISA, Power, and Policy the Emergence of Global Educational Governance*, ed. Heinz-Dieter Meyer and Aaron Benavot (Didcot, UK: Symposium Books, 2013); Sotiria Grek, "Governing by Numbers: the PISA 'Effect' in Europe," *Journal of Education Policy* 24, no. 1 (2009); Sotiria Grek, "OECD as a site of Co-production: European Education Governance and the New Politics of 'Policy Mobilisation,'" *Critical Policy Studies* 8, no. 3 (2014); Martens, "How to Become an Influential Actor"; Kamens, "Globalisation and the Emergence of an Audit Culture"; and Mary Hamilton, Camilla Addey and Bryan Maddox, *Literacy as Numbers: Researching the Politics and Practices of International Literacy Assessment* (Cambridge, UK: Cambridge University Press, 2015).

the way to legitimizing reforms, evaluating policy and sparking policy debate. Martens[52] argues the OECD achieved this through its "comparative turn" with PISA. It is somewhat surprising therefore that until the 1990s, the OECD did not welcome comparisons of educational systems which it viewed as unique to the socio-historical contexts within which they had developed. Martens[53] carried out interviews at the OECD in the early 2000s and her interviewees recount how similarly to IEA, the OECD went from acknowledging difference and in-depth studies of individual countries, to large-scale comparisons of countries along standardized metrics. Henry et al. state that in the 1990s, the OECD "saw some remarkable shifts in the development of education indicators within the OECD: from philosophical doubt to statistical certainty;[54] from covering some countries to covering most of the world; from a focus on inputs to a focus on outputs."[55] So what happened? Recounting the history of PISA and the ILSAs which fore-grounded PIAAC, the following paragraphs tell the story of how this shift in the OECD's assessment culture occurred. To do so, I draw mainly on Martens (2007), Tröhler (2013) and a recent interview with Andreas Schleicher.[56]

At a European ministerial meeting in London in 1964, it was suggested that the OECD publish a guidance handbook on the statistical factors to consider in education investment planning. Known as the Green Book, it was widely used, even though OECD staff described (in an interview with Martens in 2004) the quality of the indicators as "catastrophic" and in no way comparable. The OECD was relying on statistics provided by Member States and never questioned them even though "there were obviously dubious figures."[57] As we shall see below, UN-ESCO was criticised for similar poor data gathering and publishing in the early 1990s. The OECD did not change its approach until it was pressured into develop-ing comparable figures by two Member States dealing with internal educational crisis: the USA and France.

---

52 Martens, "How to become an Influential Actor."
53 Ibid.
54 The quote which gives the title to this chapter.
55 Henry et al., *The OECD*, 90.
56 Martens, "How to Become an Influential Actor"; Daniel Tröhler, "The OECD and Cold War Culture: Thinking Historically about PISA," in PISA, Power, and Policy the emergence of global educational governance, edited by Heinz-Dieter Meyer and Aaron Benavot (Didcot, UK: Symposium Book, 2013). The interview is from Addey's aforementioned PISA4D4Pol research project.
57 Martens, "How to Become an Influential Actor," 45.

This comparative turn starts with the Soviet satellite Sputnik, which Tröhler calls the "educationalisation of the Cold War."[58] Both Tröhler[59] and Martens[60] argue that PISA is rooted in the Cold War and that the U.S. played a key role in pushing the OECD to develop what later became PISA.

With the launch of Sputnik in 1957, it was widely acknowledged in the U.S. that their educational competitiveness was failing when compared to its enemy political and ideological model. In the decades that followed, education in the U.S. was described as being in a crisis. Education was put high on the political agenda when the report *Nation at a Risk* was published in the 1983 on the failures of the North American educational system. This coincided with the comparatively bad results of the U.S. in the Second International Mathematics Study (SIMS). Comparative educational indicators suddenly became the priority for the U.S. and through its National Center for Education Statistics (NCES), it ensured important changes in international comparative data take place, by acting directly on the organisations developing and administrating international tests. The U.S. pushed the OECD to gather and disseminate internationally comparative data on education and when its suggestions were viewed with scepticism, threats to withdraw funding[61] from the OECD's Centre for Educational Research and Innovation (CERI) were made in 1987 — as described by Stephen Heyneman, who at the time (1983) was on the Board of International and Comparative Studies in Education of the National Academy of Sciences.

> "The US delegate was said to have put a great deal of pressure and in very direct language for OECD to engage itself in a project collecting and analysing statistical education 'inputs and outcomes' — information on curricular standards, costs and trends and the like. The reaction among the staff of CERI was one of shock, and deep suspicion. Those whom I interviewed believed it was unprofessional to try and quantify such indicators, and that it would oversimplify and misrepresent OECD systems, and that it would be rejected by the twenty-four member states whose common interests they were charged to serve."[62]

Martens' OECD interviewees suggest the U.S. were keen to export its educational debate "to avoid considering that the crisis of education was only an American

---

58 Daniel Tröhler, "The OECD and Cold War Culture," 144.

59 Ibid.

60 Martens, "How to Become an Influential Actor."

61 These threats were taken seriously given the recent (and first) funding withdrawal to UNESCO in 1984 (until 2003).

62 Stephen P. Heyneman, "Quantity, Quality, and Source," *Comparative Education Review* 37, no. 4 (1993): 375.

issue."[63] The U.S. were not alone in demanding international comparative data on education: they were supported by France (at the time the French Ministry of Education was led by socialist Chevènement) which was keen to have figures showing the elitist French educational system performing poorly in order to leverage support to reform a more egalitarian education system. Demanding internationally comparable data for different reasons, Martens' interviewees state that "the OECD had to modify its programme of work on education indicators."[64] Discussions were initiated, a set of indicators were agreed on, and the International Indicators of Education Systems (INES) was established at the OECD in 1988 with an increasing focus on educational outputs (rather than inputs) and performance measurement.

Capturing the OECD's major shift, Martens argues that:

> "Prior to the establishment of INES, within the OECD section on education, this field of policy was considered a reflection of national cultural tradition, which could not be satisfactorily grasped by quantitative figures, especially not those that seek to 'measure' education. Staff did not particularly welcome the idea of conducting a project for comparative indicators in the first place."[65]

Her OECD interviewees suggest it was seen as "an American issue" and actually saw it as being dangerous and thus "purposefully avoided anything which amounted to encouraging countries to compare themselves."[66] New staff was then hired, including from IEA, and other staff members left explicitly "because of the new emphasis on how education policy was dealt with by the organisation. These changes in staff also changed the way the development of education indicators were perceived within the OECD."[67]

This pressure led to the OECD's first publication of *Education at a Glance* in 1992 (now an annual publication which Tröhler describes as the "cradle of PISA").[68] Lingard and Grek[69] highlight how in this period an OECD Policy Review and Advisory Group was created to "contribute to the diffusion of an indicator

---

63 Martens, "How to Become an Influential Actor," 45.

64 Ibid., 46.

65 Ibid., 48.

66 Ibid.

67 Ibid.

68 Daniel Tröhler, "The OECD and Cold War Culture," 154.

69 Bob Lingard and Sotiria Grek "The OECD, Indicators and PISA: An Exploration of Events and Theoretical Perspectives," (Working paper 2, Fabricating Quality in European Education, 2007, accessed May 5, 2014, http://www.ces.ed.ac.uk/research/FabQ/publications.htm).

culture within education circles."[70] It was at this point that together with Statistics Canada, the OECD developed the International Adult Literacy Survey (IALS) based on recent assessment experiences of ETS and Statistics Canada (as mentioned above). The IALS was the first international assessment of literacy to compare prose, and measure document and quantitative literacy skills of 16 to 65-year olds (exclusively focusing on the working age population) across 22 countries between 1994 and 1998. Grek[71] suggests that the IALS established a new theoretical logic for the OECD's measurement framework and "created fertile ground for the OECD to push its education policy agenda through measurement and comparison"[72] and to provide internationally comparable, scientific indicators for policy. It is in this historical context and drawing on the IALS experience that the OECD developed the ILSA that has fuelled the international assessment craze: The Programme for International Assessment Studies, PISA. The widely acknowledged father of PISA, Andreas Schleicher, describes the origins of PISA as a need to create a language which would allow countries to learn from each other:

"The origin was, when I joined this Organisation, I remember my first meeting of OECD education ministers. I don't remember how many ministers were sitting in that meeting, but it was about 22, 23 ministers, and they were all saying 'I've got the best education system in the world, and if I have a little problem left, last year I put a reform in place to solve that problem'. There was no global dialogue, no willingness to engage with other people's ideas, other peoples' missions. Education was completely a field of domestic policy and people were proud of this. And some countries actually say 'No, education is a local business', that was the attitude. And that was sort of my intention to change. We need to find a common language to learn from each other. The testing was just the instrument, but the idea was 'Let's find the language through which we can share our experience across cultural, and linguistic, and other boundaries. And it's really worked like this. What I am most proud of is that now, when ministers meet or educators meet, or when scientists meet, they may not agree but they listen to each other. And they learn from each other." (Interview with Andreas Schleicher, December 2015)

PISA was initiated in 1997 and implemented since 2000 in an increasing number of countries every three years to measure the ability of 15 years olds to apply everyday skills and competences. It was designed and developed within a policy

---

70   CERI, *Education at a Glance. The OECD Indicators* (Paris: OECD, 1995), 4.
71   Grek, "OECD as a Site of Co-Production."
72   Sotiria Grek, "Learning from Meetings and Comparisons: A Critical Examination of the Policy Tools of Transnationals," in *World Yearbook of Education. Policy Borrowing and Lending in Education,* ed. Gita Steiner-Khamsi and Florian Waldow (London, UK: Routledge, 2012), 47.

framework to meet the needs of policy actors and its rankings have become a widely used tool for national educational policy.

Although PISA is claimed to provide countries with data-based, objective evidence for policy, Bloem's[73] ethnographic study of PISA shows how the OECD went from producing and describing data during the first two PISA implementations, to producing knowledge (including policy recommendations) in order to increase the policy relevance of its assessments and the work of the OECD — placing itself at the centre of the PISA epistemic community. The policy recommendations put forward by the OECD are drawn from causal relationships, which are made without duly explaining the limits of such interpretations, as described by Hamilton and Barton, who warn of the "sweeping claims about causality from descriptive correlations and differences."[74]

Since the success of PISA, the OECD has continued to develop other ILSAs to increase the scope and reach of ILSAs. The Programme for the International Assessment of Adult Competencies (PIAAC), which further to literacy and numeracy skills, measures ICT and Internet skills, individual persistence and self-discipline, in addition to how testees feel and behave in relation to social and cultural engagement, political efficacy, and social trust, as part of a more complex understanding of human capital and its potential.[75] Further to these international assessments, the OECD terminated a feasibility study in 2012 of the Assessment of Higher Education Learning Outcomes (AHELO), which assessed scientific practicality and scientific feasibility in order to measure the knowledge and skills of university graduates in general skills, economics and engineering. As of 2012, the OECD is also developing and administrating what it calls a 'more policy-relevant' PISA, known as PISA for Development, in lower and middle-income countries, and the international assessment of early learning which is aimed at five-year olds. Although the OECD's efforts are intended to support countries improve education policies, the OECD Strategy on Development[76] highlights how the Organisation is also in the process of redefining it geographical reach in order to adapt to the shifted economic centre of gravity of the world.

---

73 Simone Bloem, "The OECD Directorate for Education as an Independent Knowledge Producer through PISA," in *Governing Educational Spaces. Knowledge, Teaching, and Learning in Transition*, ed. Hans-Georg Kotthoff et al. (Paris: Sense, 2015).
74 Mary Hamilton and David Barton, "The IALS: What Does it Really Measure?," *International Review of Education* 6, no. 5 (2000): 381.
75 Sellar and Lingard, "PISA and the Expanding Role."
76 OECD, *OECD Strategy on Development* (Paris: OECD, 2012).

This section has shown how since the establishment of INES, the OECD has seen a sharp change in its approach to assessment — going from philosophical doubt to statistical certainty. According to Martens, the "deliberate and increasing reliance on ranking and rating countries with comparative figures"[77] is what best describes the OECD's new approach to education assessment. Grek[78] argues that this new approach is what has transformed the OECD into one of the most powerful agents of transnational education governance. I add that the ILSA developments over the last ten years have seen a growing culture of trust in comparative assessment: going from reluctance to compare education performance as late as in the 1980s to unconditional belief in the validity (and objectivity) of statistical models, universal metrics, and policy solutions and best practices drawn from comparative data-based evidence.

UNESCO and its Institute for Statistics

To better understand the involvement of UNESCO in measuring learning outcomes and skills, it is worthwhile remembering that since its foundation in 1945, UNESCO has spoken the language of peace, values diversity and advocates for education as a basic human right.[79] The Organisation does serve a more pragmatic, economic agenda for national and educational development[80] whilst not moving away from its human rights approach to adopt an entirely human capital, instrumental productivity approach.[81] UNESCO and its Institute for Statistics have historically been amongst the most authoritative global actors collecting and publishing data on education. Not least, the Organisation developed a version of the OECD's IALS that would allow countries with greater differences (languages, scripts, cultures, contexts, etc.) to participate in an ILSA. It is for these reasons that it makes sense to include in this chapter an analysis of the Organisation's approach to the measurement of learning outcomes and skills over the past decades, and how it appears to have not taken a sharp comparative turn like the IEA and the

---

77 Martens, "How to Become an Influential actor," 44.

78 Grek, "OECD as a Site of Co-production."

79 Roser Cussó and Sabrina D'Amico, "From Development Comparatism to Globalisation Comparativism: towards more normative international education statistics," *Comparative Education* 41, no. 2 (2005).

80 Alexander W. Wiseman, *The Impact of Educational Achievement studies in education policymaking* (Bingley: Emerald, 2010).

81 Cussó and D'Amico, "From Development Comparatism to Globalisation Comparativism."

OECD. This chapter describes UNESCO and UIS as undecided, latecomers to the ILSA phenomenon.

At the request of US government, UNESCO ran international statistical programmes on education from its earliest days[82] with the purpose of setting standards by establishing definitions and classifications to count education and literacy, and to collect, standardize, analyse and disseminate data worldwide. Until the IEA and the OECD started to produce comparative, educational statistics, UNESCO had been the only Organisation gathering and disseminating internationally comparable statistics in education.[83] However, collecting internationally comparable statistics across the UNESCO Member States became increasingly complex (especially in terms of ensuring the same measures were behind the data being compared) and UNESCO's statistics were criticised for being narrow, unreliable and inaccessible.[84] This is where the story on the role of the U.S. (started in the IEA section), picks up again.

In the late 1980s, the US identified UNESCO's data as problematic but since it was no longer a Member State, Heyneman recounts how "the question became how more detailed information [on UNESCO's office of statistics] might be gathered without creating a diplomatic incident."[85] A report was commissioned by the World Bank and UNICEF to Jeffrey Puryear, and was presented at BICSE in 1991: it described UNESCO's statistical activities as having serious deficiencies. The report also reproached the Organisation by pointing out the statistical deficiencies of UNESCO's Member States' educational statistics. The question remained as to what could be done. As recounted by Heyneman,

> "unstated but obvious background was whether a re-entry of the United Kingdom and the United States could provide needed financial resources and technical guidance. In late 1992 (?),[86] it was decided that Jeanne Griffith should visit UNESCO and decide for herself. As a senior American government official her visit would have to be 'private.' The cost of her visit was covered by my division's budget; officially she was on vacation. Her meetings included Colin Power, the Assistant Director General for Education and

---

82 Stephen P. Heyneman, "The Sad Story of UNESCO's Education Statistics," *Int. Journal of Educational Development* 19 (1999).

83 Roser Cussó, "Restructuring UNESCO's Statistical Services — The 'Sad Story' of UNESCO's Education Statistics: 4 years later," *International Journal of Educational Development* 26 (2006).

84 Jeffrey Puryear, "International Education Statistics and Research: Status and problems," *International Journal Educational Development* 15, no. 1 (1995).

85 Heyneman, "The Struggle," 3.

86 This is not a typo. Heyneman is not sure of date.

John Smith, author of the World Education Report. At the next BICSE meeting she confirmed the essence of the Puryear report. The problem then became what to do about it. To strengthen UNESCO's statistical functions, BICSE decided it needed more detail on UNESCO's current structure and several possible options on how UNESCO statistics might be restructured.'[87]

Another report was commissioned, this time it focused on how UNESCO's statistical office might be restructured. This report, known as the Guthrie/Hansen 1995 report, was distributed widely and, according to Heyneman 'within UNESCO generated exactly the kind of positive, hopeful response as intended.'[88]

This crisis led by the U.S. under the cover of BICSE in the National Academy of Sciences, played an important role in the reconfiguration of the UNESCO Divisions of Statistics in 1999, which was transferred from UNESCO headquarters in Paris to Montreal[89] (in 2001) and restructured as the UNESCO Institute for Statistics (UIS). In 1999, Heyneman suggested UNESCO's statistical role could easily be taken over by other institutions: "What is clear is that if the new institute does not rise to the challenge, there may be other institutions waiting to take UNESCO's statistical place."[90] As we have seen above, IEA and OECD were being positioned to take up such place, this time with a comparative approach.

Cussó and D'Amico state that the World Bank and OECD criticised UNESCO's indicators for not providing 'hierarchical classifications of countries' and student learning achievements.[91] However, Cussó and D'Amico argue that UNESCO never published rankings as it contradicts the Organisation's concern for diversity and that:

"The comparability of international education statistics that prevailed over the last four decades within UNESCO seems to have been relegated to history. […]. The political objectives of the Organisation's statistical programme mainly corresponded to the planning and expansion of national education and literacy programmes. Despite their heterogeneity, countries of the south were to be measured using the very same indicators, with a view both to reflecting and comparing degrees of socio-economic modernisation and to help define the progress being made as regards development. This *comparatism*[92] was nevertheless limited by the respect for the cultural diversity in line with UNESCO's principles,

---

87 Heyneman, "The Struggle," 4.
88 Ibid., 5.
89 Cussó argues that this transfer came with priorities being given to 'political and institutional ends' (Cussó, "Restructuring UNESCO's statistical services," 533).
90 Heyneman, "The Sad Story," 73.
91 Cussó and D'Amico, "From Development Comparatism to Globalisation Comparativism," 200.
92 Highlighted by the authors.

which include steering away from standardisation in its educational activities.[93] While the Organisation did not publish any rankings of countries, the statistical comparisons were nevertheless based on a solid methodology for international standardisation including the production of comparable time series."[94]

Having led and monitored global educational commitments but also advised Member States on how to best measure adult literacy and education progress, UNESCO played a key role in discussions but also commitments[95] that moved the global education community away from indicators and proxies towards ways to measure learning outcomes, and away from dichotomous measures of literacy (literate/illiterate) towards literacy measured as continuum. Although the Organisation advises countries to measure literacy as a continuum and to monitor quality education through learning outcomes, it annually requests and publishes census dichotomous data and educational indicators and proxies. This 'schizophrenic' approach relates to the Organisation's ambiguous approach to measuring in an internationally standardized way. Although the Organisation argues that "it is difficult to argue without facts and figures and the levers and insights that comparative data provides,"[96] its measurement activities suggest the Organisation is unclear as to where it stands in relation to rankings and micro educational comparisons,[97] as differently suggested by Cussó and D'Amico.[98]

---

93 An example is the extract from the Executive Summary of 'Investing in Cultural Diversity and Intercultural Dialogue': "A curriculum shaped by the standardisation of learning processes and contents – a 'one-size-fits-all' approach – does not serve the needs of all learners, nor does it respond to the context of their lives. This is becoming increasingly obvious to a growing number of countries which are seeking alternative pathways within educational systems". UNESCO, "Investing in Cultural Diversity and Intercultural Dialogue," *Executive Summary* (2009): 15.

94 Cussó and D'Amico, "From Development Comparatism to Globalisation Comparativism," 212.

95 The Organisation has put pressure on Member States to sign up to educational commitments, like the *Belem Framework for Action*, in which all signatory countries (144) must ensure 'all surveys and data collection recognise literacy as a continuum' (UNESCO, Institute for Lifelong Learning, "Belem Framework for Action" (paper presented at the sixth international conference on adult education, Paris, December 1–4, 2009), 6).

96 UNESCO, Institute for Lifelong Learning. *Global Report on Adult Learning and Education* (Hamburg: UNESCO Institute for Lifelong Learning, 2009), 77.

97 Kamens, "Globalisation and the Emergence of an Audit Culture."

98 Cussó and D'Amico, "From Development Comparatism to Globalisation Comparativism."

In 2003, a UNESCO Expert Meeting was held at UNESCO headquarters to develop a working definition of literacy and a conceptual framework for literacy assessment.[99] It is significant that this occurred only two years after UIS had been relocated to Montreal and the reputation of the quality of its statistics was being rebuilt;[100] but also at the same time as the OECD was implementing PISA for the second time and had already implemented several adult literacy assessments. UNESCO's educational indicators and proxies were clearly leaving the Organisation behind global statistical leadership in education, making its data perceived as irrelevant in comparison to what the OECD and IEA were offering.

Claiming a space in ILSAs in 2003 when it decided to adapt the OECD IALS to the contexts of lower and middle-income countries, UNESCO can be described as a latecomer to the ILSA phenomenon. The Organisation's interest in the international assessment phenomenon can be described as twofold: firstly, it was committed to developing similar policy tools which the OECD was developing for its Member States; secondly, it needed to be part of a phenomenon that was picking up momentum and changing the global arena of policy actors setting the global education agenda. As a UIS interviewee recounted LAMP's history,[101] between 2001 and 2003 *"nothing was very clear apart from the need to get into*

---

99   This meeting followed a June 2001 UNESCO HQ meeting on EFA indicators. The recommendations put forward at this meeting included exploring the international assessment of literacy skills.

100   Heyneman, "The Sad Story."

101   Phase 1. 2001–2003. Initial ideas for LAMP were discussed but nothing was very clear apart from the need to get into the assessment field. Phase 2. 2003–2005. LAMP decided to replicate IALS/ALL, even though there were some voices of concern. These concern were disregarded by ETS and Statistics Canada. Phase 3. 2005–2006. It was confirmed that LAMP would replicate IALS/ALL because its instruments and methods were accepted as 'working globally'. The important thing was to generate data and consolidate the methodology as 'the' standard. LAMP was about to be ended in late 2006 (after the external evaluation of the UIS). This did not happen, not because the UIS wanted LAMP, but because the US government exerted pressure (the White House supported LAMP). LAMP took a new direction but was already 'half cooked'. Phase 4. 2007–2012. The UIS established a LAMP team. A more critical approach was developed to try to fix the view that LAMP was not in 'tune with its true purpose' (this is an interviewee's statement as seen in chapter five) as initially set out. There were few resources but some support from the UIS and others partners. 2012–2014. There is a financial crisis at UNESCO and LAMP's future is uncertain.

the assessment field.[102] The programme enjoyed poor political support, suffered many staff changes, and faced many methodological and conceptual challenges. Although LAMP's aims were timely in 2003, in the world of ILSAs, LAMP never gained sufficient global prestige.

What LAMP did do, was highlight the difficulties that the Organisation deals with in the age of rakings and comparative measuring learning outcomes. During LAMP's final years, UIS staff argued that UIS needed to continue its global assessment activities to legitimize its voice in the global debates and measurement of learning outcomes.[103] It was at this point (in 2012) that together with Brookings Institute, UIS established the Learning Metrics Task Force that has brought together experts from around the world to drive global education commitments on educational access *plus* learning but also to develop guidelines on how learning should be measured globally.

Although UNESCO advocates for a different approach and understanding of education, it suffers from the authority the OECD has acquired (which coincided with a serious financial crisis at UNESCO since the U.S. stopped funding the Organisation in 2012 after Palestine acquired full UNESCO Membership) with its international assessment projects and the prestige countries associate with participation. In hindsight, it will become clearer how this affected the Organisation's assessment culture.

The 1990s: The Comparative Turn

What emerges clearly from the analysis of the history of IEA, OECD and UNESCO in their international assessment activities is that 'something' changed in the 1990s, as also mentioned by Henry et al.[104] and Lingard.[105] Before the 1990s, a wider range of subjects was being tested, fewer countries were participating in a smaller number of ILSAs, and most ILSAs were research-oriented.[106] Most importantly, macro education indicators were compared but educational performance comparisons were treated with scepticism, even warned against by organisations

---

102   Interview data drawn from my PhD research on the rationales for participation of Laos and Mongolia in LAMP- fieldwork was carried out in 2012 at UIS, and in Laos and Mongolia.
103   Camilla Addey, "Why do Countries Join International Literacy Assessments."
104   Henry et al., *The OECD.*
105   Bob Lingard, "The OECD, PISA and PISA for Schools," Podcast on FreshEd, 2016. https://soundcloud.com/freshed-podcast.
106   Pizmony-Levy, "Testing for All," and Pizmony-Levy et al., "On the Merits."

like IEA.[107] As Martens' OECD interviewees reported in 2003, the OECD "purposefully avoided anything which amounted to encouraging countries to compare themselves."[108] In the 1990s this all changed, and it thus makes sense to take a deeper look into this decade.

Pizmony-Levy's[109] research captures how in 1990 the U.S. NCES pressured the IEA into developing their international assessment into a math and science study which would allow the U.S. to compare with countries relevant to the U.S. in return for financial support. Pizmony-Levy et al.[110] also highlight how in the 1990s, the IEA saw its governing body go from being represented mainly by research-affiliated individuals to government-affiliated individuals. Three years earlier, the U.S. (threatening to withdraw funding) and France (with the intention to use the data to justify an educational reform) had pressured the OECD into developing internationally comparative educational data (this saw the establishment of INES 1988). However, as Martens rightly argued,

> "while the OECD was forced into the game of developing international R&Rs by dominant states out of rational reasons, it gradually took over and the task and developed comparable, easily digestible international statistics and indicators on the basis of its own perception, which today are seen as international standards."[111]

In the 1990s, the OECD implemented the IALS for the first time in 1994 (9 countries[112] participated, another 5 countries participated in 1996 and 9 countries in 1998), the IEA implemented TIMSS for the first time in 1995 (45 countries participated), and the OECD developed PISA as of 1997. Although the OECD was pressured into an assessment culture of comparisons, Lingard[113] argues that it was in this scenario that the OECD discovered a new role for itself. This new assessment culture, which Martens[114] calls the OECD's comparative turn or governance by comparison, is what Lingard argues has given the OECD a significant role in the global governance of education and made it the legitimate establisher of international standards in education. Though "from philosophical doubt to statistical certainty" brilliantly captured the OECD's transformation in 2001,

---

107   Pizmony-Levy, "Testing for All."
108   Martens, "How to Become an Influential Actor," 48.
109   Pizmony-Levy, "Power, Conflict, and Change in World Society."
110   Pizmony-Levy et al., "On the Merits."
111   Martens, "How to Become an Influential Actor," 49.
112   In some cases, countries participate by sub-national entity or language area.
113   Lingard, "The OECD, PISA and PISA for Schools."
114   Martens, "How to Become an Influential Actor."

fifteen years later the Organisation can be described as dependent on comparative performance data.

Not of less relevance, soon after the Jomtien Education for All conference in 1990, UNESCO's educational statistical capacity to validly monitor educational progress was challenged by the U.S. — which created a legitimate voice for itself by acting through the legitimacy of the BICSE. In the early 1990s, UNESCO found itself without statistical legitimacy, whilst the IEA and the OECD were pressured into developing comparative performance data.

It is important to note that in this decade, three regional large-scale assessments were also developed and implemented for the first time. UNESCO's Regional Bureau for Education in Latin America and the Caribbean (OREALC) coordinated the Latin American Laboratory for the Evaluation of Educational Quality (LLECE) in 1997 (the first test is known as PERCE, followed by SERCE in 2006, and TERCE in 2013). The Southern and Eastern Africa Consortium for Monitoring Educational Quality (SACMEQ) was implemented in 1995, whilst in 1991 the Conference of Education Ministers of Countries Using French as a Common Language (CONFEM), implemented the Programme for Analysis of Education Systems in French-Speaking Countries (PASEC).

Finally, it is worth reflecting on what has been implicitly threaded this chapter: the geopolitical dimension within which the culture assessment shift occurred. It is significant that the 1990s also saw a major geopolitical change. As we have seen, the ILSA phenomenon can be understood as rooted in the Cold War, when two political, economic and ideological models were determined to show supremacy, not least through their educational systems (i.e. the educational crisis in the U.S. following Sputnik). When the Cold War appeared to have ended with the fall of the Berlin Wall (in November 1989), the two sides of the world were bounderless to a single process of economic globalisation, led by the U.S. (which this chapter has described as a key player in the shift towards comparing performance data). Within this political project of economic globalisation, countries (described as 'knowledge economies') started to frame their education as an economic resource, invested in to increase economic growth and global competitiveness (as given importance to by Schleicher in the above interview extract). As argued by Hamilton and Barton, ILSA are driven "by the search for universals in the relationships between literacy, education and prosperity."[115] Education becomes a currency, and measuring the learning outcomes of a country's educational system is the quantification of the currency value and its potential. Measuring all countries' education

---

115   Hamilton and Barton, "The IALS," 378.

systems and adult skills on the same metric, built upon an economic understanding of education and skills, ultimately leads to a globally shared understanding of the purpose of education, hence the ILSA phenomenon being described as a global political project (Nestor Lopez, personal communication). The history of ILSAs and the assessment culture shift discussed in this chapter call for interdisciplinary research to analyse this history in its political and economic context.

As of the 1990s, international large-scale assessments and the comparisons drawn from them were no longer questioned. The culture of assessment of international organisations and their ILSA-users had changed.

Conclusions

This chapter has considered the 1950s–2016 timeframe and in particular the 1990s as key to understanding how the ILSA phenomenon emerged and grew in scope and reach. Drawing on Martens,[116] Pizmony-Levy[117] and Addey's[118] empirical data, I have highlighted the main actors involved and the history of their education measurement activities, driven by political and pragmatic rationales. Empirical accounts clearly show how the two main organisations developing and administrating ILSAs saw a complete shift in their assessment culture. Both the OECD and the IEA departed from an approach which acknowledged difference, had an interest in-depth studies of individual educational systems, was driven by intellectual endeavour, and were research-driven large-scale studies on a broad range of school subjects. Their comparative-performance-data scepticism and philosophical doubt was substituted by a change that had started developing in the late 1980s and took centre stage in the 1990s, which Henry et al.[119] describe as statistical certainty. Without this assessment culture shift, which Martens[120] calls a "comparative turn," ILSAs could not have grown into a global phenomenon which sees a growing number of ILSAs, an increasing number of participating countries, and education policy reforms being evaluated, justified and shaped by ILSA rankings and data. This history has highlighted rationales behind this assessment culture shift and ILSA phenomenon, which have important implications for the way comparative data is used for educational policy, practice and research.

---

116   Martens, "How to Become an Influential Actor."
117   Pizmony-Levy, "Testing for All."
118   Addey, "Why do Countries Join International Literacy Assessments."
119   Henry et al., *The OECD, Globalisation and Education Policy.*
120   Martens, "How to Become an Influential actor."

Over the last ten years, the assessment landscape has been evolving further as global education actors reframe their identities and work programmes in education. Through the PISA for Development experience, the OECD has also become aware that in order for their ILSAs to impact on policy and practice, the support packages they offer (which include technical capacity and step-by-step assistance in the implementation of the programme) are not enough: what needs to be changed are the local cultures of assessment. While the Global Education Monitoring Report (the GEMR housed at UNESCO) has been using learning comparative performance data from international and regional assessments in its yearly reports, as well as its online World Inequality Database on Education, the UIS is in the process of redefining its identity by understanding what role the Institute can play within a world so dominated by the OECD and IEA international assessments. Not least, UNICEF is developing a regional assessment programme for South-East Asia.

The latest ILSA developments appear to be taking comparisons a step further, although validity concerns of performance comparisons are still legitimate questions. The history of ILSAs do not suggest that epistemological questions concerning comparisons have been resolved, they do suggest that the use of comparisons and rankings are political. This chapter therefore calls for an ethical reflection of the uses made of country comparisons and rankings in changing educational policy and practice.

Although this chapter has provided a historical account of how ILSAs appeared, developed and became a global phenomenon, whilst seeing a change in the culture of assessment of the main international organisations administering ILSA, the chapter has not resolved how this comparative turn, made of league tables and rankings, has become a widely accepted, legitimate practice. This chapter calls for further research to understand how this statistical certainty was legitimated, how the comparative turn has been used by international organisations, and how the ILSA phenomenon has changed the landscape of global education actors and the relationships amongst them.

Literature

Addey, Camilla. "Why do Countries Join International Literacy Assessments? An Actor-Network Theory Analysis with Cases Studies from Lao PDR and Mongolia." PhD diss., University of East Anglia, 2014.

Barnett, Michael N., and Martha Finnemore. Rues for the World, International Organisations in Global Politics. Cornell, NY: Cornell University Press, 2004.

Bloem, Simone. "The OECD Directorate for Education as an Independent Knowledge Producer through PISA." In *Governing Educational Spaces. Knowledge, Teaching, and Learning in Transition*, edited by Hans-Georg Kotthoff, and Eleftherios Klerides, 169–85. Rotterdam: Sense Publisher, 2015.

Boudard, Emmanuel, and Stan Jones. "The IALS Approach to Defining and Measuring Literacy Skills." *International Journal of Educational Research* 39, no. 3 (2003): 192–204.

CERI. *Education at a glance. The OECD Indicators*. Paris: OECD, 1995.

Cussó, Roser. "Restructuring UNESCO's Statistical Services — The "Sad Story" of UNESCO's Education Statistics: 4 years later." *International Journal of Educational Development* 26 (2006): 532–44.

Cussó, Roser, and Sabrina D'Amico. "From Development Comparatism to Globalisation Comparativism: Towards more Normative International Education Statistics." *Comparative Education* 41, no. 2 (2005): 199–216.

Darville, Richard. "Knowledges of Adult Literacy: Surveying for Competitiveness." International Journal of Educational Development 19 (1999): 273–85.

Deacon, Bob. *Global Social Policy and Governance*. London, UK: Sage, 2007.

Grek, Sotiria. "Governing by Numbers: the PISA 'Effect' in Europe." *Journal of Education Policy* 24, no. 1 (2009): 23–37.

–. "Learning from Meetings and Comparisons: A Critical Examination of the Policy Tools of Transnationals." In *World Yearbook of Education. Policy Borrowing and Lending in Education*, edited by Gita Steiner-Khamsi, and Florian Waldow, 41–61. London, UK: Routledge, 2012.

–. "OECD as a Site of Co-Production: European Education Governance and the New Politics of 'Policy Mobilisation.'" *Critical Policy Studies* 8, no. 3 (2014): 266–81.

Hamilton, Mary, and David Barton. "The IALS: What Does It Really Measure?" *International Review of Education* 6, no. 5 (2000): 377–389.

Hamilton, Mary, Bryan Maddox, and Camilla Addey. *Literacy as numbers: researching the politics and practices of international literacy assessment*. Cambridge, UK: Cambridge University Press, 2015.

Henry, Miriam, Robert Lingard, Fazal Rizvi, and Sandra Taylor. *The OECD, Globalisation and Education Policy*. London, UK: Pergamon, 2001.

Heyneman, Stephen P. "Quantity, Quality, and Source." *Comparative Education Review* 37, no. 4 (1993): 372–88.

–. "The Sad Story of UNESCO's Education Statistics." *International Journal of Educational Development* 19 (1999): 65–74.

–. "The Struggle to Improve Education Statistics in UNESCO: 1980–2000." Paper presented at the World Bank, May 21, 2012.

Heyneman, Stephen P., and Chad R. Lykins. "The Evolution of Comparative and International Education Statistics." In Handbook of Research in Education Finance and Policy, edited by Helen F. Ladd, and Edward B. Fiske, 105–27. London, UK: Routledge, 2008.

IEA, "Researching Education, Improving Learning." Accessed May 5, 2016. http://www.iea.nl/?id72.

Kamens, David H. "Globalisation and the Emergence of an Audit Culture: PISA and the Search for "Best Practices" and Magic Bullets." In PISA, Power, and Policy the Emergence of Global Educational Governance, edited by Heinz-Dieter Meyer, and Aaron Benavot, 117–39. Didcot, UK: Symposium Books, 2013.

Lehmkuhl, Dirk. "Governance by Rating and Ranking." Paper presented at the Annual Meeting of the International Studies Association (ISA), Honolulu, 2005.

Lingard, Bob. "The OECD, PISA and PISA for Schools." Podcast on FreshEd, 2016. https://soundcloud.com/freshed-podcast.

Lingard, Bob, and Sotiria Grek. "The OECD, indicators and PISA: An Exploration of Events and Theoretical Perspectives." Working Paper 2, Fabricating Quality in European Education (2007). Acessed May 5, 2014. http://www.ces.ed.ac.uk/research/FabQ/publications.htm.

Maddox, Bryan. "Secular and Koranic literacies in South Asia: From Colonisation to Contemporary Practice." International Journal of Educational Development 27 (2007): 661–68.

Maddox, Bryan, and Lucio Esposito. "Sufficiency Re-examined: A Capabilities Perspective on the Assessment of Functional Adult Literacy." Journal of Development Studies (2011): 1–17.

Martens, Kerstin. "How to Become an Influential Actor – the 'Comparative Turn' in OECD Education Policy." In New Arenas in Education Governance, edited by Kerstin Martens, Alessandra Rusconi, and Kathrin Leuze, 40–56. New York, NY: Palgrave Macmillan, 2007.

Martens, Kerstin, and Dennis Niemann. "When do Numbers Count? The Differential Impact of the PISA Rating and Ranking in Education Policy in Germany and the US." German Politics 22, no. 3 (2013): 314–32. doi: 10.1080/09644008.2013.794455.

Meyer, Heinz-Dieter, and Aaron Benavot, eds. PISA, Power, and Policy the Emergence of Global Educational Governance. Didcot, UK: Symposium Books, 2013.

Murray, T. Scott, and Irwin S. Kirsch. "Introduction." In Adult Literacy in OECD Countries: Technical Report on the First International Adult Literacy Survey, edited by T. Scott Murray, Irwin S. Kirsch, and Lynn Jenkins, 13–22. Washington DC: U.S. Department of Education, 1998.

OECD (Organisation for Economic Co-operation and Development). "OECD Strategy on Development." Framework presented at the OECD's 50 Anniversary Council Meeting, Paris, 2012.

–. "PISA for Development Call for Tender – Strand A and B." Call for Tender 100000990, Paris, 2014.

Papadopoulos, George S. Education 1960–1990: The OECD Perspective. Paris: OECD, 1994.

Phillips, Gary W. "International Assessment of Educational Progress (IAEP)." In Encyclopedia of Quality of Life and Well-Being Research, edited by Alex C. Michalos, 3313–15. Netherlands: Springer, 2014.

Pizmony-Levy, Oren. "Power, Conflict, and Change in World Society: The Case of International Association for the Evaluation of Educational Achievement." Lecture at Beijing Normal University, China, 2015.

–. "Testing for All: The Emergence and Development of International Assessments of Student Achievement, 1958–2012." PhD diss., Indiana University, 2013.

Pizmony-Levy, Oren, James Harvey, William H. Schmidt, Richard Noonan, Laura Engel, Michael J. Feuer, Henry Braun, Carla Santorno, Iris C. Rotberg, Paul Ash, Madhabi Chatterij, and Judith Torney-Purta. "On the Merits of, and Myths About, International Assessments." Quality Assurance in Education 22, no. 4 (2014): 319–38.

Postlethwaite, Neville. "Torsten Husén (1916-)." Prospects: The Quarterly Review of Comparative Education. UNESCO: International Bureau of Education XXIII (2000): 677–86.

Puryear, Jeffrey. "International education statistics and research: Status and problems." International Journal Educational Development 15, no. 1 (1995): 79–91.

Rizvi, Fazal, and Bob Lingard. Globalizing Education Policy. London, UK: Routledge, 2010.

Sellar, Sam, and Bob Lingard. "PISA and the Expanding Role of the OECD in Global Education Governance." In PISA, Power, and Policy the Emergence of Global Educational Governance, edited by Heinz-Dieter Meyer, and Aaron Benavot, 185–206. Didcot, UK: Symposium Books, 2013.

Stevens, Mitchell L., and Wendy Nelson Espeland. "Commensuration." Encyclopedia of Social Measurement 1 (2005): 375–378.

Street, Brian. Social Literacies: Critical Approaches to Literacy in Development, Ethnography and Education. New York, NY: Longman, 1995.

Thorn, William. "International Adult Literacy and Basic Skills Surveys in the OECD Region." *OECD Education Working Papers* 26 (2009). doi: 10.1787/221351213600.

Tröhler, Daniel. "The OECD and Cold War Culture: Thinking Historically about PISA." In *PISA, Power, and Policy the emergence of global educational governance*, edited by Heinz-Dieter Meyer, and Aaron Benavot, 141–161. Didcot, UK: Symposium Book, 2013.

UIS. *LAMP International Planning Report*. Montreal: UIS, 2004.

UNESCO. *The Global Literacy Challenge: A Profile of Youth and Adult Literacy at the Mid-Point of the United Nations Literacy Decade 2003–2012*. Paris: UNESCO, 2008.

–. "Investing in Cultural Diversity and Intercultural Dialogue." *Executive Summary* (2009).

UNESCO, Institute for Lifelong Learning. *Global Report on Adult Learning and Education*. Hamburg: UNESCO, Institute for Lifelong Learning, 2009.

–. "Belem Framework for Action." Paper presented at the sixth international conference on adult education, Paris, December 1–4, 2009.

Wiseman, Alexander W. *The Impact of Educational Achievement Studies in Education Policymaking*. Bingley: Emerald, 2010.

Martin Lawn

Governing through Assessment Data in the UK during the Late 20ᵗʰ Century: An Extreme Outlier?

From the middle of the 20ᵗʰC, with the establishment of a new school system in England, pupil assessment mainly meant teacher assessment. This took place through the marking of pupil work and accumulated in end of year reports. In the secondary school, each subject teacher added to this annual report. By the 1980s, teacher assessment became part of final secondary school examinations. Significant examinations occurred at the age of 11 to select secondary school type, and at age 16, to decide further education choice. The whole system of assessment in the state schools was dependent upon teacher experience and expertise, in the main. But by the late 1980s this had begun to change with the arrival of a standard national curriculum and standardized tests. These provided information about pupils, but more publically, about the school, and this information could be used by parents to compare schools and to make market choices where possible. Since the mid 20ᵗʰC, national school inspectors visited schools every few years to pass judgment across the whole field of its work – from the buildings, staff, curriculum and pupils. As the testing and standardisation grew, and comparisons were made, the school inspectors were reorganised with often punitive powers to raise the quality of education.

Governing the education system is an issue in all countries. Systems are created to work internally and externally, and they have to meet different purposes at different times. In the 1950s the democratic responsibilities in the system were divided between central and local government and the teachers. Over the years, the centre has weakened and excluded the other two partners and assumed a managerial role. By the 1990s, education policy and control became centralised and dominant. Over the last ten years, steering assessment policy has not been the focus of attention, instead the creation of new schools in the market, with varying degrees of central control, has supplanted the monolithic structures of the past. However tight assessment control is still the core of the system.[1]

---

1   Martin Lawn, "'Voyages of Measurement in Education in the 20ᵗʰC: experts, tools and centres," in *European Educational Research Journal* 12, no. 1 (2013): 108–119, doi: 10.2304/eerj.2013.12.1.108.

The focus of this paper is on the New Labour government in English education from the mid-2000s as it focused on school under-performance and new standards in schools [baseline assessment, key stage assessment and yearly targets for improvement]. It demanded significant improvements in the work of teachers, schools and Local [area] authorities, based upon the tested achievements of their children. The system became increasingly focused upon the performance data of the school, its production and accumulation, through which the education system became not only heavily steered but also re-imagined. My argument is that through data:

"The state, with its partners, is able to 'see' education in a way it has never been able to do so before. What was opaque to the government in the past is now transparent to governance in the present. Finding new ways of measuring system performance has meant that the state combines its illuminative capacities, 'seeing' education, with its visionary aims for the future. Transparency and vision have another effect, known to any student of measurement; what is measured is simultaneously altered. As education is seen [and re-imagined], it is simplified and re-arranged; intended and unintended effects are produced in the system. Education is being re-shaped in an accumulating series of data-produced actions throughout the system, from the teacher, the school, the local authority and the centre, with the help of private companies and specialists."[2]

Measurement and calculation have intensified and the state can 'see' more; its vision is wider, faster and has in depth focus. 'Seeing' has created a series of new mental, social and physical spaces[3] across education, which in turn is interconnected with the wide range of governing surveillance activity in English society. Yet, 'seeing' in this way leads to huge misconceptions and massive logistical and operation problems. So, while new governing actors might promote assessment data flows, they exclude the real difficulties that actors at all levels have to make to allow them to operate.

The post-war expansion and massification of schooling created a new system complexity. The rise of examination boards, the use of pupil tests, evidence for block grants [from centre to region] and the value of inspection reports became the building blocks for governing the public education system. What little governing information was available depended on manual returns and routine accounting. Schools would have to record class register information, school meals data [including free school meals], expenditure accounts, and examination data.

---

2   Martin Lawn, [b]""Voir" Comme L'État : La Gouvernance Contemporaine de L'Éducation en Angleterre, *Éducation et Sociétés, Revue Internationale de Sociologie de l'éducation*, 28, no. 2 (2011): 66.
3   Henri Lefebvre, *The Production of Space* (Oxford, UK: Wiley-Blackwell, 1991).

All this began to change as standardizing processes began to accumulate inside schooling in the 1990s with the rise of the local financial management of schools and the National Curriculum and the consequent gathering of pupil progress data. Since then England's system of governing education has used a technology supported and centralised push into data based governing of schooling, based on pupil assessments, and especially with the use of system targets and their delivery.[4] Fundamentally, what is being described here is a political process, disguised as an educational and a technological process: "Political judgments are implicit in the choice of what to measure, how to measure it, how often to measure it and how to present and interpret the results."[5]

This chapter is based upon a series of interviews,[6] undertaken as part of a large study on school inspection and quality assurance in three countries,[7] which took place in a large English city in early 2007. They act as a snapshot of a rapidly changing system of assessment, of the post-war education landscape and of ways of governing. These changes did not happen organically or evolve naturally, but by a series of disjointed, mechanical operations and the rapid rise of digitised systems. In this situation, pupil assessment was not about pupils at all, but an attempt to re-engineer the education system by measuring it. Behind the solid bricks and mortar of the schools, former significant actors [local school advisers and local government specialist officers] were being 'hollowed out' and reduced in influence by new commercial partners and software contractors working with an avalanche of data. The local authority tried to enact a 'local governing' role through data interpretation and mediation with local schools,[8] but this was becoming harder and harder as the governing centre built a new system. The aim of producing a novel governing optic by which to view the educational landscape was constantly interrupted by problems of software and organisational interoperability and constant

---

4 Michael Barber, *Instruction to Deliver – Tony Blair, Public Services, and the Challenge of Achieving Targets* (London, UK: Politico, 2007), 87.

5 Michael Power, *The audit society: Rituals of verification* (Oxford, UK: Oxford University Press, 1997), 3.

6 Three main sets of interviews were created: they were PA1, a statistician and manager of the City's research agency; PA 2, the person in charge of the City's work with the centre and the schools; and PA 3, the experienced head of the City's assessment planning and support team.

7 Fabricating Quality in European Education Systems [Fab- Q], European Science Foundation 05 ECRP FP021, 2006–2009.

8 Jenny Ozga et al., eds., *Fabricating Quality in Education: Data and Governance in Europe* (London, UK: Routledge, 2011).

pressure to produce, analyse and act upon the data. Changes to school assessment and their organisational and political problems continue and have intensified in 2016 and will endure for some time.

At the City level, the officers began to believe by 2006 that the central government could not be trusted, that the scale of change was too great and that centralisation was the only direction, and in this situation, the role, expertise and position of the City was to be excluded or under used. They began to think that they were observing, even participating in, a slow moving crash, which they could not influence:

> "I think there is an issue about scale here and accessibility and I think even as large as the City is, we are local and accessible to our schools and can have direct conversations either individually or through training or whatever. In a way central government isn't just capable for doing that, they are just such awful centralisers and obsessive in terms of legislation and initiatives." [PA 3]

New Labour Policy and the City

The large English city, with over a million inhabitants, had to manage this transition from a limited and local data collection and reporting operation as it turned into a hub in this reimagined and centralised education system. Some sense of the speed of change can be deduced from the facts that only a few years before, the little data the schools sent to the LA [Local Authority] was on either pink or blue paper forms with information about school meals [an indicator of deprivation]. With the introduction of local financial management of schools in the 1990s, fresh school digitised data and speedy transmission arrived and the City began to use this information internally as part of its school and authority improvement programmes. In the City, an Education Statistics office and a School Improvement office were established and grew quickly to advise schools about understanding data, to train teachers in report and analysis, and to aid the strategic management of the local authority. Performance indicators, based on pupil progress, began to accumulate data which was used to compare progress against the past, against other schools, and to shape the future. Termly, half-termly and weekly assessments began to create data flow around and through the permeable walls of the school.[9] Pupil performance became a public issue and its management created a new norm, system indicators, working up and down the system, as a way of

---

9   Rosemary Webb and Graham Vulliamy, *Coming full circle: The impact of New Labour's education policies on primary school teachers'work* [First Report] (London, UK: Association of Teachers and Lecturers, 2006), 46.

governing education. The constant shift of indicators and the concentration on soon to be overtaken measures did not alter the norm, built on data flow, constant adjustment, targets, rapid analyses, and future predictions.

By the years 2005/2006, the City had set up what was in fact a specialist 'data machine' with support officers, hotlines, specialist information sessions, and a data collection and analysis team. Regular circulars and bulletins were sent out to schools with information about current target setting, available comparative data and arrangements for target data collection. Colour coded forms drew attention to the targets, and return dates were highlighted. One circular listed the following: target setting and collection procedures, list of current performance data for the school, summary of performance trends and forecasts, details of workshops and reference to the PAT [Pupil Achievement Tracker] and PANDA Report on school achievement[10]. Primary school targets included minimum targets in English and Maths [levels of achievement] and this data had to be placed in the school report to parents. Additional targets for pupils in writing, reading, pupil attendance and the 'equality' gap [pupils of different ethnicities] were to be analysed and used at the school and the Local authority level.

Between the Gaps

The story of governing the education system through assessment data is the story of a gap between centralizing practices, operational snags and professional expertise and obligations. As part of its own plans as a city education department, work had been going on for several years to find ways of using assessment and other data to compare its schools and their performance. However, they were faced with the Government pilot programme when they

> "produced their first version which they call 'Pupil Achievement Tracker'... it wasn't a perfect system by any means and there were some problems with actually running the software. A lot of the data had to be put in locally which put a lot of schools off in the first place but that was the first time that there was any national system for analysing data which was more than just having school league tables." [PA 1]

---

10   The Pupil Achievement Tracker (PAT) is a pupil tracking system produced by the central government Ministry of Education. It allows schools and LAs to import their own pupil performance data and compare it with national performance data. Later PAT and PANDA were merged to create RAISEOnline [RAISE standing for Reporting and Analysis for Improvement through School Self-Evaluation]

It had the effects of complicating their City policy on assessment data

> "there are things we don't do now because it is just duplicating what is available nation-
> ally, all the things we need to continue with. What's happening so far is that because the
> national systems aren't yet robust enough and reliable enough we are still supporting our
> schools in the same way and the schools say they want that." [PA 1]

In fact, they were managing their own system, and finding ways to make the
national system work as well. RAISEOnline, the new system for self-evaluation,
was ambitious

> "they are attempting to get every single school in England, primary and secondary, thou-
> sands of schools, all the data at an individual pupil level in a massive database held on
> a server somewhere in London which then is accessed by all the schools in the country
> and OFSTED[11] inspectors, and school advisors and other people, in order to analyse the
> data." [PA 1]

This hugely ambitious operation was also late and dysfunctional

> "Somehow the [Government] is saying this will give all your 2006 data analysis in the
> autumn term which is now, at a school level. We are now at the end of the autumn term
> and there's no 2006 data in it at all. So it completely failed, massively failed, to deliver that.
> But schools say to us we've done all our data analysis for 2006, we set all our targets, we are
> doing our plans, it is no use. So the credibility of this national system will be dependent
> on two things, how accurate the data is and how soon schools get it." [PA 1]

One of the problems was that one major set of assessment data [Key Stage 4]
needed extensive data validation checks because there were so many school challenges to the assessment, and these checks happen at national level. The shift to a
digitised and privately run system, and away from the local officers, compounded
the problem with data management. So,

> "nationally they're going to have to depend on electronic scrutiny of the quality of the
> data because of the volume, whereas here [it was checked by] people. Charlie in the City
> office, for example, knows about schools, would pick up immediately if a school's result
> went up unusually or went down unusually. If the results went up or went down by 10%
> this year and they say 'but we submitted to the exam board all our business studies papers
> because we thought they were high but when we got these back'[...] but he will know
> that because he organises it. They are not going to do that nationally; they're just going
> to take whatever [...]" [PA 1]

---

11   [OFSTED standing for Office for Standards in Education, Children's Services and
     Skills].

The data is inputted by one commercial contractor and the validation checks made by another one. The contractor writes

> "to every school in the country with forms with their data in and schools at a student level have to put in the changes. So if for example a student has been re-graded, then the school has to inform the agency... they did introduce an electronic way [...] they did it online [...] we know in [City] that you got to chase schools in order to do it, cause they don't do things immediately when you ask them to, so inevitably there's going to be a time lag before you can get the data out. And that's why I am saying a national system unless they can find a way of improving the way in which they get the validation and checks done in order to provide this data to schools in the autumn term, the credibility of the system is going to disappear." [PA 1]

This very sophisticated data analysis system [RAISEOnline], pushed by the Minister in London, had to be working in a very short time but the policy actor felt that unless it improved, 'schools will delay using it and it won't have any credibility' [PA 1]. The pupil assessment data was now beginning to be integrated with new data which went into the circumstances of children attending the school. Absolute attainment measures were to be complemented by measures of the progress made by pupils – the value added data – from one key stage to another. Contextual value added included the impact of certain external factors impact on pupil progress e.g. levels of deprivation, ethnicity, second language. This means that the CVA gave a much fairer statistical measure of the effectiveness of a school and provided a solid basis for comparisons.

> "This is the new measure on which school performance is judged in comparative terms and the idea is to have a measure of student progress that enable schools to compare their performance with similar pupils nationally. So the idea is to create a level playing field for comparing performance." [PA 1]

Assessment data was further combined with another set of school factors, the size of schools, and the distribution of performance within the school, according to a very complicated formula, using about 20 variables and given different weightings. This happened centrally and the City had to assume that it was an accurate and a valid process. This process allowed the City and the centre to compare, for example, students on free school meals, of a particular ethnicity, with English as an additional language, and who joined the school late, and their attainments with pupils of the same description nationally. So, all this data could be of value to the schools, as well as to the management of the system overall.

In this situation, the City began to train teachers in the use of RaiseOnline.

The school was seen as a responsible actor, supported by the City, but the teachers had to rely on themselves to understand the statistical information about their school and what it foreshadowed or threatened. The City support office had many training sessions to train teachers in understanding the data produced by this complex process,

> "you need some understanding of statistical analysis to make sense of the data because they've introduced the statistical significance testing into all the data – which is a good thing methodologically – so if a value is statistically different from an expectation or an average it is highlighted. [For example], Box and whisker charts that you see in statistical reports, the boxes are the data points and the whiskers are the confidence lines. As long as the score falls within those confidence limits then it is within the average range but it if it falls outside then it is statistically significant but most teachers aren't going to know [...] The difficulty is to bring it back to what the implications are for teaching and learning, that is, what we do in the classroom, what do we do in lessons because of this data. There is a danger that this becomes an exercise in its own right. We will look at the data exercise and then we'll get on with the learning and the teaching. And in some ways it doesn't help because there isn't a lot, I mean on this website there isn't anything that says and this is how you use it for teaching and [...] There is a lot about what the data means and about schools' self-evaluation [...]" [PA 1]

Head teachers had to know what the data meant as it was the basis for the school inspection and could threaten the future of the school. Heads and teachers had to learn fast and develop expertise quickly. Schools varied though

> "there are significant differences in school levels, from the very basic, almost what a percentage means, through to some staff who have a very sophisticated understanding of the data and also they are able to identify flaws [meanings] in the data." [PA 1]

So, a gap emerged between the promise of a new depth of school improvement in a more efficient data system, and its actual practice. The City had to face a growing uncertainty and insecurity in the schools and the City policy actors were torn between their knowledge of the value of the system and the ragtag actuality of its operation. These actors were professionally supportive of the value of the data to schools

> "It seemed to me that if you used data really well, within the schools, you would encourage teachers to know where their kids were in relation to their own previous best ie the kids previous best and they'll be using comparative data in their minds. And enabling the kids to really move on and have a bit of ambition. Rather than 'well we've got a bad year group'... One's hope was that the data would focus everyone's effort on school improvement where school improvement was really needed in terms of an institution or a subject. One was hoping that the data used within the school would enable a farsighted head with the teachers to look at kids on entry and say – okay, what do these kids need in order to improve." [PA 3]

For both reasons, the statistical and the professional, this Unit had grounds for trying to assist the teachers

> "schools invited to come along, we explain how these models work, we provide guidance notes on the website, we show them where they can get the information and we advise them as to which ones we emphasise that look reasonable and useable, which ones the Government will insist on them using but then say to them that, as a head, we are providing you with as much information as we can because the more information you've got and the better informed you are the more you can interpret the Government line." [PA 1]

So, at one end of the scale are the heads and teachers who are capable in their understanding of the meanings of the data and how they can be used in schools and classrooms, and in a sense, they are the best pupils from the City's point of view. But there are other points on the scale:

> "that RaiseOnline is not properly understood and even then people are not so sophisticated in using it. Often you find that in the school there are certain people that often devote a lot of their time in it and are involved in it but that does not necessarily percolate through the rest of the system. And even when it does, it is often interpreted in quite a simplistic way and that's very often exacerbated by the inspection system, by inspection teams in the schools.
> So people tend to stick to the straightforward interpretation that they have significantly lower average value-added without exploring what that might mean, how the progression might look like across the stage, the extent to which that relates to particular groups of pupils [...] But in some schools and in some places you could argue that they only treat the data just as a signal system." [PA 3]

From the point of view of this specialist Unit, and from the City, there was value in the data, what it means and how it could be used in school, but there was a worrying sense that this assessment system was taking place in a rapidly changing and centralised system and a difficult work process

> "[Teachers] function within an accountability system which really constrains them in terms of reality…The situation often seems to be that people don't see this as a tool, they don't see it as something they can actually use to their advantage but it tends to sort of dictate things and they live within an anxiety almost about what judgements are going to be made about them." [PA 3]

These policy actors worried that without a punitive inspection system and the barriers of this huge data system, then heads and teachers might have little interest in understanding assessment statistics and performance processes.

> "If you removed inspection and performance tables out of the equation, the level of interest in this would be significantly lower. There would be some schools that would still be interested in doing it but a lot of schools wouldn't." [PA 1]

The actors became uncertain; they wanted schools to embrace the value of the data but recognised that without compulsion teachers wouldn't use the data, yet compulsion weakened the use and value of the data.

Operational Difficulties

At one end of the Research and Assessment Unit, there was a concern with the validity, operation and timescale of governing acts from the centre, at the other, there was the sheer daily problem of trying to support a process involving several hundred City schools.

The Unit office had one main room with several large desks, shelves with files, wall production charts, computers etc. In this room, a team of five carried out many of the main tasks of the city's data management. It was a very busy hub of activity as inquiries are sorted out or started, pupils are followed through the system, attainment levels are clarified, schools consulted and advised etc. The office is linked in a series. It works with schools within its boundaries, sometimes directly, drawing down data about the pupils or linked to primary school assessments. It works with the centre, either [the Ministry of Education] or its agencies or contractors, cleaning the data it sends to them and receiving [sometimes dirty] data back: in this relation, it is an outsider, excluded by structures over time but practically essential because of its expertise, local trustworthiness and supporting processes. The office represents a significant actor, because of tradition and expertise; it has its own democratically decided and influenced local education policies.[12]

The process had started earlier and its norm was chaos, partly because of the sheer intricacy and complexity of the process, and also the involvement of different contractors and their sometimes unskilled workers.

"By about 1997, in August, we starting to get a data feed – then we knew the [Assessment] Levels that were being awarded to the pupil that were in our schools. At that point the data was very, very ropey [poor] – there would be whole schools missing from the data feed When the mark sheets were going back to London to be imported, they were being typed in by students, names were getting transposed, they were getting mis-spelled, the English [test] results would go in separately because it was a different marker [to Maths and Science] and these marks for English, and Maths would have… a different person typing them in. On a different day, possibly at a different centre – they would spell [the pupil name differently] and then the whole thing wasn't getting matched up. And then they really messed it up, they had a company in doing the collection which might have

---

12   Author observations 2007.

been different to the other companies doing the collection. so again you've got all these big companies blaming each other – one's responsible for one thing, one for another." [PA 3]

At the City level, they felt that they had to continue to help the schools even though they were excluded from the process of collection. They continued their training processes, in this case in moderation procedures, using peer and City [schools] adviser involvement, but the City's use of teacher assessments, supplementing the test results, an essential part of their practice, was slowly excluded:

> "The Government employed private companies on contract to receive the data, from another company, check it and send information to schools. The contractor worked to the minimum specification, and checked on the final levels of assessment, and excluded teacher assessments, a useful additional check on the test mark. The City always used the teacher assessments but they began to be collected in another way, for example, they had been printed off from the school software, the school secretary would type them all in, print them off and post them to a different agency. Soon, they began to be posted later, got lost, and missed being typed." [PA 2]

This was a source of aggravation to all concerned.

> "Large amounts of information about pupils were sent from the primary to the secondary school, or when a child is going to another area. At this time, a primary school could be sending files to 40 different secondary schools, and the secondary school could be accepting files from 40 different primary schools."

The Unit could be in the middle of chaotic but vital communications, and all under very short timescales and intense transactions, and with their obligation to assist

> "[So we] agreed with primary schools that, between June 4 to June 11, they will give the secretaries time and space to type in this information, and they will load up the data on the School to School [S2S] site, and the trade-off was that the primary schools would no longer get phone calls from dozens of secondary schools, saying 'I haven't had the file on this or that kid', so the poor primary school secretary was inundated with phone calls – 'you haven't done this job yet.' They were being told by the head — don't do that, do this' So, we all got together [in the LA] and said this is stupid — with all this activity, people are getting fed up – What we will agree is that between 4th and 11th, heads in primary will give time to type these files, put them on the S2S site and send it off to each of the secondary schools – not done on paper anymore, not over the phone, it's done electronically. I can monitor that – who has loaded up their files, who has not done anything, they get a phone call from me saying 'I notice that you haven't done anything, have you been having problems?"

Again, the City officers prompt and support their schools but from their outsider/insider viewpoint

> "we print out a sheet of the results that have come from the government... you see the child's name, date of birth, the marks they got for each paper and the levels awarded, and the teacher assessment that was collected and then we send it to school [ ] the week before they come back in September with a big [note] saying *please will you check that you agree with all these marks and levels that are against each of your pupils that are in the main LA database*. From this we will be producing all sorts of reports, passing on all sorts of information to advisers, we will be using it to produce your bar charts, and to put information onto the performance web. So, it is vital that you agree with all of this. It gives them the opportunity to make amendments to it." [PA 2]

The Unit doesn't want anything to go wrong because these are still the City's schools, and because the data needs to be valid and accurate from their point of its use value in the City.

City Brokers

> "I am sort of the broker in the middle, I suppose." [P 1]

The creation of a digitised system of assessment, with clear data feeds and routes, overcame the earlier problems of missing or mislaid pupils and poor inputting of data, but it created new problems, indeed success led to new demands and intensified tasks. While the technology was bending under the burdens added to it, the City had become displaced or excluded from these new systems and was unable to assist its schools. Although confusions were widespread, the City as a regional or locally responsible authority was left in place but 'hollowed out' by the centralizing structure and power of the technology adopted. The strong central steering of the assessment and performance of schools, and continued to confirm the long purging by the centre, since the early 2000s, of the local authority, which it regarded as an unnecessary element in the system. The LA was not allowed to intervene or even advise the centre. If London called a meeting, then the City officers, in common with its colleagues elsewhere, had become audience: they were not consulted but tried to talk anyway

> "you catch them over lunch and you say there is a particular problem and they will say email me, and because City is so big, they are often waiting for our data feeds, to give them an idea about how things are going to go nationally." [PA 2]

They had become an alerting station and were not assumed to be active agents any longer. For example, the Government created a digitised system of managing pupils and their assessment data. Each pupil would be given a Unique Pupil Number or UPN, and this was done locally.

> "When a child arrives in City and is registered for a school, the school is supposed to ascertain whether they have been in a school in England before [or if] they are a new arrival." [PA 2]

The Government specifications, contained within the software, demanded perfect data input to meet the validation processes. In practice, this meant that the Office had to check everything and all data inputs and outputs.

> "There was no way you could prepare the export [of assessment data] if everything wasn't absolutely perfect – you couldn't have one thing missing, a date of birth out of the expected range, a missing UPN, you couldn't exclude – check this or that, you would get a list 'this is not right and the export failed." [PA 2]

Making the assessment data valid could take a number of people a long time.

> "You would think everything was alright and then [the software] would say a 'duplicate UPN' – a child in one school with a UPN, a totally different child with the same UPN, and you would have to get on to the two schools 'how come this child has the same UPN ?'"[PA 2]

Or it would say

> "this child has had this UPN since they came from that school three years ago, then you would have to contact that school, change the data in the system – this could take 3 days. [laughs]" [PA 2]

All data checking had to take place before the schools went on their summer vacations in mid-July.

Another confusion was the relation between the City and the emerging connectivity between the centre and the school. The assumption was that this new digitised system of reporting, supported by UPNs and the direct S2S communication site, would not only eliminate previous problems of several sites of action or responsibility, and needlessly bureaucratic tasks. But the Unit office was the only support available to local schools [apart from a central helpline] but the centre excluded it. It had no responsibility anymore but it felt it still had a duty consequently it often tried to broker or solve school problems. Politically, this was tricky as open involvement caused a suspicion at the centre that it was trying to re-establish a major role for itself. As the Unit office organiser, the policy actor described a number of incidents:

> "The [centre] helpline was phoning individual schools up to say that you have not sent us your teacher assessments – the schools were saying things like 'we sent it' – 'well, send it again.'" [PA 2]

Or

> "[The City Unit] would get a phone call [from a school]'you phoned us and said we haven't
> sent the teacher assessment'- 'no, we haven't, we don't have anything to do with that, it's
> not our responsibility, you mean the [centre]."

Or

> "'what seems to be the problem" They say they haven't received it but we have sent it 3
> times now."

The Unit had no choice but to contact the Centre-

> "'yes, there have been problems, we have lost some, some have fallen into the ether,
> sorry, can you get the school to send it again' – 'so we ring the school, please send it just
> once more."

Consequently, sometimes huge numbers of data feeds would go missing, and
sometimes entire schools, and yet, in this important part of City education, the
Local Authority Unit was not responsible, indeed a barely tolerated actor and
unable to influence or improve central operations and its contractors.

The idea of a delivery chain[13] and the flow of data along it were essential to
the new process of tight hierarchical accountability, the latest overarching mode
of governing. Even the believers in the value of assessment data in the City were
concerned about the wider vision of the new landscape of data, expressed by
government

> "there's a lot of talk about the effective use of data and you get the feeling that sometimes
> they are not talking about data in a narrow sense in terms of contextual value-added
> scores and things like that; they seem to think that data is something that can be, in terms
> of numbers, that somehow can be generated over any time scale in relation to anything
> at all and if people only engaged with these numbers then that would be the answer to
> problems of underperformance etc. and it is just not like that. I think it is overstating the
> case for the role that data can play." [PA 3]

A Data-built Landscape

The people in the Research and Assessment Unit, represented here in the work
of three policy actors, work in the City, a specific locality and a political entity in
education, with its own history, strategy and resources. Although gradually excluded from many elements of the national data management systems, they were
essential to the effective working of that same system in this period. Although data

---

13 Barber, *Instruction to Deliver.*

flows, there are physical, expert and contextual processes which enable it to do this. Increasingly these expert processes have been taken by companies, managing data processing services, and by their consultancy and strategic divisions and the public service has been displaced. They have enabled new digitised packets of data to flow around the system, following each pupil and their individual code identity; they have kept this system working more intensively hours and automated responses. While local areas had significant directors of education in their Local authorities, the new managers are hidden elsewhere. The City may try to enact a 'governing' role through data interpretation and mediation with 'its' schools, in order to assist and support over-whelmed schools but some smaller authorities with fewer data skills may be more dependent on the centre and less able to offer independent strategic and contextual support.[14] The capacity of the centre, the local and the school to produce and analyse a wide range of school data has increased beyond anything known earlier. Although they were no longer system 'partners', the digitisation of education, and its future governance, could not happen effectively without the work of the Unit

> "In the City, its efforts go into data management and increasing its local value. Without the hard work of the office, data cannot fulfil their governing and performance functions. There are physical, expert and contextual processes which enable them to flow; without them, flow is halted. Data easily jams and this demands sophistication of use from people, they manage data, and argue about it, to widen their space of manoeuvre. Data is constantly re-imagined. People re-engineer its flow paths, its constituent objects, its protocols and its manuals. This is partly problem based [policy and material problems of flow] and partly, a related scientific imagination [the capabilities and potential of data and systems]. It has to be coded to flow. Without coding, it is either not data or it is local. Flow demands constant engineering and physical effort from many actors. The metaphor of a "delivery chain" simplifies this process and turns it into a symbol of the new education order, and at the same time renders the complex processes and crude interventions which keep its working invisible."[15]

In fact, the 'delivery chain' depended on policy actors or agents who were excluded from the 'chain' and yet were necessary to it.

Measuring the English education system has depended upon the sheer quantity of assessment data produced by and about children and school performance. So, data has enabled a new optic through which to view the education system, and in turn, it has facilitated the creation of a virtual representation of the system through

---

14 Ozga et al., *Quality in Education.*
15 Martin Lawn, [a] "Governing through Data in English Education," *Education Inquiry* 2, no. 2 (2011): 286, doi: 10.3402/edui.v2i2.21980.

data, which many education actors in England now treat *as* the actual system. The act of 'seeing', of making things governable, alters the observed.

In this snapshot of City officers working at a particular time and place, dealing with the problems of assessment policy and operation, an argument can be made about the meaning of the case. Firstly, assessment policy reflected deeply a political process of constantly defining and redefining what to measure, how to measure and how to interpret the assessment of the system. Secondly, a complex system of education was redesigned through the creation and control of data, which involved new planning cycles, performance targets, service manuals, middle management, definable teacher skills, new accounting software and most of all, new working relations across the system. Thirdly, that the effect of these actions produced a new governing process of education [and across the public service], dependent upon an amassing of big data which could reimagine the system. This reimagining of education allowed a new landscape to be built in which older relations between pupils, teachers and local authorities could be excluded slowly. Fourthly, it is the case that in each element of the education system new contradictions and confusions are still created as others are resolved.

This case study can be used to show how assessment data can be extended, integrated and linked to other data to provide micro management of the education system. It has superseded older system information like teacher's conditions of work or grants to local authorities as a way to manage the system. Now it involves the automation of work processes, the creation of private data management companies and the panoptic gaze of central managers. It links together marketisation, choice and schools.

It does not explain why the English education system should have taken this form, why it centralised and excluded, and why managerialism replaced democratic accountability. But it does suggest that even a subject like the assessment of pupils cannot be divorced from the politics and culture of its society, and cannot be treated purely as a psycho-pedagogical phenomenon.

Literature

Barber, Michael. *Instruction to Deliver – Tony Blair, Public Services, and the Challenge of Achieving Targets.* London, UK: Politico, 2007.

Goldstein, Harvey. "Education for All: the globalisation of learning targets." *Comparative Education* 40, no. 1 (2004): 7–14. doi: 10.1080/0305006042000184854.

Lawn, Martin. [a] "Governing through Data in English Education." *Education Inquiry* 2, no. 2 (2011): 277–288. doi: 10.3402/edui.v2i2.21980.

–. [b] ""Voir"Comme L'État : La Gouvernance Contemporaine de L'Éducation en Angleterre. *Éducation et Sociétés. Revue Internationale de Sociologie de l'éducation* 28, no. 2 (2011): 65–76.

–. "'Voyages of Measurement in Education in the 20[th]C: experts, tools and centres." *European Educational Research Journal* 12, no. 1 (2013): 108–19. doi: 10.2304/eerj.2013.12.1.108.

–. "'A Systemless System: Designing the Disarticulation of English State Education." *European Educational Research Journal* 12, no. 2 (2013): 231–41. doi: 10.2304/eerj.2013.12.2.231.

Lawn, Martin, and Sotiria Grek. "'Figures in the (land)scape: Hybridity and Transformation in Education Governance in England.'" In *Re-reading Education Policies: Studying the Policy Agenda of the 21st Century*, edited by Maarten Simons, Mark Olssen, and Michael Peters, 568–83. Rotterdam: Sense Publishers, 2010.

Lefebvre, Henri. *The Production of Space.* Oxford, UK: Wiley-Blackwell, 1991.

Ozga, Jenny, Peter Dahler-Larsen, Cristina Segerholm, and Hannu Simola, eds. *Fabricating Quality in Education: Data and Governance in Europe.* London, UK: Routledge, 2011.

Power, Michael. *The audit society: Rituals of verification.* Oxford, UK: Oxford University Press, 1997.

Webb, Rosemary, and Graham Vulliamy. *Coming full circle: The impact of New Labour's education policies on primary school teachers' work.* [First Report]. London, UK: Association of Teachers and Lecturers, 2006.

Authors

Addey, Camilla (PhD, Postdoctoral Researcher). Centre for Comparative and International Education, Humboldt-Universität zu Berlin/Germany. International Large-Scale Assessments; global education policy: camilla.addey@hu-berlin.de

Alarcón, Cristina (PhD, Research Associate and Lecturer), Institute of Education Studies, Humboldt-Universität zu Berlin/Germany. Transnational/comparative history of educational and psychological knowledge; history of assessment and experts: cristina.alarcon@hu-berlin.de

Berdelmann, Kathrin (PhD, Postdoctoral Researcher), German Institute for International Pedagogical Research, Library for the History of Education, Berlin/Germany. Historical research on educational practices, qualitative methodology and methods; research on time, space and materiality in classrooms: berdelmann@dipf.de

Bongrand, Philippe (PhD, Associate Professor), ÉMA Research Centre, University of Cergy-Pontoise, University of Paris-Seine/France. Socio-history of the schooling process; home-schooling: philippe.bongrand@u-cergy.fr

Buchardt, Mette (PhD, Associate Professor), Centre for Educational Policy Research, Department of Learning & Philosophy, Aalborg University/Denmark. Transnational history of Education; Comparative Welfare State history; history of church and religion: mb@learning.aau.dk

Flórez Petour, María Teresa (PhD in Education, Assistant Professor), Pedagogical Studies Department, University of Chile. Assessment policies in connection to history, politics and ideology; Assessment for Learning; validity in assessment: mtflorez@u.uchile.cl

Gurova, Galina (MA, Researcher). Faculty of Education, University of Tampere/Finland. Education policy and governance; quality assurance in schools; education in Russia: galina.gurova@gmail.com

Hutt, Ethan (PhD, Assistant Professor). College of Education, University of Maryland, College Park, Maryland/USA. History of Education in America; history of testing and quantification: ehutt@umd.edu

Lawn, Martin (PhD, Honorary Professor), Fellow of the Academy of Social Sciences, University of Edinburgh/UK. Transnational histories; history of educational sciences; Europeanisation of education: m.lawn@btinternet.com

Lundahl, Christian (PhD, Professor of Education). School of Humanities, Education and Social Sciences, Örebro University, Örebro/Sweden. Assessment in education; transnational/comparative history of education: christian.lundahl@oru.se

Méndez, Alicia (PhD, Senior Researcher) University of Buenos Aires. Argentina. Formation of elites; ethnography of meritocratic trajectories: aliciamzv@yahoo.com

Piattoeva, Nelli (PhD, University Lecturer), Faculty of Education, University of Tampere/Finland. Education policy and comparative education; Russian education system, governance by numbers: nelli.piattoeva@uta.fi

Rengifo Correa, Ángela Adriana (PhD, Research Fellow and Lecturer), School of Literary Studies, University of Valle, Cali/Colombia. History of concepts; history of assessment in Colombia; reading and writing teaching methods: angelaadrianar@gmail.com

Schneider, Jack (PhD, Assistant Professor), Department of Education, College of the Holy Cross, Worcester, Massachusetts/USA. Educational policy; school reform; intellectual history: jschneid@holycross.edu

Tanaka, Koji (Professor Emeritus), Institute of Education, Bukkyo-University of Kyoto/Japan. Curriculum Instruction and Assessment; history of assessment and experts: koji-t@bukkyo-u.ac.jp

Tveit, Sverre (University lecturer), Department of Education, University of Agder, Kristiansand/Norway; (PhD student), Department of Education, University of Oslo. Research interests: Transnational and comparative studies into the validity, comparability and legitimacy of educational assessment: sverre.tveit@uia.no

Vogt, Michaela (PhD, Junior Professor), Institute of Education, Ludwigsburg University of Education/Germany. Qualitative research; historical educational research; childhood studies, empirical research on inclusive education: michaela. vogt@ph-ludwigsburg.de

Waldow, Florian (PhD, Professor of Comparative and International Education), Institute of Education Studies, Humboldt-Universität zu Berlin/Germany. Institutional and historical dimensions of pupil assessment; educational transfer; international education governance: florian.waldow@hu-berlin.de

Ydesen, Christian (PhD, Associate Professor). Department of Learning and Philosophy, Aalborg University/Denmark. Transnational/comparative history of education; minority education; history of assessment and experts: cy@learning.aau.dk

Studia Educationis Historica

Bildungsgeschichtliche Studien / Studies in the History of Education /
Estudios de Historia de la Educación

Herausgegeben von/ edited by

Marcelo Caruso, Eckhardt Fuchs, Gert Geißler, Sabine Reh, Eugenia Roldán Vera, Noah W. Sobe

www.peterlang.com